Aberdeenshire Library and Information Service
www.aberdeenshire.gov.uk/libraries
Renewals Hotline 01224 661511

30

HEADQUARTERS

1 5 MAY 2008
2 9 JUL 2008
0 4 NOV 2008

2 9 OCT 2008
0 3 DEC 2008
2 6 FEB 2009
2 9 APR 2009

2 0 OCT 2009

HEADQUARTERS

2 4 JAN 2011
1 1 MAR 2011
08 APR 2011
12 APR 2011

ABERDEENSHIRE
LIBRARIES

- 9 JUN 2011

WITHDRAWN
FROM LIBRARY 2 7 DEC 2014

1 3 SEP 2016
2 4 OCT 2017
1 2 JUL 2019

ABERDEENSHIRE
LIBRARIES

- 5 DEC 2016

WITHDRAWN
FROM LIBRARY

2 1 JAN 2020

0 9 MAR 2020

1 0 JUN 2022

Shennan, Margar

Our man in
Malaya : John
Davis, CBE,   959.
5

1808314

ABERDEENSHIRE
LIBRARIES

WITHDRAWN
FROM LIBRARY

D1187947

Our Man in Malaya

Our Man in Malaya

John Davis CBE, DSO, Force 136 SOE and Postwar Counter-Insurgency

Margaret Shennan

SUTTON PUBLISHING

First published in the United Kingdom in 2007 by
Sutton Publishing, an imprint of NPI Media Group Limited
Cirencester Road · Chalford · Stroud · Gloucestershire · GL6 8PE

Copyright © Margaret Shennan, 2007

All rights reserved. No part of this publication may be reproduced, stored in
a retrieval system, or transmitted, in any form, or by any means, electronic,
mechanical, photocopying, recording or otherwise, without the prior
permission of the publisher and copyright holder.

Margaret Shennan has asserted the moral right to be identified as the
author of this work.

British Library Cataloguing in Publication Data
A catalogue record for this book is available from the British Library.

Hardback ISBN 978-0-7509-4710-7

Shennan, Margare

Our man in
Malaya : John
Davis, CBE, DSO,
                959.
                  5
1808314

Typeset in Photina MT.
Typesetting and origination by
NPI Media Group Limited.
Printed and bound in England.

For Helen,
Patta, Bill, Humphrey and Tom,
to whom this story now belongs

Contents

Acknowledgements

The career of John Davis was inextricably and paradoxically intertwined with that of Chin Peng, the leader of the Malayan Communist Party (MCP). For more than fifty years their mutual respect overcame their ideological differences.

I am deeply grateful to Chin Peng for his contribution to this biography of his friend and adversary.

Serendipity plays a large part in the evolution of this book. In 1999, while writing *Out in the Midday Sun: The British in Malaya, 1880–1960*, I was struck by the wartime heroics of a police officer called John Davis. After a mutual acquaintance gave me his telephone number, I was able to question John Davis further about his wartime experiences. I did not know then that in 1954–6 he was Senior District Officer (SDO) in Butterworth, Province Wellesley, which was 'home' to me during eight of my childhood years.

Meanwhile, pursuing information about one of John Davis's closest friends, the late Guy Madoc, I made contact with Madoc's daughter, Fenella, who, I then learned, was married to John Davis's nephew – also John Davis. After establishing these fortuitous connections, we – Fenella, John, my husband, Joe, and I – met up in London. The outcome was a tempting invitation to write a biography of John Davis, focusing on his years in the Far East. In the spring of 2000 we met John Davis himself and his wife at their home, together with members of their family. I was assured of their complete cooperation and was given carte blanche to use the Davis private archive, a priceless, eclectic collection of papers that formed the basis of my research and enabled the authentic voice of John Davis to echo down the years.

My gratitude to the Davis family for this opportunity is immense. I thank them for their frankness, cooperation, enthusiasm and hospitality. Talking to John and Helen at length during many visits was enlightening and a great deal of fun. Conversations with their daughter Patta and their son Humphrey invariably produced fascinating insights, such as Humphrey's revelations about Kim Philby and his account of the last meeting between John Davis and Chin Peng, at which he and his wife Dilla had been present. My warmest thanks go also to John and Fenella for setting everything in motion, and for their patience and sustained interest in the project.

I thank Professor John Broome and Mr Nicholas Broome for allowing me to make full use of Richard Broome's *A Memoir (Wartime Experiences)*, their father's detailed record of 1942. I am much indebted to John Loch MCS and Michael McConville MCS for their information and advice, including their personal insights and constructive comments on the manuscript; similarly my sincere thanks to Anthony Short, the leading British authority on the Emergency, for reading the manuscript and for giving me the benefit of his extensive knowledge of the period. Lastly I am extremely grateful to Mr Ian Ward, Media Masters Publishers, Singapore, and Mr Wah-Piow Tan, who have facilitated communications with Chin Peng.

Many others have talked to me about John Davis or helped me with particular matters. My thanks go to Stephen Alexander, Terry Barringer, Helen Bruce, Laura Clouting (Imperial War Museum), A. Cradock, Maurice Dunman (The National Archives, Kew), John Edington, Mary Elder, Peter Elphick, P.W. Giles, Vanessa Harrison (BBC Radio 4), Lynn Keeping, J.S.A. Lewis, Mrs B. Matthews (school librarian, Tonbridge School), Maj Alex Mineef, the Revd Geoffrey S. Mowat, Dr Philip Murphy, Rowland Oakeley MCS, Judy O'Flynn, Penny Prior (Foreign and Commonwealth Office), Professor Jeffrey Richards, the late Harvey Ryves, Brian Stewart MCS, Hubert Strathairn, Roderick Suddaby (Imperial War Museum), Nicholas Webb (archivist, Barclays Group), Joan Welburn and the late Professor Oliver Wolters.

Finally, I thank my husband Joe for his advice as a fellow historian and for his unstinting support, even while he was busy writing another book.

Margaret Shennan

Prologue

On the evening of 24 May 1943 a long, dark, low shape appeared on the horizon some 10 miles to the north of the Malayan island of Pulau Pangkor. An astute observer might have identified the hull of a submarine that was surfacing for a specific purpose in the Malacca Straits. Aboard Submarine O24 five Chinese secret agents waited expectantly as a stocky British Army officer resolutely surveyed the stars and the rise and fall of the land to the north of the headland of the Haunted Hill, Tanjong Hantu. Capt John Davis was leading the first special operations landing on the Malayan Peninsula since the surrender of Singapore to the Japanese fifteen months before.

This new initiative would be a significant enterprise, carried out under the agency of the Special Operations Executive's (SOE's) Malaya Country Section, and a great deal rested on its reconnaissance and intelligence-gathering success. If all went well, and communications were restored between Ceylon and Malaya, the present operation, code-named 'Gustavus I', would be the prelude to a series of sorties to put Chinese agents into Japanese-occupied Malaya. Select parties of volunteers, specially trained in the skills of sabotage, intelligence gathering and guerrilla warfare, would be infiltrated under the command of European officers. In addition, Capt Davis had two further objectives: to discover the fate of a number of Europeans who had volunteered for behind-the-lines operations during the ten-week Malayan campaign and might still be surviving in the jungle; and, last but not least, to make contact with the Chinese Communist guerrillas in Perak, led by a remarkable youth whose wartime alias was Chin Peng, and harness their anti-Japanese zeal to the Allied cause. In implementing the last aim Davis was drawn into political relationships that would profoundly affect his career. The wartime comradeship he was to forge with Chin Peng in life-threatening circumstances during the next two and a half years would be replaced, within a similar time span, by mortal conflict and finally, in old age, by a kind of reconciliation.

As he stared towards the Malayan coast on that May evening Capt Davis, formerly an officer of the Federated Malay States Police Service, was all too aware of his responsibility for making the right operational decisions. Time and again he had rehearsed the outline of the Segari Hills from an old pilot's book until he knew it by heart. But there was no knowing what might be waiting there, and suddenly the implications of a blind landing struck home. He and his handful of Chinese volunteers would be alone, facing the unknown; so it would require all the luck in the world to paddle several miles in flimsy, collapsible canoes known as folboats, beach them at the correct point and find cover before entering the dark hinterland unobserved. And luck threatened to desert them when one of the folboats was slightly crushed while being fed through the torpedo-loading hatch. Though this was a not uncommon problem, it was frustrating to a hard-pressed team. Capt Davis was relieved and grateful to the Dutch submarine crew who worked on deck in the dark to repair the damage.

As the little team of SOE men prepared to leave the submarine under cover of darkness, the Dutch skipper, Lt Cdr W.J. de Vries, caught a flash of apprehension on Davis's face. He felt compelled to intervene. Exercising his due authority as commander, he offered the British officer his unequivocal support if he decided that the risks were too great and that, for the sake of his men as well as himself, they should call off the operation. 'Look. Come back with me, there'll be no loss of face,' he assured his fellow officer. The gesture was sufficient to revive Capt Davis's morale. He felt 'a tremendous determination to go ahead with the thing, also a tremendous feeling of gratitude' to his Allied colleague 'for taking that point of view'.[1] De Vries accepted Davis's decision to proceed and wished him well. He explained that he would turn the submarine so that it pointed in the direction of their destination; and as soon as they were clear he would take it out backwards. 'I will just slip away and then you're on your own.'[2] Davis nodded: the die was cast.

They were still 5 miles offshore at 8.30 p.m. when the little party began the long haul by canoe. John Davis was satisfied that his team represented a good mix of skills and temperaments. With him in the leading folboat was Ah Piu, a tough character, a former mechanic, whom he had selected as his bodyguard. Another pair brought up the rear: Ah Tsing, who would be valuable as a speaker of the common dialect of Pangkor, and Ah Ying, a keen young graduate of a Chinese military school. In the middle folboat were two good friends. Ah Han knew Perak well and had experience behind the lines in Burma, and Ah Ng, an intelligent and pragmatic individual from a Chinese–Borneo family, had been picked by Davis to be leader of the little Chinese party.[3] For much of the time Ah Han and Ah Ng struggled to control their canoe which was yawing badly. Although the weather was fine, with little surface swell, the sea was like ink and they ran into unexpectedly strong currents; at one point Ah Han fell into the water. Otherwise there was just one heart-stopping moment when suddenly, in the distance, they heard the 'phut, phut, phut' of engines . . .

Davis's first thought was of Japanese motorboats on night patrol. He tensed, wrestling with the implications, before it came to him in a flash that the Chinese fishing fleet would be putting out for a night's work from Pangkor. As the sound receded, the six paddled on with relief towards the Segari shoreline, but it was nearly midnight when the gentle lap-lapping of shallow water heralded the end of their journey. Wearied by their exertions, they rolled from the folboats, mustering enough energy to drag themselves on to dry land. Ahead was a short, sandy beach, beyond a canopy of scrub and jungle, 'so quiet, so desolate', John Davis recalled. And all around the air was filled with a lovely familiar smell, the soft, warm, musky scent that told him he was back home in Malaya.

Once they had pulled the folboats into the scrub, concealing them with the gear, the men requested a soothing midnight bathe. After a fortnight's confinement in the submarine they waded eagerly into the sea, wallowing in its freshness until in sheer exhaustion they staggered back to the shore. Finally, when the night watch had been set, the beach became an inviting bed for the rest of the dog-tired party.

At the first streaks of dawn Capt Davis ordered a survey of the shore to ensure it was clear; then he reminded everyone to dismantle and camouflage the folboats. It was barely light on 25 May when Davis and his men, still tired but eager to start, shouldered their packs at the ready. Each was carrying 70lb in weight on his back, which included rations and weapons.[4] With Davis at their head, they set off along the deserted shore, looking for a natural break in the vegetation that would indicate a way through to the interior. As they stared eastwards they were dazzled by the sun, and the land, dark with shadow, was all the more obscure. In those few unguarded moments Davis and his men almost blundered into a Malay couple approaching noiselessly along the sand. Everyone looked aside instinctively as they passed and hurried on in silence.

Davis managed to control his surprise. Since he was satisfied that he and his Chinese agents had taken proper precautions, he wanted to believe that no harm would come of their brief encounter with two locals on an early morning walk. But he would never know for certain whether the Malay couple were spies and informants assigned to watch this part of the coast. Whatever the truth, Davis knew it was vital that the SOE party pushed inland and found a secure bolt-hole in the Segari Hills.

They made slow headway and were patently suffering from the effects of their confinement in the submarine as they cut their way through dense undergrowth. Luckily Davis had years of jungle experience behind him. His senses were tuned to the sights, smells and sounds of a tropical forest, to potential dangers and the advisability of keeping to high tracks and avoiding gullies. Eventually they came across an abandoned palm-thatched hut, close to a stream and screened from a nearby rubber estate. Though it was almost roofless, it provided them with basic living quarters thanks to the unusually dry weather in June. They struck camp on Bukit Segari and took stock of their situation.

Since April 1943 the presence of Japanese troops in the townships of Perak had been more noticeable and confrontations between the Communist guerrillas and Japanese forces had been on the increase. There was a build-up of police activity in the Lumut–Segari–Pangkor area as Japanese counter-intelligence anticipated the infiltration of Allied agents along the Perak coast. After being warned of probable Japanese attacks Davis and his men had to move camp several times to different sites on Bukit Segari, but they knew the advantage lay with the occupying forces and their superior numbers.[5]

John Davis had no illusions as to his fate if he were taken prisoner by the Japanese. As a British officer he could expect little mercy. But as he rose in prominence, promoted to the rank of major in July 1943 and later designated Adm Mountbatten's representative and head of Force 136 in occupied Malaya, he knew he would be treated as a spy and subjected to degrading humiliation, starvation, torture and execution. Yet, being a natural optimist, he believed that bad news was generally worse in the contemplation and best countered by taking physical action. In simple terms, 'In war, if you saw a job that needed to be done, you got on and did it.' This explains Davis's total involvement in the 'Gustavus' enterprise, with its paradoxical and heroic turn of events.

John Davis was an iconic figure who played a singular part in thirty years of Malaya's history. Yet, partly because of his own reticence and modesty, John's extraordinary contribution is little known, his story untold. His career in the police, the Army and the civil service coincided with the distinctive phases of a country in evolution, changing its identity from a colony and protectorate to an independent, democratic federation. He recognised the difficulty after the Japanese war of balancing the political and economic ambitions of Malaya's multiracial population, particularly the Malays and Chinese, with Britain's resumption of her imperial role. But the two positions were obviously irreconcilable. So, too, for many years were John Davis and his erstwhile wartime ally, Chin Peng, who launched a bitter Communist insurrection on the people of Malaya in 1948.

Throughout the so-called Emergency John Davis worked to bring the rural Chinese into the government's orbit, ending their sense of alienation. He also pitted his considerable energy and know-how against the Communist guerrillas of the Malayan Races' Liberation Army (MRLA), some of whom he had been responsible for training and infiltrating into the jungle during the Japanese war. In 1955 the Malayan government appointed Davis as Chin Peng's Conducting Officer at the Baling peace talks. When these failed, Davis tried to persuade him to surrender in a mysterious nocturnal meeting, wrongly said to have been their last. The Emergency was resumed, but from the eve of Malayan Independence in August 1957 John Davis masterminded the counter-insurgency strategies in Johore and Kedah that finally, by 1960, eliminated the last guerrillas on Malayan soil, defining the end of the Emergency.

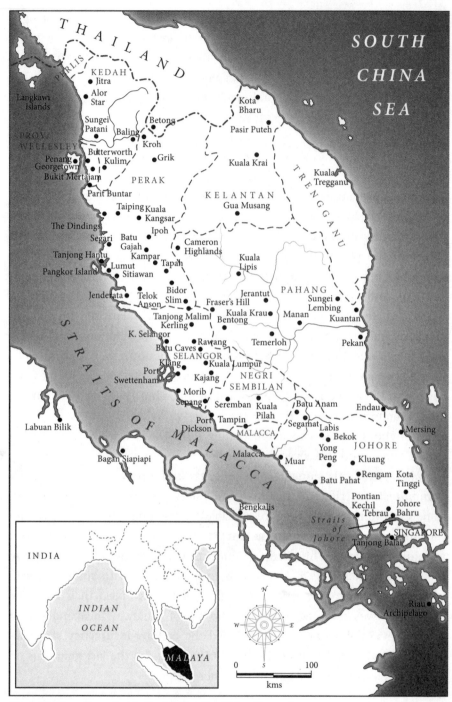

Map of Malaya from *Out in the Midday Sun* (John Murray).

Chapter 1

The Approach of War
in the Far East

John Davis was born in Sutton in 1911 into a comfortable Edwardian family with roots south of the Thames Estuary. He was a complex man, blessed with phenomenal luck, longevity and good looks. The eldest of three sons of a successful Barclays Bank manager in the City, John possessed many of the qualities expected of the English public-school man: self-assurance, natural sporting prowess, modesty and a commitment to traditional British values of loyalty and patriotism, duty and service. Besides these attributes, his housemaster at Tonbridge pointed to his cheerful disposition and gift of leadership, recommending him unequivocally for an overseas post somewhere in the British Empire.

There was no hint here of another John: stubborn, argumentative and independent-minded; a colonial officer who was attracted by radical ideas and colourful eccentrics, someone who habitually questioned convention – not to mention the decisions of the Establishment Office – who had more than a touch of the maverick in him. He remembered long afterwards his CID (Criminal Investigation Department) chief in Ipoh saying that he did not mind his *being* a Bolshevik so long as he did not *behave* like a Bolshevik in the police service.

John's connection with the Malayan Police began at the end of 1930 when he was selected as a probationer in a party of ten young men to serve in the Federated Malay States and the Straits Settlements Police. The leisurely sea voyage to the East provided ample opportunity for the recruits to bond; John formed a lifetime's friendship with one in particular, Guy Madoc.

After six months' training in Kuala Lumpur and temporary posts in Selangor John's career began in earnest in February 1932, when he was sent to Pahang to be Officer Commanding Police District (OCPD) of Kuantan. Here he experienced his first real contact with Communism, one of his duties being to lead official searches for members of the proscribed party. Five months later he became OCPD of Pekan, the seat of the Sultan of Pahang. This was a large, rural constituency and its ethnic composition of farmers and fishermen was predominantly Malay, as were almost all his constables, with whom he established a genuine rapport. From them he acquired his fluency in Malay and learned much about the people, culture and way of life.

In 1933, however, John faced a critical moment when he was selected to spend two years in Canton learning Chinese. At the end of this time he was notified of his promotion to the rank of Assistant Commissioner of Police, Federated Malay States. Returning to Kuala Lumpur after home leave in 1936, John found he had to readjust to provincial life in the tin-producing state of Perak. After eight months in the 'Chinese' town of Ipoh as the Assistant Officer Overseeing Detectives in the CID office, he moved in August 1937 to be OCPD of Taiping and Matang.

From his quiet Malayan backwater in 1937 John Davis kept assiduously abreast of international developments. Since he had close friends in Canton, he took the volatile situation in China very much to heart, fearing the likelihood of an escalating Sino-Japanese conflict in the Far East that would involve Great Britain. And if the West supported China with economic sanctions against Japan he predicted the outcome would be 'the next world war'. Political trends in Europe were just as worrying. Fascism was flourishing and when Hitler engineered the union – *Anschluss* – with Austria, and German forces dismembered an impotent Czechoslovakia in 1938–9, John despairingly began to question Chamberlain's appeasement policy and his own youthful enthusiasm for pacifism and idealism.

Germany's next blow came at the end of August 1939 with the news of the Nazi–Soviet Non-Aggression Pact signed between Russia and Germany. From John's perspective this was a diplomatic absurdity that could not last, but for its duration the Chinese Communists in Malaya would be encouraged to be more militantly anti-British. From this point the political crisis mounted rapidly in Europe. On 1 September Hitler launched a major assault on Poland, and as guarantors of Polish integrity Britain and France had no alternative but to issue an ultimatum. When no withdrawal was forthcoming, both countries declared war on Germany. It was 3 September and the Second World War had begun.

Many people saw this as the end of an era. John, like many Malayans, found the reality difficult to comprehend. He offered to join the Army but was turned down because the Malayan government had decided the economy could not afford the exodus of European volunteers such as had occurred in 1914. The official line in Singapore was reassuring – Malaya would be a comfortable side-seat for the duration – despite evidence to the contrary. From September 1938 to the Nazi–Soviet Pact relations between Britain and Japan steadily deteriorated. And soon a note of unease crept into John's words: 'We are still living in a complete pre-war paradise – a fool's paradise it may well turn out to be.'

In December 1940, after receiving notice that he was to leave the Federated Malay States Police Service, John was transferred to the Straits Settlements Police and posted to Singapore. He was in two minds about the change. He had once described Singapore town as 'very hot and full of people who had nothing better to do than drink gin and talk nonsense'. Furthermore, the police accommodation above the Sikh Barracks on Pearls Hill was anything but comfortable, being subject to 'the incessant noise, the muffled roar of millions in conversation, cars, trains and blaring synthetic music from a cinema opposite and a dance hall a little further down'. Common sense, however, told him to make the best of it, and in retrospect this relocation proved to be a significant career move. His posting was to the Detective Office in the CID with responsibility for bribery and corruption cases. He joined in time to wind up the police enquiry into the Loveday case, a serious scam involving an Army officer responsible for awarding defence contracts. With their infinite faith in the integrity of the officer class, the European community had been badly shaken by the trial.[1] On completing his report John was promoted to Assistant Superintendent of Police in Charge of Investigations. His task was to oversee Singapore's police divisions and appraise their work in relation to serious crime. The workload was immense and it was a relief to be told in July 1941 by the Inspector-General of Police, Arthur H. Dickinson, that he was to be transferred to Special Branch, which was housed in the same block in Robinson Road.

Dickinson had already noted John's particular abilities and had singled him out for an intelligence role in internal security. In due course John was told he was to be moved to the Defence Security Office to a 'cover' job in counter-intelligence. Although based in the same building as Police HQ, the Defence Security Officer and his Assistant were military officers appointed by the War Office and MI5. To counter the divisive structure of the police forces it was decided there should also be a Civil Security Officer, and Arthur Dickinson had been appointed to this post. In his view, the intelligence system would have benefited greatly if the Defence Security Officer's role had gone to a dynamic young man with a first-rate mind. John's superior officer was a former Royal Marine, 'a delightful old colonel' but 'not exactly a live wire'. He gave his new officer a fair degree of latitude in his investigations, but it became clear to a newcomer like John that the Defence Security Office had become a hub of clerical rather than counter-espionage activity.

The intelligence world was sufficiently complex to warrant a short explanation. The police Special Branch and the Defence Security Office were but two of several organisations operating in Singapore at this time. The armed services each had their own intelligence organisation – Naval Command had Naval Intelligence, Air Command had the Air Security Service and Malaya Command had the Military Arm. However, in addition to these, the Far East Combined Bureau, officered by members of all three services, was charged with coordinating intelligence and counter-intelligence. There is no doubt that in the 1930s the means of protecting British intelligence in the country was fragmentary and underfunded. It was also an exclusive world, based on the 'old boy network'. It was undermined by personal rivalry and duplication of effort. In contrast, Japan's intelligence network in South-east Asia was concentrated in the hands of the Military Attaché in the Japanese Embassy, Bangkok, and the Consulate-General, Singapore.

John's new front role as Services Liaison Officer for Police was to address yet another weakness of the British system: the overall lack of liaison between police organisations. He was given responsibility for forging links between the civil and military police in the investigation of sabotage. Keen to be proactive, John approached his opposite number in the Air Security Service, Maurice Browne, with a proposal to test the security of Kallang airfield, in the south of Singapore Island, which was the base for two squadrons of Brewster Buffalo fighters of the Royal New Zealand Air Force. John brought in a fellow police officer, Claude Fenner, who suggested they should consult Capt Freddy Spencer Chapman, an expert on clandestine operations. The objective in this instance was to test how many times it was possible for a man to get through Kallang's perimeter fence undetected. After conducting a number of practical experiments for breaking through, all they demonstrated was a woeful lack of any effective security.

At this time John was also involved in the investigation of a fatal bomber crash over Singapore. Contrary to the official assumption that this must be a case of sabotage, the work of a pro-Japanese fifth column, he identified the perpetrator as a seriously disturbed aircraftsman in the ranks. Measures to counter fifth columnists in Singapore were, however, very much within his remit. Even more than its airfields, the island's state-of-the-art naval base was highly vulnerable. It had been built over seventeen years at a cost of some £63 million, and the vista of this great arsenal with barracks, dry and floating docks, machine shops, cranes, storage tanks and heavy gun emplacements made it a prime target for sabotage. Though the details have been lost over time, evidence suggests that in his liaison role John was involved in pre-emptive action to protect the base.[2]

The decisions on Singapore's strategic defence had been made during the 1920s, when it was thought that an attack on the island was likely to be seaborne. Most of the island's impressive range of fixed gun emplacements was therefore directed towards the sea. As events proved, the real danger to Singapore would come from a major enemy onslaught from the north, down the length of the Malayan Peninsula. At the critical test in 1942 there was a lack of the correct ammunition for those guns that could be turned against a landward attack.[3] However, once it was apparent that Japan had embarked on imperial expansion into South-east Asia, the need for sound defences on Malaya's northern and eastern flanks should have been obvious. The warning came when Japanese troops marched into French Indochina in 1940.

Economic deficiencies were the driving force for Japanese expansionism. Japanese companies had shown determined interest in Malaya's rich mining settlements, such as those near Dungan and Endau, on the Trengganu and Pahang coasts. By mid-summer 1941 the threat was more focused when the British censor intercepted a detailed Japanese report on the harbour facilities at Endau, and the tides and loading arrangements. The British had taken some steps to protect vulnerable sites. Fixed defences – observation posts, pillboxes, dannart (barbed) wire, artillery emplacements – were concentrated on salient points overlooking the eastern beaches, the approaches to the coastal towns and around the airfields. (From the defensive standpoint the interior of the Peninsula was protected by impenetrable jungle, so it received scant attention.) But the efficacy of the east-coast defences had yet to be tested. Malaya Command had casually assumed that the Japanese were unlikely to attack from the South China Sea between November and February, at the height of the north-east monsoon. When Special Branch picked up information on fresh Japanese activity around the Pahang–Johore border, the unthinkable now seemed possible.

It was against this darkening backcloth in late November that John and a colleague in the Defence Security Office went on a reconnaissance operation in the guise of two businessmen. Their aim was to assess the capability of defences on the south-eastern coast of Malaya. John was anxious to consult a friend who knew the area intimately. Lt Cyril Windsor of the Malay Royal Naval Volunteer Reserve was secretly working for Naval Intelligence. He might be able to shed light on verbal reports of unusual late night shipping activity in Endau and the sighting of suspicious vessels, believed to be Japanese submarines.

In the meantime, John had been asked in July to take on another assignment of particular sensitivity. He greeted the request quizzically, taking it to be one of those hush-hush jobs he distrusted, 'all atmosphere and sometimes precious little else'. But if he sounded flippant, it was simply to deflect the curiosity of others. He was to take on the difficult responsibility for intelligence relating to the MCP, in particular acting as case officer for Special Branch's most infamous secret double agent. This was none other than the Secretary-General of the Malayan Communist Party (MCP), who operated under many aliases but would be best known as 'Lai Tek'.[4] For fifty years John played this secret so close to his chest that no-one, neither close friends nor family, knew anything about it.[5]

Born in French Indochina of Chinese and Annamite blood, Lai Tek had been an informer for the French Securité in Saigon until the early 1930s. He claimed to support the Vietnamese Communist Party and to have helped Ho Chi Minh in its organisation. He is also alleged to have served as an agent of the Soviet Comintern and the Chinese Communist Party in Shanghai. At any rate, after his French cover was blown, the services of this astute, duplicitous, enigmatic character were acquired by a British Special Branch officer. Under a veil of official secrecy (not least because the MCP was a proscribed organisation), Lai Tek was acting as an informer in the pay of the Singapore Special Branch by 1934. His revelations enabled the Singapore Police to arrest and banish key members of the MCP's Central Executive Committee, which cleared the way for his promotion through the Communist hierarchy and his election to the highest post in the MCP in April 1939.

To run an agent of Lai Tek's professionalism and exploit the political potential would challenge an experienced Special Branch officer. The timing, however, was to John's advantage. Since Hitler had chosen the summer of 1941 to launch an all-out German attack on Russia, the Nazi–Soviet Pact of 1939 became a dead letter. Communism switched its full hostility against Fascism and Imperial Japan, and the primary objective of the Chinese Communists in particular was the defeat of the Japanese. So just as John was working to establish a constructive relationship with Lai Tek, Malayan Communists were ready to cooperate with the British colonials. Secretly Lai Tek volunteered MCP resources to the British in the event of war with Japan. His offer of help was initially turned down by a Malaya Command confident of its invincibility. It fell to John Davis, his case officer, to soothe the Secretary-General's pride and regain his trust for future cooperation with the MCP.

There were two other intelligence organisations operating in South-east Asia that would involve John Davis.[6] First, the Secret Intelligence Service (SIS), the operational arm of MI6, was the oldest of the departments of British Military Intelligence, responsible to the War Office (though funded by the Foreign Office). The War Office, it should be said, had tacitly acknowledged there might be a case for government-supported covert warfare when it sent Lt Col Alan Warren of the Royal Marines to Singapore to consider the viability of special operations in the Far East. In 1940 the Far Eastern wing of SIS, known as the Inter-Services Liaison Department (ISLD), established an office in Singapore. The *raison d'être* of the ISLD was pure intelligence, the gathering and collating of information on people and organisations likely to prove a threat to the security of Britain's Far Eastern possessions. Always intensely secretive about its agents and its operations, SIS/ISLD was considered by Air Chief Marshal H.R.M. Brooke-Popham, Commander-in-Chief Far East, to be the weak link in the Intelligence system, at least until a new head was appointed in the spring of 1941, a shadowy figure called G.C. Denham.[7] To the detriment of SIS, however, there was insufficient time for him to achieve dramatic improvements in the ISLD before the conflict with Japan began.

Meanwhile, in the summer of 1940, as European governments capitulated one by one to Hitler's armies, 'a small, tough British fighting service' had been formed in London to work with the Resistance forces.[8] This was SOE, which came to be something of a rival of the ISLD. Outside the control of Whitehall, it was a creature of the Ministry of Economic Warfare in Baker Street, Marylebone, which was headed by a Labour member of Churchill's Cabinet, Dr Hugh Dalton. If the ISLD claimed to be concerned with 'pure' intelligence, what marked out SOE, apart from its heavy reliance on civilian volunteers, was its function, defined by John Davis as 'action-based intelligence work'. In his view, if the primary purpose of SOE was to undertake operations such as resistance, sabotage, propaganda, deception tactics and so on in occupied or enemy territories, success depended heavily on sound intelligence, the result of careful surveillance and information gathering.

Initially, SOE's target area was Nazi Germany, but in November 1940 a decision was taken to extend operations to the Far East to counter Japan's determined expansionist policy. After some delay, in May 1941 SOE's Singapore Mission was launched under a contrived cover of carrying out a study of economic and industrial trends. The whole operation – code-named the Oriental Mission – was spearheaded by a civilian, Valentine St J. Killery, who, like Dalton, was an old Etonian. A senior figure in ICI, he had a rich background of commercial experience in the Far East. His able deputy, Basil Goodfellow, with whom John was to work very closely and who became a personal friend, also came into the Oriental Mission from ICI. However, it seems there was little love lost between senior Intelligence officers in the armed services and Oriental Mission men, the latter being dismissed as 'bloody civilians', whose covert activities might rock the boat. There was, additionally, a deep distrust of irregular warfare among Malaya Command, and in consequence a proposal from the Oriental Mission to train guerrilla parties for behind-the-lines operations in the Malayan jungle was turned down as late as October 1941 by ACM Brooke-Popham, with the support of Maj Gen A.E. Percival, GOC (General Officer Commanding) Malaya Command. One reason given was that public morale would suffer if there was a perceived need to train guerrillas!

Nevertheless, a major achievement of the Oriental Mission was the establishment in July of a special training school for covert operations under Lt Col J.M.L. Gavin. It was sited at Tanjong Balai, an isolated headland on the south coast of Singapore Island. In view of the intransigence of the Malayan High Command, for the first five months No. 101 Special Training School (STS) handled a largely 'foreign' clientele, in that its recruits came from Hong Kong, French Indochina, Burma and Southern Siam. (For instance, most of the two dozen SOE operatives placed in Southern Siam by December 1941 were trained at No. 101 STS.) It was only after a fieldwork expert, Capt Freddy Spencer Chapman, joined the school that he and Gavin worked together on a detailed plan to infiltrate stay-behind groups in Malaya. Their intention was to exploit the diversity of experience and talents of Malayan volunteers, whether they were European or Asian, servicemen or civilians, just so long as they were willing to accept the risks of covert operations. But various pressures, including lack of time, prompted the Oriental Mission to compromise and settle on all-European and all-Asian groups. There was, therefore, a need for Chinese-speaking officers to direct the all-Chinese parties.

It goes without saying that leadership, whether in pure intelligence, counter-intelligence or guerrilla warfare, requires special skills and unusual qualities and experience. Arthur Dickinson was not the only senior officer to see in John many of the essential attributes: another was Killery's second-in-command in Singapore, Basil Goodfellow. He was instrumental in prompting John to produce a pithy curriculum vitae to justify his selection for leading SOE operations in Malaya. In that document, written in the summer of 1942, John made it clear that he was ready to pledge his full commitment to special operations, since he was unmarried and had no dependants. He had always enjoyed good health, was physically very strong and had no desire to settle down to an office job. He could draw on eleven years' experience of police work in all parts of Malaya, which had given him 'a particular knowledge of the Malayan countryside and jungle'. Furthermore, he was one of a small band of police officers who was fluent in Malay and Cantonese and had learnt Mandarin for several months, and, with 'suitable opportunities to practise it', could become 'fluent in that dialect in a very short time'. As a resident of Canton for two years he could claim 'a fair experience of travel in China', including wartime visits to the Kuomintang (KMT) capital, Chungking, and the strategic city of Kunming, which controlled the Burma Road and air links between south-west China and the Allies in India. The ancient Chinese city of Canton, which was also a European treaty port, was an extraordinary mixture of East and West. To be exposed to both a cultural antithesis and one of the great civilisations of the world had been a defining experience for the young police officer. Finally, he had nothing to lose, he observed wryly. 'I lost all my possessions in Singapore beyond a kit bag of clothing, and all my bank balance is frozen till the war ends.'

Academic aspirations had also been a new experience to John. Daily tuition by a corps of scholarly Chinese teachers, leading to examinations at three stages, imposed on the cadets high demands of concentration and self-discipline. He also matured rapidly, as if his China days were in effect a substitute for the university education he had missed. He had time to extend the parameters of his thinking and challenge the social and political assumptions of his youth and background. From a new friend, Robert Bruce, he acquired an interest in politics, in Socialism in particular, and began to work out his own utopian ideology. In addition to Bruce, John met a number of refreshingly different people and made some good friends in the Malayan circle: Innes Tremlett and Ian Wylie in the police, and from the Malayan Civil Service Noel Alexander, Geoffrey Davis and Richard Broome, to whom he became so close that the others jokingly referred to him as 'Tweedledee' to Broome's 'Tweedledum'.

John's claim to 'particular knowledge' of Malaya was well justified, since he had held positions in Selangor, Pahang and Perak. Collectively these states covered a large swathe of the Peninsula from coast to coast.[9] Since there were few roads in the Kuantan district of Perak – and almost none in Pekan – John regularly spent hours with his constables cycling or slogging the 20 or more miles on foot between settlements. Later he familiarised himself with the more developed west-coast belt and the urban communities of Perak and Selangor, where the tin towns traditionally attracted a high proportion of Chinese workers and harboured gang robbers. It was fortunate that he enjoyed active policing and leading a police party in hot pursuit of cut-throats in the Perak Hills.

Over time, John developed a rare overview of the topography of the Peninsula. In his last Perak post, Kuala Kangsar, he was responsible for policing the valley of the Perak River from the estuary to the middle of the Peninsula and north to the limestone country around the Siamese border. Away from Perak's urban scene he was at his happiest sailing in the Malacca Straits, that and yomping up and down spurs of 2,000–3,000ft with a friend or 'bagging' a peak like Gunong Korbu or Yong Yap.[10] He loved the wild, remote areas and the jungle-covered mountains of the central range where Perak, Pahang and Kelantan meet; where man-made clearings revealed the presence of the shy, kindly aboriginal people. He and his friend Guy Madoc took their 'jungling' very seriously. John relished a challenge that exercised all the senses and tested physical stamina, intelligence, competitiveness and judgement. Subsequently, many of the lessons learned while enjoying his leisure pursuits in peacetime contributed to his survival in the Japanese war.

The gloomy political situation in 1941 produced a year of hectic diplomatic activity. With their troops already occupying northern French Indochina, the Japanese skilfully exploited hostilities between Siam and her neighbour to negotiate important concessions that would lead to the utilisation of Indochina's southern airfields and port facilities. In February, Prime Minister Churchill told President Roosevelt that Japan was intent on war with their countries. In Malaya blackout practices were held. The colonial government introduced petrol rationing and income tax, which John considered 'a mere flea bite'. Moves towards a military build-up that began in April may have reduced British anxieties, but the majority of Australian and Indian troops were scarcely trained for jungle warfare. The truth is that, even through the next crisis in July and on into the autumn, Britain and America were playing for time, relying on economic sanctions and still hoping for a diplomatic resolution to Japanese ambitions. But a change of government in Japan in mid-October heralded more extreme policies: by November the talk was mostly of war. Even so, John still only gave the odds on war as 'fifty-fifty', for he could not believe that the Japanese would take on both the United States and the British Empire simultaneously. However, five days later the Japanese presented the Americans with their final peace proposals, to which the US government responded on 26 November with counter-demands that Japanese forces should be withdrawn from China and Indochina.

From this point events moved very quickly. Repeated reports came in of Japanese aircraft making high-altitude flights over Malaya's main range. On the evening of Saturday 29 December cinema screens flashed notices to all service personnel to return to their bases, and the following day civilian volunteers were told to report to their local headquarters. Public gloom lifted briefly on 2 December as Britain's Naval Task Force – Force Z – at last reached Singapore waters. The ships steamed into view in a single line, silhouetted against a backcloth of blue sky and green islands. The battleship HMS *Prince of Wales* and the battlecruiser HMS *Repulse*, escorted by the destroyers HMS *Electra*, HMS *Express*, HMS *Tenedos* and HMAS *Vampire*, made their way up the Johore Straits to the Naval Base. They had been sent at Churchill's insistence to defend Malaya. But the aircraft carrier HMS *Indomitable*, which should have been there to provide vital air cover, had run aground a month before in Kingston Harbour, Jamaica, and no other carrier could be spared.

Four days later an RAAF Hudson reconnaissance aircraft spotted three ships some 200 miles off Kota Bharu, sailing northwards towards the Gulf of Siam. Within the hour, two convoys of troop transports with naval escort were sighted steaming in a westerly direction. The chiefs of staff assumed they were heading for Thailand, but monsoon rain and mist played havoc with visibility in the next critical hours. On 7 December the *Sunday Tribune* printed a Reuter report on the sighting of Japanese transports off Cambodia Point. The editor saw this as a bad omen, as bad as the failure of a lone Catalina to return to base after a reconnaissance mission. Officers in Special Branch and the Defence Security Office had been warned that 'things were likely to happen'. They were told to stay within the limits of Singapore town, where they could be contacted by telephone if 'the balloon went up'.

John pondered the situation over and over that morning. In common with friends like Richard Broome, he could not bring himself to believe anything so grave could occur. His mind was partly on the boat races due to take place that day. He persuaded his Malay assistant to bring the boat he had bought earlier in the year to Pasir Panjang, which he judged was within the town limits. It was a good day's racing. When evening came without any message, John was satisfied all was well. He went to bed feeling confident and relaxed. Like most of the residents of Singapore, he was sound asleep when the first wave of Japanese bombers struck in the early hours of Monday 8 December.

Chapter 2

A Taste of MI6

Sixty years on John Davis could still remember the sequence of reports that shattered the prolonged peace and complacency of colonial Singapore. There was something crude, sickening, and even banal about a stick of bombs that, with hindsight, accelerated the collapse of Europe's colonial hegemony and brought about a turning point in the history of the modern world. Three bangs on one side of the police house, followed by nothing – just a pause – then three bangs on the other. John put the time at around 4 a.m.

Sirens wailed and explosions alternated with ack-ack fire. Searchlights fanned the moonlit sky, but from Pearls Hill he observed that far from being blacked out, the lights in the centre of the town were still shining. He followed orders to go immediately to Police HQ. 'We had a rendezvous to go to . . . but when we got there, there was nothing to do . . . Nobody knew what was happening. We spent the rest of the night drinking coffee and talking . . .' John heard later that although the main targets had been the airfields of Tengah and Seletar, the populated districts and the commercial area around Raffles Square had also been damaged, causing 200 civilian casualties.

Neither he nor anyone he knew had anticipated the dramatic speed and extent of the Japanese onslaught, which only became apparent in the course of that Monday. Ominously on the previous night four Japanese destroyers had turned south, reaching their destination off northern Malaya by midnight to reveal a deadly game plan. After preliminary shelling of Kelantan's coastal defences, in the early moonlit hours of Monday 8 December, assault barges disgorged troops of Gen Yamashita's Twenty-fifth

Army on to the beach near Kota Bharu. This was followed a few hours later by coastal assaults on the Thai ports of Singora and Patani.

Meanwhile, across the dateline in Hawaii, Japan had launched what John described as a 'terrifyingly successful' air attack on the United States Pacific Fleet lying peacefully at anchor in Pearl Harbor. America would grieve the loss of 2,330 servicemen who died that day. The eight battleships in port were all hit; five were sunk. Two destroyers and nine other ships suffered a similar fate and 140 aircraft were destroyed. The only solace was that three aircraft carriers of the United States Pacific Fleet were away at sea and missed the conflagration.

On the six o'clock news that fateful morning, Singapore Radio announced the stark but obvious fact that Great Britain and the United States were now at war with Japan. Reports flowed in of more Japanese successes. Some hours later on 8 December Thailand surrendered. While the people of Singapore assessed the damage they had suffered, there were further amphibious landings on the airfield at Hong Kong and on American air bases in the Philippines. All the same, John remained confident, and like many British Malayans he presumed the fighting could be contained in the north of the Peninsula until the British Army proceeded – in Governor Sir Shenton Thomas's inept expression – to 'shove the little men off'.[1] The worst that could happen, John felt at this stage, was that hostilities might drag on, resulting in restrictions and shortages, 'with all the fun taken out of life'.

In the next twenty-four hours, however, the enemy's grip tightened on Northern Malaya. The British unit sent too late to hold the Ledge, a key defensive position in Thailand, was forced back to the border by crack Japanese troops and tanks. More seriously, the damage inflicted by bombing raids on Malaya's northern airfields and the destruction of precious aircraft meant that the British rapidly lost control of the air. Dire consequences followed. On the evening of Monday 8 December Force Z had slipped away from Singapore under cover of darkness and turned north to intercept the Japanese task force off the Thai and Kelantan coasts. Without fighter cover Adm Sir Tom Phillips took a calculated gamble, compounded by his decision to change course to investigate an unverified report of an enemy landing at Kuantan.[2] The next day the British warships were spotted by Japanese reconnaissance aircraft and shadowed off the Pahang coast. Unprotected from the air, the *Prince of Wales* and the *Repulse* were sitting ducks as bombers and torpedo aircraft of Japan's 85-strong 22nd

Air Flotilla swooped upon them with deadly accuracy. Both fighting ships were crippled, then mortally hit and finally sank to their graves beneath the waves of the South China Sea. They took with them 860 officers and men, including Adm Phillips and Capt J.C. Leach of the *Prince of Wales.*

The news began to percolate later in the day, though curiously John did not hear about it until the following morning. Claude Fenner, a fellow resident of Pearls Hill, came in to see him carrying the morning paper, which he solemnly handed over. Staring at the headlines John was overwhelmed. Rarely in his life did he experience such a brutal shock. In a flash the hopes of yesterday evaporated. Instead he was filled with a sense of helplessness that events were veering out of control.

This emotion was reinforced by a strange happening a short time later. 'I was called to the top of the Detective Branch,' John recalled, 'and we watched a most extraordinary phenomenon in the Western sky just at dusk. It looked like a great huge ball of fire as if coming from some tremendous explosion right in the distance . . . We examined this phenomenon, we took bearings on it suggesting it was Venus, which it turned out to be, as it sank below the horizon – but we couldn't believe it.' He admitted to being disturbed by the portent. It was as if the natural world was corroborating the human disaster that had just afflicted Britain.

Throughout Malaya public morale was plummeting dramatically. In London, on receiving the grim news of Force Z's fate, Churchill was fearful of the implications. 'There were no British or American capital ships in the Indian Ocean or the Pacific . . . Over all this vast expanse of waters Japan was supreme and we everywhere were weak and naked.'[3] In popular tradition Britannia had ruled the waves for two centuries or more. Now at a stroke that hegemony had been destroyed. Wednesday 10 December 1941 was Britain's 'day of infamy'. No one felt it more keenly than John Davis.

Driven by the seriousness of the early disasters, the civil and military authorities in Singapore agreed to enlist the support of Malaya's Chinese community against China's national enemy, Japan. Belatedly Malaya Command accepted the value of a body of guerrillas to fight behind the lines in the jungle. One source of young, able-bodied, Chinese zealots eager to fight the Japanese was the MCP. While the colonial government was still unwilling to acknowledge publicly any association with Communism, Special Branch acted as an intermediary behind the scenes. John Davis was certainly involved in negotiating the arrangements because of his familiarity with the case history of the Party's Secretary-General.[4] In any event, shortly after the declaration of war, agent Lai Tek, speaking on behalf of the MCP Central Executive Committee, repeated the offer of the previous July to provide recruits for covert operations. This time the colonial authorities responded positively. There followed a cloak-and-dagger meeting on 18 December in a poky upstairs room in one of Singapore's back streets. Present on the Communist side were the Secretary-General and another unidentified MCP member – both wearing dark glasses, 'to complete the air of conspiracy' – while Freddy Spencer Chapman represented the Oriental Mission.[5] The second British officer present was a Chinese-speaking member of Special Branch, whose identity has been confirmed recently as John Davis.[6] The events of that day would have repercussions for the duration of the Japanese war and arguably well beyond. The British agreed to release Chinese Communists from prison in return for the MCP's guarantee that they would supply suitable recruits to be trained in guerrilla warfare at No. 101 STS. There was no time to lose. The first group of volunteers was to be collected at a pre-arranged venue in Singapore on 20 December.

A little time before this John had received an unexpected request through the Deputy Defence Security Officer, Maj Jimmy Green of MI6, to come and meet the head of SIS. Green explained that John had been recommended to MI6 as a fluent Chinese speaker. The service had an acute lack of qualified linguists to assist with the preparations for 'behind-the-lines' operations. Was John prepared to help the ISLD in Kuala Lumpur? He was assured that Arthur Dickinson, his mentor, would be kept informed of his movements and there would be no objection from the military. Seeing no reason to demur, John agreed.

A fortnight into the war, on the afternoon of 22 December, he climbed into a cramped de Havilland passenger biplane and flew up to Kuala Lumpur. 'I remember sitting on packing cases,' he recalled later. 'The top of the plane had been literally broken through and a chap with a Lewis gun shoved it through the back, and as we landed we were told to look for bomb holes and warn the pilot if there were any.' The reason, it transpired, was that the airfield had been bombed earlier that day; and since it was now serving as an advanced base for the men and supplies salvaged from the northern airfields, the capital of the Federated Malay States was poised to be the target of increasingly heavy enemy attacks. But on this occasion their luck held and the aircraft made a good landing.

Elsewhere, however, the outlook was grim. After a mere week of war Kedah, northern Perak, Province Wellesley and Penang Island had all been abandoned to the Japanese. In the east the general retreat by rail from Kelantan was completed on the 22nd as John flew to Selangor. Yet in Kuala Lumpur III Indian Corps HQ bustled with activity, and people were still busily at work despite disruptions caused partly by an influx of civilian refugees from the north. The mood here was in stark contrast to the mounting chaos in central Perak, where hard-pressed British and Indian troops, unable to stem the Japanese advance, were withdrawing down the Perak River.

On his arrival John took stock. He had been told the officer in overall charge of clandestine operations and related intelligence matters in Kuala Lumpur was Lt Col Alan Warren, a tall, tough, bristly commanding figure and a staff officer at GHQ Singapore. But John was referred first to a Maj Rosher, MI6's Secret Intelligence Officer in the city, who desperately needed assistance with the deployment of Chinese and European operatives in the field. If the speed of the Japanese advance brought one benefit, it was, John noticed, the spontaneous cooperation between officers in the various intelligence agencies. He learnt that Lt Col Warren had taken over the Chinese school in Batu Road as another SOE training school for local Communist recruits; and Maj Rosher and a Special Branch officer, R.O.W.M. 'Towkay' Davis, were liaising with the local Communist leader, Tan Chen King, in organising groups of young Communists for guerrilla training. At the same time the Signals Officer for the Oriental Mission's special operations, Capt Jack Knott, was helping Maj Rosher to set up a W/T unit that would convey intelligence from outstations near the front line to the main signals base at Kranji in Singapore. In addition, assisted by an officer of the Malayan Forestry Department, J.C.K. 'Jungly' Marshall, the Head of Special Branch in Kuala Lumpur, John Dalley, was recruiting volunteers for a special jungle force of guerrillas to be known as Dalley's Company (Dalco for short).

Meanwhile, the day after his arrival, John Davis was directed to attend an SIS conference arranged by 'Towkay' Davis and some local Communists, to discuss how their volunteers could best be deployed. It was agreed that the first priority was to send stay-behind reinforcements to eastern Pahang where Kuantan airfield – evacuated over-hastily by the RAF on

9 December – was in danger of falling into enemy hands. The order to hold the airfield until a counter-attack could be launched came from Maj Gen Percival, GOC Malaya Command, but to implement it would require some very disciplined, brave and well-trained men. At the top of the SIS/ISLD agenda, therefore, was a plan to transport a detachment of young Chinese Communists to Kuantan and send them undercover into the jungle as near as possible to the airfield. John was enlisted to accompany them and give them their orders in their native tongue, a move intended to raise their spirits and give them some well-deserved encouragement.

Since the success of a counter-attack would depend on maintaining W/T communication with Singapore, a second feature on the ISLD agenda was to establish a stay-behind party, complete with W/T set, among the tree-covered hillsides rising above the river at Sungei Lembing. In addition, there was concern at III Indian Corps HQ in Kuala Lumpur as to what was happening in the state of Trengganu, to the north of Kuantan and Sungei Lembing. The only intelligence to come from this area was now a fortnight old. It had been reported by an MCS officer called Walter Cole, a member of the Malay States Volunteer Reserve attached to the Argyll and Sutherland Highlanders, who had since disappeared.[7] John learned that another intelligence-gathering unit, complete with W/T set, was to be placed in southern Trengganu, and a Malayan Civil Service officer in the Malay States Volunteer Reserve, Mervyn Sheppard, was to be in charge of planting both W/T teams. Sheppard, like John, was a serious jungle walker, and two postings in Kemaman during the 1930s had given him inside knowledge of the area.

Meanwhile, later on 23 December, after the SIS conference broke up, John went off to the Batu Road STS to collect equipment, arms and ammunition for the Kuantan operation. While he was there he bumped into Freddy Spencer Chapman, who was busy equipping himself for a secret raiding party the following day on the Trong River. He invited John to join him but of course he had to decline. John spent Christmas Eve finalising the Kuantan arrangements. In the evening he went over to the Selangor Club, better known as the 'Spotted Dog'. There were few people about and the atmosphere was strangely subdued until he was warmly greeted by a police subordinate from Perak days, Harvey Ryves, and his wife. John told him briefly that he had come up from Singapore on a special job, so he would not linger: his mind was very much on the Kuantan operation the next day.

On Christmas Day 1941 the ISLD party drove east across the jungle-covered hills by the Genting Simpah Pass into Pahang. John was at the wheel of a Ford car, and with him were Maj Rosher and Capt Knott. They followed behind a lorry, loaded to the roof and driven by a young Sikh Army driver. In addition to a British instrument mechanic, two Chinese W/T operators and a party of Chinese Communist would-be guerrillas, the lorry also carried their equipment, a generator, W/T transmitter, stores, arms and explosives. John was familiar with the route and the weather conditions. As the road twisted past sheer hillsides and around hairpin bends wet with monsoon rain, they had to look out for another hazard, the chance of being spotted by Japanese aircraft out on reconnaissance. It was important to John not to lose sight of the lorry, but in trying to tail it he unintentionally pressed the driver too much. Each in turn increased their speed until finally the lorry veered out of control and slipped over the side of the road down towards a ravine. The Sikh driver was concussed and broke his arm, one of the W/T operators gashed his thigh, the W/T transmitter was damaged and the vehicle itself was a write-off. The passengers were hauled out and eventually taken back to Kuala Lumpur in varying states of shock. The rest of the party, including John, slunk back into town, consoling themselves that it could have been a good deal worse and what they had just experienced was a typical mishap of war.

As it was Christmas the Intelligence community gathered for dinner somewhat later at the Station Hotel. The news that Hong Kong had surrendered to the Japanese that day had not permeated to all those present. Mervyn Sheppard was in ebullient mood despite the fact that his colleague on the prospective mission to plant W/T parties had just cried off. As he sat listening to the table talk John was reserved, still somewhat shaken by the day's events. At one point in the conversation Sheppard raised his voice and loudly declared to everyone present that 'the one chap he'd really like to go with him was John Davis'. Under the circumstances John felt forced to agree to his request despite some reservations that he had unwisely committed himself to taking part in three operations, not one. Much later, he revealed that 'Fuff' Sheppard's cocksure impulsiveness made him uneasy – and John never totally trusted a man with an ego. He scarcely slept that night, talking over his worries into the early hours with a former colleague in the Federated Malay States Police Service, but there was no way back.[8]

By now the mission to plant the clandestine party by Kuantan airfield was becoming a race against time. Throughout Boxing Day Maj Rosher's unit worked feverishly to build a new transmitter and receiver with spare parts, and by 27 December a second lorry was loaded with equipment and men. This time there were no serious problems crossing the Main Range, although they were slowed down by the archaic river ferry at Jerantut. When Rosher's party, which included John, reached Kuantan, the whereabouts of the enemy was still unclear. In addition to lack of intelligence, Brig G.W.A. Painter, the senior British officer, was dogged by contradictory orders. Later they discovered that the Japanese had embarked on a two-pronged attack from Kelantan to Pahang, one following the railway track, the other keeping to the coast. They were still north of Kuantan when Rosher's party reached the western outskirts where the airfield was located. After John had briefed the Chinese volunteers on tactics in anticipation of a Japanese attack, he gave them orders to transfer the equipment and arms and prepare to take up their positions inside the surrounding secondary jungle. Then, as soon as the young men had taken effective cover, John drove Rosher, Knott and a Chinese W/T operator back to the little settlement of Sungei Lembing.

It was now 28 December. Sheppard had meanwhile agreed arrangements with Vincent Baker, the manager of the Pahang Consolidated tin mine there. His assistant, Brian Tyson, and a local planter, Maurice Cotterill, would help Sheppard to recruit reliable locals for a stay-behind party and find a suitable site for linking up with the signals base at Kranji.[9] Leaving Tyson and Cotterill to sort out the practicalities, on 29 December John and Mervyn Sheppard, with a *jelutong* tapper as their guide, set off on the third stage of the ISLD mission. Their objectives were to ascertain the Japanese position and also whether another secret W/T station could be established in southern Trengganu. Their destination was the old tin mine at Bundi, 30 miles north of Sungei Lembing, which would take them through some awe-inspiring jungle punctuated by limestone caves. The two men set themselves a good pace but the weather conditions were foul and they were forced to rest overnight in the jungle, wrapped in mackintosh capes. In the circumstances the distance was a severe test of stamina, and they knew there was always a chance of running into a squad of Japanese troops probing southwards, not something John wished to dwell on, given the stories of excessive Japanese brutality that were already circulating.

They reached the mining complex on 30 December and immediately set up a surveillance. Detecting an atmosphere of high tension, they decided to lie low in the surrounding secondary jungle until the dead of night when eventually the mine manager, Yong Hon Fa, would slip out to meet them. They talked in subdued voices amid the undergrowth for an hour or so, discussing the possibility of infiltrating a guerrilla group into the mine and bringing in explosives, arms and ammunition in support. John was less confident than Sheppard as to whether the plans were realistic but it was only after the war that they learned of the dire outcome. A Chinese dresser at the mine somehow discovered the plan and reported it to the Japanese. As a result several workers were arrested and tortured.[10]

In an effort to keep to schedule, the two Englishmen trekked back hotfoot to Sungei Lembing the next day, New Year's Eve. Bad news awaited them. Kuantan had been attacked at dawn the previous day. Maj Rosher, who had returned to Kuantan to locate the signals station, ran into enemy machine-gun fire directed at the ferry, which was loaded with a company of the Garhwali Rifles evacuating the north bank. Rosher managed to get back to report that the British were on the point of abandoning Kuantan and were withdrawing 22 Indian Brigade west to the town of Maran. This news prompted the remaining Europeans in Sungei Lembing to leave immediately.

The second piece of bad luck was that Tyson's W/T transmitter appeared to have a faulty valve so would not work. John and Sheppard agreed to do their best to get a replacement. Darkness had fallen when the pair suddenly realised how hungry they were. They scoured the empty mine bungalows for food, scraping up a New Year's supper of cream crackers and a half bottle of champagne. Tyson and Cotterill were on the point of disappearing to their jungle hideout, following Baker and his sister, but in a last gesture of defiance Tyson and Rosher destroyed a bridge across the Kuantan River.

By now it was apparent that to linger would be foolish, and escape was vital before the Japanese appeared. At first light a friendly Malay guided the British party out of Sungei Lembing by a little known route over a 3,000ft jungle-covered ridge. Their path followed the line of the Pohoi River to the bridge of the same name and the main Kuantan–Maran road. There was no sign of military activity. It was not yet dusk so they hid in reeds along the riverbank until they were able to flag down a British Army lorry, which took them as far as the mining town of Raub, the latest headquarters of

22 Brigade. After further delays and more lifts they all got back to Kuala
Lumpur in early January.

In the week that had elapsed since the ISLD party had set off for Pahang
the war had continued on its disastrous course. In Kuala Lumpur John was
told that Kuantan had actually fallen on 2 January and with it the airfield.
The fate of the ISLD's Chinese guerrillas was unknown. In the western belt,
the town of Ipoh had been lost on 28 December. As the New Year dawned,
the ridges guarding Kampar were engulfed in bitter fighting and it proved
impossible to hold the town, which was also occupied on 2 January. On the
3rd the British began to fall back to their next line of defence at the Slim
River. Since this was only 80 miles north of Kuala Lumpur, preparations
had already started for a mass evacuation of the capital.

In the midst of preparing for another strategic withdrawal Lt Col Warren
still had time to authorise the new valve and spare parts needed by Brian
Tyson's stay-behind party, but locating any parts in the chaos proved
impossible. John decided to return to Singapore, put in his report to the
ISLD and take a deserved breather. He would rejoin Sheppard as soon as he
could and offered to pick up the required spare parts from No. 101 STS.

The train from Kuala Lumpur moved at a snail's pace, repeatedly delayed
by blockages on the line. Normally John would have found the situation
intolerable but on this occasion he was overwhelmed by physical and
mental exhaustion. He had no idea how many miles he and Sheppard
had trekked on minimal food and sleep at the height of the monsoon,
continuously anticipating a head-on encounter with enemy troops. Now his
body's natural reaction was to shut down. Remarkably, the air-conditioning
in his carriage was still functioning, and he slumped into a dream-laden
sleep. Kuantan brought back powerful images of the *Prince of Wales* and
the *Repulse*. He was haunted by their loss, appalled by the implications for
Britain's maritime supremacy and the imperial traditions on which he and
countless generations had been nurtured. 'I think this broke my morale,' he
said sententiously.

By the time he reached Singapore, however, he began to recover. This
was as well since his first task was to placate an angry Arthur Dickinson:
MI6 had failed to inform him about the circumstances of John's absence.

Dickinson, of course, accepted John's explanation of why and where he had been but was fairly dismissive of the value of stay-behind parties. Still feeling the need to unwind, John and a friend, Geoffrey Davis, went on a long ramble over the deserted Japanese golf links near the Tanglin Barracks. The older man was a sympathetic listener and a calming influence. For the first time John questioned the step he had taken in joining the ISLD. He had decided that Maj Rosher's set-up was inefficient and this irritated him even more than his habit of calling everyone 'Old Boy'. Later that day John's spirits rose further on receiving a message from Richard Broome – Tweedledum to his Tweedledee in their carefree Canton days – asking John to meet him at Batu Anam in Johore. There was still unfinished business with Sheppard and Tyson, but as soon as that was over, John decided, he would search out Richard. Luckily, Sheppard had acquired the replacement valve at Command HQ, Johore; all they had to do was ensure they reached Tyson and Cotterill in their hideout above Sungei Lembing.

Sheppard drove north again with John until they reached the little town of Segamat. Here Sheppard stopped and told John he intended to continue on foot to Sungei Lembing with the valve and some plastic explosive. John baulked at the idea, considering it to be sheer madness. He suggested sending a message by a carrier to Tyson and Cotterill, asking them to make their way down to Johore where they could probably link up with Allied troops. Sheppard did not look well, so John accompanied him as far as the Keratang River, where he found two Chinese peasants willing to take a message to Sungei Lembing. He felt he had now acquitted his obligations to the Special Intelligence Service. As for Mervyn Sheppard, who clearly had a fever, John tried again to dissuade him from going any further and suggested they should return to Segamat. Sheppard refused and they parted company. Later John learnt he had been forced to abandon his attempt to reach Tyson and Cotterill.[11]

At Segamat John caught up with the news of the previous few days. On 6–7 January the British had suffered their most humiliating military defeat of the campaign so far, at the Slim River. It was clear that nothing could save Kuala Lumpur now. John's only consolation was that another message from Richard Broome awaited him in Segamat, repeating the request to meet. Their reunion, however, came quite unexpectedly. By sheer coincidence Richard spotted John walking down the main street of Segamat. It was 10 January. Neither would forget the date, for the next day the demoralised British abandoned Kuala Lumpur to the invincible Japanese.

Chapter 3

SOE and the Oriental Mission

At the same time as John flew to Kuala Lumpur at the request of SIS, Richard Broome received a summons to the Singapore headquarters of the Inter-Services Liaison Department (ISLD). It appeared that SIS was looking for someone to maintain their Singapore office, though Richard was surprised to be told there was only one W/T communications unit operating in the field.[1] Then, on hearing that an order had gone out withdrawing secret service agents from Malaya, he was distinctly unimpressed by the apparent pusillanimity of SIS/ISLD; and yet he felt a flat refusal to join the organisation would seem unpatriotic.

However, as he left the ISLD office he was accosted by Basil Goodfellow, Killery's deputy, who confirmed in plain language that it would be unwise to get involved with 'that lot' and invited him to join SOE instead. Goodfellow hustled Richard back to their offices in the Cathay Building, a tall modern block near the Singapore waterfront, where he proceeded to explain the activities of the Oriental Mission and SOE's No. 101 STS. Impressed by Goodfellow's intellect and enthusiasm, Richard agreed to join SOE, which needed someone to convey groups of Chinese guerrillas up-country and launch them behind the lines.

Richard anticipated that the work would be gruelling and dangerous, but he found it oppressively lonely, too. After his first mission he tackled Goodfellow about sharing the work with John, who was then on his way to rejoin Mervyn Sheppard. Their whereabouts being unknown, SOE had to put out a hue and cry to locate John. Meanwhile, Richard had left the chain of messages, aware that he owed John a frank explanation of a decision that would affect both their futures. As it turned out, John needed little persuasion. In wartime, he observed, normal procedures were irrelevant; there was no time for pussyfooting and you made your own decisions. Quite simply, he was ready to leave SIS/ISLD. Since Richard wanted him to join SOE, he agreed to switch services. Through his work in Special Branch he knew the Oriental Mission, its strategy for guerrilla operations using Chinese Communist volunteers and the 'sabotage school' at Tanjong Balai – No. 101 STS – for training men for covert warfare. John thought of the young guerrillas he had taken to Kuantan airfield as Richard explained that his job entailed 'picking up these fellows [from No. 101 STS] and taking them in lorries as near as we could get to the front line, finding hiding places in the jungle, giving them all their stores, trying to give them a bit of spirit by making speeches in Cantonese and waving [a] fist, and then coming back and collecting the next lot'.[2]

Richard's first party had been placed on 5 January at Serendah, north of Kuala Lumpur. Its members were dedicated Communist volunteers, young, keen and highly disciplined, ready to sacrifice their lives to defeat the Japanese. This spirit was badly needed in a war that had turned disastrously against the British, for in the five days separating Richard's missions the Allied front had crumbled. Indian troops had abandoned Serendah in the face of heavy air and artillery attacks, and III Indian Corps HQ was in the process of relocating to the town of Segamat in northern Johore. When he met up with John, Richard was heading for Tampin, a natural junction on the border of Malacca and Negri Sembilan, with another lorryload of Chinese guerrillas.[3] It seemed sensible that they should join forces immediately and complete this second operation together; but it was a frustrating journey, pushing northwards against the flow of the retreating Allied traffic. When at last Richard drove into Tampin, it had the shuttered air of no man's land. They carried on a mile beyond the township until stopped by an anti-tank unit whose gunners warned them the Japanese were somewhere ahead, advancing south, which was why they proposed to clear off at dusk. Once they had gone, the Oriental Mission party would constitute the Allied front line, a distinction, Richard observed dryly, that he and John could well have done without.

After reconnoitring the jungle outskirts the two Englishmen came across a municipal rubbish dump with an incinerator that could serve as a temporary hiding place. Leaving the guerrillas to transfer their supplies, Richard and

John returned to the centre of Tampin to meet Lt Col Warren, who had driven in with an additional lorryload of Chinese to join their contingent. It was almost dark when these reinforcements reached the incinerator site. When Richard reminded them all that Japanese troops might appear at any time they quickly moved most of the heavy stores, piling them in an improvised dump in the jungle. After that it was time to snatch some sleep. John took charge of all the Chinese fighters for the night as Richard was required to drive Warren back to Segamat. Some of the Chinese went off to an abandoned planter's bungalow nearby; others slept near the incinerator. John rolled underneath a lorry to keep out of the heavy night rain and dozed till dawn. He met up with Richard later at Segamat.

Early that morning the thirty-strong party of Communists prepared to disappear into the jungle. They seemed refreshed and on their mettle. The group leader, Lai Fuk, a brave young man, rose within a year to command the 5th (Perak) Regiment of the MPAJA, and their Chinese interpreter was to take over as leader of the Negri Sembilan guerrillas. John gave them some last-minute instructions in cheerful, rousing tones. A Signals Officer in the SIS, watching him in a similar situation a few days later, 'envied him his easy relationship with the Chinese'.[4]

As John casually eyed the party preparing to leave, Lai Fuk mentioned that he had no means of timekeeping. This was a serious oversight and without hesitation John slipped off his wristwatch and handed it to him. 'I'll be able to get another in Singapore,' he gestured. They shook hands warmly and John wished Lai Fuk well. This small incident might have been forgotten but for a sequel eighteen months down the line.

Mission accomplished, John and Richard were keen to get back to Singapore to prepare for the next operation. The island was no longer a comfortable place to be. By mid-January the naval base and airfields had become the prime focus for enemy air attacks. John had a taste of the impact of aerial bombardment upon unarmed civilians when he was trapped in SOE's high-rise offices as bombs fell all around. The speed of the Japanese advance compelled the Oriental Mission staff to be decisive and pragmatic. The initial two-week training course was pared to the minimum. John and Richard also modified the infiltration tactics so that latterly the guerrillas were simply dropped as near as possible to a supply dump and were instructed to filter up the line as and when they were able. Even so, they found that by the time the next Chinese parties were ready their projected locations had been overrun, thanks to the enemy's dual advance down the Peninsula by the coastal and inland trunk roads. Some doubling up of parties became necessary: so, for instance, the third Communist contingent was joined by a group of ISLD Chinese from Kluang, making a total party of some sixty guerrillas. Their point of infiltration was Kampong Chaah, near Labis, northern Johore, an area of oil palm and rubber interspersed with dense jungle.[5]

For John the following fortnight was a kaleidoscope of disconnected events. He had one close shave outside Kluang when his car was chased by an enemy aircraft. As he made for the shelter of a nearby rubber and oil palm estate a dispatch rider pulled alongside but swerved, crashing his motorcycle into the side of John's Chevrolet. In a separate incident, while aiming for the coast road back to Singapore, he and Richard almost stumbled into a battle for the west-coast port of Batu Pahat. Smoke was drifting from recently bombed buildings and shops set alight by looters; and beyond, to the south-west, came the sound of firing around Kampong Minyak Beku. They watched through binoculars as a company of the 2nd Malay Regiment came under a ferocious mortar attack from an advance raiding party of Japanese Guards.

For the rest, only fleeting impressions remained of an unreal, unsettled existence in which, in Richard's words, they spent 'a day or so at the line bumming meals and beds here and there between hectic breaks back in Singapore'.[6] John recalled a Bofors battery dug in at Ayer Hitam crossroads, which was later the scene of some heavy fighting. Occasionally they bumped into an intrepid individual on the one-way trek down to Singapore. At Johore Bahru John met John Dalley, former Head of Special Branch in Kuala Lumpur. While held up by a logjam they sat on the grass verge and discussed seriously how Chinese volunteers could be deployed in the defence of Singapore. Their conversation bore fruit. Within days Dalley had raised a Chinese force of civilian irregulars, the legendary Dalforce, who were to fight with supreme courage almost to the last man.

By 18–19 January the Muar–Segamat front had collapsed and the rail and road junction of Kluang in central Johore became the new focus of the Allied line. But that, too, was short-lived. On the 22nd John was in Singapore waiting to collect another group of Chinese to be deployed near Kluang when Lt Col Warren told him to leave immediately for Johore to organise a supply dump. On reaching Rengam, 12 miles before

Kluang, John's sixth sense told him to leave the stores at Dalco HQ while he cased the situation ahead. What he saw and heard at Kluang was hardly reassuring. Maj James Barry, Rosher's successor, was about to evacuate the ISLD HQ and Training School on reports that the Japanese were only 11 miles away.[7] John had to act fast. He secured Barry's help with manpower and transport to shift the Oriental Mission's supplies of arms, ammunition and food from Rengam to a jungle access point some 12½ miles off the main Kluang–Mersing road. John made his own way to the spot and waited to take personal delivery. Then he supervised the transport of the supplies to a safe hideout in the hills by two parties of Chinese volunteers. They completed the task by dawn on 24 January. But it became clear later that this operation, like many others, was a waste of effort because the Japanese prevented the Chinese guerrilla party from reaching their source of supplies. Plans to deploy several other Chinese parties behind the lines were similarly foiled. In the final count the number of supply dumps hidden in the jungle exceeded the number of stay-behind groups, which in John's recollection was only four, totalling between 160 and 165 men.[8]

John, meanwhile, drove back with a sense of urgency to Singapore. He hoped to raise one more load of supplies and a sabotage party for infiltration in the hills north of Kota Tinggi, the only part of Johore with suitable jungle cover and still in Allied hands. It was another race against time as the decision on a staged withdrawal of all Allied forces to Singapore would be made on 26 January. Unfortunately, the monsoon rains had flooded Kota Tinggi, and progress was further delayed by an aerial bombardment of the town on the evening of the 28th. It was not until the 30th that fifty-eight guerrillas were all positioned. John now had 25 dangerous, rain-drenched miles to cover from Kota Tinggi back to Johore Bahru. In the confusion he found the bridge at Tebrau had been blown by engineers of the Johore Volunteers, forcing him to abandon his lorry on the north bank and paddle across the river. It was approaching daylight on the 31st when the dishevelled figure of John Davis reached the outer bridgehead and the causeway. He remembered seeing pipers of the Argyll and Sutherland Highlanders before being hastily waved through, but he missed the bagpipes and the roar of the demolition charges. He sensed that the Oriental Mission had reached a defining point. 'When the Singapore causeway was blown on 31 January 1942 the island of Singapore was invested, all communications with the mainland were severed.' The dilemma reverberated in John's head: had contact with the Peninsula become impossible, or could a viable tactical solution be found?

Both Richard and John were keen to know whether they had succeeded in laying down a framework for behind-the-lines resistance. One man who would have an answer was double agent Lai Tek, but it seems that John lost contact with him during January. So before reporting to Basil Goodfellow the two friends repaired to John's apartment to work out their own strategy for re-establishing links with Oriental Mission guerrillas. Clearly any attempt across the Johore Straits would be suicidal, but a back-door, night-time entry from the Malacca Straits might be feasible.

At a meeting with Basil on 2 February they explained their idea of finding a base on the east coast of Sumatra as a springboard to re-enter Malaya. They were still talking when two members of the Oriental Mission appeared and joined in the discussion. Frank Vanrenan and Ron Graham, ex-planters with Freddy Spencer Chapman's European party, had failed to rendezvous with their leader at Tanjong Malim, but had managed to escape to Sumatra. Now they were wondering how to rejoin him on the Malayan Peninsula. Their problem was that after losing contact with Chapman his fate was unknown. However, since all four men were thinking of a clandestine entry on Malaya's west coast, John and Richard suggested they should work out a joint action plan. Outside the fighting zone, Sumatra would obviously be the key to a successful plan, with Dutch cooperation.

Goodfellow passed on the gist of these discussions to Lt Col Warren, who was already working on other plans. One was to establish a supply line on the islands between Singapore and Sumatra, with a southern base at Rengat on the Indragiri River. If the worst were to happen it could serve as an escape route for Allied personnel to Sumatra's west-coast port of Padang. Warren, meanwhile, approved the idea of a two-pronged operation run by Broome and Davis and Vanrenan and Graham. He decided it could be combined with an intelligence-gathering mission and the deployment of the last ten Chinese guerrillas still waiting at No. 101 STS. As Goodfellow was busy organising the evacuation of the STS to Rangoon, Warren offered to use his naval contacts to find transport for this Sumatran operation. He came up with a Chinese motor *tongkang* called the *Hin Lee*, a reeking, diesel-driven coaster that was still carrying a perishable cargo of sugar and coconut oil: a cockroaches' delight, John recalled.

There was no time to spare. At her mooring by Clifford Pier the little ship was loaded up for the journey. Departure was set for Thursday 5 February. The sky over Singapore was darkened by palls of smoke rising from burning oil tanks at the naval base. That morning in the Outer Roads, Japanese dive-bombers had pasted the troopship *Empress of Asia* with deadly accuracy.[9] She lay to the rear of an incoming convoy that had delayed the *Hin Lee*'s departure, adding to the chaos as she continued to blaze for hours. Conditions on the *Hin Lee* were already grossly unpleasant. Crammed on board were Vanrenan and Graham; two RNVR officers, Lt Alex Lind and Lt Brian Passmore, and the crew; survivors from the *Prince of Wales* and the *Repulse*; and an NCO of the Gordon Highlanders. With them were ten Communist 'graduates' from No. 101 STS with Richard and John in charge; Jamal bin Daim, who was John's Malay orderly; and Ah Chuan, Richard's Chinese 'Boy'.[10] The Chinese were directed to the forward end, the Europeans to the cabins in the aft. Vanrenan was in charge of the armoury while Lt Lind, a fluent Dutch and Malay speaker, had overall command; Lt Passmore had been deputed to take her out to sea.

The *Hin Lee* left the wharf as darkness fell. Passmore swiftly detected trouble with the anchor cable and winch. The ship dragged, the engine was running hot and a stench rose into the air. In addition, there was no sign of the marker buoy to guide them through the minefield to open sea. Realising this, Passmore dropped anchor for the night and early the next morning he brought her back to harbour. Seeing that it would take some time to deal with the *Hin Lee*'s defects, John pondered his own problems: some unfinished official business and the fact that he only had the clothes he stood up in. He seized the chance to slip back to Pearls Hill, retrieve some clothes and polish off the business. When he returned an unexpected sight greeted him. Relative order had replaced the stinking chaos of the night before. The Harbour Board engineers had been helpful. A chart table was up, the ship had been cleaned, there were fresh food supplies and stores, and a prominent figure was on board. Lind had been relegated to second-in-command and Lt Col Warren was very much in charge, having decided that he could usefully direct operations from outside Singapore.

Just after 4 p.m. on the 6th the *Hin Lee* nosed her way a second time past Keppel Heads, avoiding the ghostly wreck of the *Empress*, which lay aground. Darkness fell as they steered between the southern islands of the Riau Archipelago, and over Little Karimun John observed the anomalous beauty of the tropical sky. With moonrise it was a calm, clear, starry night as the *Hin Lee* was set on her westerly course. Once off the Sumatran coast it was a matter of hiding by day and travelling by night, hugging the swampy coastline northwards from Selat Padang. At Bengkalis they traded a cargo of sugar, leaving again in time to reach Bagan Siapiapi on the afternoon of 10 February.

These four days were an uncomfortably tense time. They not only faced danger from the air and of running aground on mud flats and mangrove swamps, but their W/T battery acquired from Signals personnel in Singapore went dead, so they had no means of communication. At Bengkalis they picked up the disturbing news that Singapore town was being systematically shelled. On a personal note, John and Richard had become increasingly irritated by Warren's authoritarian military style and his tendency to exclude all but Lind from strategy discussions. On one occasion John's argumentative streak got the better of him and he dared to question Warren's directive. Warren responded furiously: 'Look here, Davis, these are my bloody orders!' John found it difficult not to smirk.[11]

Bagan Siapiapi, once an old pirate haunt but now a busy fishing port, made an obvious base for a Malayan incursion in view of its proximity to the coastline of Selangor, Negri Sembilan and Malacca. On meeting the British party, the Dutch administrator, Controlleur Visscher, and the harbour-master, were most welcoming but seemed oblivious to the seriousness of the Japanese threat, especially to Palembang, the centre of the Sumatran oilfields and refineries.[12] However, Warren persuaded Visscher to use his good offices to fix transport and supplies – petrol, food and fresh drinking water – for the Oriental Mission. The Dutchman undertook to pay for the hire of a motor boat, diesel oil and three junks which, with three skippers and two crews, would be available to the British until 12 March. Vanrenan and Graham were to sail in one vessel to the Kuala Selangor area with the aim of locating the rest of Chapman's party. In their coaster Richard, John, and their Chinese party would make for Sepang on the Selangor–Negri Sembilan border, in the hope of contacting friendly locals who would help them to contact other Communist guerrillas.[13] Richard was allocated a tommy-gun, two rifles, six grenades and around Straits $1,000 in cash. In their absence Warren proposed to sail north to Labuan

Bilik, where the two junks were expected to rendezvous with the *Hin Lee* within the next ten days.

After a frantic rush the junks left Bagan Siapiapi on the afternoon of 12 February. It was John's thirty-first birthday. They anchored in the estuary for the night, setting sail before dawn on Friday the 13th. While becalmed by light breezes they snatched some sleep, after which John primed the grenades and they talked over tactics to deal with aircraft or patrol boats. Spotting landfall on the 14th they were annoyed to find themselves 35 miles north of their intended destination. The next thirty-six hours proved frustrating, and when they reached the Sepang River after dark on Sunday 15 February their boat ran aground. Two of the Chinese were sent ahead as scouts, four men were left on board, while Richard, John and the rest of the party walked in bright moonlight over the sand and took refuge in an empty beach house to which they were directed by friendly Chinese. Here they spent an execrable night amid sandflies and mosquitoes, but at least they felt safe from the enemy.

Early the next morning the Chinese went off as scouting parties. A few hours later the Chinese schoolmaster in their party returned with important news, picked up in a nearby township. On 15 February the Japanese had issued a proclamation closing all ports of entry and prohibiting movement of all fishing vessels. Rumour had it that this was to prevent the escape of Allied troops on the run.[14] Since the embargo clearly posed a serious danger to white men, they were advised not to linger. John, however, was all for continuing inland in the hope of securing a system of contact with the guerrilla leaders. Richard, on the other hand, advocated a speedy return to Sumatra, armed with such intelligence as the Sepang guerrillas could provide on the spot.

All that day, the 16th, members of the local relief committee arrived with strategic information. They reported that military activity was centred on Klang and Port Swettenham, the entry point for major supplies. Some 15,000 Japanese troops were said to be in Klang, but those in Kuala Lumpur and Seremban were mostly in transit. Kuala Lumpur airport was functioning and a huge petrol dump had been set up on the Pudu–Sungei Besi road.

During the day a Communist representative of the MPAJF also appeared with the news that the trained parties put in by Richard and John had wasted no time. Anti-Japanese recruitment had been strong. Successful guerrilla action against enemy transport was reported from northern

Malaya, and two guerrilla centres had been set up in Selangor and Negri Sembilan. Several thousand men were allegedly active around Titi Kong, from which they had stormed the Kuala Pilah police station to free five Australian soldiers at a cost of thirty Japanese casualties. The guerrillas had also demolished a number of bridges. However, the price of this guerrilla activity was high. Two bridge-blowing incidents drew savage reprisals in which hundreds of Chinese were massacred. The Kuala Pilah attack resulted in the execution of eleven captured guerrillas, and after the Seremban–Kuala Lumpur railway was sabotaged the Japanese declared the line a prohibited area, warning that trespassers would be shot on sight.

The aim of Japanese propaganda and policy was to divide and rule. To win the support of the Indians and Malays civil government had been restored, using the original Malay ADOs (Assistant District Officers) and police wherever possible. Indian prisoners were treated humanely compared with Australian prisoners of war quartered in Pudu Gaol. The targets of retribution were Malaya's Chinese population and European 'Imperialists', who were used as forced labour. In the towns leading Chinese were compelled on pain of death to serve on peace maintenance committees with Malays and Indians. It was axiomatic that all European and American property and merchandise had been seized. Malayan government money, however, was still in use in an economy that was fast running down. Business was grinding to a halt, deprived of supplies; industry, notably rubber and tin mining, were at a standstill. And a black rumour originating in Seremban declared that Singapore had fallen.

Despite the piecemeal nature of this information it convinced John that 'the spark of anti-Japanese resistance had been ignited'. As a step towards establishing communications and exploring the matter of Allied support, he and Richard agreed that half a dozen Chinese activists should return with them to make contacts in Sumatra and arrange for arms and W/T sets to be smuggled back to the Peninsula and thence to Singapore. They would leave that night as soon as their ship had been brought from its moorings. Some anxious hours remained ahead for at dawn their junk was still in sight of the Malayan coast and the wind was persistently fickle. It was not till dusk on the 19th that they reached Labuan Bilik. Then, to crown everything, they were fired on by coastguards in the estuary.

But there was worse to come after they had disembarked. A visibly shocked and depressed Lt Col Warren broke the news that on 15 February Singapore had fallen to the Japanese. Though not unexpected, it was a mortal blow, for the island had been in British hands since 1819. ('The party is over,' scribbled John, in the trite expression of the day.) Warren's bemused entry in his log, 'Trying to appreciate our position,' played down SOE's plight. Their promises of material assistance to the guerrillas, contacts, W/T communications, everything was invalidated by the loss of Singapore. The Oriental Mission's operational base no longer existed. And last but not least, a painful thought struck John: '95% of my friends were in the bag.'

By 16 February a grave situation had also developed in Sumatra with the Japanese seizure of the oil installations at Palembang. Warren's priority now was to move the personnel of the defunct Oriental Mission to the west coast to ensure their escape. As a preliminary step Lind and Passmore took the *Hin Lee* 80 miles upstream to block the river in anticipation of the enemy advance. On 22 February Warren left Labuan Bilik for Padang with some of the Oriental Mission party, including Richard Broome.

An impassive John watched them drive away. He had been ordered to stay behind to await the return of the junk with news of Vanrenan and Graham. As the days passed he felt he was living in a vacuum, with only the company of Controlleur Jonsen, a cultured and hospitable young Dutch officer, to make it bearable. The junk reappeared on 27 February and the two-man crew recounted their experiences to John. On the 14th they had reached the mouth of the Sungei Buloh but it was low tide so they could not put Vanrenan and Graham ashore. They were taken instead by *sampan* upriver and landed near a small mosque. From there the pair set off inland, having instructed the crew to wait four days before leaving, to give them time to return if their plan proved abortive. In fact, the junk waited six days but there was neither a message nor sign of Vanrenan and Graham. In the end a motor boat with four Japanese soldiers and two Malays appeared and questioned the crew as to their business. Luckily they did not search the junk, and after a warning to clear off the two Chinese left post-haste. They made for Bagan Siapiapi where the police detained them for questioning. This accounted for a further delay.

Reluctantly John accepted they had no means of contacting Vanrenan, Graham, Spencer Chapman or any of those left behind in the Malayan jungle. Details of the fate of the two planters only emerged after the war. They had been captured not long after being put ashore and were incarcerated in Pudu Gaol, Kuala Lumpur. Just as John prepared to depart, Richard appeared. He had been sent by Warren to wind up SOE affairs in Labuan Bilik and escort John and the others from the *Hin Lee* to Padang. But before leaving he and John briefed the six Chinese agents they had brought from Sepang and arranged for their return to Malaya. Finally, with the remaining stores and equipment, the party set off in two lorries supplied by the Dutch. The journey down the rugged, mountainous watershed of Sumatra was easy and uneventful; but at Fort-de-Kock it was made memorable by a single image, the surreal vision of the hotel orchestra playing serenely to the dining guests.

It was 2 March when they reached Padang. The town had a bedraggled air. A week earlier it had been packed with British and Australian troops waiting for ships to take them to Colombo or Java, and there was considerable confusion and change of command. Now the flood of servicemen and civilians had slowed down. A British India liner, the SS *Chilka*, was expected at any time for what was likely to be the final evacuation of personnel.

Richard and John made for the Enderaach Club, which served as the British headquarters and officers' mess, before reporting to Warren on the inconclusive outcome of the Vanrenan–Graham operation. As they were members of Warren's staff, their orders were now to assist him with the last phase of the evacuation. Their first duty was to meet a troop train and take responsibility for Lt Col Arthur E. Cummings, who won the Victoria Cross, though severely wounded, in the retreat from Kuantan. They ensured his safe transfer to a Dutch passenger ship that took fifty of the last evacuees from Padang. A few days later news reached the port that the *Chilka* had been torpedoed on her way to Sumatra.

Anticipating the evacuation of SOE personnel, Warren had set aside Oriental Mission funds for the purchase of a suitable boat. John and Richard were deputed to help with the provisioning and John, additionally, to make the final transport arrangements. The two went down to the harbour to look over the sailing boat. For security's sake and to pre-empt the threat of a boom being placed across the harbour by the Dutch, they advised she should be moved several miles up the coast to the shelter of some islands.

With the capitulation of the Dutch East Indies to Japan on 8 March, Warren could no longer delay activating the Oriental Mission's contingency plan. He ordered all the SOE officers to assemble that evening in a large colonial property on the edge of Padang where he addressed them bluntly. The Japanese were expected at any time, so they must leave and make a bid for Ceylon. Some other officers would accompany them on the voyage. Everybody had been chosen on one criterion, their potential value to the war effort. Meanwhile, in another room the second group waited edgily, drinks in their hands, until summoned to join the SOE party. As Warren spoke the atmosphere was highly charged. They were to sail in utmost secrecy that night, with Richard Broome in overall command and Lind in charge of the ship.[15] All were ordered to go: no man could demur. They would face considerable risks but he believed they had a sporting chance. He wished them all good luck. Finally, he announced that as the senior British officer in Padang, he would be remaining behind, a decision representing an act of considerable courage.

As everyone emerged into darkness and pouring rain, John pointed to a line of pony traps to take them to the rendezvous 7 miles up the coast. Journey's end was a cluster of fishermen's huts, whose Malay and Chinese occupants were roused for the beach reception. After paying off the *tongah* drivers, John introduced himself to the additional officers and offered them a drink of water.

By now the rain had stopped, the moon had risen and the night was clear. Out at sea a mile or so away, the outline of a sailing ship at anchor was visible, and on the shoreline long canoes were waiting to take the escape party in relays to the *prahu*. By midnight all but John of the SOE men were aboard. He followed in the last canoe.

Richard Broome recorded in the log, '3.25 a.m. 9.3.42. Up anchor and set sail with light southerly breeze.' Their bid for freedom had begun.

Chapter 4

'Lucky John'

Daylight was breaking as the *Sederhana Djohanis* proceeded along the Sumatran coast some 3 miles offshore with eighteen hopeful men aboard and three members of the original Malay crew. Those fortunate enough to have snatched some sleep roused themselves, eyeing with interest their new colleagues and the racy-looking craft that was their refuge. In colloquial English her name was 'Lucky John'.

She was a large traditional Malay sailing ship, some 16ft broad and 45ft long at the waterline, extending steeply to 65ft at the stem and stern, excluding the 20ft bowsprit. 'The hull was excellent but very saucer-like,' noted John, purpose-built for coastal trading but quite unsuited to ocean voyages. There were two small decks fore and aft, the rest of the hull being covered with a penthouse roof over the sleeping quarters and ballast, giving protection against rain, sun and more unheralded dangers. Finally, in seafaring parlance, 'she carried an enormous spread of canvas; jib and foresail, mainsail on a 50ft mast and mizzen on a 35ft mast. She had no keel or centre-board. She would sail beautifully in the lightest of breezes'.[1] But sudden squalls were a feature of these waters and in the aftermath, when the wind had dropped, the saucer-like shape of the old *prahu* had a frightening effect. 'She did her best to roll herself to pieces in the most appalling jerks,' John recalled. Then the stomach and skill of every man on board would be tested. However, they had a good stock of stores, sufficient for an estimated forty-two days at sea, and Warren had provided a small armoury of rifles and revolvers, ammunition and a couple of Lewis guns. First-aid materials, medicines, equipment, cigarettes and rations had all

been bought with Oriental Mission money. John was satisfied they had
ample food: stacked tins of bully beef; 'and, when you got tired of the
salmon then there was [more] bully beef, and to be quite frank, milk, sugar
and tea, and quite a few tins of oddments as well'. Finally, lashed around
the main mast were kerosene tins of fresh water in addition to two drums.

His companions on the *Sederhana Djohanis* were by any reckoning a
bunch of unusual individuals whom chance had brought to the attention
of Alan Warren. John considered he and his comrades were the lucky ones;
there were many equally deserving in Singapore who had no opportunity
to escape. What mattered now, however, was that under Richard Broome's
restrained style of leadership the eighteen aboard the *Djohanis* should bond
together as a strong team. Everyone knew it would take a determined,
cooperative effort to reach the Indian subcontinent across 1,600 miles of
potentially hostile seas. So grumbles were largely directed at the weather,
and for the most part tempers were cool and good humour prevailed. The
more perceptive of the ship's company knew that much of the credit was
due to the quiet efficiency and good example of their leader, and – when
it was called for – his instinctive courage. Though slight in frame, Richard
had powerful arms. The company was to watch in awe when, amid high
seas, he swarmed up the mainmast like a lamplighter to deal with the peak
halyard which had broken in a gale. He succeeded where a number of
others had tried and failed.

Richard's first task in command was to divide them into two watches
for the voyage. Confident of his many years' experience as an amateur
yachtsman, he supervised the starboard watch himself, putting a
charismatic Gordon Highlander, Capt Ivan Lyon, in charge of the port
watch. After he implemented Warren's plan for an SOE escape route from
Singapore and the islands across Sumatra, Lyon's reputation was high, but
John had also heard about his exploits as 'an ocean yachtsman – a really
magnificent sailor who seemed to hold our sails together just by the glint
in his eye'. There was tacit support for his acting as sailing master during
the voyage. Richard was unconcerned that John's experience was with
small boats. He was an automatic choice for the starboard watch, together
with Alex Lind and Brian Passmore from the *Hin Lee*. Alongside them were
Maj Bill Waller RA, a staff officer at HQ Singapore, and Lt Douglas Fraser,
an ex-planter and pilot of the Malayan Air Force Volunteers and unofficial
aide to Maj G.H. Rowley-Conwy RA, who had led the successful escape

of his battery from Singapore. Rowley-Conwy perceptively picked up on John's qualities. 'Davis', he remarked, 'possessed a self-assurance that was majestic and although his knowledge of sailing was perhaps less extensive than that of Ivan Lyon, he did not hesitate to advise forcefully on many questions of seamanship. He had a magnificent physique and he was soon doing the work of two men on the little ship.'[2]

Lyon's watch included Lt Geoffrey Brooke RN, a survivor of the *Prince of Wales*, who had worked under Warren in the evacuation of Penang and latterly had been in charge of 400 men housed in the Malay school in Padang; a Merchant Navy officer, Garth Gorham, whom they collectively called 'Columbus', an experienced China hand and a fully trained navigator; and two naval officers from the hapless tanker *Trang*, Lt H.E. 'Holly' Holwell RNVR and Lt Richard Cox, who had selflessly assisted the refugees gathered at Dabo. Cox was an experienced sailor, having crewed before the war in one of the last fully rigged ships to go round the world on the Australian run. With them were Capt G.J.C. Spanton of the Manchester Regiment, who had left Singapore with Maj Waller in a rowing boat, and a Eurasian Military Intelligence Officer named Lt 'Tojo' Clarke, who was a fluent Japanese speaker; being half Japanese he was arguably the most valuable but most vulnerable in the party.

Warren had already indicated that Maj H.A. 'Jock' Campbell should be quartermaster. He had picked Campbell, an assured organiser, to work with Lyon on the Singapore–Sumatra escape route.[3] Now he was exempt from the watch and was to be assisted as quartermaster by the party's medical doctor, Maj L.E.C. Davies RAMC. The final places on the *Djohanis* went to the SOE Asian pair on the *Hin Lee*. Richard Broome would not part from his Chinese 'Boy', Ah Chuan, and John insisted that his loyal Malay Police orderly, Jamal, had earned his place.[4] They more than justified their passage by selflessly undertaking to stay on deck to steer the ship if she came under enemy observation. They would pose as innocuous Asian sailors plying a peaceful trade as a cover for the sixteen British officers down below. Ah Chuan also took on the job of ship's cook, and though prone to seasickness, he never let the company down. As the ship's log for 9 March noted, in Richard's scrawly hand, they started well with 'a good breakfast of sausages and eggs'.

Next Richard briefed everyone on the plan, which was to take advantage of the shore breezes to sail as far north as possible between the Sumatran coast and the adjacent cluster of islands. Then they would strike west across the Indian Ocean, making maximum use of the failing north-east monsoon. It was imperative that they made good progress before mid-April and the advent of the south-west monsoon, which would drive them directly to Japanese-held territory. More immediately, however, they faced two dangers: the capricious weather that could conjure a squall out of the ether and the lurking menace of coral reefs. On her second day out the *Djohanis* encountered both, and in the wild winds the ship's boom broke. As a farewell gesture the Malay crew lashed the splintered boom together and took her into sheltered anchorage by the isle of Pulau Panjang. After helping the officers to buy a large bamboo replacement for the boom, they then 'departed, heaping the blessings of Allah on our heads, but firmly convinced that we were all completely mad!'[5]

The Malays must have known a succession of *sumatras* was imminent. The first crisis broke the following day. The wind suddenly dropped to a flat calm, producing a violent reaction in the *Djohanis*. She simply 'rolled like hell', the lashing round the main mast breaking loose and threatening the loss of all their precious water. John, among the rugby players, reacted instantly, yelling to everyone to form a scrum around the mast. The weight of their bodies held the stack in place until the worst was over and they saved all but one tin.

However, after an appalling night and morning Richard was seriously worried about the state of the sails and gear. John agreed: they were 'rotten to the core. This was the nightmare of the trip . . . you could see as many stars through the mainsail as you could see in the open.' Mending torn sails and splicing ropes were continuous and unenviable jobs for the men of both watches. Some of the Army officers had neither experience nor aptitude. Rowley-Conwy, for one, looked on with grudging admiration as 'Davis was stitching with his usual air of competent authority'.[6] There were still other pressing repairs but Richard was conscious that they might be in enemy waters, so he was reluctant to draw attention to their *prahu* by putting in to the large island of Nias. He chose instead a more obscure anchorage, where the men went ashore to bathe, replenish their fresh water and wood supplies, and attend to repairs.

All of a sudden the throb of an approaching engine sounded the alert. It seemed too good to be true when a friendly Dutch tug, bound for Sibolga, came into view and the captain offered them a tow. He warned them of the daily presence of Japanese reconnaissance aircraft, but later, when all seemed quiet, the tug set off, towing the *Djohanis* northwards. Despite a bit of a roll as she went through another squall, Richard was grateful for an excellent night at the rate of about 4 knots. By early morning on 13 March they had completed some 65 miles with the Dutchman's help – a real stroke of luck – and in one last kind gesture he presented Richard with some new rope for the rigging before heading away.

The *Djohanis* was then lying in the lee of the little island of Pulau Ilir. It had the air of a tropical paradise, tempting the landlubbers to take a closer look, as well as enabling them to replenish their water supply. John offered to row them ashore in the dinghy and watched amused as Rowley-Conwy and co. clambered out like eager schoolboys, scampered through the surf and ran across the beach. They disappeared into the lush undergrowth beyond, only to stumble out a few minutes later in furious retreat, bitten and bloodied by clouds of vengeful mosquitoes. Back on the *Djohanis* a mounting sense of urgency replaced all other considerations. They needed to press on to the last large island of Simalur, before turning away from Sumatran waters and striking west towards Ceylon.

Progress was not easy in the face of variable winds and contrary conditions. Squalls carried the little ship racing under bare poles, but when they died she was left to wallow in flat calm and to roll intolerably. A massive thunderstorm brewing to the east on the 15th blew up into a force 6 or 7 gale. Once more the men almost lost their water supply, lashing the drums in the nick of time. There were a number of small islands to be cleared and one large coral reef, a malevolent habitat of shark, from which they had to pole their way to safety. Then, on the 16th, a second easterly squall hit them as the north point of Nias came into view, sending the *Djohanis* bowling along at 7 knots with everything straining. As helmsman John was rewarded with a tot of whisky for his commendable control. Though there would be many squalls to come, they named these two Big and Little Willy.

In that first week they covered 300 miles, adjusting to the deafening thunder rolls that heralded relentless downpours. At least the rainstorms enabled every man to fill his belly and catch gallons of water for their store. By 18 March they had left Nias well behind and had bypassed Simalur. Richard set course north-west, hoping to pick up the last of the north-east monsoon. At noon on the 19th they were all cheered by the news that in

24 hours the *Djohanis* had covered nearly 100 miles – until the drone of aircraft suddenly wiped away their smiles. Leaving Jamal at the helm and Ah Chuan at his side, the rest ducked beneath the penthouse canopy and held their breath until all was clear. A Japanese reconnaissance aircraft passed on eastward, apparently unconcerned. But the incident presaged two unwelcome developments, both half-expected.

The winds had grown lighter. There was an increased roll, and soon it was clear that the *Djohanis* was becalmed. On 21 March Richard wrote in the log, 'Calm (absolutely flat) all morning and very hot. Most demoralising. Where is the monsoon?' Over the next few days thirst and lassitude tested the most even-tempered individuals. Touching on his rising sense of futility, John confessed, 'One never really expected to get anywhere . . . Your mind went a complete blank.' After nature teased them each evening with majestic sunsets, John dreamed all night of gallons of beer and sweet ice-cream cones. The hidden fear was that in this immobilised condition the ship would be a sitting target for roving enemy aircraft. They had good reason to worry. On four successive days Japanese aircraft had roared overhead. On 20, 21 and 22 March they came twice a day, around breakfast time and again around lunch, forcing everyone under cover to swelter in the heat. It appeared that the Japanese were curious but satisfied, for they took no action, and on the fourth day a single aircraft appeared just once, at 12.45 p.m. Afterwards, banks of darkening cloud began to build, suggesting an imminent weather change. When a small cyclone engaged the *prahu* at dusk, it swept her, supercharged, over the waves and wreaked havoc with her gear. In the next few days the men's spirits alternated between utter exasperation, as yet another change of wind direction stalled their progress, and dawning hope that they might just be escaping from the 'aeroplane belt'.

Then slowly the talk came round to the chances of landfall. When they wakened on 29 March the company was more cheerful. Richard was optimistic that the wind would soon be steady and favourable. It was still only 7.40 a.m. – the sea was calm and breakfast preparations were under way – when a distant throbbing reached their ears. It was high in the blue depths of the sky but approaching from the east. As it quickly changed to a deep-throated roar the thought flashed through John's head that this was the most critical moment yet. Lind just had time to shout a warning and the officers massed under the penthouse as a twin-engined

bomber approached with the obvious intention of opening fire. Visible
at their stations in the stern, Jamal and Ah Chuan flung themselves flat
face-down as the pilot brought the aircraft down to some 300ft and circled
his prey three times before pumping out five long bursts of machine-gun
fire. The bullets splashed into the sea around the ship, peppered the sails
and penetrated the *atap* roof, splintering several stones in the ballast. But
strafing was often the first line of attack, the prelude to bombing. Each
man held his breath and in a state of suspense waited for an obliterating
explosion. In this traumatic moment it seemed impossible that the roar of
engines was diminishing. Yet remarkably the drone had lost its edge, then
grew steadily fainter. John found it incomprehensible that the attack had
not been sustained. The whole company looked around and counted their
luck: no casualties, no damage to the water containers or to the ship's
hull. However, according to the old adage, troubles come in threes. There
remained the fear that the same pilot might return at any time to finish
the job, and meanwhile light winds made it unbearably hot and hampered
their hopes of escaping from the scene. Their only defensive action was to
reorganise the space beneath the canopy to create some sort of air-raid
shelter and whenever they could, to garner every spare drop of water.

Being becalmed in tropical seas brought some painful side-effects:
sunburn, sepsis, excessive thirst and various infestations. 'Lying on a heap
of ballast with cockroaches biting one's toes may not sound nice,' admitted
John, but neither were his septic ulcers that 'Doc' Davies was also treating.
Just as insidious was the men's creeping exhaustion: 'There was so much
working of the sails to do and naturally we did not get any stronger day
to day.' Advised by the Doc, Jock Campbell had devised a way to boost
morale by increasing rations from their stockpile or supplementing the
drink allowance from its lowest ration of a third of a pint – one cigarette
tin – when spirits were dangerously low. 'The other rock bottom occasion',
John recalled, 'was when we found our navigation watch was fast and
our position was 130 miles behind what we thought.' He felt that it was
unfair to blame Garth Gorham, who had unknowingly given over-optimistic
reckonings of their position. His only chronometer was an ordinary
wristwatch, the W/T set was in danger of failing and the spare battery
from an old car proved useless. They were therefore unable to pick up a
reliable time signal or to receive regular bulletins about the state of war;
and consequently their morale took a bruising.

April saw the *Djohanis* making slow headway against the familiar pattern of light winds interspersed with squalls. In mid-morning on the 5th they heard aircraft in the distance but fortunately none came into sight. Richard's log on the 6th noted succinctly, 'Everybody very exhausted,' and it was calculated that they were still 300 miles short of Ceylon. Then once again good and bad news seemed to coincide. By 9 April they were making fair progress after picking up the north-east monsoon, when in mid-afternoon they caught the drone of an aeroplane. Lulled into wishful thinking, someone shouted that the single-engine fighter must be an American reconnoitring from a British base in Ceylon. But as the pilot banked into a late dive, to their horror the hostile red blobs of Japan's emblem came unmistakably into view. On deck Jamal and Ah Chuan watched as still as stone while the aircraft approached low from the stern as if to look them over deliberately. Below, sixteen men waited for bursts of machine-gun fire. Then the aircraft climbed to repeat the intimidating manoeuvre, but again, amazingly, not a single shot was fired. It was after the fighter disappeared in a westerly direction that relief gave way to disturbing thoughts. Where was it based? Was there a Japanese aircraft carrier in the vicinity? If so, it suggested the presence of escorting cruisers and destroyers – a whole fleet, perhaps – a hypothesis confirmed the next day by rumbles of distant gunfire over the horizon. But there was a worse scenario. If the fighter was operating from a land base, rather than a carrier, did this mean Ceylon had fallen? And while they pondered these questions the dying north-east monsoon was wafting their *prahu* ever nearer to that island . . .

Their fortune reached a fine balance three days later. 'At 11 a.m. we sight two tankers on N.E. course to port. Great excitement,' the log recorded. The party was divided as to whether the ships were British or Japanese, and though Richard agreed to signals, the tankers ignored them and sailed away. If John and the rest were disappointed, with hindsight this was a massive stroke of luck. They had just missed a pair of enemy tankers that had been refuelling the Japanese fleet for an attack on Colombo. Then, an hour after the tanker sighting, the log recorded more excitement. 'At noon we sight land in expected place, dead on bow!' After thirty-five days at sea there before them was Adams Peak and the coast of Ceylon.

The sight of land called immediately for a celebration: at lunch there were extra tins of fruit, jam, sausages and cheese. For the rest of the day and the following one, too, the winds were still from the north-east. Keeping in sight of land the *Djohanis* proceeded to aim for the port of Galle or Hambantote on the island's southern coast. But by dawn on the 14th the land had disappeared – they had gone too far – and redressing the situation was made impossible by a fickle turn of wind direction. Exasperation showed on their burned and bearded faces. Then, John explained, 'It finally changed again, forcing us to make straight for a barren and difficult shore, instead of a port. Only 2 miles from shore, when we were making a very doubtful anchorage with breakers', serendipity took a hand. A ship was apparently heading towards them. Joy erupted over the *Djohanis*, a little prematurely.

The *Anglo-Canadian* was a 5,000-ton Welsh freighter out of Barry but bound for the Indian port of Bombay. In trying to attract her attention, the *prahu*'s company had unfortunately sent out mixed messages and in the ensuing uncertainty Capt Williams ordered a 4in gun to be trained on the *Djohanis* lest she was an enemy decoy. There was an uncomfortable pause before the cargo steamer signalled to the sailing ship to come alongside, and Jacob's ladders were lowered. Next came the mad scramble to ascend: desperation, weakness, heartfelt relief; John felt them all. It was perhaps the most dangerous moment of the voyage. He nearly missed the ladder and two men fell into the sea and had to be hauled out. But then came a solid deck underfoot and a huge mug of tea thrust into every pair of hands. After that John remembered two things. One was his anger when he saw Jock Campbell buttonhole Capt Williams, as if to convey that he – not Richard – was in command of the *Djohanis*.[7] The other memory was pure bathos. Since an unmanned ship was a danger at sea, it was agreed the *Djohanis* would have to be destroyed. Broken by the guns of the *Anglo-Canadian*, she finally disappeared into the glow of a tropical sunset. Too late, John recalled that in his haste to reach safety, he had left his wristwatch on board!

Over the next five days everyone luxuriated in comfort, good food and clean quarters. The healing process kicked in as they made up for lost sleep and caught up with the world news. As they had feared, the war in the East was now a dispiriting saga of Japan's remorseless advance. Without a reliable W/T set they had not fully appreciated how Japanese naval and air forces were beginning to close in on the Indian subcontinent, focusing on the island of Ceylon and the Bay of Bengal.[8] The officers of the *Anglo-Canadian* confirmed how two days earlier their gun crews had fought off

Japanese dive-bombers for six hours in the port of Vizagapatam. Their ship was only saved from a direct hit by the chance failure of the bomb to explode, but seven other vessels had been sunk. As they listened, it was obvious that the two tankers that had been spotted from the *Djohanis* were hostile ships, and had the Japanese responded to their signals all eighteen men on board the *prahu* would now be prisoners.

John discovered later that this matched the fate of the last escape party under Col F.J. Dillon RAMC, which had left Sumatra on 16 March. They had followed the same route as the *Djohanis*, and had covered about 300 miles when they were observed by a Japanese reconnaissance aircraft on 1 April. A few days later they were intercepted by an enemy tanker and taken on board as prisoners. In an ironic twist, the party was then carried off to Changi prisoner-of-war camp in Singapore in time for Lt Col Warren to observe their arrival. He had just been transferred as a prisoner to Changi direct from Sumatra.

John also learned subsequently of the fate of the armada of little ships that fled Singapore on Black Friday, 13 February, only to be caught at sea between the Riau Archipelago and the Bangka Straits in their vain attempt to reach Java or Australia.[9] Hundreds of Malayans, enduring great hardship, reached Padang by SOE's escape route, but failed in their bid to reach Ceylon. Although it was not a unique epic, the voyage of the *Sederhana Djohanis* was a heroic story of human triumph over adversity. 'Lucky John', an old sailing ship built by Malay craftsmen to hug familiar coasts, had been steered by alien hands, whipped by damaging gales, becalmed, machine-gunned and driven off-course, yet carried her company of eighteen officers and men nearly 1,700 miles to safety. Yet John was inclined to make light of the experience when he heard of the sufferings of the many held in Japanese hands. 'Ours was never hell,' he insisted, 'most people's was never anything else.'

They reached Bombay on Sunday, 19 April, and gazed from the Roads on the heart-warming sight of British ships of the Eastern Fleet at anchor.

As soon as their feet touched dry land John and Richard needed to clarify their futures.[10] With relief John was told by the Malayan government representative that the Colonial Office recognised their existence in terms of salaries and employment. Richard was immediately in touch with Basil Goodfellow, who already had an office in Meerut, at the headquarters of the Ministry of Economic Warfare. A week later Basil met the two in Bombay. He told them about his own circuitous journey to India, during which he met a group of Singapore Chinese known for their anti-Japanese activities. Among them was a dynamic character called Lim Bo Seng, whose future would soon be intertwined with John's and Richard's. Then Basil de-briefed them from their departure on the *Hin Lee*. They told him the substance of the intelligence they picked up at Sepang, including the evidence of a nascent Resistance movement. Both made it clear that they wanted to continue working in special operations and aimed 'to do something about Malaya'. Basil assured them he would support them to the hilt. He wished he could be more positive about the Malayan front, but he warned them that 'we were looked on as refugees from a debacle in which we had acquitted ourselves badly, and the whole Singapore end of the organisation [the Oriental Mission] was in disgrace'.[11] John deeply resented this blanket criticism of the Oriental Mission.[12]

However, a few days later, the two friends were summoned to Delhi to meet the head of SOE's India Mission. Colin Mackenzie was by all accounts an impressive man of outstanding intelligence, who had the requisite qualifications for high office and commanded enormous respect from high and low.[13] His territorial remit included Afghanistan, Tibet, eastern Persia, the Russian Caucasus and China – but not Malaya. Nevertheless, in view of Japan's sweeping conquests in South-east Asia, and the consequent threat to Assam and India's eastern seaboard, Basil Goodfellow hoped that the India Mission's purview would change. But initially Mackenzie was not encouraging, He told John and Richard bluntly, 'India is not interested in Malaya.' As a consolation prize John might be given a job to do with the Chinese domiciled in India, but Richard was advised he should probably return to the Colonial Office. Since neither man found these suggestions appealing, they set their minds on an alternative course. In the meantime they took a fortnight's leave in Kashmir to recover from their turbulent voyage and to cool down from the fierce heat of the plains.

At the end of the trip John heard he had been promoted to the rank of captain with effect from 5 May. This was encouraging, but to remain in special operations he still needed a written offer of employment from the India Mission. He prepared a written justification for his appointment to the

Ministry of Economic Warfare, spelling out the areas of activity for which he felt suited. In the short term, while resident in India, he would like to be responsible for 'collecting a small party of suitable men to be landed' and take them into Malaya to re-establish communications. In the long term he would expect to be involved in organising 'a force of Malayans of all nationalities' to pre-empt or accompany a future force sent to attack Malaya, the purpose being 'to act as guides, propagandists etc.' He made it clear that he was keen to take a lead in special operations, preferably in Malaya but failing that, China, where his linguistic proficiency and experience could be used, though he understood that operations conducted by Z Force were currently at a standstill. In plain language he indicated that he did not want a safe administrative post in India, since he had no knowledge of the country.[14] He hoped that whatever the nature of a proposed undertaking, it would be possible to involve Richard Broome, as their close friendship and mutual interest in matters Chinese made for a solid working partnership.

At the end of May Goodfellow arranged for John and Richard to travel together to Calcutta, where the India Mission had an office and a W/T station. John was waiting for confirmation of his secondment to the Ministry of Economic Warfare Liaison Office. Mackenzie had outlined a mundane job for him to suit his own purposes. He was to track the Chinese domiciled in India 'to see how far they would be useful to the Indian organisation'. Richard's position was unclear but he made himself useful decoding and encoding messages and meeting VIPs who descended on Calcutta.

There was just one spark of hope in the brief Mackenzie had given John. As an afterthought he conceded that John could keep 'a secondary eye, if he liked, on Malaya'. That was all John needed. He resolved to exploit Mackenzie's concession to the best of his ability, with Richard's help and Basil's support. Their ideas took a while to crystallise but he was confident a project centred on Malaya would emerge in the months ahead.

Chapter 5

The India Mission and the Malayan Project

Shortly after John and Richard arrived in Calcutta, the British situation in India discernibly deteriorated. The war had moved into a critical phase, with Japanese pressure on the gates of India, the jungle hillsides of Assam's border with Burma. This coincided with growing internal anti-imperial clamour, inspired by Gandhi, that the British should 'quit India'. John reckoned that 'things will take a considerable time to sort themselves out'. He was thinking not only of the containment of Japanese forces and the concentration by the India Mission on defensive measures. He was concerned about the diminishing prospect of special operations in Japanese-occupied areas of South-east Asia, such as Malaya. Meanwhile, in Calcutta's execrable heat it was difficult to find anything good to say about their situation. As John tersely remarked, 'Nothing to do but wait, wander from office to office and become a hotel lounge lizard.' Their only relaxation was an occasional visit to the cinema.

He and Richard had been given accommodation with four or five others in the upstairs floor of a ramshackle mansion in Merlin Park, Ballygunge, which also housed the India Mission W/T station. The quarters were none too comfortable and the food was bad, though boredom drove John to eat far too much of it. Downstairs they set up their own office, which officially came under Basil Goodfellow and the India Mission, though it would be transformed in the coming months into a Malayan Office. In these early days at least, there was a 'nice and cheery' atmosphere in the place. John enjoyed a touch of mothering from four charming 'girls' who ran the office. (Three, he noted, were married.) Besides some 'fun and games' they produced iced cakes for tea, apparently responding to the appetite of the strikingly good-looking, laidback officer and his quiet friend who had appeared in their midst.

The war, however, dominated conversation. The evacuation of Burma was hot news, as exhausted survivors of the Oriental Mission's Burma Section joined a nucleus of Far Eastern escapees and refugees who were gathering in Ballygunge.[1] The India Mission W/T station in Merlin Park was still in touch with two signals stations inside Burma, Fort Hertz and Kalewa, while maintaining regular contact with Meerut, Chungking and Colombo. The station was unquestionably strengthened by the arrival of Capt Jack Knott, whose wide experience made him the obvious choice to be SOE's Chief Signals Officer. Richard worked alongside Knott for a short time, and even John made himself useful, decoding and listening to what was assumed to be the last news to come out of Burma before it fell to the Japanese. Indeed, for a while the two friends became totally hooked on wireless telegraphy and enjoyed both 'acrimonious arguments' and 'many a hearty laugh' over the signals.[2]

By comparison, John's first official job in Calcutta, set up by Mackenzie, was decidedly boring. At his base in police HQ, he had to plough through lists of Calcutta's Chinese residents in the hope of finding some who would be suitable for clandestine warfare. It was depressing to find no inclination in the city's Chinatown to give up a comfortable existence, nor any interest whatsoever in Malaya or covert operations. John became increasingly restless, hankering after 'a definite objective'. Fortunately, in the second half of July Basil Goodfellow joined them and life noticeably picked up for John and Richard as the vital 'Malayan objective' was clarified after long discussions. Their talks were given real point in July–August 1942, when Basil set up a new body within the India Mission. This was the Malaya Country Section and initially its only members were Goodfellow himself, John Davis and Richard Broome.

To restore communications with Malaya was their first priority, and this could only be done by infiltrating one or more parties into the Japanese-occupied Malayan Peninsula. The strategy would require the support of a body of suitable Chinese volunteers, which in turn might well involve a search across the length and breadth of India. As a preliminary move John and Richard were sent in late July to Bombay, where an SOE office received new arrivals to the country. Although the recruitment of volunteers was their immediate concern, it was only the preliminary stage in a complex process. They had to organise the operation, train the operatives, transport personnel, arms and W/T equipment and set up the reception and infiltration of agents in enemy-occupied territory. John had already made his intentions clear. He saw it as his duty to lead a special operation to Malaya. In doing so he had no intention whatsoever of ousting Richard, who was older and senior to him in the colonial service. However, as he was quick to point out, whoever went in first would have to land 'blind' and face innumerable risks. Being single, he was more expendable than Richard, who was a married man with a family. John was also the physically fitter at the time and he had the important advantage of being more familiar with the Malayan jungle. So for all these reasons it was agreed between the three that John should lead the first mission, and once given the all-clear, Richard would join any subsequent sortie.

Once these points were clarified John was impatient for action. Since it was generally agreed that the majority of operatives should be indigenous to their country of mission, the next step was to locate suitable volunteers among Asian Malayans. The search began for high-calibre recruits, young men who were fit and strong, could face the rigours and dangers of working in the field as 'the eyes and ears of any party', and would be able to assimilate the range of skills needed for survival and for successful sabotage and intelligence work. Initial attempts to recruit Malays in Britain failed to raise any volunteers, so hopes turned to a KMT organisation of Chinese seamen in Calcutta, a pool of around 5,000 potential recruits. They were currently being welded into a service corps by two Chinese Malayans, a prominent Straits businessman named Lim Bo Seng, whom Goodfellow already knew, and his associate Chuan Hui Tsuan. As Chinese patriots and nationalists, in the run-up to the Second World War they were involved in anti-Japanese activities and the raising of relief funds for China. It was because of Bo Seng's high profile in Singapore that the British ordered him to escape before the surrender.[3]

As it turned out, the Chinese seamen in Lim Bo Seng's charge were a disappointment: John found only one whom he considered at all suitable, Ah Piu, who became his bodyguard. The search was therefore hastily widened. From the files of Malayan organisations lists were elicited of other dockyard personnel, police, teachers, government clerks and men in the armed services, Indians, Malays and Chinese, in addition to Eurasians and

Europeans who had escaped from Malaya and spoke one or more of the country's languages. Most men could be eliminated on grounds of age, health or physique. But at Colaba Camp in Bombay they located a few ex-Malayan planters who had fought in Dalforce, and some Sarawak Chinese with work experience in Singapore. At Karachi they interviewed nine Chinese with naval experience. They also carried the search to Madras, Bangalore and Colombo, interviewing a handful of men here or a single promising individual there, and acting quickly to enlist a man when they came across a potentially valuable volunteer.[4]

For a while the problem of recruitment was a major stumbling block. Consideration was given to using Chinese-speaking officers from Z Force, though there were obvious drawbacks, since few had any prior experience of Malaya.[5] A more profitable measure might be an appeal to Chinese exiles from Malaya living in Nationalist China, such as students studying at universities and in similar institutions. Their intelligence, motivation and youthful resilience would be invaluable to SOE. In August Goodfellow telegraphed John to let him know there were 400 trainees at Chungking Overseas School. John offered to fly to the wartime capital to interview prospective volunteers if official sanction could be obtained for his entry to Nationalist China. Goodfellow, however, came up with a better solution.[6] He arranged to meet Lim Bo Seng, who was on the point of returning to Chungking. During their meeting the Chinese industrialist expressed his keenness to cooperate by interceding on behalf of the Malaya Country Section, using his connection with KMT commander Gen Tai Li, head of the Chinese Secret Service. Bo Seng was confident that there would be no official hindrance to the recruitment and transfer of volunteers to India. To everyone's relief he was proved right. That first meeting in August 1942 was followed by another at which Goodfellow introduced Lim Bo Seng to John and Richard. These two encounters were another milestone. Over a matter of months the quartet of Goodfellow, Lim Bo Seng, Broome and Davis established bonds of trust and friendship that made for a formidable unit. As Richard put it, the team was 'nicely balanced', with John's bullheadedness and tenacity of purpose, Basil's organising ability and facility for dealing with high-level VIPs, and Lim Bo Seng's energy and fanaticism. His own contribution, he believed, was 'a certain capacity for judgement', a degree of cynicism that could be a useful brake, and 'a nose for "bull" in all its forms'. In fact Richard came across a worrying amount of fraud and 'bull' involving public money, which he attributed to the fact that the India Mission was run by businessmen rather than professional administrators.[7] But the Malayan scheme that John and he initiated with Basil and then implemented with Lim Bo Seng was arguably the most cost-effective operation to come out of the India Mission since their collective efforts eventually brought about the successful landings of Force 136 personnel on the Malayan Peninsula.

In 1942 the scheme was still in gestation. Though an early decision was needed on the matter of training facilities, it was impossible to tell how many volunteers would come forward. Colin Mackenzie believed the numbers enlisted would not warrant establishing a new school for basic training. Instead, a special wing was equipped at the former Guerrilla Training Unit, re-named the India Mission's Eastern Warfare School, in the rocky Western Ghats near Poona, to provide basic field training, instruction in sabotage, weaponry and handling of small boats. In October John and Richard were sent to view this complex as a potential camp for the Malaya Country Section. It had all the necessary facilities, barracks, mess, offices, classrooms, conference rooms, training field and parade ground and was under the command of Maj Mike Kendall, who had served in China but had attended one of the first courses at No. 101 STS in Singapore.

The Eastern Warfare School was set in majestic surroundings. The adjacent hill-fort of Singarh had in past centuries been both a Moghul and a Maharatta stronghold, and its granite fortifications and massive gateway were the work of Italian mercenaries. The site was spectacular, some 4,000ft above sea level, with views over the Poona plain to the high stronghold of Rajgarh, while 2,000ft below lay Lake Kharakvasla. Yet in dull light the lush greenery of the valleys was lost from view and the bare, craggy landscape resembled a desolate moonscape.

On their first visit in October John extolled the perfect weather and the ambience: 'cool nights and all the walking in the world . . . It took me about three days to get as fit as I have ever been and at the end of ten I was physically positively dangerous.' But with all its virtues, Singarh would not have acclimatised the recruits to tropical Malaya. A decision on the location of an Advanced Operations School and final training and holding camp for the Malayan operatives was badly needed. Ceylon was the obvious choice, since its climate and vegetation had an affinity with that of Malaya. Furthermore, the island was a natural base for submarine operations; and in the absence of aircraft capable of making the round trip from the Indian subcontinent to and from Japanese-occupied South-east Asia, submarines were the only feasible form of transport. On behalf of Goodfellow, John and Richard went to Ceylon in August to reconnoitre the island. After looking at various possibilities they favoured a site at Arugam Bay on the north-west coast for the Advanced Training School. Otherwise they made little progress. The Ministry of Economic Warfare Liaison Office in Colombo was merely an embryo set-up, and the Commander-in-Chief Ceylon, Adm Sir Geoffrey Layton, was sceptical of special operations, which was initially disheartening. But things began to change in the first half of 1943 after a reorganisation of the India Mission. Ceylon then became home to the new Force 136 Group B, which included the Malaya Country Section, under the command of Col Christopher Hudson RASC.[8] However, in August this was still some months away.

In November John was ordered back to Calcutta by Basil Goodfellow. There was no sign of Lim Bo Seng, but on the principle that no news is good news they had to presume that he was simply delayed in Chungking and would probably arrive some time in December with his first group of overseas volunteers. The Malaya Country Section had already been joined by a couple of valuable recruits. One was Peter Dobree, a former Malayan Agricultural Officer, who met with John's warm approval. He was disappointed to learn that 'Jungly' Marshall had failed to come as expected, but before the end of the year Claude Fenner would transfer to the Malaya Country Section from West Africa, which greatly pleased him.

Meanwhile, on his return to Calcutta John had found Basil in a depressed and distracted frame of mind. He even spoke of their Malayan project as being 'hopelessly premature', a view that John instantly repudiated. He noticed, however, that during his various absences from Calcutta the atmosphere in the India Mission offices had definitely changed, and not for the better. Calcutta had become a sub-mission of the India Mission, housing the three country sections of Group A, Burma, Siam and French Indochina. It was obvious that this expansion, preparatory to the formation in March 1943 of Force 136, had brought a sizeable influx of bureaucratic personnel. In John's opinion, under Mackenzie's deputy, Gavin Stewart, the place had been taken over by uncongenial newcomers with inflated functions. He was dismissive, for instance, of the central head of the country sections and the new General Conducting Officer for the Chinese. The proliferation of offices and sections with the inexorable drive to centralise operations brought increased paperwork.[9] There were, in Basil's words, 'too many bosses and too much attempted control from headquarters' but no compensating improvement in communications. John's reaction was naturally blunt: 'reorganisation is the key word everywhere and so of course everything is a balls-up'. 'An Imperial balls-up,' agreed Basil emphatically, for like John he bridled at the threat of interference in the running of the Malaya Country Section. John predicted, 'We have a short but sharp fight ahead of us to preserve our essential independence,' but he was quite confident of success, taking heart from the obvious belligerence of Basil, who was 'itching for the fray'.

In mid-November John went off to Colombo to stake out progress on the marine and jungle-training facilities and transport for the Malaya Country Section personnel. The news was not very encouraging. Although Cdr R.M. Gambier, the senior officer in charge of British submarines, was sympathetic towards a Malayan mission, even the best-laid plans sometimes fell victim to the grand strategies of war. For the second half of 1942 while Rommel's forces held Tobruk, British strategy focused on North Africa and the desert campaign. Consequently, the eight submarines in Mediterranean Command that had been promised by the Admiralty as Far Eastern reinforcements had not yet arrived; nor would they for many months to come. The Ministry of Economic Warfare's Liaison Office in Ceylon was therefore entirely dependent on the cooperation of the Dutch authorities, although at the time there were only two or three Dutch submarines available (not to mention a serious lack of spares and maintenance facilities). In addition – and this was critical in John's estimation – the priority given to conventional *offensive* submarine operations in the Malacca Straits and their western approaches almost minimised opportunities for irregular operations on the Malayan Peninsula. So John discovered within a couple of hours of arriving in Colombo that his plan for a Malayan sortie was 'completely scuppered in one fell swoop'. Inevitably he was keenly disappointed, though in breaking the news to Richard he tried to sound reasonably upbeat. 'First blow – the Navy are very sorry but they cannot do our first operation . . . They are being most helpful and considered the matter very carefully, so I am afraid we must accept the position . . . I hope to go and see the flotilla Commander again and get definite data of what he can do on which we can build up some other scheme. I have some vague ideas out of which we may be able to concoct something.'

The other disappointment was less serious. Brig G.H. Beyts, the senior officer in charge of operations, had turned down Arugam Bay in favour of a coastal site near the town of Trincomalee. John accepted his decision. He respected Beyts and enjoyed accompanying him to inspect the chosen site which, John admitted, had many favourable features. For all that, he was anxious that Richard should check the details of the plan and synchronise the Singarh courses with the projected opening of the Trincomalee camp.

The only other matter that was still on John's mind was the lack of news from Lim Bo Seng. 'I am not worrying,' he reassured Richard. 'I think if left alone he will do his stuff.' In any case, since the original timetable had been dropped, the urgent need for the Chinese agents to complete their training had temporarily diminished. Basil Goodfellow, meanwhile, was agitating for a meeting with John and Richard 'to talk over the ideas and developments of the last two months', but their travel schedules made it difficult to arrange. In early December John returned to Singarh to keep up his fitness with strenuous walking and hill climbing. Some Chinese volunteers were waiting to start training there.

In the interim Goodfellow heard from Lim Bo Seng. He had been in Kunming and Kweilin as well as Chungking, where his recruits were now gathering. Basil told John he was trying to arrange a charter aircraft or US Army Air Force transport to bring the Chinese Malayan volunteers to India before the end of 1942. A modern bungalow in Calcutta and a holding camp some 30 miles upriver had been set up to receive them. Richard was to act as their escorting officer for the long westward train journey to Poona and the final lap to Singarh. After an interesting trip to Colombo in the New Year, John was back at the hilltop fort in readiness to receive Lim Bo Seng and his party.[10] As Malay speakers, the latter would be distinguished from other groups of Chinese recruits by their code name, 'the Dragons'.[11]

Although the Dragons had received military training in China a carefully tailored course had been devised for them at Singarh. In addition to basic training, Goodfellow insisted they should be instructed in propaganda, surveillance, subversion and the use of ciphers and codes suitable for Chinese agents in a Malayan situation. In an account of their preparation, one of the Dragons listed 'shooting skills, assassination, raid attacks, canoeing, explosives and bombing, undercover communications, intelligence gathering, camouflage, map-reading and guerrilla warfare', adding that 'shooting and bombing were two of the more important topics'.[12] After this there would be a re-grouping of personnel and those selected for an imminent amphibious operation would transfer to Ceylon.

In January 1943, while the training programme was going ahead, the planning process entered a new phase. A scheme for three amphibious groups to land parties on Malayan soil had been discussed and agreed. In the first, originally called Operation 'Pirate', John was to take a group of five Chinese to the Port Swettenham area to facilitate contact with the Sepang guerrillas. However, that was only one of four principal objectives. Another was to establish and maintain a direct submarine link with Col Christopher Hudson and Basil Goodfellow in Ceylon. A third goal was to set up an intelligence system, manned by the Chinese agents, and the last was to discover the fate of the Oriental Mission's European parties, and if possible to make contact with any individuals who might still be at large. Since it became apparent that a sequence of sorties would be necessary to achieve these objectives, the code name 'Gustavus' was adopted for the series, the first phase being Operation 'Gustavus I'. As with all untried operations, a fall-back position was devised in the event of unforeseen difficulties. But if the original plan proved successful, Richard would join John and his party in a month's time with two Chinese reserves. In the third phase, led by Claude Fenner, John would return to Ceylon to give a full intelligence report, while Fenner remained in Selangor with Richard.

There remained one outstanding issue, and that was the availability of submarines for the amphibious operations. As the two senior officers responsible for the Malaya Country Section, Hudson and Goodfellow negotiated arrangements with the Dutch representatives in Ceylon. The first sortie under John Davis was scheduled to leave in early April 1943. So far as he was concerned, everything was in hand.

There was no indication of a problem until the last week of March, when suddenly his plans were dealt another body blow. A terse warning from India Mission HQ in Meerut was followed by a top-secret letter to John dated 21 March from a furious Basil Goodfellow in Calcutta. 'I received yesterday a telegram from HQ warning me that there was likely to be a further postponement of the sortie allotted to "Gustavus",' he told John. 'I need not tell you how angry I am about this, and angry in particular that the reason appears to be that our colleagues have been given priority over us.' The 'colleagues' were members of the Far Eastern branch of SIS, the ISLD, with which John was familiar. Although SIS/ISLD operated under formidable secrecy, it depended on the same submarines as SOE's India Mission to transport operatives in Far Eastern waters. Unknown to Goodfellow and John, ISLD had set up an intelligence operation timed for early April (but known as Operation 'May') to infiltrate seven Chinese agents to Ipoh via Telok Anson on Malaya's west coast. This was to be followed by a second to Kuala Lumpur a month later (Operation 'Moon'). The first would have clashed with John's sortie, the second conceivably with Richard's. On the face of it ISLD had deliberately kept the SOE leadership in the dark.

To compound John's frustration other problems had arisen due to the unfavourable war situation. In Burma an expeditionary force sent from Assam to Arakan towards the end of 1942 was forced to withdraw to Chittagong in May 1943 after a powerful and sustained Japanese counter-attack. Consequently, there seemed no hope of imminent Allied counter-offensives in South-east Asia. Mackenzie and Stewart had reassessed tactics and argued that there was no case for special operations in Malaya involving the infiltration of British officers before the middle of 1944. Indeed, the services of experienced officers would be more useful in the run-up to an Allied invasion, whenever that might be. Finally, they feared that continuous submarine communications could not be guaranteed, so the chances of withdrawing British officers from Malaya could be seriously jeopardised. It was Basil who had to put the unpalatable reality to John. 'It will therefore be necessary to have an alternative plan under which you do not remain ashore in "Gustavus I" or any other of the early sorties. I know how difficult it will be for you to face the men with a change of plan like this.' Even if 'Gustavus I' were not postponed, Basil urged John to work out an alternative plan to put the Chinese agents ashore alone, if possible with W/T set and operators. He assured him of his help in resolving these issues. He had already alerted Lim Bo Seng to the proposal to send in all-Chinese parties. Anticipating the Dragons would take this badly, Bo Seng's presence would be invaluable to soothe their fears and resentments.

A draft of John's riposte to Basil Goodfellow's letter has miraculously survived. It was addressed to Colin Mackenzie as head of India Mission, with a copy to Basil, and stated his case in unequivocal terms. First, in

John's opinion it was too late to change his plans now. In any case change would be highly undesirable, for it would diminish European influence and control of the proposed Resistance organisation: 'I feel that the removal of European participation from the first parties would hopelessly jeopardise their chance of success.' He admitted that a European presence increased the immediate risk of discovery, whereas a Chinese could fade more easily into the country. However:

I should point out that

(1) Their loyalty would be almost entirely sacrificed thereby.
(2) Their incentive to return would be largely removed.
(3) The party would suffer from lack of leadership and drive . . . The security of any future W/T communications would be greatly endangered.
(4) The presence of a European is a guarantee of their bona fides when negotiating. They would probably not otherwise be believed.
(5) I am the only link with our former communist contacts.

I do of course agree that you do not want to jeopardise the lives of Europeans with local knowledge unnecessarily. I would point out however that there is no question of anyone else entering the country unless I have been successful. Whether or not you continue to send Europeans in will depend on my report.

Mackenzie can rarely have received such a forthright missive from a junior officer. On the issue of submarines, he defined precisely the ways in which they were essential to Operation 'Gustavus'.[13] But he reserved the main thrust of his letter for the sturdy defence of the use of European officers on special operations, insisting that his life alone was on the line.

Whatever Mackenzie's reaction, it appears that John won the argument because Operation 'Gustavus' went ahead and the leadership of European officers became a hallmark of SOE operations in Malaya. The one concession John had to accept was the rescheduling of 'Gustavus' for May instead of April.

In their final few days of training and bonding John led his Chinese party on a last trek through empty mountain country to the hill fort of Torna and back to Singarh. A farewell party for the team was punctuated by a particularly violent storm over Mount Singarh. If some of the disappointed

Chinese took this as a bad omen, it did not affect John or his party. The next day they went by train to Ceylon, where they stayed on the depot ship, HMS *Adamant*. The weather was extremely hot, but Cdr Gambier made them feel welcome while they spent the last few days on their final preparations. In particular, they practised the essential manoeuvres for disembarking from the submarine and managing their folboats.

To safeguard all participants in amphibious operations, Hudson and Gambier had worked out the principles of their *modus operandi*, which everyone had to observe. To avoid unnecessary risk to the submarine, while on board the whole party accepted the command of the submarine captain. If at any point the vessel was in danger, the captain had discretionary power to abort the operation, but once the party left the submarine the party leader took over command for the rest of the operation. It was also understood that to avoid compromising a special operation, the submarine involved would refrain from any aggressive action during the twenty-four hours before and after its completion.

Accepting these conditions, John and his pioneers embarked on Submarine 024. Their stores, folboats and equipment had already been loaded. Lt Cdr W.J. de Vries of the Royal Dutch Navy was in charge as the boat stealthily departed on schedule.

John felt satisfied with their preparations; now everything was in the lap of the gods. The date was 11 May 1943, as he set his sights on achieving the first SOE sortie into Japanese-occupied Malaya since he and Richard Broome had sneaked into the estuary of Sepang back in February 1942.

Chapter 6

Operation 'Gustavus'

In the folk memory of the 'Gustavus' team, the voyage by submarine was an unpleasant necessity. Cruising on the surface of the sea for three days allowed them to acclimatise, but after that 024 was submerged all day and there were only brief spells at night to take in the air. With six extra bodies, five of them packed into the crew's quarters, conditions were very cramped and difficult. The heavy atmosphere and stodgy food dulled the senses, making it hard to keep alert.

In the early hours of 19 May a small enemy vessel was sighted some 60 miles off the northern tip of Sumatra. Suspecting it was an anti-submarine trawler, de Vries decided to keep it under surveillance, and while shadowing the ship in squally weather an enemy merchantman came into view. This invited a snap torpedo attack, which John watched with interest through the periscope. The action was inconclusive and there were no further encounters before they reached their operational area of Selangor.

In the Malacca Straits submarine manoeuvres were limited by the shallow coastal waters, and landings hampered by miles of dense mangrove swamp. Thus the party's plan was to stay in deep water, target a suitable junk out in the fishing lanes and move in by folboat to hijack the vessel. With or without the cooperation of the junk crew, they would hope to land at a secluded spot in the vicinity of Port Swettenham, and from here John hoped to make contact with the Sepang guerrillas. But if in doubt about the security of their operation, he had orders to return the junk crew by submarine to Ceylon as prisoners.

At first all went well. Through the periscope John spotted a lone junk, which the submarine proceeded to stalk until nightfall. Then under cover of darkness the six SOE men disembarked, paddled over to the boat and boarded it. Despite their surprise at being hijacked, the Hailam crew seemed amenable enough and offered to take their abductors to a large Chinese fishing settlement near Port Swettenham. John eyed them warily, his suspicions growing by the minute as they painted an over-rosy picture of life under occupation. In consultation with his Chinese agents he decided it was too risky to go ahead, and reluctant to burden Lt Cdr de Vries with a bag of vociferous prisoners, they simply left the crew on their junk, returned to the submarine and proceeded with a contingency plan to land further north at Segari in the coastal region of West Perak, known as the Dindings.[1] The Dutch captain turned his submarine around and made for a point north of Pangkor. The story of their blind landing and striking camp in the Segari hills, recounted in the Prologue, needs no re-telling.

The British in India knew nothing of the situation in Perak after a year and a half of Japanese occupation. General intelligence was required about the strength and dispersal of the Resistance and of enemy forces, as well as the state of the economy. The Chinese crew of the hijacked junk had insisted that a Resistance movement existed, but John wanted confirmation, so the first task of 'Gustavus I' was to establish contact with local people. John was hopeful that the Chinese of rural Perak would help his KMT agents, if only out of a visceral hatred of the Japanese.

He dispersed his Dragons singly, each with a different brief. The first to leave was Ah Ng, the senior among the KMT agents. Posing as a refugee on the run from the Japanese, Ah Ng won the confidence of a rubber-tappers' overseer living near Segari, and once Kong Ching and his wife ascertained that he was not a Communist guerrilla they became invaluable allies, covering his back on a number of occasions. John trusted Ah Ng to keep the camp supplied with food and bring news of conditions outside the jungle. The common complaints he picked up were of food shortages and an economy approaching standstill, a Japanese dollar being worth a third less than an illegal British dollar.

Meanwhile, John gave his approval to Ah Han's intention to make for Ipoh where he had family contacts, while the youthful Ah Ying was to find menial work at a coffee shop in the township of Segari, where he hoped to pick up useful information from customers. After Ah Ng's departure John turned his mind to the imminent problem of linking up with the next submarine that would bring in the follow-up mission, 'Gustavus II'. He had already decided this would be Ah Tsing's task, and after providing him with the requisite dollars, John sent him off to Pangkor via Lumut to acquire a boat for the prospective rendezvous. Posing as an aspiring fishmonger, Ah Tsing caught the Lumut ferry.

On landing at Pangkor Ah Tsing paused uncertainly, just long enough to arouse the suspicion of a sharp-eyed Malay policeman. With luck and skill, however, he managed to bluff his way through by inveigling himself into the confidence of a fellow passenger, a local shopkeeper. This man not only vouched for Ah Tsing but introduced him to the leading figure in the local Teochew community, a wealthy fish merchant named Chua Koon Eng. A man of influence, Chua convinced the Malay police that Ah Tsing was his nephew and took him under his protective wing. Playing the role of a smart young fish-trader and carrying a parcel of fresh fish as proof, Ah Tsing later returned to the jungle to report to John. He knew the procedures for a safe rendezvous had to be set up in the next three weeks. As time was pressing Ah Tsing decided he had no alternative but to use trading trips down the coast as a smokescreen for acquiring a suitable boat. But his activities would take more than a cool head and theatrical skills. He urgently needed practical help, so he decided to enlist Chua's cooperation, swearing him to secrecy before revealing his role in the 'Gustavus I' operation. In response Chua acquired a suitable junk for the rendezvous and provided two loyal Hailams as crewmen. John was pleased with this progress and felt Ah Tsing had done well.

While the ball was set rolling in these various ways John remained at the jungle hideout with Ah Piu. It was essential he avoided exposure while his agents were settling into their new roles. He hated the inactivity but he knew that until contacts were established there was little he could do. He listened regularly to the news from India on a small portable receiver that he had carried from the landings site. All India Radio served another important purpose: it confirmed in coded language the date and place of the expected submarine rendezvous. But for one with John's restless temperament, the waiting was difficult to bear, particularly after he developed an irritating fungus infection. It bothered him that Ah Ng was devoting too much energy to everyday needs such as finding food and insufficient to the business of making intelligence contacts.

News was beginning to percolate about the anti-Japanese forces, and John was eager for more information. From Ah Tsing – indirectly through Chua – he learned there were 800 guerrillas in the Sitiawan area, just south of Segari, and Ah Ng had heard that Communist guerrillas were active elsewhere in Perak. But without a two-way W/T set John was unable to pass on this kind of information to India Mission HQ. In the end he decided it was imperative that he returned briefly to Ceylon to make a full report to his superiors and confer with Richard and others, leaving his team to carry on unimpeded in his absence.

At dawn on 22 June the junk that Chua had supplied left Pangkor to pick up John and his bodyguard from Segari beach. As a diversionary cover for the submarine rendezvous they were to take a cargo of rice to Port Swettenham, so after putting John and Ah Piu ashore on one of the uninhabited Sembilan islands near the agreed rendezvous, the junk proceeded south to Selangor. By a stroke of bad luck the weather turned stormy, and the pair sat huddled all night in scrub near the shore trying to protect themselves from the rain and cold. John's fear was that the rough seas would delay the junk's return. However, although it was late, after being picked up they still spent the next two days at sea waiting for the submarine to appear.

When the time finally approached, the crew put up the recognition signal, a scarlet blanket draped over the port side, and later raised and lowered the sail. John long remembered the frustration of that first rendezvous: he stared out at the sea from dawn, spotting after a couple of hours a hopeful streak on the water that disappeared, then reappeared nearer only to re-submerge at the sight of smoke on the horizon and the approach of unidentified vessels. It was not until dark that a periscope emerged. 'Soon after nightfall we heard what appeared in the stillness of the night to be incredibly loud rumbling and gurgling, splashing quite nearby and then silence.' Suddenly the submarine's silhouette was seen some way off, and soon after they heard the splash of paddles and a folboat slid alongside the junk. John waited excitedly but in his eagerness almost caused a disaster. In the heat of the moment he had forgotten there should be a coded exchange, so when mutterings of 'Ivy clings to the wall' rose from the folboat he shouted back, 'Don't be damn silly.' At this 'they promptly sheered off and there was an uncomfortable fumbling of guns. I then realised that I had failed to give the password', he admitted. 'I had forgotten it of course but got near enough to reassure them that we were not a trap and that we did not harbour a platoon of Jap soldiers with their bayonets sticking in our backs.'[2] Claude Fenner, the Conducting Officer, and Richard Broome then came aboard to speak to John about transferring to the submarine, and to introduce him to Lt Cdr Valkenburg.

The original purpose of 'Gustavus II' was to take John out and replace him with Richard, along with three more of Lim Bo Seng's agents, Ah Lim and Shek Fu, and a first-rate W/T operator, Lee Choon, who were all waiting on board.[3] However, unable to forewarn Ceylon that there should be a change of plan, John had to inform Richard and Claude that this was *not* the right time for a second landing. He had decided to leave his four Dragons to continue their work, while armed with an intelligence report and samples of Japanese currency notes, he needed to return to Colombo with Claude, taking Richard, Ah Lim, Shek Fu and Lee Choon with him. John's decision was final, so with the pick-up completed, they headed back to Ceylon, reaching Colombo without mishap on 6 July. John felt satisfied. From an operational standpoint 'Gustavus I' and 'Gustavus II' could be rated successful.

The first bombshell for John on his return was that Basil Goodfellow was leaving the Malaya Country Section for a bigger job at the Ministry of Economic Warfare. The news was a hard blow: Basil had been their 'universal provider' since January 1942. But his replacement would be Maj Innes Tremlett, whom John and Richard had known for ten years since they learned Cantonese together in China. Tremlett joined the two at Mount Lavinia briefly to hear first-hand news of Malaya. At his de-briefing in Colombo John repeated to Col Hudson how the Chinese guerrillas trained at No. 101 STS had built up a largely Communist force, the Anti-Japanese Army (AJA). There was also a wider non-combative organisation, the Anti-Japanese Union (AJU), actively supplying AJA fighters in the jungle with food and money.[4]

During John's short spell in Ceylon a radical reorganisation of the command structure was under way, although a public announcement that

Adm Lord Louis Mountbatten was to be the new Allied Supreme Commander of South East Asia Command (SEAC) came after John was back on Malayan soil. But it was significant for him, and all Far Eastern personnel, that SEAC would shortly take control not only of all regular forces but of all clandestine organisations. Consequently, the Malaya Country Section would no longer be under the Ministry of Economic Warfare's Liaison Office, India Mission or India Command, but would operate as Force 136 under SEAC. Moreover, with his experience of Combined Operations Mountbatten was more sympathetic towards an organisation like SOE than the vast majority of service chiefs. The effect for John in personal terms would be important. He was already effectively the Head of Mission, Malayan Operations, but he would soon receive Mountbatten's endorsement. And in July he heard that he had been promoted to the rank of major, though he took such matters lightly. 'I belong to one of the most famous regiments of the Indian Army – the General List!' he joked to those at home.

John had originally expected to undergo another spell of physical training of several weeks, but this fell through with his own decision to rejoin his agents in Perak on the next submarine sortie. In fact he only had three weeks to prepare himself for the revised plan, in which Richard would follow within a month. Their primary objective would be to make contact with the Communists at the highest level and come to an agreement for future cooperation. Operation 'Gustavus III' was due to begin on 27 July, when the Dutch Submarine 023 under Lt Cdr Valkenburg's command would collect the party at Trincomalee on completing seaborne training. It had been decided that John would take in Richard's three agents who had sailed on 'Gustavus II' to reinforce his original four, although he knew this was not an ideal arrangement. The risk factor and associated stress of special operations were always considerable; relationships between an officer and his men were of paramount importance, and Ah Lim, Shek Fu and Lee Choon did not know John as well as they knew Richard.

In addition, as they began their final preparations a crisis blew up that not even Colin Mackenzie could control. On 23 July John was contacted urgently by Col Hudson, acting under orders, to bring forward their departure to the next day. At the time no reason was given but later he learnt that a Japanese warship was to be intercepted and sunk between the Andaman Islands and its destination, Singapore. Since 023 was the only submarine available 'Gustavus III' had to accommodate the Navy's demands. When the head of the Malaya Country Section told him, John's main concern was the reaction of Richard's Chinese agents. Although he accepted the imminent departure he felt bound to protest; and had he known then that en route to Malaya the submarine would develop a series of mechanical faults that nullified the attack, John would most certainly have refused to proceed. As it was, the party had to take all their supplies and equipment and fly the 140 miles to Colombo by whatever aircraft was available. And John's fear, that in their haste a mistake or an omission would occur, was justified when the signals plan was delivered to the wrong quay. This time it was Hudson's turn to fume at the inefficient staff work.

Without any further delay Claude Fenner escorted John by fast boat to the submarine. The Chinese party was aboard and Lim Bo Seng was waiting to wish his Dragons goodbye. It was 10 p.m. on 24 July when 023 left Colombo harbour at the end of a nightmare that neither John Davis nor Christopher Hudson would ever wish to see repeated.

On 4 August the submarine reached the waters between Pangkor and the Sembilan Islands and prepared to rendezvous. The agreed signals identified Chua's junk with Ah Tsing on board; below, John discovered later, were Ah Ng and one of his guerrilla contacts who had come to escort the party. After dark Claude Fenner made contact by folboat and assisted John in supervising the transport of equipment and stores from the submarine to the junk. There was a brief alarm at the noise of a motor and flashing lights, but the rendezvous was completed and before the two boats went their separate ways John handed Claude some general intelligence from Ah Ng, together with information on the Resistance, and some Chinese newspapers to take back to Ceylon. 'Gustavus III' made a safe landing not far from their original site of Segari, where they also rested for the night.

Before leaving the next morning for Bukit Segari they buried the cumbersome Mark III W/T among the stores, intending to arrange their conveyance at a later date. Speed and caution were essential as they cut their way through the dense vegetation. Their caution paid off for they came across a burnt-out hut and a sealed water well, indicating recent enemy activity by soldiers or police. John insisted they took a diversionary route to their old camp. It was a wise move because Japanese counter-intelligence had been alerted to the infiltration of Allied agents along the Perak coast. On 9 August, two days after the SOE party reached their destination, the Japanese-controlled press issued a sinister warning of possible air raids and submarine bombardments, and, more significantly, 'the landing of a small group of soldiers in an out-of-the-way place from craft in pursuit of certain aims'.[5]

To Ah Ng's credit, he had been in touch with the Sitiawan guerrillas in John's absence, so that on reaching their camp the 'Gustavus III' party was met by four Communist guards who had been assigned to protect John. Their leader, Cheng Kiang Koon, seemed both able and cooperative, and his manner encouraged John to ask for an official meeting with a representative of the AJA.[6] Before the end of August news reached the camp that a high-level official of the Malayan People's Anti-Japanese Army (MPAJA) was on his way to see Maj Davis. The Communist Acting Secretary of State for Perak duly appeared. He was impressive, calm and quietly spoken, a natural leader with a political mind. He was also remarkably youthful-looking but not unusually so for someone still short of his nineteenth birthday. He introduced himself as Chen Chin Sheng, but his real name was Ong Boon Hua and his best-known alias Chin Peng.

To establish the bona fides of the British officer who met him, Chin Peng held out a watch and asked if John recognised it. 'Of course, it's mine!', John replied instantly, explaining how he gave it the leader of the Tampin stay-behind party. In response Chin Peng told him that the Communist leader, Lai Fuk, had been ambushed and killed by the Japanese two months before. But on a happier note he was able to confirm that Spencer Chapman was alive and with the Communist guerrillas in Pahang, and though John's anthropologist friend, Pat Noone, had joined the Perak guerrillas at their Chemor camp, he understood that he had recently crossed into Kelantan. Chin Peng also gave John general information on the Resistance movement, confirming that the MPAJA was now a countrywide organisation, consisting of semi-independent groups.[7] However, in the light of Japanese reconnaissance activity in the Dindings, Chin Peng advised John that the 'Gustavus' base camp should be moved without delay from Segari to a safe location on the Perak side of the central range. John readily accepted his offer to arrange the transfer as soon as possible after Richard Broome's arrival, scheduled for late September.

Submarine 024, with Lt Cdr de Vries in command, left Ceylon on the 12th with Richard and his Conducting Officer, ex-rubber-planter Capt F.P.W. Harrison. The rendezvous was south of Pulau Rumbia in the Sembilan Islands, where the boat surfaced on the morning of 23 September. The junk was easily spotted and John was identified making the recognition signals.

He had with him two AJUF (Anti-Japanese Union Forces) bodyguards and Cheng, the Sitiawan guerrilla whom he had arranged should act as courier and return by submarine for further training in India.[8] All went well until 4 p.m. when an enemy merchant convoy appeared, sailing towards them from the south. Realising that de Vries had a duty to attack, Richard Broome agreed to a compromise. 'He [de Vries] would surface as soon after dusk as possible and put me straight off in a folboat with only such stores as I could take with me,' Richard reported, 'and would wait till I reached the junk, after which he would immediately leave to chase the convoy.'[9] John, it seems, was decidedly annoyed that their operation would be prejudiced, and when Richard reached the junk he refused to comply and insisted on returning to the junk with Cheng to give Harrison a verbal report. This took up precious time so that a large quantity of valuable goods had to be left on 024 and returned to Ceylon. Nevertheless, John and Richard – or Dee and Dum to use their code names in the official records – made landfall safely near Segari beach and with the help of the bodyguards buried the Mark III W/T and other heavy stores on the jungle fringe before making their way to camp.

As good as his word, on 30 September Chin Peng appeared there to meet John Davis and update the British officers on the arrangements for the move. A starting date of 8 October was agreed. The 'Gustavus' party would be escorted by two AJUF guerrillas, Ah Lau and Dark (or Black) Lim, who were attached to John, and his KMT staff, Ah Han and Lee Choon. Chin Peng also wanted to reassure John that he had arranged for the 'Gustavus' leaders to meet a fully empowered Communist representative in due course; also that he would bring Spencer Chapman to the new camp as soon as it could be managed. John was relieved and delighted to hear this. He took to Chin Peng's manner – his quiet reasonableness – without being disarmed by it, and he felt instinctively that he could trust him. As a measure of the rapport between them Chin Peng assured John of his goodwill, pledging the MPAJA's cooperation in their common struggle and their willingness to take over the protection and support of 'Gustavus' to free the Dragons for intelligence work.

Meanwhile all minds were concentrated on the move: none too soon because Japanese coastal activity suddenly intensified. The SOE men were not to know the reason, but the enemy had been badly rattled by a daring attack on their shipping in Singapore harbour on the night of 26/27 September. Operation 'Jaywick' was the work of a group in Special

Operations Australia, commanded by an officer well known to John and
Richard: Capt Ivan Lyon.[10] As a rare example of a successful sabotage
mission to Malaya, it boosted the Allied war effort. Sadly, however, when
Lyon attempted to repeat the triumph a year later, it was a total disaster.

Since July 1943, with the help of the other Dragons, Ah Ng had also been
active and had initiated an external intelligence-gathering network. As a
cover for his activities he had started a commission agency in Ipoh from an
office at Chop Kuan Aik Chan, 77 Market Street, with an additional branch
at Lumut and agents in Kuala Lumpur and Singapore. Taking advantage of
an economic climate driven by rampant shortages and corruption,

> the emphasis of the agency was on a 'get rich quick and no questions asked' basis,
> dealing mostly in black market foodstuffs smuggled from Siam through Lumut. It
> included a share in a project for making lubricating oil from resin, a junk trading
> business which enabled us to keep our submarine RVs and an arrangement with
> a Jap official by which so called Siam gold was smuggled up to Ipoh and sold to
> him, thus enabling us to cash our gold.[11]

As he pocketed his 'commission', little did the Japanese realise that he was
actually financing an enemy intelligence system. The thought gave great
satisfaction to Ah Ng. However, aware of the danger of over-exposure, Ah
Ng felt additional experienced hands were needed to help run the business.
Although Ah Ying had moved to Ipoh to assist him, Ah Ng had parted with
Ah Han, who was too well known in Ipoh, as well as being identifiable from
a slight limp. He had therefore returned to the main base camp to be John's
right-hand man. In September Ah Lim left camp to establish himself as Ah
Ng's agent in Lumut, and Shek Fu, who went first to Lumut, then became
a shopkeeper in Tapah. In the meantime in Ipoh Ah Ng had enlisted the
help of two friends of Chua who were influential in the town's Chinese
community.[12] They were not told about the true purpose of the commission
agency, but a third recruit, an articulate young Ipoh journalist, Mo Ching,
was taken fully into the organisation.[13]

John and Richard fully appreciated the dangers facing the 'Gustavus' party as they crossed Perak, but Richard's subsequent account was factual and low-key.[14] Between the coast and the foothills of the mountain range lay a substantial area of impenetrable swamp-jungle, so Chin Peng's plan was that they should bypass this to the south and travel inland up the Perak River. To reach this point, however, they first had to retrace their steps to the Segari coast and rendezvous with the boat that would take them to the Perak estuary. As a security measure, instead of accompanying the party Chin Peng met them at stages on the route. 'It was a march of 4 hours from our camp to this beach and we arrived there about midday, but to our great disappointment no junk arrived that day,' wrote Richard. 'We had an unpleasant night, with pouring rain and no food, and the conviction [grew] that the game was up and we should become fugitives in the scanty Sigari [sic] jungle.' The junk did not arrive until mid-afternoon the following day, but once on the open water they struck a northerly breeze which took them through the Dindings channel at a good speed in the course of that night. They had adopted a high-risk strategy in taking the inner course rather than the open Malacca Strait, but it proved an astute decision, for they passed unnoticed under the noses of the Japanese. The wind, meanwhile, continued to propel them up the Perak River in broad daylight past Bagan Datoh, until they anchored at Jenderata at 11 a.m.

At this point the party suffered their first setback. It was after midnight before they moved up a small creek to contact a group of AJU carriers who led them through Jenderata rubber estate to a vegetable garden. Here a temporary hut had been built for the rendezvous with Chin Peng, though it was a Malay area, where delay spelt danger. By ill luck the Communist leader had gone down with malaria, and for five days and nights the place became a virtual prison for the waiting party, stifling in the midday sun and plagued after dusk by a myriad mosquitoes. Late on the fifth night they set off once more, along the jungle edge and through a stretch of swampy rubber to a Malay *kampong*, but progress was slow. Here, too, there was some panic when they stumbled their way beneath a house on stilts, waking the Malay occupant, who luckily took them for a wild pig. After a day's shelter in the jungle, they crossed the Telok Anson–Bidor road in darkness, negotiated the Gloucester rubber estate and the Bidor River by a rickety wooden bridge, finally making it over the Degong road. A well-earned day of rest awaited them at a safe house in the midst of a

Chinese agricultural area but, as Richard recounted, their respite was brief. The next night in the darkness 'our guides lost their way and their heads and we spent three hours paddling about in the swamp, waking scores of Malays and leaving tracks like a herd of elephants. Eventually at dawn, when things looked pretty desperate, we found a small piece of jungle behind some rubber, about 30yds wide, where we lay for the day very uncomfortably with some Tamil cultivators about 20yds away'.[15]

John said little about the journey, except that it was 'the most awful trekking of my life'. He *hated* not to feel in control. Trudging through 'appalling swamps in the pouring rain' or lying about in the heat of the days 'as a preparation for a night of hell' was something best forgotten. But he could not forget his fear at being led into a crowded Chinese coffee-shop, nor the relief of learning that it was an AJUF meeting house as he was plied with coffee and cakes. They were on the last lap. That night they crossed the main highway near the Tongkah harbour tin mine and reached some Chinese labour lines on the pipeline. A stiff three-hour jungle walk the next morning, involving a climb to a level of over 2,000ft, finally brought the exhausted party to their new camp near the summit of Blantan hill. By the end, at least three – Ah Han, Lee Choon and Richard Broome – had succumbed temporarily to an unknown fever, but John dished out aspirin and they slowly recovered.

The 'Gustavus' party quickly appreciated Blantan's situation. On a fine day there were magnificent views, east to the mountains of the main range and westwards, Bidor and Tapah in the foreground, across the coastal plain and the meandering Perak River to Pangkor and the Sembilan Islands, set in the bluish haze of the Malacca Straits. The rainforests of eastern Perak were effectively guerrilla territory. Chin Peng had picked the isolated site and the camp was prepared on his orders. To look after the 'Gustavus' team a fifteen-man Communist bodyguard was installed, commanded by an English-speaking Chinese, Ah Yang, 'a bulky bespectacled student who . . . was unbelievably erudite, having read all of Marx, Engels and Shaw'.[16] If his lack of humour and secretive, surly manner did not endear him to the British, they gave him full credit for his efficiency in organising their food supply and their protection.

Before the end of October the inexorable timetable of the Malaya Country Section was weighing on John's mind. He and Richard discussed the next submarine operation, 'Gustavus V', scheduled for early November, bringing their KMT friend, Lim Bo Seng. Though he still felt groggy Richard insisted on keeping the rendezvous planned for 6 November. John accompanied him from Blantan to the main north–south road, where Richard was to pick up a car and continue to the coast, but to their surprise Chin Peng appeared, warning them of enemy patrols. The Japanese must have had wind of something because they were setting up roadblocks between Bidor and Telok Anson. The three men did not know that the infiltration of Lim Bo Seng by submarine in the Telok Anson area had been betrayed to the Japanese Kempeitai and this unquestionably accounted for the build-up of Japanese military and police activity from the beginning of the 'Gustavus' operations.[17] From his own information Chin Peng judged it too dangerous for a European officer to take part. He insisted on standing in for Richard. While the two Englishmen returned to Blantan, Chin Peng proceeded to the coast.

Despite minor hiccups the rendezvous off Kuala Bernam was kept, but in the light of Chin Peng's concerns about the Japanese presence, Lim Bo Seng refused to let Capt Harrison or anyone else land. Instead, Harrison and the Conducting Officer, Fenner, were given the message that the MPAJA had asked for money and medicine, and 'Gustavus' had requested another rendezvous for 9–11 December. Lim Bo Seng then joined Chin Peng on the junk after completing the transfer of stores (including two new light-weight B Mark II W/T sets). They had hoped to make a quick getaway, but good as the guerrillas' organisation was in some respects, they had no means of transporting bulky stores 50 miles across a countryside at risk from troop patrols and informers. So again the stores were left behind, this time at Jenderata, to be transported inland later. Chin Peng, however, had arranged for a car to wait for Lim Bo Seng and they were driven to a point near Tapah, from which they walked up to Blantan to be reunited with the British party.

The request for a December rendezvous had been made in case it was necessary to reinforce the Davis party or pull out any members: Richard's health, for instance, remained problematical. Operation 'Gustavus VI', in December, was the first by a British T-class submarine. Lt Cdr L.W.A. Bennington, commander of HMS *Tally-Ho*, was not an enthusiast of special missions and he had to contend with a defective periscope. Nevertheless, with Harrison and a Chinese agent on board, the submarine reached the Sembilan Islands on 9 December and patrolled the area for two more days. In the absence of a junk displaying the correct signals Harrison and the agent landed on the island of Pulau Lalang South to search for an emergency message in the 'Gustavus' 'post-box'. On finding nothing Bennington aborted the operation and headed for home.[18]

However, there was to be one more sortie early in January 1944, 'Emergency Gustavus VI', when *Tally-Ho* returned with reinforcements for 'Gustavus'.[19] Aboard the submarine were officers Claude Fenner and Jim Hannah and eight Chinese agents. Richard was originally to meet the party but Ah Ying was concerned about enemy shore patrols, and again it was Chin Peng who met Fenner from the folboat and handed him a toothpaste tube containing secret information and a warning not to proceed with landing. In return the Chinese leader was handed a dried fish, with messages concealed inside the brain cavity, to be taken back to Blantan. With these exchanges the rendezvous was concluded on the 5th and for Bennington the operation was rounded off satisfactorily when *Tally-Ho* sank a Japanese cruiser north of Penang Island.

For the 'Gustavus' mission the year 1943 ended with interesting developments. In November Lim Bo Seng had brought two important items of news, and in December Chin Peng delivered on his last promise to John. On Christmas night Freddy Spencer Chapman miraculously walked into Blantan to join his former colleagues of the Oriental Mission; and there was just time to ensure the glad – but top-secret – tidings were relayed by submarine to SEAC. This would be followed in the New Year by the arrival of an important plenipotentiary from Communist HQ to take part in high-level talks with the British mission. Nevertheless, if the year 1943 ended on a constructive, even euphoric note, the tempo and tenor of events were about to change dramatically. The year 1944 soon developed into a roller-coaster year as the initial high peak gave way to an alarming descent into a grim, impenetrable trough of silence.

Chapter 7

Force 136 in Turmoil

When Lim Bo Seng came to Blantan in November 1943 he brought an important official document. It confirmed John's authority and clear mandate to negotiate a military treaty on behalf of SEAC with the Communist Plenipotentiary, who was expected shortly from Central HQ. 'The Plen' was duly shown these credentials:

> Admiral Lord Louis Mountbatten, G.C.V.O., Supreme Allied Commander, South East Asia Command, has received with pleasure reports of Major J.L. Davis confirming the enduring anti-Japanese attitude of the peoples of Malaya, which has continued through a long and most difficult time . . . He now appoints until further notice Major J.L. Davis . . . as his representative in Malaya for the purpose of aiding and strengthening all those elements who can be counted on to assist in the preparations for the final ejection of the Japanese from Malayan territory.[1]

The Communist leader who arrived at Blantan on 30 December to negotiate with the British party was introduced by Chin Peng to John and his colleagues as Mr Chang Hung, the elected representative of the MCP, the AJF and the AJU. No mention was made, however, of his role as Secretary-General of the MCP. The moment of meeting was, in John's own words, perhaps the most 'difficult and strange' of his life, because he instantly recognised Special Branch's most valued double agent, Lai Tek, whom he had been responsible for managing before the outbreak of war. When he took on that role John had entered a world of extraordinary secrecy and deception. Now, in that split second, he had to control his body language to hide any hint of recognition. Spencer Chapman also knew Chang Hung's real identity but kept his own counsel. If Lai Tek's record had been revealed at this point, the meeting on 30 December would certainly have dissolved in confusion and recrimination. To John's considerable relief Chang Hung retained a totally impassive expression, as one might expect of a skilled dissembler, though John found it frustrating that they had no opportunity to talk in private. In fact, in a highly sinister twist the Communist Secretary-General had expanded his operations since March 1942 to become a triple agent, working for Japanese military intelligence and the Kempeitai. No one in British Intelligence, not even John Davis, could have known of this development.

Despite these treacherous undercurrents the discussions at Blantan went ahead as planned over two days, 30–1 December 1943. John formally introduced his colleagues, Capt R.N. Broome and Tan Choong Lim (alias Lim Bo Seng), the senior Chinese officer, serving as interpreter in English and Mandarin, who were also SEAC's military representatives. Though he was present, Maj Spencer Chapman was not accredited; nor was Chang Hung's sole colleague, Chin Peng, a signatory to the agreement. The British officers had been told that 'no questions of postwar policy were to be discussed and that our whole mission was military'. However, in his perceptive way Richard observed a paradox, that the underlying aim of the Force 136 mission was 'a political operation more than anything else'.[2]

Chang Hung seemed amenable to the Allied request for cooperation. The British made it clear they expected the Communists to keep up anti-Japanese feeling, to undertake limited fifth-column activity and to emphasise in their propaganda the need for complete cooperation with the Allied invading forces.[3] The British officers anticipated the invasion taking place in six months, giving time to prepare for combined action. In return for his support, Chang Hung requested arms, ammunition, medical supplies, including doctors, military training and financial assistance to the tune of Straits $50,000–70,000 per month. John responded as honestly as he could. A plan for shipping arms and medical supplies was drawn up but he foresaw a shortage of doctors. Measures would be taken to train sufficient military instructors.[4] He had already raised the matter of finance with the authorities and awaited a reply.

The negotiators obviously had their own agendas. Beneath the civility Richard detected an 'air of cautiousness and possibly of cynicism' in the

Communist response, and Chin Peng also sensed a 'sinister aspect' to the proceedings.[5] To the British what mattered most was Chang Hung's agreement to cooperate with Allied forces during the re-taking of Malaya, though he adroitly prevaricated over extending cooperation to the post-invasion period, when the British Army would be responsible for peace and order.[6] John discerned a political manoeuvre by Lai Tek, a delaying tactic to protect his position. For all that, Richard was satisfied 'the Plen [Plenipotentiary, alias Chang Hung], a man of considerable intelligence, meant to stand by everything he said'.[7]

The Blantan Agreement covers only a couple of sides of an exercise book but it is a remarkable document. Lacking the verbiage of many international treaties, it was negotiated in a hut amid primeval jungle. The motive was the defeat of the common enemy, Japan, but the subtle sub-text of the agreement was the complex relationship between Lai Tek, John Davis and Chin Peng. At the time John and Richard were satisfied that Force 136 had scored a vital success in securing Chang Hung's cooperation. His acceptance that the Communist Party 'will follow the instructions of the Allied C-in-C [Commander-in-Chief] in so far as military operations in Malaya are concerned' was regarded as a considerable tactical achievement.[8] But there were personal gains for Lai Tek in terms of his reputation and self-protection, and the Chinese Communists drew valuable benefit from the training and equipping of their guerrillas. However, the legacy of the Blantan Agreement lingered beyond Japan's surrender, adding to the postwar economic confusion in Malaya and the separation of British and Communist Chinese interests. The end-game was the Communist insurgency against colonial Britain.

Of the two items of news brought to Blantan by Lim Bo Seng, the second was strictly political. It concerned the Indian Nationalist leader, Subhas Chandra Bose, a swashbuckling sympathiser of the Axis powers, a man driven by hatred of British imperialism.[9]

Early in 1943 he returned from Germany by submarine to the Far East, and with Japanese support assumed the leadership of the moribund Indian National Army to serve alongside Japan's forces. Then soaring ambition drove him on 21 October to declare a Provisional Government

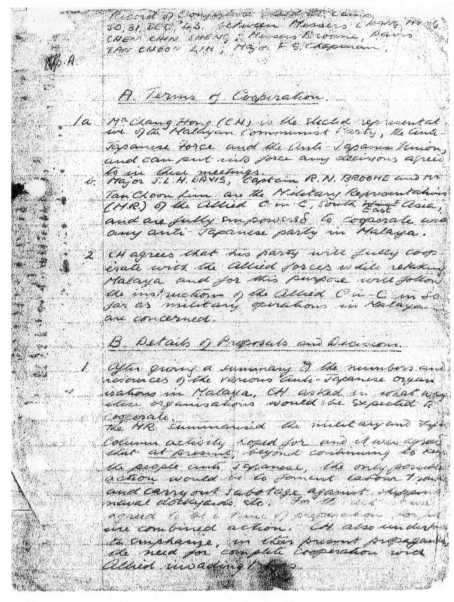

The Blantan Agreement, signed by Maj John Davis, Richard Broome and Tan Choong Lim – alias Lim Bo Seng – representing SEAC, and Chang Hung – alias Lai Tek –

representing the Malayan Communists, December 1943. *(Reproduced with the permission of The National Archives, Kew, HS 7/165)* of Free India (Azad Hind), of which he became the self-elected premier and head of state. Not content with this, three days later he declared war on Great Britain and the United States. But before this final step he had already aroused the British government to serious pre-emptive action. By implication an order to initiate a special operation had been received in New Delhi, for in September a top-secret telegram to Colin Mackenzie urged 'GREATEST SECRECY IS NECESSARY REGARDING X AND THAT WE SHOULD NOT ATTEMPT OPERATION UNLESS CONVINCED OF SUCCESS AND THAT IT CANNOT BE TRACED TO BRITISH SOURCE.' While suggesting that the unidentified plan might be 'too wild cat' he conceded that 'WE ARE MEDIUM FOR SUCH ACTIONS AND MUST DO ALL IN OUR POWER TO ASSIST H.M.G.'[10] Subhas Chandra Bose's incautious declaration of war on 24 October simply advanced the justification for retaliation.

Col Christopher Hudson, as head of Force 136 Group B, was summoned urgently to Meerut for further orders. The next 'Gustavus' mission, with Lim Bo Seng on board, was due to leave Ceylon the following day. The Chinese leader was hastily contacted. To his primary function of reinforcing Force 136's intelligence network was added a last minute order to organise the assassination of Subhas Chandra Bose. As soon as he arrived at Blantan camp Lim Bo Seng disclosed this bombshell to John and Richard. The three discussed the implications. John accepted that political assassination was a function of SOE but he was highly indignant that the order should be given to Lim Bo Seng on the point of his departure on a different mission. He described it later as 'a typical vague Meerut idea' that was 'thrown at him just before he left on his operation'. He insisted that it could only be valid on a 'should opportunity arise' basis, and to suggest it should take a higher priority was quite unacceptable. It would put Lim Bo Seng and surviving members of his family in Singapore in increased danger and could also have an adverse effect on the outcome of 'Gustavus V'. So, on the assumption that 'any action on it was a vague possibility of the future', they agreed to put it on the back burner. In fact the opportunity never presented itself, so the assassination never took place. That saved the reputation – in John's words – of a 'great hero of the non-Communist Malayan Chinese'.

Freddy Spencer Chapman's appearance at Blantan on Christmas night 1943 reunited the men who had spearheaded the Oriental Mission's behind-the-lines operations. In the two years since the Malayan Peninsula was overrun Chapman had lived a charmed life, enduring close brushes with the Japanese, periods with very little food and no European company and a series of deadly illnesses that would have killed lesser mortals (including the blackwater fever that had delayed his arrival at Blantan). In order to survive he had thrown his lot in with the MPAJA guerrillas, and in return for protection he had trained them in guerrilla warfare.

John had high hopes that Freddy had news of European stay-behind-parties or individuals stranded in the jungle that could be conveyed by submarine to Ceylon. But Chapman, an eternally restless character, had moved around the Peninsula making passing contacts and had little up-to-date information on other Europeans, such as Frank Vanrenan and Ron Graham.[11] Chapman heard that his explosives expert, John Sartin, had been taken prisoner, and his companion Clark Heywood had been killed in July 1942 in a running battle with Japanese troops on the Karak–Menchis road. By that time Freddy had lost touch with three more of his original party, Frank Quayle, Bob Chrystal and Bill Robinson, who were joined by Pat Noone at the Perak guerrilla camp east of Chemor.[12] Freddy was fearful of the fate of his other European volunteers, such as the five-man party under Lt William Stubbington encamped north-east of the mining town of Raub. Stubbington and 2/Lt Guy Rand were both killed on 17 March 1942 after a surprise Japanese attack between Merapoh and Jerantut. There was mixed news, too, of the Sungei Lembing pair, Brian Tyson and Maurice Cotterill, whom Freddy met in Johore at New Year 1943. He was much heartened by his first sight of Englishmen for six months, so it was a double blow when a week later Tyson died of pneumonia and Cotterill refused to cooperate with Freddy on a plan of escape. Of the other six Oriental Mission European stay-behind groups nothing firm was heard until after the war.[13]

Spencer Chapman and Frank Quayle were not the only Englishmen to be told by the anti-Japanese forces of the presence of John's SOE party in Perak. Among the British still hiding in Johore, protected by Chinese guerrillas, were the ISLD unit under Maj Barry, whom John had come across at Kluang in the last week of fighting on the Peninsula. On 23 December 1943 Barry received two somewhat garbled letters from the MCP Secretary-General, who called himself 'Lao Wu', the first dated August

1943, claiming contact with Allied HQ in India, and stating that another group with radio equipment had been sent to Malaya. 'You know Major Davis and Major Chapman who are with us now,' he added. The second letter, dated 15 December 1943, referred to some English 'technical friends' sent to establish contact with other agents.[14] The imprecise language of these messages was misleading, but had he known that his whereabouts was being discussed by others, particularly by the super-agent Communist Secretary-General – Lao Wu/Chang Hung/Lai Tek – John would have been deeply worried by the security implications. At the end of 1943, however, the 'Gustavus' network at Blantan was quite unaware of the surviving SIS/ISLD group in Johore and their contacts with the Secretary-General under any of his aliases. Nor did they know of any alleged orders that as SOE operatives they should become involved with Barry's party.

Believing that their presence was a carefully guarded secret, John and his colleagues lived at Blantan comparatively undisturbed. For relaxation they had books and playing cards, and they had enough medicines and money to maintain a supply of fresh meat and vegetables from the plains. John's long familiarity with the jungle enabled him to feel comfortable with his surroundings and at ease with the aboriginal people, the *orang asli*, who lived in clearings near the camp like silent, discreet shadows. Ah Han was John's mediator *vis-à-vis* the bodyguards. On an everyday basis the AJUF men were usually helpful and behaved correctly towards the Force 136 officers. But John had no illusions that the Communist Party members among them were indoctrinated to believe that 'deceit in the name of the party is absolutely legitimate and expected', and from time to time he became 'terribly irritated with that'.[15] In compensation, both he and Richard found the higher command dependable and straightforward, especially Chin Peng, who was (in Richard's words) 'the only Communist we felt to be totally reliable and also an extremely pleasant character'.[16] John could guess what the KMT Chinese thought of the AJUF guards, and vice versa, but Chin Peng revealed in his memoirs that he had identified Tan Choon Lim (that is to say, Lim Bo Seng) as a KMT agent and 'that Tan and I viewed each other with considerable skepticism [*sic*]'.[17] Yet there was surprisingly little trouble, because as Ah Han said later, 'There was no question of politics in the jungle. Our primary aim was to get rid of the Japanese.' More than ever, security had to override other considerations.

By New Year 1944 aerial reconnaissance by enemy aircraft was noticeably increasing. Although their target was believed to be the guerrillas' patrol camp at Bidor, the lack of air cover and Blantan's relative proximity to the jungle edge made the camp vulnerable. John accepted that another move was necessary. Feelers were put out to the local *orang asli* and a disused clearing was found above the confluence of the Woh River and its tributary, the Ayer Busok. Like most of the tribesmen, the elderly diminutive headman was fearful of the Japanese but he kindly agreed to their taking over the site for their camp.

More secluded and secure than Blantan, Pa Kasut's house became their home for the next four months. In March AJUF guides brought Frank Quayle to the camp. He was a resourceful, decent, straightforward, cheerful character and an asset to his fellow officers. The wisdom of the decision to move was confirmed when the Japanese embarked on a murderous campaign of wholesale burning and slaughter among the *kampong* dwellers along the jungle fringe.

Unfortunately, this happened when the submarine link was proving unreliable. The timing of Ah Ying's departure from Blantan in late December had been set by the impending arrival of 'Emergency Gustavus VI'. This operation was prior to the negotiations between Chang Hung and the Force 136 party, so regrettably SEAC were not informed of the successful conclusion of the Blantan Agreement. In February 1944 Operation 'Remarkable I' arrived in Malayan waters on HMS *Tally-Ho* with a mixed party of special operations personnel.[18] Ah Ying undertook to make the rendezvous in place of Chin Peng, who was ill, but after three days' patrolling, from 17 to 19 February, *Tally-Ho* had made no contact. More worrying, Lt Cdr Bennington reported enemy patrol vessels and heavy sea traffic around Pulau Jarak and Kuala Bernam. In mid-March Operation 'Remarkable II' fared similarly. Once again Ah Ying failed to make the rendezvous, so Claude Fenner and Jim Hannah returned to Ceylon with their load of arms and stores. The apparent breakdown in the monthly submarine system was compounded by the inability to establish W/T communications with Ceylon. John and his Force 136 party were now effectively cut off from all contact with SEAC.

The difficulty of bringing the W/T transmitters and equipment up from the coast had also been worrying John for some time. AJUF had agreed to organise carriers, but Japanese control of the plains prohibited attempts to bring the large transmitters up by lorry, and for several months the

30lb sets remained in their hiding place at Jenderata. In addition, John was concerned that running the external organisation of 'Gustavus' was imposing an intolerable burden on Ah Ng. He had succeeded better than could have been expected and had acquired a lorry, a private car and the leading share in a motor boat operating between Singapore and northern Malaya. He had also been close to winning a lucrative Japanese contract for one of his agents to supply vegetables from the Cameron Highlands to the Imperial Japanese Navy in Penang. He had extended his contacts to include several high-ranking Chinese detectives, some of whom were satisfactorily compromised to ensure that they would warn him of any threatening Japanese activity. The danger, in John's opinion – and Richard and Lim Bo Seng agreed – was the network's unavoidable dependence on Ah Ng and the fact that none of the other outside agents were of his calibre. Ah Tsing, in John's view, though 'a big, rather clumsy youngster', had done a wonderful job in setting up the submarine rendezvous, but after his initial burst of effort his nerve and energy began to flag. This threw more responsibility on Ah Ng, as well as on Chua Koon Eng (who was not, after all, a Force 136 agent but knew a great deal about the organisation), and ultimately on Ah Ying, who was brave and resourceful but lacked the employment credentials for a good cover. Ah Ng's agency was also short of capital to guarantee it was on a safe and sound footing. Equally, as the failing submarine rendezvous halted the supply of funds, a cashflow problem loomed. Hopes of extending the external intelligence network beyond Perak into other states were put on hold. The only solution seemed to be to send Ah Ng to Singapore to seek financial help from three old friends of Lim Bo Seng.[19] Ah Ng was given a thorough briefing by Lim Bo Seng before he left.

This trip, however, was not a success. One good friend appeared too frightened to respond, while the other two prevaricated. Lim Bo Seng had arguably underestimated the impact of the crippling extortion imposed on the Chinese by the Japanese. Hiding his disappointment, he discussed with John and Richard whether to leave Blantan and join the KMT agents on the plain. They put no pressure on him either way, knowing – as he did – that he could be taking a heavy personal risk. But he decided it was his duty to give positive leadership to his men by going into the Chinese community, with a tacit understanding that he would return to camp as soon as he had completed his task. John recalled his friend's fighting talk and great self-belief, especially in his capacity for raising money. They bowed to his decision. Lim Bo Seng left Blantan on 1 March 1944.

Posing as Ah Ng's uncle, he was temporarily installed in a house in Ipoh. He planned to organise a safe hideout on a friend's rubber estate on the Cameron Highlands road, from which to direct the intelligence network. Both Richard and John saw no immediate danger, nor had any warning of a possible threat been received from their AJUF guard. So when they came, the blows were insidious, calculated and crushing.

In mid-March the Japanese landed a force of 200 troops on Pangkor, where they already had an undercover observation post. On the 21st a contingent of military police appeared and made a rigorous motorboat search of the surrounding islands. Although Ah Tsing was there, Ah Ying had left some days earlier to wait at sea for the rendezvous with 'Remarkable II'. On 22 March a military cordon was thrown around Pangkor, but by then Ah Ying was back at Pa Kasut's to report the failure of the rendezvous and deliver a letter to John from Lim Bo Seng, saying that Ah Ng had left Ipoh for further financial discussions in Singapore. Ah Ying also reported how Chua Koon Eng had received a mysterious visit from two men claiming to be from the Resistance army. When they demanded Straits $25,000 with menaces Chua refused to be drawn but, on the grounds that discretion was the better part of valour, he left Pangkor immediately. However, it seems that he was already being tracked because the next evening, 23 March, he was arrested by the Japanese at Telok Murrok, interrogated and in terror confessed to all he knew about the 'Gustavus' organisation. Ah Tsing's arrest followed the next day.

Confronted with Chua, looking bowed and broken, he confirmed what Chua had told his captors. Ah Tsing was taken to the Japanese counter-espionage headquarters in Ipoh. He expected rough treatment before being thrown in a cell, but while under surveillance he was treated surprisingly well as a preliminary to 'softening up' and 'turning' a captured agent. In townships like Lumut the tension was palpable. When Ah Lim heard about Ah Tsing's capture he was convinced he was being held as bait to reveal the whereabouts of Maj Davis. However, on 26 March, acting with commendable presence of mind, Ah Tsing made a daring escape when his two women minders were temporarily distracted.[20] Seeing his chance, Ah Tsing made for the bathroom. He climbed down two storeys from an open window and made a quick getaway by a passing taxi. When Ah Tsing revealed he was an escaping guerrilla, the taxi driver drove at full speed to Bidor. There the agent borrowed his fare from local AJUF guides sitting in the coffee shop before making off post-haste into the jungle. Once at Pa Kasut's camp he poured out all he knew to John and Richard. With Chin Peng's help urgent messages were sent by courier, warning Lim Bo Seng and other members of the network. Meanwhile Ah Lim was arrested in an Ipoh hotel on the 26th and two days later Shek Fu was picked up in Tapah.

Unfortunately it proved impossible to warn Lim Bo Seng in time. It emerged later that he and Mo Ching tried to escape in a private car but were stopped and arrested on the outskirts of Ipoh. Finally, Ah Ng was cornered when returning from Singapore. According to Ah Lim he tried to kill himself before being arrested.[21] In the meantime, Chua was released after revealing all he knew and was allowed to resume his business activities under strict Japanese control. The two boatmen from the SOE junk were also picked up by the Kempeitai and forced to reveal the venues of the submarine rendezvous. Luckily for Force 136 the men did not know the dates or the revised recognition signals essential to trap a waiting submarine. All the same, one of the boatmen hanged himself afterwards. It was never established who revealed the presence at Segari of the buried Sten guns and the Mark III W/T set, but soon after their retrieval by the Japanese the Stens were used by a contingent of Indian police in a massacre at Bidor.

In these swiftly executed steps the Japanese destroyed all John's hopes and plans, but worse in human terms, all Force 136's external network of KMT agents. Nothing was more painful than recording 'Our men simply disappeared, and nothing has been heard of any of them since'.[22] The inquest into the disaster came later when John and his team had time to think and piece together bits of information, but the full explanation was not revealed until 1945. However, the seizure of Lim Bo Seng was an instantaneous blow to the future of intelligence work in the Peninsula, as well as a cruel personal tragedy; and inevitably the impact on Force 136's inner circle, hiding in the jungle, was profound. John admitted, 'My morale was absolutely shattered, and I'm sure everybody else's was.' Further, the realisation dawned that in their state of isolation they would be ever more dependent on their AJUF allies. At the same time it would be impossible for the foreseeable future to fulfil their treaty promises on material, financial and personal aid to the MPAJA. Their only consolation was a modest supply of medicines and sufficient money to last for about a year. At the first opportunity John suggested to Chin Peng that AJUF should try to borrow funds on the strength of his position as the authorised representative of Mountbatten and SEAC, which the Chinese leader agreed to do. But ultimately, according to John, the only hope of survival was to display characteristic British phlegm, just as the only hope of re-establishing contact with Ceylon was the retrieval of the W/T sets from their hiding place at Jenderata, which called for patience.

Among the officers, Freddy Spencer Chapman's passion for adventure made him the least suited to the waiting game. John and Richard hit on a solution: Freddy should undertake a search in the high jungle wilderness for the one Englishman whose whereabouts was still a mystery: the anthropologist Pat Noone. Armed with a letter of introduction, maps and information on relevant mountain routes, and guided by aborigines, on 13 April Freddy set off to Sungei Siput with Black Lim as his escort.

Within days of his departure another submarine rendezvous was attempted off Pulau Jarak. Operation 'Remarkable III' was carrying reinforcements for John's internal party, but in view of the collapse of the external organisation there was no chance of Ah Ying making the rendezvous. So after waiting from 22 to 24 April without seeing signs of a reception committee or the correct recognition signals, the submarine commander reverted to an emergency plan. Despite the severe risk, two Chinese agents came ashore by folboat to make a successful blind landing on Pangkor in the early hours of the 25th. Cheng Kiang Koon, the AJUF guerrilla whom John had sent to India for training, had returned with one of the Dragons, Chang Teh Cheok. With the help of the MPAJA they made their way by early May to Pa Kasut's camp, bringing some much-needed gold and new instructions about the submarine schedule. All but Freddy and John greeted them warmly. John had been taken ill at the end of April with suspected leptospirosis. He was still very sick, and at the same time malaria was rife in the camp when a message arrived from Chin Peng about 20 May to say that at last the stores from Jenderata had reached Blantan. Despite Richard's reservations John insisted on accompanying him to meet Chin Peng at their old camp to arrange the last transit lap to Pa Kasut's.

It was agreed that John and Richard should take Ah Tsing and the newcomers, Cheng and Chang, with most of the AJUF guard to carry the stores from Blantan. While they were away Black Lim arrived back at Pa Kasut's. He had been sent with a message for John from Chapman, who was continuing his searches alone. Although Lim reported the rumour that Noone had been killed by the Temiar people, nobody, including John, would believe his story.[23] Meanwhile, at Blantan John learnt that the heavy equipment was still at the foot of the hills. The lighter stores, with two batteries and a hand generator, were waiting, so these were sent on ahead. The two Force 136 men remained behind at Blantan for talks with Chin Peng, who had become the pivotal support of Force 136. In particular, John wanted to arrange with him for Cheng to keep the next submarine rendezvous so that he could take back a report of the catastrophic collapse of Force 136's external network. The two Chinese left Blantan on 29 May but their mission was prevented by large-scale Japanese military activity from making any contact with 'Remarkable IV'. John underestimated the great depth of concern in Ceylon for the safety of his party. He had no idea that Maj Innes Tremlett, as head of Malaya Country Section, insisted on going in the submarine HMS *Tantalus* to the rendezvous on 11–12 June. When this failed John assumed correctly that, in view of the excessive risks, submarine links with Force 136 would be suspended. Consequently some time elapsed before Colombo knew of the major intelligence disaster in March and the success of the April landings.

On 30 May John, Richard and six of the guard set off back to Pa Kasut's camp. But after crossing the Telom River they came across alarming signs on the track: a series of campfires, still warm, that could only be attributed to Japanese troops. They worked out that the enemy had come in from the 7th mile on the Cameron Highlands road before camping at Kuala Telom, and from there they had proceeded to attack Pa Kasut's camp that morning. Since it was too late to warn the camp, the small party retraced their steps to Blantan to intercept the carriers with the two Mark II W/T sets and have them dumped in the jungle. Luckily they found two aboriginal huts where they lay low for a few days, while some of the guards went off to locate the rest of the Force 136 party. Through local tribesmen they learnt that an enemy force of 200–300 men were still in their camp: roughly a quarter were Japanese, the remainder being Indians and Malays. However, the good news was that all the Force 136 men had escaped unharmed, and some friendly *orang asli* would take a message to them by secure new tracks. After two more days, when it seemed safe to assume the enemy had withdrawn, John's party set off for Pa Kasut's to assess the situation.

It was a desolate and depressing sight. Their camp had been completely destroyed and the jungle all around for a radius of a quarter of a mile had been laid low where the ground had been systematically searched. Richard reported:

Our material losses were serious . . . The batteries and hand generator which had just arrived had been hastily thrown into the undergrowth and were easily found by the Japs. A large amount of reserve food and medicines and miscellaneous stores . . . was lost. Worst of all we lost our security bag which Quayle, when the alarm was received, buried in the undergrowth some distance from the camp. The unexpectedly long stay of the Japs in our camp (five days) enabled them to find it. It contained all our money, all the rest of the medicines, 'Gustavus' signals plan, Chinese codes and certain notes on our dealings with AJUF. Fortunately DEE [John] had taken all other documents for our conference with CTP [Chin Peng]. Nevertheless, the loss was very serious indeed.[24]

Considerably depressed by these discoveries, particularly by the loss of the security bag, John hurried off to find the survivors. After their reunion they found a temporary home in a large aboriginal house at Juit, above the Kuala Telom. Here they learnt more about the attack. The men in the camp had luckily received a good ten minutes' warning from their sentry, which guaranteed their escape. John had issued a general order not to fire unless essential, to avoid being drawn into a running battle with Japanese troops. Instead they should concentrate on escape. News percolated through to them that the destruction of Pa Kasut's had been part of a major six-week drive. The headquarters of the 5th (Perak) Regiment of the MPAJA were repeatedly harassed and arbitrary round-ups and atrocities occurred all along the route from Slim to Sungei Siput. The Japanese had actually diverted troops for temporary deployment against the guerrillas, soldiers who were en route to Assam, where the Japanese tide from Burma to India was finally turned at Kohima and Imphal.

The few weeks at Juit were the start of 'a pretty grim period with practically no food except tapioca, the world's worst diet'. Malnutrition, exposure, fever and infection each took their toll to some degree. There was a spell when sentry go was decided not by the clock, but by the period each day when a person knew he should be free from fever. John was reluctant to dramatise their sufferings when compared with those of the KMT Dragons imprisoned by the Kempeitai. Weakened by hunger strike and repeated torture, deprived of medical aid and water, Lim Bo Seng died in Batu Gajah Gaol on 29 June 1944. Looking back, there was no doubt in John's mind that June 1944 was the nadir of the fortunes of Force 136 in Malaya.

Chapter 8

Freeing the Airways

In July 1944 Force 136 moved to another campsite. The sheer effort left John close to physical collapse, something he had never experienced before. On one particular day he was appalled to find 'not a limb in my body would move'.[1]

He and his men owed their continued safety to Chin Peng. The Communist leader had arranged the construction of their new home and the party's transfer from Juit, carried out by Ah Yang and the AJUF guards. Their latest camp, Gurun, was built in primary jungle at about 2,500ft up the mountainous shoulder of Gunong Batu Puteh, but it had none of the panoramic views of Blantan. The clearing was deliberately small to preserve air cover, and the claustrophobic atmosphere was aggravated by drenching downpours and mountain mists.

The Force 136 hut was built about 100yds from the guards' hut and housed the dozen men in John's party.[2] The floor was earth and the one-roomed hut was simply constructed of bamboo, rotan and jungle *atap*, with sleeping benches, table tops and bench seats of flattened bamboo. For security's sake there were front and rear entrances, and in the centre, beneath the square fire area, a secret chamber had been constructed as a safe box.

At night the Force 136 men slept with Webley 38 revolvers and Stens at hand on the sleeping bench. Ah Yang was a punctilious guard. His daily whistle for reveille cut through the darkness at 5.30 a.m., dawn being the time the enemy was most likely to attack. John and his men, shivering with malnutrition in their threadbare clothes, would huddle round the fire in the early morning and again in the evenings. By day they tended to stay within the camouflage of trees and undergrowth.

The next six months seemed a 'very long dead period', dreary, frustrating, pervaded by monotony. Curiously, however, the slowdown in the body's metabolism helped each man to cope. 'When you're emaciated with malnutrition time goes very, very gently, plans evolve slowly,' John recalled. Each member of the party worked out his own way to keep active, mentally as well as physically. The KMT Chinese spent afternoons playing mah-jong. Quayle could be found working away with his hands. Freddy liked to go hunting. Richard was a man of many talents, among which were playing chess, singing and taking a leading part in the camp socials. John, however, was not an actor, a vocalist or a handyman. In fine weather he went on walks looking out for some unusual foliage or hoping for a view of the forbidden world beyond Gurun. In the rainy periods he would read, though the choice had been arbitrarily reduced to four books, the New Testament, a school collection of essays, a book on farriery and Dickens's *Pickwick Papers*.

The problem of communication constantly gnawed at him. The glad discovery that their two Mark II W/T sets were in perfect condition was countered by finding two gallons of water inside one of the packing cases: consequently the pedal generator, two small receiving sets and all spares were ruined by damp. And as the motor generator proved too heavy to transport, there was still no means of contacting SEAC's base in Ceylon.

Their isolation also produced mood changes and emotional tensions that affected personal relationships. Freddy Spencer Chapman found John's style of leadership incomprehensible. 'Davis always refused to ration the food for the same reason that he refused to allocate and divide up the essential chores among us – namely, that he hated any sort of organisation and what he called "militarism" and never gave an order if he could possibly help it.'[3] At the same time, while recognising Freddy's strengths, both John and Richard were sorely tried by his self-obsessive personality. Privately, John doubted whether someone as self-centred as Freddy, and as wedded to dangerous adventures, had the qualities for leadership.[4] Meanwhile Freddy felt that John was constantly brooding on the disastrous sequence of events that had overtaken Force 136 and the fate of Lim Bo Seng. In the future Lim Bo Seng's widow would tell John about her husband's deep fatalism.[5] How far his sense of foreboding might have affected his actions or clouded his judgement is a moot point; but deprived of information John could only ponder interminably on what went wrong.

Together he and Richard tried to analyse the catastrophic loss of the external network. In planning how best to deploy the Dragons there was neither the time nor the manpower to build a secure system of autonomous cells. 'The whole weakness of our organisation was the unavoidable dependence of all our outside men on Ng,' wrote Richard in his report.[6] Simple negligence had dire results. Over-frequent visits by agents exposed Ah Ng, an error repeated when Lim Bo Seng joined the network in Ipoh. Another outcome was the necessary reliance on individual volunteers with no *a priori* loyalty to the Resistance. For instance, John and Richard guessed it was likely that Chua Koon Eng would break down if arrested, as indeed he did. But it was distasteful to John to question the integrity of people who had selflessly volunteered to serve Force 136. He accepted that some individuals would always crack under torture, or the mere threat of it, but this did not necessarily mean they were despicable human beings. His idealism ran deep. He once made the curious remark that 'in warfare one has to be fairly naïve' and take people on trust.[7] It may seem an over-casual attitude for a Resistance leader, but it could explain his reluctance to pursue individual traitors.

Yet the question remains, why were Japanese counter-intelligence forces so successful against Force 136 in the first half of 1944? In any organisation hit by a series of sudden, crucial and apparently inexplicable security breakdowns, the presence of a well-placed mole must be a probability. In due course it became clear that this accounted for all Force 136's adversities in Malaya. In addition to successful aerial reconnaissance, the destruction of the Force 136 camp was put down to information received from a Malay detective-turned-informant stationed at the 7th Mile. When the identity of the principal mole was revealed, however, no blame could be attached to the way John Davis ran the Malayan operation. But it was no consolation to him that another man's treachery deprived postwar Malaya of the leadership of Lim Bo Seng, the one man who could have become the strong but politically moderate voice in the Chinese community of the future.

The isolation preyed on John. For all internal communications the Force 136 party was dependent on the slow-moving Communist courier system. In late September a runner from Central HQ reached Gurun with a letter from John Cross, one of Maj Barry's ISLD party in Johore, seeking 'an understanding' with the Davis party. Dated 30 April 1944, the missive was already five months old. John delayed committing himself for security reasons, intending to take soundings from Ceylon as soon as W/T links were re-established, and to respond accordingly. But when he finally wrote in December 1944 he had to admit 'we are not in contact with outside and have not been for over eight months'.[8]

It was a deeply frustrating time. Nothing illustrated this more than the fate of their transmitter equipment. One of the two B II sets brought to Blantan was in perfect condition, despite having been buried in a swamp. All it needed was power. John had asked as a matter of urgency for some fresh batteries and the repair of their dynamo, but they were still waiting for both as November approached. It was difficult to apportion blame, but Chin Peng was suffering periodic bouts of fever at this time and the intervals between his visits had lengthened from four to six or eight weeks. Richard, on the other hand, blamed the delays on the guerrillas' lack of influence with the urban Chinese; for when the dynamo eventually came with the assurance that it was serviceable, it still would not work. Another attempt to bring up a car battery also failed. However, in the interim Frank Quayle had cannibalised an old bicycle frame to set up a rough-and-ready pedal generator. So when at last the much-needed batteries came through, the mood at Gurun changed dramatically.

It was 5 November 1944, a date John was unlikely to forget. He and Freddy were out in the jungle collecting sweet potato leaves when they heard an unfamiliar drone and rumble and what sounded like gunfire overhead, suggesting aeroplanes in combat. Furiously, they searched for a gap in the trees and a clear patch of sky, but in vain: it was the excited voices back in camp that told them of an indefinite number of Allied bombers high in the ether, chased by Japanese aircraft. Here was the first intimation that the fortunes of war had turned. By sheer coincidence that same afternoon Ah Yang's men reached camp with the car batteries. It was a moment of exaltation for Lee Choon, who had patiently waited for sixteen months to do the job for which he had been trained. The workable W/T set was retrieved from its hiding place, and by slinging an aerial between Ah Yang's flagstaff and Force 136's hut and tuning in, he managed to raise the first sounds from the set. Huddled round, John's colleagues listened in mounting excitement as All India Radio came on air with the news that Singapore had been bombed that morning by thirty 'Superfortresses', all the aircraft returning safely to base.[9] The broadcast gave them the warm feeling of reconnection with the world.

Intermittently over the next few weeks – for they were still dependent on the vagaries of the battery supply – they caught the headlines of more bulletins. From their recollections of 1942–3 the war in the West hinged on changing fortunes in North Africa. Now they learnt with incredulity that the Allies were advancing on three major fronts. In north-east Europe the Red Army was established at the Vistula, while in the Balkans Soviet forces had taken Belgrade and entered the suburbs of Budapest. In the south, Greece was liberated, Allied armies had occupied Sicily and driven the Germans from the leg of Italy. Meanwhile, from their landings on the beaches of Normandy on D-Day, 6 June, the Western Allies had triumphantly thrust their way across France to reach the Belgian port of Antwerp and the historic city of Aachen, the first on German soil to fall. At the same time the tide had turned against the Japanese in the Pacific and in South-east Asia. By July 1944 they had suffered severe reversals in New Guinea, Assam and Burma, the Mariana Islands and the Philippines. John dared to hope that the Allied invasion of Malaya, which had proved chimerical in 1944, was still high on SEAC's agenda.

The need to reassure Ceylon that his base party was alive and ready to act on instructions transcended other considerations. On 20 December a message from Chin Peng brought John encouraging news of another European-led Force 136 operation, code-named 'Carpenter'. Commanded by a former Johore rubber-planter, Maj Paddy Martin, the party had sailed from Western Australia by submarine, reaching Malaya on 28 October. As a result of Carpenter's liaison with the MPAJA, an operative had been able to transmit the excellent news to the Malaya Country Section on 16 December that John Davis and Richard Broome, with Spencer Chapman, were safely hiding in Perak. Four days later, when John heard about Carpenter, he immediately requested that a return runner should convey an urgent message to SEAC. It was imperative that Signals staff in Ceylon were alerted to the imminent prospect of 'Gustavus' commencing transmission. The news was duly relayed by Carpenter on 19 January 1945. A week later Maj Martin was killed in a Japanese ambush, and command of his mission was taken over by Maj D. Sime.

In their first three months at Gurun the food line had been cut, forcing everyone to live on tapioca and jungle produce provided by the *orang asli*. There was no doubt that the Japanese strategy was to starve out the Resistance by severing their food supplies. However, both morale and the quality of life had improved once the AJUF guards were able to bring in stores from Jenderata, foodstuffs and medicines, including a precious quantity of drugs, quinine and M&B (May & Baker, a sulphonamide drug preceding penicillin). In addition, the two technical experts on site, Lee Choon and Frank Quayle, were at last able to tackle the transmission problem. When a second, much-used car dynamo reached camp on 11 January 1945, the pair set to with a will, applying their combined knowledge and ingenuity and working relentlessly to adapt the dynamo to the pedal generator so that it would charge batteries. Eventually they created a functional but highly labour-intensive machine, the chief drawback being that it required everyone's total energy to build up the charge.[10] Nevertheless, by 'pedalling in turn all our waking hours we managed to work up enough juice to transmit', said John triumphantly. Now everything rested on Lee Choon, all that is except the one imponderable factor – whether Ceylon would recognise their compromised Mark III signals transmitting on Mark II frequencies. John himself was quietly optimistic, remembering the reassuring words of his colleague, Jack Knott. 'We shall continue to listen for you each day both on your old signals plan and on the new one. This will go on ad infinitum – you need have no fear of us ceasing to call and listen to you.'[11]

Lee Choon made his first attempt at transmission on 28 January. A few days later, on 1 February 1945, the signals station at Colombo picked up the call sign from Gurun. They had used a simple emergency code, accepting that after such a long silence their signal would almost certainly be viewed with suspicion as being conveyed under duress. SEAC had already anticipated such an eventuality and had established a special Deception Branch under Col Peter Fleming to counter enemy-controlled transmissions.[12] 'There followed a series of strange hints and personal remarks in messages to us which I could not make head or tail of,' John admitted, 'but Richard Broome, who has a more subtle mind, suddenly realised they were intended to test us out.' Just as Deception Branch was about to be called in, Tremlett and Claude Fenner at the Ceylon end urged Signals to put out one or two more idiosyncratic messages. Fenner recalled that in the 1930s John had been known to close police colleagues as 'Titus' and on one occasion Mrs Dickinson, the wife of the police chief Arthur Dickinson, had greatly embarrassed him by asking him the origin of the nickname.[13] John had always detested the name and banished it from memory, so when Signals asked for news of 'Titus', he was nonplussed and decided it was a reference to some obscure SOE operation. Then came a question about 'Dum' and 'Tam', which referred of course to Richard ('Tweedledum') and Tamsin Broome, and suddenly the penny dropped. In response the two men did their best to concoct a convincing reply. Their answer included a blunt warning from Richard to 'keep my wife out of this' and ended with an inspired coup de grâce: 'If you're not satisfied now, you bastards, come and pedal this bloody machine yourselves.' At the Ceylon end they knew no self-respecting Japanese would use such language. The Davis team was surely back on air!

In Force 136 a legend soon grew from the story that an anonymous but bright young FANY operator had been twiddling the knobs of her radio set when she picked up their call sign. She thought it came from the 'Gustavus' party and reported her discovery, only to be mildly rebuked by a disbelieving sergeant. 'She saved our lives,' was Richard's verdict.[14]

However, forty years later the legend was disputed by a former Royal Corps of Signals operator in Force 136, who worked in the Colombo signals station. Geoffrey Bence contacted John Davis to give him the definitive version that, alas, involved no young FANY operator. He wrote apologetically:

Despite the fact that you had not been in contact, a listening watch was still kept and this tended to be a very boring task to be given. I was on the listening watch when to my amazement I heard the call sign. The signal was very weak and fading badly. Having realised it would be almost impossible to receive a complete message, owing to the way the signal faded in and out, I quickly called two other Operators [both male, one being Harry Cullen] . . . to tune in to your signal before I made contact. The three of us then took the message . . . the three copies were put together and [the] cipher girls – they *were* all FANYs – did a marvellous job in de-cyphering the message.

According to Bence, security in Force 136 was always very tight and none of the signals operators was ever told the contents of the deciphered messages. 'However, the contact with you was so exceptional and generated so much interest,' Bence reassured John, 'that the information leaked out.'[15]

The situation had been transformed since 'Gustavus I' landed blind on the Dindings coast in May 1943. They were not only in W/T contact with SEAC but by February 1945 it was possible for SOE to undertake airborne operations, using new Mark VI Liberator aircraft to drop parachute parties and supplies into Malaya. At last John was also able to report to Ceylon that in December 1943 he had carried out his instructions to make an agreement with the MPAJA on the matter of military cooperation. In conveying the terms of the Blantan Agreement, he indicated the importance of honouring their commitments as to arms, ammunition and military training; in addition, he requested food and medicines. The very prospect of being able to fulfil the terms agreed with the elusive leader of the Chinese Communists in Malaya would, he knew, raise the morale and credibility of his Force 136 team.

The practical difficulty of maintaining the pedal generator remained, but in the following weeks they burned the midnight oil encoding and decoding signals as the air waves crackled with the flow of vital intelligence and commands to and from Colombo. One of the early signals carried the news that John and Freddy Spencer Chapman had been awarded the Distinguished Service Order from 31 March 1944. John's citation praised his 'outstanding services under difficult and dangerous conditions . . . with the ever-present threat of discovery and death at the hands of the enemy'.[16] Although he appreciated the honour, he was more absorbed by the excellent news that a relief parachute drop would be made by the end of the month. Combining their collective hard labour and Lee Choon's skill John's party managed to come up on every slot in their transmission schedule while the arrangements were finalised. The task of leading Operation 'Funnel' went to Maj Jim Hannah: both he and his second-in-command, Maj F.P.W. Harrison, had been Conducting Officers for 'Gustavus' missions. Hannah had at his disposal two first-class W/T operators for the enterprise which, after a late postponement at the Ceylon end, was set for the night of 26/27 February.[17]

Instructions had been sent by Colombo for 'Funnel's' reception. The site chosen for the dropping zone was a jungle clearing near Tapah, some 8 miles as the crow flies from Gurun camp. John had overall control at the Perak end, but the ground work was largely covered by Ah Yang and the guards working under his direction. They needed around 100 porters to remove the huge containers from the dropping zone and conceal them in the jungle from enemy patrols, so to assist the Gurun guards Chin Peng recruited a contingent from the neighbouring Bidor patrol of AJUF, as well as a party of between thirty and forty *orang asli*. John had established good relations with these jungle tribesmen, whom he had always found to be 'wonderful people', immensely hospitable and highly skilled with their hands. Now and in the coming months they took on an invaluable role as carriers for Force 136.

When the day of Operation 'Funnel' dawned, the dropping zone had to be marked out with flares delineating the letter 'T'. Leaving Freddy (who was still far from well) to guard the camp, John, Richard and Frank Quayle set off in the early morning to build five bonfires of dry timber on the site. The expected time over target was midnight, and at the first sound of the approaching Liberators the bonfires would be lit. But a long day of hard labour was followed by an agonising wait. 'When the time came we listened and listened,' John recalled, 'but nothing happened and our morale went down again to the absolute bottom.' One hour passed, then a second, and it was not far short of 2.30 a.m. when they caught the distant drone of an aircraft coming in from the coast. From the air Perak lay glinting in the moonlight. 'We immediately set alight these flares,' said John, 'and they leapt about twenty feet in the air.' To the Liberator pilots the jungle seemed suddenly ablaze. Then 'the aircraft came round and dropped first of all the men – Jim Hannah and his W/T operator, Reg Humpleman – and two others . . .'[18] Shortly after a second Liberator followed and another cluster of parachutes drifted down to dispense supply canisters over the ground. By this time Hannah was shaking hands with John and Richard. Humpleman missed the dropping zone and landed in a mine working, from which he emerged soaking wet but unharmed. His colleagues were more fortunate. The last to land was the stocky figure of Maj Harrison; just behind the other W/T operator, their smart appearance in stark contrast to the ragged, skinny Resistance men. The instant the operator was on his feet he marched over to Richard, saluted crisply and offered him his open cigarette case. 'I'd been waiting for one of these things for about a year and it was about time too,' Richard responded wearily. But there was a gleam in his eye as he looked into the triumphant face of Ah Chuan, his former house boy. It was a heart-warming reunion. After escaping to India and joining the Royal Berkshire Regiment with Jamal, Ah Chuan had set his heart on accompanying Richard on 'Gustavus'. By remarkable persistence he eventually succeeded in his ambition to return to Malaya as a Force 136 agent.[19]

The next three hectic days were spent bringing the contents of the containers to the camp. John much appreciated the new weapons, small US M1 semi-automatic carbines that were superior to their old Stens. There was a welcome quantity of gold earmarked as operational funds, which he handled personally, complaining bitterly at its weight as he struggled uphill back to camp. Having suffered intermittently from malaria and other fevers, Richard was greatly cheered by the medical stores, especially the mepacrine. Among the loads they also found a welcome variety of tinned food, clothes, shoes, and the small luxuries of books, cigarettes and tobacco, and for John and Richard eighteen months of precious mail from home.[20]

In addition to family news came the notification that John and Freddy had been promoted to the rank of lieutenant-colonel. Freddy could not hide his delight, but out of respect for Richard Broome and for his brother Geoffrey, John showed little reaction. Since the European war was almost over, the projected date of the British invasion of Malaya was likely to be brought forward. He was very concerned to know the command structure that SEAC planned for Force 136 to assist the British reoccupation. Although the Chiefs of Staff and Supreme Allied Command, South East Asia (SACSEA) were turning their attention to arming the guerrillas for the coming campaign, there were still a number of political decisions to be made. Colombo's plans to send in arms, ammunition and supplies to the MPAJA was conditional on AJUF's acceptance of the presence and operational control of a network of British liaison officers. After the first drop by Operation 'Funnel' John was keen that AJUF should confirm their undertaking so that progress could be made with training and arming the guerrillas.

Anticipating heavier responsibilities ahead, John braced himself to be briefed by Hannah and Harrison on the situation in the wider world. More urgently, he wanted to know what, if any, developments had taken place in Force 136 since the landing of Operation 'Carpenter' in Johore. He may have suspected the truth, that policy decisions regarding the Malayan Resistance had been made of which he was completely unaware. In fact he only appreciated the full picture after the war when he saw some of the documentation.[21]

Since the capture of Lim Bo Seng and the KMT Dragons, Force 136 had no contact with any KMT Chinese in Malaya. Discouraging rumours reached SEAC of KMT banditry in the Grik region of northern Perak and sporadic fighting between KMT and MPAJA guerrillas in Kelantan. These reports dampened hopes of constructive KMT Chinese participation in the Resistance, leaving the possibility of Malay involvement. Certainly they could 'form a useful intelligence organisation'.[22] John tried to remain impartial, but he feared that 'the Malay police have not been whole-heartedly pro-British and the younger ones willingly cooperated with the Japanese'.[23]

After his reconnection with SEAC John heard that a decision to support the Malayan Resistance had already been taken with the support of Innes Tremlett. John also learned that several attempts had been made from the autumn of 1944 to infiltrate reinforcements into northern Malaya to build up the Malayan Resistance. In August 1944 a submarine party under Capt Peter Dobree and Capt Ibrahim bin Ismail had made an unsuccessful attempt to land on the coast near Kedah Peak. Ibrahim's second attempt, Operation 'Oatmeal', on 31 October, in which he and a small group of Malays flew by Catalina to the waters off Kelantan, foundered through a combination of bad weather and local informants.[24]

Meanwhile, Dobree's first successful blind landing by aircraft – Operation 'Hebrides' – was made in mid-December east of Grik, after which he gathered a group of agents and raised volunteers in northern Perak for an *Ashkar Melayu Setia* (*AMS*), or Loyal Malay Army. This occurred while John was still unable to communicate directly with Colombo, so he knew nothing of the development. Dobree's landing was followed in the New Year by Maj G.A. Hasler's drop into Kedah. Then, a few days in advance of Operation 'Funnel', Maj G.A. Leonard parachuted into Pahang, east of Merapoh, close to the Kelantan border; there were two further drops east of the central range, one near Kuala Lipis in Pahang, led by Maj J.A. Richardson, and a second east of Raub by Maj Derek Headly, formerly of the Malayan Civil Service. John had no idea then that Richardson's party included his former police orderly, Jamal, who like Ah Chuan was trained by the Malaya Country Section.[25]

It must have been obvious to SEAC that any change of SOE policy in favour of the Malays would have immediate implications for John and Force 136, as well as longer-term consequences for Malaya. He was unquestionably taken aback to be told that there were other European-led Malay parties already operating relatively close to his camp, and the news produced 'considerable confusion' among his team. He had been authorised by Mountbatten to align AJF with the Allied cause, a policy with serious implications for resources. At the news of Malay parties, his Chinese allies were understandably 'quite bewildered'. In his subsequent report to SEAC Richard Broome spelt out the difficult situation into which John and Force 136 Malaya had been thrown. 'We were terrified of their [i.e. AJUF's] playing one of our parties off against the other,' he complained. 'Moreover, *it was essential if we were to have any sort of control over AJUF's activities that we ourselves should not lose face by being ignorant of the presence or objects of our own parties in the country, or having to confess that we had no power to control them.*'[26] In addition to these worries, the rivalry between SOE and ISLD affected the progress of the Malayan Resistance.

John's disenchantment with the Far Eastern wing of the SIS has been touched on already. So, too, has the fact that circumstances in Malaya forced SOE to concentrate on intelligence-gathering once Japanese counter-intelligence virtually ruled out operational activities such as sabotage. The fact that two British rival organisations were carrying out intelligence work simultaneously and in the same area was bound to create tension, especially when the pooling of transport, specialist personnel and signals staff were added to the equation. No doubt John's disapproval of ISLD lay deep in the feverish atmosphere of wartime India, when SOE had constantly been forced to compete for slender resources for its Malayan mission. Being a highly competitive individual he also resented ISLD's claim to precedence. He contended that while ISLD protected its own interests, it was less scrupulous about the security of other special service personnel. To protect mutual security senior officers in Colombo and Calcutta reached an agreement that when joint submarine ventures could not be avoided, procedure must ensure that one party should not compromise the other's activities. However, John was aware that procedures were one thing, operational situations quite another, and he remained stubbornly averse to Combined Operations. In point of fact, the unsatisfactory conclusion of 'Gustavus Emergency' suggested a lack of trust on both sides.

It is evident from his correspondence that John had some knowledge of ISLD operations.[27] Nevertheless, during the time that his mission was incommunicado he apparently made almost no attempt to approach these parties as intermediaries, deliberately resisting contacts that could prejudice his own team further. Indeed, the collapse of his external organisation made him more wary of the possibilities of compromising his team at Gurun.

It was SEAC's plan for an invasion of Malaya that brought moral pressure on all the services to cooperate, and John saw his chance to lead the intelligence field. The organiser of ISLD infiltration into Malaya was not a faceless boffin, but one of Freddy Spencer Chapman's original SOE stay-behind party, Boris Hembry. Early in 1945 joint action had been started between officers of ISLD and SOE's Force 136. In Johore ISLD's Operation 'Mint' was working with SOE's 'Carpenter' to monitor Japanese shipping, and in Perak Maj Desmond Wilson of ISLD was involved in intelligence-gathering with SOE's Peter Dobree. John, however, was singularly irritated when an ISLD unit arrived in the Bidor area in January 1945, just before Jim Hannah's party. His concern grew when Operation 'Evidence', led by Maj George Brownie, an old Malaya hand (whom John had down as 'a flamboyant type'), proceeded to establish an ISLD intelligence station on his very doorstep at Kuala Blantan, only a few miles from Gurun and AJUF's No. 4 Patrol camp. When contacted by Brownie, offering to pass on signals to Colombo, John replied firmly in the negative.

It was only when the build-up to Malaya's D-Day began in earnest that John accepted that he would have to be proactive. He secured from AJUF an understanding that they would cooperate fully in helping existing and future ISLD parties, and in a further agreement, Force 136 and ISLD agreed to 'work in complete co-ordination' and abide by the principle of 'one war, one effort'. John's status was made clear to the 'Evidence' team when they were informed by their Calcutta Office, 'Davis is now at Central HQ and is acting as our rep. He will bring pressure to bear to ensure full assistance is given to you.' In other words, ISLD's intelligence units were coming under the tactical command of the GLOs (Group Liaison Officers) of Force 136 and John as its senior officer. All negotiations with AJUF were also to be made by these GLOs.[28] In the same month two ISLD officers, Maj J.N. Harvey and Maj P.A. Wilson, paid a tactical call on John at Force 136's Bidor camp on their way to set up ISLD operations in Selangor.

Long after these events, John tended to shy away from questions on the relations between SOE and ISLD. He disclaimed knowledge of the joint ISLD/SOE observation post in Johore, and recollection of ISLD parties in Malaya before the very end of the war. Timely amnesia, perhaps, drew a veil over a once contentious subject. However, by the summer of 1945 the balance between the two organisations had altered significantly. ISLD was reduced to playing second fiddle to SOE's Force 136 in Malaya with regard to personnel, resources and influence.[29] But once the Japanese war was over, John Davis, who had no taste for triumphalism or personal unpleasantness, simply preferred to forget the wartime rivalries.

Chapter 9

War and Undeclared Peace

In the spring of 1945, all the efforts of Force 136 had been directed towards receiving the reinforcements and aid promised in the Blantan Agreement. Unfortunately the two supply drops to the Perak guerrillas, planned for March, had to be postponed because of another breakdown in MPAJA communications. Chin Peng was suffering from typhoid and in his absence the guerrilla patrol leaders were at their most elusive; their unwillingness to take the initiative made it impossible for John to arrange reception parties for the parachute drops. His frustration turned to concern that the AJUF collaboration might be wavering. He was also anxious to clarify his own position vis-à-vis AJUF, and establish how, in practice, the 'Malt' network – the code-name for the Force 136 network that was to implement cooperation between the MPAJA and the British – and AJUF were going to collaborate. Consequently it was a considerable relief to John when Chin Peng reappeared at Gurun on 1 April to discuss with him the time, place and the arrangements for a second jungle conference between Force 136 and the Communist leaders. He was cheered when they agreed the meeting would take place as soon as 16–17 April.

Meanwhile, in his usual robust way, John tackled the authorities in Colombo about his status as the head of the 'Malt' network. He felt strongly that during the build-up to the Allied invasion 'Malt' should have authority over the Force 136 GLOs in matters of liaison with AJUF. Fortunately, on 13 April a message came back clearing up the ambiguities. He was to command the Group Liaison Team (GLT) attached to MCP Central HQ, which was to be the liaison link between Force 136 and

AJUF in the run-up to the Allied landings. Afterwards, the Task Force Commander's instructions would be conveyed by John to MCP Central HQ. This meant that he could approach the coming conference fully assured of his authority.

The venue for the second conference was a specially prepared jungle camp seven hours' hard walking from Gurun. John had no problem with the distance but Richard, who was far from fit, found the going very tough. Jim Hannah, who was taking over from John as GLO Perak, stood in place of Lim Bo Seng and Col Itu was present as commander of the 5th (Perak) Regiment of the MPAJA; otherwise the representation was the same as at the first conference in December 1943.

Over coffee on the first night John chatted informally with the Communist Plenipotentiary, the man generally known by his alias of Lai Tek. They were, of course, old acquaintances from pre-war days, when John had been given the job of 'handling' the MCP Secretary General, Special Branch's most valuable secret agent. This made it all the easier the next day to agree on ways and means of implementing their original treaty. The portents were good. As excitement mounted in Europe at the imminent prospect of a great Allied victory, 'the Plen' was encouraged to urge his side to 'get on with the war', so Richard reported. 'The atmosphere from the beginning was one of complete understanding and there was no bargaining whatsoever.' 'The Plen' was frank about AJUF's powers and limitations, and there was no point of disagreement.[1]

Some 3,300 AJUF guerrillas could be expected under arms in the next three months and this number could be increased. AJUF HQ agreed in principle to appoint a commander-in-chief to 'keep in constant personal touch with Colonel Davis' as the senior British Liaison Officer. Until the new commander was officially named, Chin Peng was appointed acting head – Kaput – of the MPAJA. Under the new command structure British GLOs and a GLT were to be attached to each AJUF regiment; at the same time a Patrol Liaison Officer and team were to be attached to each AJUF patrol. These teams would include W/T operators, interpreters and one medical doctor per group to cover all the patrols. Code-names were introduced into the new communications system by which all GLO teams had their own W/T station to communicate directly with Colombo. A specified quota of arms, ammunition and demolition devices was to be provided; financial subsidies and food supplies were to be arranged by the Liaison Officers.

Finally, the tactical decentralisation of AJUF was agreed, together with the independence of the groups and patrols during the build-up and training period. After Malaya's 'D-Day' the guerrillas would receive their orders via their GLOs from the Allied Task Force Commander.[2] At the conclusion of the talks the British officers were clearly jubilant. They looked forward to a future without the 'suspicion, shilly-shally and secretiveness' of the kind that had sometimes sullied relationships in the past.[3] John was surprisingly frank in his report:

> This meeting was a great affair . . . AJA managed to buy up all the pigs and poultry in the countryside. FUNNEL gold must have helped. A guard of honour 100 strong was provided and two days were given up to conferencing, feasting and cordiality. RNB [Richard Broome] passed out on the way down, was given a spoonful of rum to revive him and . . . he managed to take the salute of the guard of honour in royal style, firmly supported by two aides de camp. I ate myself silly. The whole atmosphere was one of the greatest confidence and optimism. The break up too was ceremonial. CTP [Chin Peng] wore the only tin helmet known to exist in Perak . . .[4]

It had already been decided that Broome and Spencer Chapman should return imminently by submarine to Ceylon. Both men needed to recuperate, but they could also provide SEAC with first-hand accounts of the military situation inside Malaya. After the conference Chin Peng arranged their route to Pangkor, and they left camp with their guides at dawn on 27 April. John was subdued at the prospect of Richard's departure and the end of the special collaboration and comradeship of 'Dee' and 'Dum'. He insisted on accompanying them down to the plain with Chin Peng, but reined in the urge to go further as he was expecting an important parachute drop near Bidor on the night of the 28th. Meanwhile, he had to meet the reception party for the two British officers, Maj Abbot and Capt A.P. Grant, who were due to land with supplies for the Perak guerrillas. Chin Peng joined John at the dropping zone, but the landing met with mixed success, and in a surprise enemy attack many of the stores were lost.

In the next few weeks John, as head of 'Malt', waited for 'the Plen' to fulfil his promise to sanction a fully empowered representative of the MCP, a permanent *Kaput*. As the acting representative, Chin Peng was amicable and efficient. He and John still enjoyed extraordinarily good relations, but as May and June came and went without news of the promised appointment John became suspicious. His antennae made him question whether there was an MCP Central Executive Committee with fixed military headquarters. Knowing the protean nature of 'the Plen', by July both John and Innes Tremlett were moved to the conclusion that 'Central' was following its own secret political agenda. Certainly John had real doubts as to whether the MCP ever intended to accept a form of central authority led by a British officer. Would the agreements be repudiated as soon as the MPAJA acquired sufficient arms and supplies from Force 136's parachute drops? Was the MCP leadership preparing for subversive activity after the war? Fortunately the suspense was eased in late July when Chin Peng was finally officially appointed *Kaput*. Relying on the latter's word and plausible explanation about a personnel shortage at headquarters, on 1 August John signalled this news to Ceylon. All would soon be well: the *Kaput* organisation to liaise with 'Malt' would be up and running by the end of the month. 'CTP has promised me that directly he gets full control he will instruct all other GHQ men to meet their respective GLTs so that much of this behind the scenes feeling may be eradicated. I think we should be content with this,' John told Tremlett. 'In actual fact things appear to be progressing satisfactorily in most areas.'[5]

John was referring to the local situation. In Europe the war had ended on 8 May with Germany's surrender, and VE-Day had been marked in camp by raising a Union Jack brought in by one of the airborne parties. In Malaya the parachute build-up had started in May. John reported that 'the skies opened and we had a steady stream of supplies and personnel, and the arming of Perak proceeded smoothly'.[6] As more men joined 'Funnel' more responsibilities rested on John's shoulders. In a move to pre-empt ethnic tension he pressed SEAC in early July to take conciliatory steps by dropping leaflets declaring equal rights for Malays, Chinese and other domiciled peoples, and news-sheets in Malay, Chinese and English. He also had to meet incoming Liaison Officers and their teams, ensuring their safety and assessing weapons supplies against requirements.[7]

Another urgent problem was the soaring inflation in towns and villages and the impact on food supplies. At one point when his men were driven to live off jungle roots again, John signalled Ceylon, 'Food situation deteriorating alarmingly, Lay in large stocks. Help reinforcements.' A later request went out for 'Patrol Deficiency Food', bully and cheese. When one problem was dealt with John moved on to the next, often in the company of Chin Peng. He was even known to officiate in Perak camp hospital as the new untried weapons had resulted in an increase in accidents among the patrols. Overriding these matters, however, was the serious military training of the guerrillas, daily squad drill followed by instruction and practice in the skills of handling guns and throwing grenades. 'Colonel Davis inspected the patrol and was very pleased with the results,' one Patrol Liaison Officer reported. His experience and knowledge 'invariably kept me on the right lines and indeed at times prodded me on to them'.[8]

'Funnel' and 'Carpenter' were only a prelude, however, to Operations 'Galvanic', 'Multiple', 'Beacon', 'Tideway', 'Sergeant', 'Humour' and 'Siphon', and a strategic build-up of parachute drops in Selangor and Negri Sembilan, where the invasion forces were to land. These liaison groups were reinforced by half a dozen special Gurkha groups with British officers, and from late July by groups of guerrilla veterans from the European theatre. The 'men from the sky', as the *orang asli* called the parachutists of Force 136, braved many hazards. From the Liberator base at Jessore in northern India they faced an interminably long, uncomfortable flight before dropping through night skies into obscure jungle clearings. Some sustained injuries in landing, others missed the dropping zone by several miles and had to take cover and re-group before trekking inland to find protection in the jungle. Often they had to search for the dropped containers while avoiding enemy troops or 'puppet' patrols sent to flush out new arrivals. Occasionally there were short, sharp, armed clashes, though fearless characters like Jim Hannah enjoyed the adrenalin rush of a military encounter with the enemy.

Later, John was often asked what sort of men volunteered for Force 136. In his self-effacing way he went too far in playing down the heroic qualities of these men. Anxious to dispel the impression that they were 'swashbuckling and insensitive' colonial types, he insisted they were just 'very ordinary, rather frightened but absolutely dedicated to the job'.[9] In fact the rigours of Force 136 demanded a great deal more. Typical of the best was Lt Col Douglas 'Duggie' Broadhurst, GLO with the 1st (Selangor) Regiment of the MPAJA, 'a remarkably cool customer in war' who had also fought behind the lines in Timor, Borneo and the Philippines.

Privately, John regarded him as 'a wonderful, gentle, whimsical, light-hearted companion and friend'. But 'Duggie' was never an ordinary man. Nor, indeed, was his leader, or the majority of the officers and men of Force 136.

By July–August 1945 the British had dropped parties the length of the Malay states. As training proceeded, spirits were high. In Selangor, for instance, Broadhurst testified to 'an air of gusto and enthusiasm' pervading the camps.[10] Patrols were being formed ready to attack the Japanese and sabotage targets, such as road and rail communications, the full length of the western plain and across into West Pahang as soon as the signal was given. In five months Hannah had over 800 guerrillas under his tactical control and in Selangor, over a shorter period, Broadhurst had around 700 trained AJUF fighters. The situation was repeated in Negri Sembilan, where Claude Fenner was GLO, and in Ian Wylie's command area in Johore. Altogether Force 136 landed some ninety British officers, who with support personnel brought the total to around 400. In addition, supplies of arms and ammunition for around 5,000 guerrillas were dropped into Malaya.[11]

As soon as the liaison arrangements with Chin Peng were clarified in July, John decided to leave Perak for Selangor to be near the new MCP Central HQ, and at the heart of the action when the expected invasion occurred. With Tremlett's approval Broadhurst was alerted, and on 2 August John set off on foot with his bodyguard and W/T operator to join the Selangor GLT. It was a long trek made against pressure of time and the constant danger of enemy contact as they skirted the mountain spine by way of Sungkai and Slim. W/T reception along the foothills was very poor and for ten days John had little contact with Ceylon, although from All India Radio he picked up news that powerful American bombs had been dropped on Hiroshima and Nagasaki. Meanwhile, 'Galvanic' patrols were experiencing similar difficulties with transmissions. However, while John was en route, Broadhurst did receive one crucial circular signal about the atomic bomb. But he found it difficult to grasp the implications 'beyond that it was very important and would probably rapidly bring the war to a conclusion'.[12] In the meantime, as they pressed south, John found himself off air for two days, from 10 to 12 August. This proved critical. On 11 August all the GLTs received a second, unprecedented signal from SEAC, warning that in the wake of the two atomic attacks on the Japanese homeland, Japan's surrender was imminent, though this information was not yet official.

Some hours later, on 12 August, John and his companions reached the nearest 'Galvanic' camp at Kerling. He introduced himself to Peter Maxwell, the British officer in charge, before enquiring about Broadhurst and proceeding with his usual patter. Maxwell looked blankly at John, puzzled at his irrelevant remarks. 'I don't think you can have seen this, sir,' he replied, handing John a piece of paper with a deciphered message, adding, 'We've been told to stand by and wait for the declaration of Japan's surrender.'

The news caught John off-guard and for a few seconds he was dumbfounded. A lesser man might have felt foolish, but he shrugged off the irony with good grace. After striving tirelessly for over three years for Japan's defeat, it seemed he was the last senior officer of Force 136 Malaya to receive SEAC's historic order, heralding the impending victory of the Allies in the Far East.

News that Emperor Hirohito had accepted the conditions of surrender spread like wildfire after 15 August. A jubilant Duggie Broadhurst and his team met John as he marched into their jungle camp east of Ulu Yam. Duggie was struck by John's 'very high spirits and mental and physical vigour'. They were all heartened by a signal from Adm Mountbatten, the Supreme Allied Commander, South East Asia Command, to the effect that 'Victory is now at hand', in which he warmly praised the contribution of Force 136 in Malaya. Anticipating family reunions and the saving of countless military and civilian lives on both sides, Duggie Broadhurst was emphatic: 'The prospect of peace was dazzling.'[13]

As it turned out, their elation was short-lived. Frustration quickly set in when it was realised that, for all their preparations, the Resistance was to be sidelined. The stand-by signal of 11 August had placed immediate limitations on Force 136. The GLOs were ordered to 'take no action other than to ensure that Japanese arms did not fall into the hands of the AJA'.[14] These stay-put orders operated even on the 15th, VJ-Day, producing gloom, depression and bitter, ironical guffaws in the Group Liaison HQ in Selangor. Confined to camp, short of food and without cigarettes or alcohol, theirs would be a cheap-jack celebration of victory over Japan.

John quickly sensed a potentially disastrous anti-climax was looming. He was more aware than anyone of the pent-up energies of the MPAJA and Force 136, created by their intensive preparation 'to emerge, hit hard and cause the maximum disruption to the Japanese behind their lines'. An early SACSEA warning to all Liaison Officers to avoid clashes or bloodshed and to keep out of all towns and districts where there was a Japanese presence was, in John's view, untenable. And he had the temerity to say so, reminding SEAC on 19 August, 'It was inimical to British Government prestige that its representatives should still lurk in the hills.' He attributed the antipathy among members of SACSEA towards the AJF to entrenched mistrust of Communism.[15] But he argued that the enforced inactivity of the guerrillas on SEAC's orders would have a catastrophic effect upon MPAJA morale and discipline. There was a real danger that they would abandon their jungle camps. It would then be impossible for Force 136 to maintain influence over them, and acts of summary justice were likely to follow, reprisals against isolated Japanese troops, collaborators and profiteers, and the looting of food stocks. Repeatedly John urged SACSEA to honour the April agreement to bestow the status of SEAC troops on the MPAJA regiments and to provide them with subsistence, equipment and a clear and active function with specific tasks. In the uneasy interim, however, between Japan's surrender and the expected Allied invasion, John could only control his Communist allies through his well-honed skills of persuasion or by a degree of expediency: 'We tried to ease the situation', he admitted, 'by getting them as much food as possible.'

Unfortunately for Force 136 other factors weighed more heavily with the decision-makers. In London John's warnings were treated with uninformed scepticism by staff in SOE HQ and the Colonial Office.[16] More significantly, Gen Douglas MacArthur, America's Commander-in-Chief South West Pacific Forces, had insisted there should be no landings and no formal surrenders in any Japanese-occupied territories until he had presided over the principal peace-signing ceremony in Tokyo Bay. This was scheduled for 31 August, but an ill-timed typhoon put it back a few days. It meant there would be a three-week delay before the arrival of British and Allied forces in Malaya, long enough for anarchy to take hold. Even if Mountbatten opposed the postponement of Operation 'Zipper', he had to accept that British interests were secondary to those of the United States. Meanwhile, the political hiatus created by America's timetable perpetuated a dangerously flimsy balance in Malaya and Singapore, a power vacuum, a condition of neither peace nor war.

To Force 136 officers, however, all the politicking was inexplicable. They simply knew that delays in conveying the ceasefire order were followed by an announcement by Gen Itagaki, commander of the Japanese Seventh Area Army in Singapore, that hostilities would continue. At worst there would be fighting, at best an unpredictable situation. Then, on 22 August, MPAJA HQ ordered the guerrillas to move into townships, so SEAC conceded at last that GLOs could take over conditionally in areas outside Japanese occupation.[17] It was fortunate that the next day the Japanese High Command ordered an immediate ceasefire, but delays continued in the field, and only on the 26th was a Japanese delegation sent to meet Mountbatten's representatives. In this highly volatile state of affairs John received an urgent signal from Colombo. The Japanese authorities were ignoring the order to surrender, despite the repeated transmission of the terms over the air waves. As head of Force 136 John was instructed to communicate the terms directly to the Japanese Command in Kuala Lumpur.

In response he made for the nearest township, Serendah, where he used the railway telephone system to convey the surrender terms to the Japanese governor of Selangor and took the precaution of repeating them in a written message. The reply – that the governor had no hand in the matter and could do nothing about the situation – confirmed what the British believed, that the Japanese authorities were still stalling. Although the responsibility for law and order remained with the Japanese according to the surrender terms, John was acutely aware that when Force 136 patrols came out into the open, enforcement would be difficult and the chances of a flashpoint were high. For this reason he decided to move into a strategic position in Serendah. With Broadhurst's group team in support, and Maj Philip Thompson-Walker's patrol already camped nearby, on 24 August John set up 'Malt' HQ there, jointly with 'Galvanic' officers and men. In addition to his personal staff, Broadhurst had a strong Gurkha support group under Maj John Heelis and a large body of well-dressed, uniformed MPAJA guerrillas, the 1st (Selangor) Regiment, under the Selangor State commander, Liew Yau. While the local MPAJA patrol with Thompson-Walker's team took over the police station, the 1st (Selangor) Regiment was bedded into the derelict Boys' Home on the south side of Serendah. John and Duggie made themselves at home in a bungalow a quarter of a mile south of the town.

1. Colonel John Davis CBE, DSO. *(All photographs Davis family collection)*

2. The Malaya Section Training Camp at Fort Lion, Singarh, near Poona, India, where Force 136 was trained for clandestine warfare.

3. Officers of the British merchant ship, the *Anglo-Canadian*, with their guests from the *Sederhana Djohanis*. John Davis is on the back row, second from the right.

4. John Davis with two of his most trusted Dragons of the 'Gustavus I' party, Ah Han (left) and Ah Ng.

5. Former shipmates reunited in Delhi, April 1942. Left to right: Richard Broome, John Davis, H.A. 'Jock' Campbell and Ivan Lyon.

Left: 6. Practising linking up between submarine and folboat in the open sea off Ceylon. John Davis is in the rear of the folboat.

Below: 7. A reunion of British officers of the Malaya Country Section at Mount Lavinia, Ceylon, July 1943, after Operation 'Gustavus I'. Left to right: Claude Fenner, John Davis, Richard Broome and Basil Goodfellow. The latter was head of the Malaya Country Section.

8. The disbandment ceremony of the 1st (Selangor) Regiment of the MPAJA, 5 December 1945. The inspection of the HQ Patrol by Lt Gen Sir F.W. Messervy, GOC Malaya (centre), with Col John Davis (behind Messervy), Lt Col Douglas Broadhurst, General Liaison Officer (head visible behind guerrilla patrol leader) and Liew Yao, CO 1st (Selangor) Regiment.

9. Early August 1945, the last phase of the Second World War and Japanese Occupation. John Davis (far right) and his escort pose before a Japanese government notice near the Slim River on their way south to join the Force 136 contingent in Selangor, in anticipation of the British invasion of Malaya.

10. John Davis (second in line), appointed Malaya's NVLO by Gen Templer in 1952, en route with local officials to inspect a New Village site.

11. The Second World War victory celebrations in London, June 1946: a part of the Malayan contingent standing on the steps of the Albert Memorial with Col John Davis and Lt Col Douglas Broadhurst. All were formerly MPAJA except for Ah Han (back row, first right).

12. The Baling Talks, 1955. Before the Peace Talks, Chin Peng, MCP Secretary-General, was met at Gunong Paku by his wartime ally, John Davis, serving as his Conducting Officer. They posed for this photograph, along with the Communist leader's two associates, Chen Tien and Rashid Maidin.

13. Cordial handshakes between Malayan government ministers and British senior officers reflect the goodwill established at the prospect of Malayan Independence in 1957. Left to right: unidentified senior police officer, Tunku Abdul Razak (later successor to Tunku Abdul Rahman as Prime Minister of Malaysia), John Davis, Tunku Ya'acob.

14. John Davis (left) in traditional Chinese dress with Lim Bo Seng, leader of the KMT Chinese Dragons.

Happily, during the next few days their material conditions suddenly improved with air-dropped supplies of food, cigarettes and alcohol. But John was still worried about the fragility of the ceasefire. Although Japanese troop movements were passing unmolested along the main road and rail trunk route, on one occasion a twitchy-looking Japanese NCO defensively produced a light machine gun on Serendah station. The threat only receded when the soldier was bundled back aboard his moving train – gun and all – by Broadhurst's men.

It seemed to John that the Japanese military were 'stiff and aggressive' towards the Chinese, treating them as bandits. He decided they were pursuing 'some sort of policy of trying to separate Force 136 officers – "goodies" – from the MPAJA – "baddies" – whom they pretended they had a duty to clean up in order to hand over Malaya in good condition to the Allies'. They were also smarting severely after an incident on the Perak border, between Slim and Tanjong Malim, when a convoy of Japanese troops on the way to surrender had been ambushed at a road check by Chinese guerrillas and thirty-four soldiers had been killed. Consequently, when Capt Shimizu, the military commander in Kuala Lumpur, heard that more 'bandits' had descended on Serendah, he sent a company of troops from Rawang to clear them out and restore order. He meant business: the soldiers had battle equipment and were wearing rubber sneakers. John explained what followed in Serandah on 31 August:

When just before dawn one morning we, at the HQ, were woken by a violent outburst of firing from the village [and] shortly afterwards a runner from the patrol arrived with the information that a Japanese force had attacked without warning, killed the sentry, rushed the police station and seized two British liaison officers [Maj Thompson-Walker and his second-in-command, Flt Lt Jimmy Robertson]. The MPAJA had scattered to the surrounding buildings and were keeping up a sporadic resistance. Immediate and, if possible, non-aggressive action was needed to regain control and prevent the incident from spreading. Fortunately I had a Union Jack . . . so with Broadhurst and Lau [sic], the Chinese commander of the MPAJA, and with our Gurkha support group flying the flag but with arms at the shoulder, we set off down the road just as dawn was breaking. We brushed aside two Japanese sentries that tried to bar our way as we approached the police station and by the time we arrived had worked ourselves up into such a state of simulated anger and

indignation (we were in fact very nervous) that we must have been quite
impressive. Anyhow, the bluff worked, the Jap [*sic*] company commander
quickly handed over the two British officers and agreed to call his men off.
This, however, was easier said than done as they were busily engaged with
the MPAJA, who were still holding out in the buildings ahead. It took a good
half hour of flag waving, shouting and blustering before we got the two sides
lined up facing each other along the main road, still glowering but at least
under control, and the incident was over.[18]

Whenever John wrote or spoke of this confrontation he played down his
own role, insisting that a combined effort by the officers present had saved
the day. Yet what started as some sort of distant shemozzle would have
escalated into a serious Japanese–Chinese shoot-out but for his spontaneous
intervention. When it was clear from the continuing sound of gunshots
and hand grenades that the Japanese officer-in-charge ('a stupid-looking
stooge', 'completely bewildered', according to Broadhurst) had lost control
of the situation, John dashed forward. He stood firmly between the lines
of firing Japanese troops and the MPAJA guerrillas, and, with a histrionic
display of bellowing and flag-waving that overawed the Japanese officer as
much as all the other observers, forced everyone eventually to a ceasefire.
This instinctive act of courage on John's part brought to a satisfactory end
a military clash that could have re-ignited a state of open warfare. Instead,
it was clear that the initiative was once again back in British hands. The
war with Japan was effectively over.

Chapter 10

Peace and Disbandment

John was determined to show that Force 136 had a grip on the situation. Since the SEAC signal of 29 August instructed all field parties to safeguard against lawlessness, John and Duggie Broadhurst demanded to see the Japanese authorities. The Japanese officer in charge at Serendah, anxious to be helpful, telephoned to Rawang for a staff car for John. It arrived bearing Capt Shimizu and a Japanese police officer to the scene. At the risk of angering the Chinese guerrillas, the British officers agreed that a few Japanese troops should remain in Serendah to warn off other units passing through the main north–south route. Then John and Duggie piled into the vehicle and, with an escort of guerrillas in a lorry and the Union Jack and Communist standard fluttering, drove to Kuala Lumpur.

Lining the roadside, goggle-eyed villagers stared incredulously or smiled broadly. At the Batu Road entrance to the capital where heavily guarded barriers had been erected there was a short delay, but long enough for large crowds of happy, grinning Chinese to gather in welcome. When they reached the military headquarters in the Batu Road school, the guerrillas were provided with a good meal while the two British officers confronted the Japanese commander with the ceasefire situation, forcing him to apologise and justify the day's actions. Shimizu resorted to bluff. ('The affair at Serendah but "Ha, ha", what else could he do?') He insisted that he had had no orders to recognise the officers of Force 136. It was agreed, however, that with an MPAJA patrol in support, Force 136 should move their headquarters to Kuala Lumpur. Here they would take over a luxurious house once owned by a lawyer, which the Japanese had just vacated. By the afternoon the atmosphere had become quite conciliatory, but standing in Shimizu's office, John and Duggie realised how close they had sailed to the wind when they spotted a map accurately marked with every Force 136 dropping zone and most of their camp sites in Selangor.

John was sufficiently concerned about the earlier provocative incident near Tanjong Malim that he decided to check the situation in Perak personally. He had also been instructed by SEAC to investigate prisoner-of-war camps and prisons, and to initiate a search for war criminals. The Japanese commander in Kuala Lumpur provided him with a car and a staff officer, 'a nice, English-speaking fellow', and they left Broadhurst in charge at the top of Batu Road. Driving that evening through Kuala Kubu close to the Japanese military camp John heard troops chanting their usual evening prayer for the last time: according to his aide, the order had finally penetrated to rural outposts that Japan's war was over.

In Perak John did a quick tour of the British Liaison Teams to discuss the situation. Although the Japanese had been slow to acknowledge the surrender here too, John was pleased that Jim Hannah was now in control. The 5th (Perak) Regiment of the MPAJA had moved from the jungle fringes to the kampongs and smaller towns, and Hannah had increased the force to 1,200 men by bringing less disciplined guerrillas from outlying areas under his command. He had contacted the Kempeitai in Tapah, where a large body of troops and military police were concentrated, and by judicious bluffing persuaded them to arrange transport to Ipoh to enable him to reach a ceasefire agreement with the Japanese commanders there. John was now satisfied that no serious clashes had been reported. However, he decided to send his loyal staff officer, Ah Han, across to Kelantan to investigate reported violence between the MPAJA and the KMT Chinese. In addition, before leaving Ipoh, he tried to discover the fate of his 'Gustavus' agents, but in the end had to delegate the task to Hannah, who later questioned Kempeitai officers and learnt of the death of Lim Bo Seng.[1] The others, Ah Ng, Shek Fu, Ah Lim and Mo Ching, had been released from prison and had allegedly left the country, a fabrication by the secret police to cover their tracks.[2] John had also made enquiries about Cheng, Agent 108, whom he had planned to employ as an interpreter. He discovered that Cheng had moved from Sitiawan to Ipoh at the end of 1944 and was shocked to learn shortly afterwards that he had been murdered.[3]

As he was leaving Ipoh news broke that John was to be promoted to the acting rank of full colonel as from 9 September. He was relieved as much as pleased, suspecting correctly that there would be many tests of his authority in the coming weeks. Meanwhile, he had immediate instructions to return south to contact the Japanese authorities over preparations for the formal surrender of Singapore on 5 September. In Selangor he heard that Penang's surrender had been received aboard HMS *Nelson*, but in deference to Gen MacArthur's orders the Royal Marines did not land on the island until the next day. After conferring with Broadhurst in Kuala Lumpur John arranged to meet the Japanese surrender delegate at Seremban to convey SEAC's instructions. His task was made easier by the diplomacy of Claude Fenner, the GLO, who had already established a degree of trust with the Japanese governor in Negri Sembilan, which proved invaluable in the transfer of power. Continuing south John also conferred with Lt Col A.C. Campbell-Miles at Segamat and Ian Wylie in Johore Bahru. He wanted to assess the peacekeeping arrangements in Johore and the extent of Japanese cooperation, following a serious racial clash between Malays and Chinese in the Muar–Batu Pahat area in late August. John reached Singapore just in time to watch the ceremony aboard the cruiser HMS *Sussex* with the handing over of the signed document of surrender by the Japanese delegates, Lt Gen Itaguki and Vice-Adm Fukodome, to Mountbatten's representative. The following morning men of the 5th Indian Division landed on the soil of Singapore and marched in triumph through the town past rapturous crowds.

The brief visit gave John the chance to meet Maj Gen H.R. Hone, a Colonial Service officer appointed to be the incoming head of Civil Affairs in the BMA (British Military Administration), with whom he would work over a short but intensive period. But he had another duty too. That evening he made his way to Sime Road where the civilian internees were based. The picture emerging from the Changi complex was one of horrifying Japanese cruelty and neglect. As John went in search of his old friends, he was haunted by the thought that some would have died from malnutrition or disease. Since the first rumours of surrender, time had dragged interminably for the Allied prisoners. Still gaunt and emaciated, but with hope restored as medicine and food parcels began to arrive, several internees were sitting as usual in their hut, waiting desultorily on events, when suddenly a stocky but very smart-looking officer walked in out of the blue. He was in full khaki uniform with a DSO [Distinguished Service Order] ribbon on his chest. Guy Madoc gasped, 'Good God, it's John Davis! He joined the Force with me . . .' John's reply was lost in the drama of the moment, but before leaving he promised his friends that he would signal Ceylon and request all next-of-kin be informed. Six days later a telegram was sent by a SEAC officer in Colombo to John's father in England. 'FOLLOWING FROM JOHN STOP HAS SEEN GUY MADICK [sic] NOEL ALEXANDER GEOFFREY DAVIS MACNAMARA GAFFER HARVEY RYVES AND MANY OTHERS ALL REMARKABLY FIT AND HAPPY INFORM EVERYONE LOVE TO ALL.'

John had other reasons for being in Singapore. He had received an urgent request to contact a SEAC officer, Maj R.J. Isaacs of Military Intelligence, at the newly established Field Security Force HQ in Balmoral Road. Recently parachuted into the country, Isaacs had already embarked on preliminary investigations of Japanese war criminals. One of the detainees in Changi, Marmoru Shinozaki, was anxious to be as cooperative as possible. A pre-war press attaché in Singapore, he had been taken from prison after the Japanese surrender to serve the British as an Army interpreter to interrogate his own side.[4] Among the Japanese prisoners questioned were two notorious Kempeitai operatives, Sub-Lt Yamaguchi and Sgt Maj Shimomura, who had been assigned to shadow Special Branch Agent Lai Tek, known to them as Wong Kim Geok, and to gather information from him to pass on to their superior, Maj Sartoru Onishi. As highly sensitive facts began to emerge about the MCP Secretary-General, Isaacs wanted corroboration from Wong's pre-war case officer in Special Branch, now Col Davis of Force 136.

At this meeting with Isaacs, John found himself listening to revelations unknown even to Tremlett, his superior in the Malaya Country Section. At one point Isaacs handed him a photograph and asked if he could identify the man in the picture. 'Yes,' John replied, as he looked at the face of the MCP representative with whom he had made the Blantan Agreement. 'It's Chang Hung.' But the man of many pseudonyms was also 'Mr Wright', which transliterated into variants – Loi Tak, Lai Te and Lai Tek – in addition to Wong Kim Geok, Lao Wu and 'the Plen'. He was, of course, the self-same character who had passed information about members of the illegal MCP to Special Branch before the war and had cooperated with the British authorities up to the end of 1941; and the Lai Tek who had supplied them with dozens of keen young Communists to train as guerrillas in No. 101 STS, the very recruits whom John and Richard Broome had escorted to their destinations behind the enemy lines.

Between the end of the Malayan Peninsula campaign and the fall of Singapore, Lai Tek went to ground, though a good deal of mystery continued to surround this ruthless yet charming character. At the personal initiative of Maj Onishi, Lai Tek was traced by radio detector and quietly arrested in March 1942. To pre-empt interrogation the Communist leader readily agreed to collaborate with the Kempeitai and for the rest of the war he served as their chief Chinese informer, betraying countless MCP colleagues to save his own skin. He was allowed to continue in his official role, enjoying freedom of movement and various perks provided by the Japanese, including a car, to keep in contact with members of the Communist Party on the Peninsula.

The full, horrifying implications of this remarkable Japanese intelligence coup were only just beginning to emerge at the time of John's first conversation with Maj Isaacs. For, unaware that their leader had become a spy and secret informer for the Japanese, Lai Tek's MCP comrades had diligently reported to him on their activities and movements throughout the Japanese Occupation. He consulted in particular a few trusted aides among Communist leaders in the states (one of whom was his alleged favourite, Chin Peng, State Secretary of Perak); these men innocently passed on to Lai Tek significant information from the field. In return he fed selected intelligence to his Kempeitai guardians to devastating effect. In short, his machinations almost wiped out the Chinese Communist leadership in Malaya. Furthermore, after he had ensured the elimination of the Central Executive Committee, the power of decision making was effectively concentrated in Lai Tek's hands. At Japan's surrender the Kempeitai gave him the option of escape from the country, but he chose to go into hiding and await the return of the British, having decided that it was in his and his party's interests to renew his old contacts with Singapore Special Branch. Once he had achieved this, he poured out details of criminals, and crimes committed by the Japanese during the Occupation.

There was much more to the story of Lai Tek that emerged over time. Despite his later denials, from spring 1943 he had told the Kempeitai about the infiltration of Force 136 agents by submarine and had revealed their landing sites and overland routes to the interior. These disclosures account for the press reports of the presence of British agents and explain the increased naval activity around Pangkor and police and military attacks on *kampongs* along the jungle fringe of Perak. Chin Peng must have briefed him fully on the 'Gustavus' intelligence network, and after visiting the jungle headquarters of Force 136 under the alias of Chang Hung, he knew the precise locations of their camps. More significant than this, however, was the fact that as Chang Hung he had been the sole Communist negotiator of the two jungle treaties, so that he had a total overview of the plans for cooperation between the MPAJA, Force 136 and SEAC leading up to the British seaborne invasion of Malaya.

Shinozaki also laid the responsibility for Lim Bo Seng's fate on Lai Tek. Force 136's Chinese leader was the Kempeitai's prize catch, his fate sealed by his KMT connections and his public record of hostility to the Japanese. In addition, armed with inside information, Yamaguchi and Shimomura were able to pick off Lim Bo Seng's fellow KMT agents. Japanese counter-intelligence was a ruthlessly efficient and inhumane machine, and repelled by emerging evidence John insisted to Isaacs that before Lim Bo Seng's body was brought to Singapore in December 1945, Yamaguchi and Shimomura were sent back to their cells in Changi Gaol to await trial for war crimes. Yet with the luck of the devil, Lai Tek managed to evade exposure for eighteen more months amid the confusing climate of postwar Malaya.[5]

Meanwhile, on two or three occasions in the autumn of 1945 John and Lai Tek attended meetings together on the issue of disbandment. The Secretary-General was in a conciliatory mood, after forbidding his Party to side with the Japanese Army against the British colonials. On 25 August the MCP Central Executive Committee had put forward an eight-point programme for the Party anticipating democratic government in Malaya and cooperation with the Great Powers in a new organisation for world security; and on this evidence John was inclined believe in Lai Tek's emollient intentions towards Britain. Decades later, John still took the line that if Force 136's European officers had come through the war unscathed, it was because of Lai Tek's residual loyalty to his British spymasters: 'He'd been playing throughout the war this extraordinary role – keeping them quiet, looking after us.' Reflecting on their postwar encounters, John admitted that at first Lai Tek made no mention of his activities as a triple agent. 'But he himself raised it with me one day,' said John. Then, 'He simply said, "You realise, of course, that I have always been absolutely anti-Communist?" Being in the pay of the British, "I've never let the British down. I've always been working with you.'"[6]

Although he did not challenge it, the first assertion must have seemed preposterous to John, until he reflected on what little was known of Lai Tek's early years in the French Sécurité. As to the second point, he knew Lai Tek could easily have betrayed a number of British officers to his Japanese masters, including John, Richard Broome and Freddy Spencer Chapman: indeed, the possibility had crossed John's mind. Curiously, John shared a tendency with his supremo, Adm Mountbatten, not so much of being 'soft on Communism' but of an over-readiness to assume the best of those with whom he had dealings.[7] His last words on Lai Tek reflect John's quirky individualism:

> I personally find a character like that – a person who has spent the whole of his life as an informer or traitor, or whatever word you like to use, for one side or another, then doubly, develops a strange sort of character. You can't dislike a man intensely just because of that – you've got to look behind and understand a certain amount about it. And I don't think Lai Tek let us down: we couldn't have got anywhere without him.[8]

John was back in Selangor in time to link up with Duggie Broadhurst to witness the Allied landing, code-named Operation 'Zipper'. By 8 September excitement had built up near the coast at Klang. Large crowds, milling around, cheered in derision at a departing truck of Japanese troops. That night John picked up Chin Peng and met Broadhurst's party at Telok Datok, and they moved in the pre-dawn hours of 9 September down to Morib beach. It was a familiar scene to John, flat, lonely contours of sand and sea, one of his first discoveries in 1931. At first light there was no sign onshore of the Japanese, but the Force 136 party gazed seaward in some awe at the unprecedented sight of the vast Allied fleet, lights ablaze, anchored in placid waters. Fighters flew low along the coast, spotted the little Force 136 group and wiggled their wings. Soon after with a roar of engines the landing craft came in, wave after wave, depositing Indian soldiers of the 25th Division on the shore.

In the course of the fine early morning they were joined by Maj Gen G.N. 'Daddy' Wood, GOC 25th Indian Division, and a Beach Landing Officer. As they watched, the first of the heavy landing craft appeared, carrying trucks, tanks, jeeps and heavy equipment. The Beach Landing Officer, a Royal Navy officer, pointed out an obstructive sandbank where they would need to take avoiding action. The initial craft made it through sand and deep water gullies, but pandemonium broke out as the rest began to flounder in thick mud, and the beach was soon littered with 'drowned' vehicles. This sector was a tactical fiasco that would have become a major disaster had the landing been opposed by Japanese gunfire.[9] However, the Force 136 men kept their opinions to themselves. That afternoon, Col Davis and Lt Col Broadhurst attended the surrender negotiations with senior Japanese officers before being taken out to Vice-Adm Harold Walker's flagship, HMS *Nelson*, for an evening celebration. To complete their sense of well-being after several *stengahs* and a good dinner, they sailed for shore past the twinkling lights of the British fleet. The long-awaited, flawed invasion was soon over.

The next day John and Duggie sped back to Kuala Lumpur, where there was still something of a power vacuum. The atmosphere in much of Selangor was tense, but more controlled than other parts of the Peninsula where effective Force 136 influence had never penetrated over the Chinese. In Kelantan and northern Perak nationalist KMT gangs, little better than bandits, stole food supplies, occupied police stations and indulged in kidnapping and murder, while in East Pahang renegade Communist guerrillas were taking unilateral action.[10] Yet where the guerrillas were acting under the terms of the April agreement, they gave valuable assistance to their Liaison Officers especially after 11 September, when they were recognised as SEAC troops.

Finally, on 13 September Allied forces entered Kuala Lumpur in the wake of the Japanese surrender. From that time the Army's takeover of power proceeded with reasonable speed as transport and supplies became available, but to solve the temporary manpower shortage Force 136 officers were enlisted as Civil Affairs Officers. By the beginning of October the BMA was running most of populated Malaya, although until that process was completed a great deal rested on the personal authority of the Force 136 officers in handling both the MPAJA and the Japanese. Under John's overall leadership they did a 'magnificent job'.[11] Knowing it would not be easy to keep a grip on guerrilla discipline and morale he relied heavily on his close understanding with Chin Peng to assist Force 136 in maintaining law and order. He urged the same cooperative spirit on all Liaison Officers in a confidential instruction: 'It is imperative for the wellbeing of this country', he wrote, 'that nothing should be allowed to affect the closeness of our relations with and therefore our influence over MPAJA.'

John's optimism was rewarded when former guerrillas, wearing British Army uniforms with MPAJA caps and insignia, assisted Force 136 officers to guard and escort lines of Japanese troops at surrender ceremonies. Throughout these uneasy times he led by example, as, for instance, at the Perak surrender ceremony where he was photographed with comrades Chin Peng, Col Itu and Lau Liu, the Bidor patrol leader. In public acknowledgement of the MPAJA's contribution a detachment of guerrillas was invited to take part in the victory parade in Kuala Lumpur, at which Lt Gen O.L. Roberts, GOC XXXIV Corps, took the salute. Although John was never excited by choreographed displays, it was a satisfying moment when the corps commander stepped down from the saluting base to meet British officers and members of the MPAJA. Typically, on the dais Col Davis modestly positioned himself behind the front row of officers.

For the next three months Kuala Lumpur was John's base. After years of jungle life he was hyperconscious of his luxurious accommodation. 'I am presently living in a magnificently appointed house with tiled bathroom, hot water laid on etc.' he told his parents in his first letter for months. 'But my total belongings still consist of two shirts and one rucksack and I still eat Chinese food, so I have not totally degenerated.' Malaya Command relied on him as a troubleshooter, a role he relished for its freedom, responsibility and excitement. He was constantly on the road, travelling to hotspots from Kedah to Kuantan and south to Johore. In early November he was directed posthaste to Negri Sembilan to investigate a grim outbreak of ethnic violence at Padang Lebar. Forty-two Chinese villagers had been murdered by local Malays, creating deep alarm in the Chinese community. Without hesitation John offered tactical advice to Malaya Command: respond immediately with troop patrols and low-flying aircraft to prevent further racial frenzy that might spread like wildfire throughout the country.[12] To Broadhurst John was indefatigable. Watching him set off by jeep with his new staff officer, Duggie remarked admiringly, 'A person of less patience and determination would have very soon felt completely exhausted.'

September to December marked a spell of unremitting activity, and to judge by the incoherent, scribbled fragments in his pocket notebooks John had a host of different problems on his mind. There are dark hints of trouble in 'a waterless cookingless electricity rubber store [sic] . . . bitter feeling – angry slackening discipline', and apropos police collaborators, 'Can the names of torturers be published?' A draft telegram to Innes Tremlett questioned 'my position here since the re-occupation is a little obscure'. There are pages chequered with names, Chinese, Malays, Indians, British officers; lists of addresses and telephone numbers, including those of the Kempeitai and MPAJA HQ, Force 136 officers and an ISLD 'house'. With the names of Communist leaders are places, dates and directions, draft character references, official passes and instructions to Liaison Officers, orders on government rice supplies, statements of accounts, monies received from Ceylon to hand over for MPAJA salaries, and a few light-hearted remarks, such as his thanks to the brigadier who brought the 'trappings' for his colonel's uniform (adding, 'Pity you did not send a cap badge with the red hatband and buttons with the red tape!').

Privately, John conceded that though the war was over he found aspects of life 'bewildering and upsetting'. He had expected the BMA to behave responsibly, but as crime multiplied – and he himself discovered two separate episodes of theft by the military – their trigger-happy methods resembled those of an army of occupation rather than liberation.[13] Force 136 had a particular grievance. In October Fourteenth Army high-handedly commandeered the best properties in the Maxwell Road area occupied by Force 136, and on 29 October removed the whole contingent, John included, under protest to inferior billets at Petaling Hill. Angry men drew the conclusion that special operations were inferior to Regular forces. As it was, Force 136 morale plunged at the end of September when Innes Tremlett and his aide were killed in an air crash on a return flight from Singapore to Ceylon: Tremlett had been planning the transfer of the Malaya Country Section to Malayan soil. The widespread frustration among Force 136 officers that had been building up during the interregnum even reached the ears of Colin Mackenzie, who did his best to raise their spirits for the last phase of their Malayan service.[14] John knew many of his colleagues were disgruntled and impatient for release, and all shared private regrets that they missed the chance to show what their Chinese guerrillas could actually do. But he found himself constantly having to defuse other situations such as misunderstandings between the MPAJA and the BMA.

There is no doubt that he sympathised with the MPAJA troops who suffered when the Army failed to deliver on promises of food, equipment and amenities. Supplies varied from one area to another, but the inequities caused much hard feeling. The trouble often centred on the hard-line attitude of the military police and Field Security Force men towards minor breaches of military conduct by MPAJA guards, and the same units invariably attributed strikes and disturbances to the guerrillas.[15] It disturbed John that 'everyone appeared seriously infected by the "anti-Communist" bug' and only wanted to see the back of the MPAJA. He was infuriated by some of the middle-ranking officers who were uninformed, obtuse and insensitive and treated the Communist guerrillas as 'a public menace to be tolerated only until they were disbanded'. It was clear they knew nothing of the circumstances that had brought Britain and the Communist Chinese together in 1941 to cooperate in Japan's defeat and Malaya's salvation.

While dealing resolutely with these issues, John was simultaneously involved in the disbandment of the guerrilla forces. With the end of all hostilities, general demobilisation was under way and on 15 November Force 136 Malaya ceased to function as an operational unit. But before SOE officers left the country they had one last duty to perform in assisting the BMA with the disbandment of the Resistance groups. John's experience and his knowledge of the Resistance leaders were seen by the military as an important asset. From 23 September, when he was summoned by Lt Gen Sir Miles C. Dempsey, GOC Fourteenth Army, to the top-level conference on post-occupation policy towards the MPAJA, he was involved in all the decision making and became the principal British intermediary.[16] Victor Purcell MCS, a long-standing Chinese expert also involved, acknowledged the part 'Colonel Davis' played in 'a continuous coming and going between Force 136, the MPAJA, ALFSEA [Allied Land Forces South East Asia] and the BMA between September and 1st December'.[17] John simply remembered 'dashing about, [the] smell of petrol and everlasting conferences'. On at least two occasions he was accompanied by 'the mysterious M.P.A.J.A. [*sic*] leader with many aliases . . . the "Stalin" of the Malayan Communist Party' – which was how Purcell described Lai Tek. At other times Chin Peng was with him. All the while the key question in John's mind was on what terms would the MPAJA accept disbandment? The Communists tried various ploys, but the British stood firm on all demands of a political nature.[18] Lt Gen Roberts also flatly refused financial demands such as back pay for the time spent by guerrillas in the jungle. Looking back on these negotiations, 'It was a ticklish period,' Purcell confirmed, in which the MCP resorted to both the pressure of labour unrest and agitation and a 'peaceful offensive' on the BMA.

The talks over terms were bound to be protracted. Although there was virtue in keeping the Communists guessing, John felt that hard-line bargaining would prove counter-productive. He favoured a process of subtle probing. Discussion focused finally on economic matters, gratuities, aid for resettlement, rehabilitation, training and support for ex-servicemen and dependants. With the offer of a generous final gratuity and the distribution of campaign medals, he hoped that Chinese honour would be assuaged and during the disbandment the GOC's orders would be obeyed. As an additional sweetener the BMA promised assistance with employment, education and vocational training, although John was concerned that no promises should be made that could not be fulfilled. In the end the Communist leaders appeared to give their tacit agreement to the handing in of all arms to coincide with an ex-gratia payment to every guerrilla. However, John still had to convince his own side. At first Maj Gen G.R. Hone, Chief Civil Affairs Officer (CCAO), was non-committal about the proposed terms. Brig H.C. Willan, the Deputy CCAO in Kuala Lumpur, firmly opposed them (for 'fair and understandable reasons', John accepted). As it turned out, Purcell's strong support was crucial, for it finally persuaded Maj Gen Hone to agree. By mid-November the arrangements were complete. Disbandment of all units of the MPAJA, the Malay *AMS* and the KMT would take place at various centres across the country, beginning on 1 December 1945.

The ceremonial arrangements and celebrations were designed to give honourable recognition to the contribution of the Resistance, but the nub of the terms was the payment of a gratuity of Straits $350 to be paid to every guerrilla who handed in his arms. Lt Gen Sir Miles C. Dempsey's successor, Lt Gen Sir F.W. Messervy, agreed to take the salute at the Kuala Lumpur ceremony and to issue an address of thanks. In addition, local citizens contributed enthusiastically with processions, a grand concert and receptions for the MPAJA. John's task was to ensure agreement between his Force 136 officers and Malaya Command on a whole range of practical matters from transport, billeting, rationing and policing of the guerrillas in the run-up to 1 December, to detailed arrangements for the formal parades, the collection of arms, the receipt of documents and gratuities to the demobilised men, and the social functions that would follow the disbandment parades. The military authorities expected the ceremonies to be 'extremely impressive', from the initial march past and presentation of campaign ribbons, to the climax on 5 December when arms were handed in and gratuities paid.

In spite of some British misgivings disbandment was successfully accomplished.[19] There was no bloodshed, and the only aberrant guerrillas were 99 KMT men in northern Perak who absconded with their weapons to Thailand. John felt satisfied when some 6,000 members of the MPAJA were demobilised and 5,500 weapons were surrendered to the British, over 700 more than Force 136 had originally issued.[20] To ease the transition to civilian life after disbandment AJA ex-servicemen were encouraged to join the MPAJA Old Comrades' Association, a new organisation conceived initially to assist with housing and feeding homeless and unemployed members.

In Purcell's view the fact that 'Davis and his Force 136 officers . . . luckily believed in their MPAJA men' guaranteed success. Derek Headly, a GLO, was more effusive in his praise. 'This peaceful demobilisation was *entirely* due to the *personal* regard that Chin Peng et al. had for you,' he told John. 'I think there is a case for arguing that the trust which you . . . evoked from the Chinese Communist leadership in Malaya was *unique* in the world for Communist/non-Communist relationships.'[21] But in 1945 it was rash to predict that political stability would follow the reintegration of the guerrillas into a civilian population, for the Japanese triumphs of 1941–2 had seriously undermined British prestige and proved a catalyst to nationalism in South-east Asia. Disturbing developments in Java and Vietnam prompted Colin Mackenzie's appeal to Force 136 officers to be constructive and conciliatory.[22] In his own reflections on Malaya's political future John never claimed unerring political accuracy. Perhaps his natural optimism persuaded him that the smooth disbandment 'substantiates . . . my conviction that the MCP are not planning armed disorders in the country but intend to press their aims by political methods. The vast majority of AJA rank and file are not politically minded.' He went on to say that the Communist leaders 'have shown remarkable ability and sense of responsibility during the war. Many of them have gained the admiration and firm friendship of the British Liaison Officers working with them.' However, he recognised the economic devastation caused by the Japanese Occupation and the political challenge facing the British, of satisfying legitimate aspirations and harnessing the talents of the same leaders 'under conditions which must preclude full franchise and responsible government for a long time ahead'. The political comfort of Malaya, he predicted, would 'depend on the successful solution of this difficult problem'.[23] The problem and the solution would occupy John's energies for the next fifteen years.

Chapter 11

Home Interlude

The loose ends of war dogged John Davis until he boarded the aircraft for home. His departure had been delayed three times, on the last occasion by an unfortunate, petty, political brouhaha.

Shortly before Japan's surrender the Supreme Allied Commander, South East Asia Command, Adm Mountbatten, made clear his intention of presenting the guerrilla leaders personally with campaign medals. Chin Peng was one of several Chinese officers to be awarded the Burma Star and the 1939–45 Star. The award ceremony was originally scheduled for 13 December, a week after disbandment. However, Mountbatten insisted on the presence of massed bands, which were not immediately available, so the occasion was put back to 6 January. It took place on the steps of the Municipal Building in Singapore in the presence of the high-ranking officers of SEAC and Allied Land Forces South East Asia (ALFSEA). Afterwards the guerrilla leaders were to be entertained over two days with impressive demonstrations of British air and sea power by the RAF and Royal Navy.

A contemporary account states that the ceremony went well: 'The Guerrilla Leaders comported themselves with dignity and there was no hitch in the proceedings. The whole party then repaired to Government House and consumed gin.'[1] The trouble began the next day.

John was completely unprepared for the hostile reaction of the Communist leaders when he arrived at their hotel with an escort. 'The following morning at 8 o'clock the [three] AJA leaders refused to attend any demonstrations, and also declined to give their reasons for doing so.

This resulted in a vast amount of high-level recrimination, Air Marshal and Lady Parke objecting strongly to being kept waiting on the airfield for over an hour.'[2] John was outraged. In his moral code, honour was repaid by honour, not by insult. He had always shown respect to the Communist leaders in public and indicated his gratitude to Chin Peng for his assistance in the war.[3] Later the Communist leaders explained that they were protesting against BMA injustice, notably the treatment of Soon Kwong, the MCP chief in Selangor, but John, bitter and unmoved, was determined that amends would be made.[4] Lai Tek was visibly ill at ease in John's presence, in the light of his secret reinstatement as a Special Branch agent. It was he who relented first to John's demand, giving his comrades, Chin Peng and Liew Yau, no alternative but to follow suit. 'The outcome was an apology (in writing) from the AJA leaders to the Supreme Commander which, in addition to expressing regrets for having offered him what apparently amounted to an affront, stated that they did not feel they could accept further hospitality at the hands of the Military Authorities.'[5] John felt the incident would never have occurred had the original schedule been kept, but since he was never notified of further public repercussions he presumed the matter was considered closed.

Meanwhile, before he flew home, John's advice was sought on a host of matters by the Military Administration. There were still unresolved issues relating to MPAJA claims to back pay, pensions and compensation: these were handed over to ALFSEA. Then there were pressing questions over the future of the KMT Dragons, whose terms and conditions of service had never been clearly defined by SOE in the early days in India.[6] Coupled with this matter was the delicate but confused question of Britain's obligations to the widow of Lim Bo Seng and their seven children. John felt personally that Force 136 had a duty to assist them financially, and on the eve of departure he was told to use his stopover in India to press Force 136 HQ in Meerut on the British government's obligations. But for two more years, during which the Lim family's case was transferred to the War Office in London, John was involved in protracted correspondence on their behalf.

John also felt concern for the aboriginal tribesmen who had repeatedly helped members of the Resistance. In his view the time was ripe for the British government to show its gratitude with simple rewards such as agricultural tools and medicines; and for the five headmen who had rendered conspicuous service to the 'Gustavus' party a gift of engraved shotguns. A year later he was disgusted but not surprised to learn that nothing had come of his recommendations.[7] John reacted similarly to the loss of his kit and personal effects for which SOE refused to accept financial liability, though they had been left in safe keeping in Poona and Colombo during his absence on mission. Perhaps most galling, however, was the cavalier destruction of Force 136 records, including his own papers, at the winding up of the organisation.[8]

On arrival in England John reported immediately to SOE HQ in Baker Street. Granted two months' leave after five and a half years away on active service, he headed home to his family. They had been on his mind ever since he received the precious cache of letters by the first jungle drop a year ago. He had dearly wished that he could have comforted his parents at the news that his brother was missing, presumed killed, but it was moving to discover how highly respected Geoffrey had been in his chosen field of orthopaedic surgery. John was still adjusting to all the changes around him, not to mention the heady taste of freedom to come and go and do as he pleased, when another official directive arrived. The Colonial Office wanted him to prepare to cut short his hard-earned leave and be ready to return to Malaya.

While considering his long-term future John had already decided against returning to Special Branch or to any section of the police service. Initially he felt it would be uncomfortable to rejoin a force whose Asiatic policemen had been compelled to fight members of the Resistance, including himself. Later, he put it a little differently: he wanted to deal with the future and not with the past. At any rate, with a career change in mind, he had approached Maj Gen Hone in November 1945 for a transfer to the BMA, as a route into the Malayan Civil Service as soon as the country returned to civil government. At the same time he told the Commissioner of Police, Col Langworthy, of his intentions and was assured by Victor Purcell of his support. Hone found the request reasonable enough but indicated that even the head of a successful wartime mission would have to go through the usual Colonial Office channels.

On reaching England John also wrote to his old boss, Arthur Dickinson, and they discussed the prospects ahead. John accepted that 'independence was the unspoken premise' of the postwar political scene, so that the future of Britain's presence in Malaya was uncertain.[9] Some Europeans confidently believed that it would last two or three decades, and even the Malay politician, Dato Onn bin Jafaar, spoke in 1948 of self-government in terms of twenty-five years ahead.[10] Others, anxious about their career prospects, hoped for at least fifteen years. John never put a figure on his expectations, but he was young enough to look forward with optimism. He repeated his opinion to Dickinson that police morale and public confidence in the Malayan force were at a low ebb and he wanted to get out. Tactfully he made no specific mention of the bitter rift emerging between those British officers who had to pick up their careers as best they could after remaining at their posts and suffering internment, and those who had broken rank to escape and continue the fight, bolstered by service commissions.[11] John had friends in both camps; he himself was fireproof since he had left Singapore on SOE orders. But he knew that if personal relations were soured, morale and discipline would suffer and service in the Malayan Police would no longer have its pre-war attraction.

On the other hand, entry to the administrative corps of the Malayan Civil Service – the colony's elite – would bring personal career enhancement. John also felt that thanks to his war experiences he could contribute valuable insight into the political Left, which would be beneficial to the Malayan government.[12] He apparently saw no paradox in an ex-police officer with an irrepressibly restless and unorthodox streak joining a traditional colonial administration. He even went so far as to admit to Dickinson that, 'Like many people who have been in the resistance "line", I hate Communism but love Communists – or at least those people who have been led by Communists to resistance throughout the war.'[13] Dickinson responded with a warning: 'I have no doubt you will be criticised . . . A good Police Force is far more important now than a good MCS,' and 'Were I your Commanding Officer I would not allow you to go if I could help it.' Others felt the same about John. A touching plea came from a Chinese police inspector in Perak: 'Please try to come back to us soon to help us . . . We are very, very short-handed and what we require now is senior and very experienced officers like you who can understand this country and its local conditions to pull us out of the chaos which we are going to have very shortly.' Assessing John's experience of intelligence work, Dickinson said, 'In my mind I had put you down for an M.S.

[Malayan Security Service] job', but his final advice was to 'wait and see till you get back what you should do'.

John, however, was disinclined to wait. On 4 February 1946 he wrote to Edward Gent, the incoming Governor, enclosing a handwritten letter to the Secretary of State for the Colonies.[14] Nonetheless, he little expected the swift response that arrived within the month, asking him to hold himself in readiness to return to Malaya by air at short notice. If, as expected, the BMA handed over power quite soon to a civil administration, there would be a pressing need for experienced Malayan officers. All those under fifty who were fit were asked to return for a short tour, with the warning that they should expect 'difficult and arduous conditions' during the period of reconstruction. Rising to the challenge, John agreed to make himself available to return at any time after 15 April.

A small green diary for 1946 demonstrates just how much John packed into his leave. The newly formed Special Forces Club, which he was invited to join, gave him a congenial social base in London, where preparations were being finalised in May for the victory celebrations, the great national event of the early summer. The climax on 8 June would be the victory parade through the centre of London, ending with a spectacular fly-past, while the afternoon and evening would be given over to an incomparable programme of mass popular evening entertainment in the parks and across the capital. National pride made it imperative that Britain put on a good show as a statement of self-belief in all its citizens, not least the peoples of the Empire. Among the groups due to participate was a mixed Malay and Chinese contingent from Malaya, representing twenty-one services, including the Malayan guerrilla forces. John had been asked to deal with the latter among the 190-strong party of visitors aboard the SS *Orontes*.

In the month before the ship docked on 16 May John braced himself to take on the job of troubleshooter. He had been contacted by a frustrated official in Singapore's Chinese Secretariat, alerting him to potential trouble from the MPAJA representatives: they had been extremely 'bolshie' about matters of rank, status and conditions of conduct in the forthcoming visit, and though they eventually gave way, the message had reached London that the Communists were difficult to manage. Shortly afterwards, John was called to the Colonial Office to talk over the problems of handling the MPAJA visitors.[15] He had been half expecting the summons, knowing that in Malaya and Singapore Communist anger over the Soon Kwong case had continued to simmer. The MCP's policy of so-called peaceful agitation prompted a rising tide of strikes and stoppages, notably a 24-hour General Strike on 29–30 January 1946 organised by the General Labour Union to demand the release of Soon Kwong. Two weeks later, when a rally was held to coincide with the anniversary of the fall of Singapore, the BMA intervened decisively with arrests and a show of force, and other rallies in Labis and Mersing in Johore were dispersed by British troops. Meanwhile, John could only hope that the new constitutional framework of the Malayan Union, published in a White Paper at the end of January and due to supersede the BMA on 1 April 1946, would ease Chinese grievances.

As the victory celebrations approached John was asked to visit the camp in Kensington Gardens where the Malayan contingent was housed. He was greeted by a beaming Ah Han, but without his 'Gustavus' partner, Ah Ng. In the absence of Chin Peng, the most familiar ex-AJA officers were Col Itu, Chan Yeung Pan of the 1st (Selangor) Regiment, Deng Fuk Lung of the 2nd (Negri Sembilan) Regiment and Liew Yau, President of the Ex-Comrades' Association. Before the official programme began a number of outings had been arranged. John took the visitors to Lords to watch the MCC play All India at cricket, and to the BBC, whose Chinese Editor wanted to record the personal wartime experiences of the Chinese guerrillas. When it came to the parade, however, John offered his place to Douglas Broadhurst, who was delighted to march with the Malayan contingent. Afterwards they met up with the MPAJA and KMT Chinese to have their photograph taken on the steps of the Albert Memorial in Kensington Gardens.

Some of the Chinese were obviously enjoying themselves. Chien Tian, a former leader of the Johore guerrillas, appeared at ease socialising in the British style; he developed quite a taste for half a pint of bitter. Although others, like Itu, were brooding on the situation back home, John felt on balance the visitors were having a good time, 'as much as their Communist consciences would allow – or perhaps a little more'. He elaborated the point to a friend:

The visit of the AJA passed off without incident. In fact they thoroughly enjoyed themselves though they have been at considerable pains to deny it since they have been back. I fear any intentions they had of assassinating the King or blowing up the Houses of Parliament rather faded away before the delights of four cinema shows a day and ice creams during the intervals!

One way or another, in the course of his leave John received a fair amount of information about the Malayan situation. It was still a matter of concern to him that 'the guerrillas had been subjected to a great deal of criticism, some fair, much unfair'. While in London, Liew Yau harangued him on a complaint that had been festering since January, the British authorities' refusal to meet the full expenses of the MPAJA leaders whom Lord Mountbatten had invited to attend the award ceremony in Singapore. In May 1946 Victor Purcell also contacted John in London. 'There are a number of things I should like to tell you about the MPAJA members and the happenings of the last five months,' he wrote. 'Perhaps we can meet?'[16] In July Nona Baker, the only European woman known to have spent the war in the jungle under MPAJA protection, wrote to him with hearsay evidence from two of the guerrillas visiting London. They complained of 'poor conditions in Malaya', 'particularly the official attitude to the MPAJA'; that membership of the MPAJA ruled them out of getting jobs. 'Is this true?' she asked John anxiously.[17] Unemployment was certainly a thorny issue for which the MPAJA Ex-Servicemen's Association and the British authorities each carried some of the blame. Since disbandment official arrangements for rehabilitating guerrillas had been deliberately blocked by MPAJA hardliners, who refused to cooperate with designated British officers. But the British had also failed to establish the vocational training centres that had been promised in September 1945, and coveted positions such as transport drivers or food inspectors were only available with the support of Force 136 Liaison Officers. A limited number of MPAJA men received trading licences. Most drifted back to rural occupations. A minority turned to lawlessness.

Jim Hannah was another correspondent keen to keep John informed about the turn of events in Malaya. A voluble idealist, he was one of a very small number of British officers to trust and be trusted by former MPAJA comrades. Hannah felt personally involved in Malaya's recovery and wanted to see 'a happy settlement' that would reconcile conflicting ethnic and political interests. To this end he seriously considered going into public relations, nursing the unrealistic hope that John might join him in his venture.[18] In fact, during John's prolonged absence on leave Hannah set up a small private investigation service in Ipoh, using local informants and exploiting his links with the British police, the *orang asli* and his ex-AJA comrades. He openly professed willingness to help any former Communist guerrilla with legitimate needs but firmly renounced those who used their war service as an excuse for wrongdoing, a position John broadly shared.

In letters to John, Hannah poured out all his frustration and disapproval of developments in Malaya: the power of uncontrolled elements, including the MCP's intimidation of the *orang asli*, the mistakes of an over-taxed police service, the government's inertia and neglect of constructive policies. He regaled John with anecdotes of traitor-killing incidents, murders of police informants by the Communists, violent clashes with the KMT, collusion between the MPAJA and gang robbers and the hoarding by the Communists of illegal weapons. More seriously, he talked of a 'Reserve Army' of ex-MPAJA guerrillas, which, in his uninhibited language, 'contains an amazing assortment of prize bastards . . . who are causing trouble'. In addition, jungle camps were being prepared in the hills above Bidor and Tapah, not far from the wartime Resistance camps, in case the government suddenly outlawed the MCP and the secret army needed to go underground. He itched to deal with the fanatics. 'I get wild with them. I keep urging the Police to dispose of Lau Mah, legitimately or otherwise, as with his removal half the trouble would stop.' As to the more reasonable leaders, Hannah took the initiative himself by inviting Itu and Lai Tek, the Communist Secretary-General, to his house in Ipoh to talk things over. They met for six hours under cover of darkness. He did his best to convince the comrades that pursuing their political objectives of a Malayan republic by violent means would not succeed. He urged John to deal with the looming confrontation in Perak:

If John Davis was worth his salt he could come back to Kinta and sort the whole thing out. If I had your knowledge of the country and the Chinese, I could do it myself. It is all a question of separating the bad from the good. There are a lot of decent Communists who could be persuaded to work for the good of Malaya but there are a lot of opportunists . . . if you had any idealism you could, with your flair, be another Raffles . . . You enjoyed every minute of the time you spent in here . . . and you made a success of it. You've got a terrific name here now but unless you are coming back to keep it up or enhance it, it would seem a great pity to me. The work is here . . . this spot is bristling with problems . . . not just petty routine problems but the whole future of Malaya . . . For God's sake drop me a line when you know what you are going to do . . .[19]

Knowing Jim Hannah's tendency to exaggerate, John would take this outburst in his stride. Yet Hannah's warnings were valid, especially his revelation of a secret army with caches of arms hidden deep in the jungle. Proof came in February 1947 when a MPAJA dump of nearly 300 firearms and 20,000 rounds of ammunition was discovered by police in the hills near Kuala Lumpur, a significant enough haul to be reported in the British press.[20]

John shared Hannah's commitment to keeping lines of communication open with the Communists. Aware that he and the Communist leaders had been mutually silent since the stand-off over Soon Kwong at the Singapore award ceremony, John felt he ought to take the initiative and write to Chin Peng from England, which he did early in 1947. While referring obliquely to the current tensions between the MPAJA and the government, John emphasised the importance of maintaining their own wartime camaraderie. He asked Jim Hannah to convey the letter to Chin Peng, who replied as soon as he could:

Dear Davis,

It is really delightful to receive your letter of 4th January 1947 sent via Col. Hannah. I am very grateful to you indeed. But I hope you will kindly accept my apologies for not sending you an early reply as by the time I received your letter I was busy at home preparing the celebration of the Chinese New Year. I was sorry too to be unable to accompany the others for the Victory Parade owing to my personal affairs. It is true that the AJA relations with the Government are not always very satisfactory. I quite see your opinion and personally I am in sympathy with what you feel. In my personal opinion I agree with you that the great comradeship of the war years is not only unforgetable [sic] but should also be maintained . . . Since you will be returning very soon I hope I will be able to see you. Hope you will enjoy a pleasant trip on your way to Malaya and with my regards to . . . all my friends,

Yours very sincerely,
Chen Ping [sic][21]

The letter was, as John expected, friendly and soothing, skirting diplomatically around the difficulties that the MCP and its satellite organisations were causing the colonial administration. The Chinese New Year celebrations concealed the mounting tension in the Communist leadership, as the methodical uncovering of Lai Tek's treachery was reaching a critical point. In the circumstances it is surprising that Chin Peng had the time to reply. The long saga of Lai Tek's career as a secret agent was to climax in the three months before 6 March 1947, when he failed to appear at an important meeting of the Central Executive Committee. By then the renegade had ransacked the MCP's finances and disappeared without trace. His comrades never saw him or the funds again. It was probably fortuitous that John was on home leave when the serious questioning of Lai Tek's leadership of the MCP began. It led to Chin Peng's devastating exposure of Lai Tek as an arch-traitor and ultimately to his taking over as Secretary-General in May 1947. Some months later the deposed master agent was strangled by a Communist killer squad in Bangkok. Contrary to custom he was silenced without prior interrogation.[22] Had Lai Tek been put under duress by interrogators, he might have revealed John's identity as the Special Branch officer who 'ran' him before the Second World War.

With the world conflict over, after 1945 ex-servicemen and -women everywhere were finding what it meant to be civilians again, revisiting old haunts, rediscovering friends and lost loves. John felt he had much to catch up on since he was last at home in 1940. Now, at the age of thirty-five, he was strikingly handsome, athletic, at the height of his physical prowess. If comparisons can be made with archetypal British heroes, he was 'in a James Bond kind of mould', and 'had the jut-jawed good looks of the last generation of British imperialist actors, such as Jack Hawkins, Anthony Steel and George Baker, like whom he craved action in the great outdoors'.[23] One of John's early ports of call was to the home of his father's old friend, Charles Ouin, in Sutton. Their two families had enjoyed holidays together in the 1920s, and though the eldest daughter, Helen, was three years younger than John, theirs had always been a special friendship. From 1930, when John left for the Far East, to the approach of war, they had corresponded regularly and Helen had cherished every moment of his home leave. Now, in February 1946, John was keen to see her, though he anticipated a strained meeting. The war had disrupted normal links between them. John's movements from 1942 were cloaked in official secrecy and after her transfer to the Caribbean by the Censorship Office he had no precise record of Helen's whereabouts. Their separation seemed final when John heard in India that she had become engaged to be married.[24] However, the relationship was short-lived: Helen's fiancé had died suddenly of acute appendicitis. In November 1945 she returned to England and was working in London as a filing clerk for the British Council when John arrived home.

It was instantly apparent that she had changed. She was now a mature, vivacious 32-year-old, tall and slender, with a clear, expressive gaze and finely moulded cheekbones, her face framed by thick, wavy brown hair. She was unquestionably beautiful in an individual way. If John was excited by rediscovering Helen, he was perplexed for some time by the absence of news of an educated, Christian Chinese family, the Lams, who had befriended him in his pre-war years in China. One of the daughters, Rose, was a frail slip of a girl when she was recommended to John as an excellent Cantonese language teacher. After hiring her help with conversation lessons he was intrigued and gradually captivated by her unusual charm, intelligence and intuitive morality. Their friendship blossomed further, though even at his most emotionally involved John was aware of the political incorrectness of a union with Rose Lam. The family moved to Hong Kong, and some months before the outbreak of war with Japan he wrote to her to break off their relationship. It was not until the spring of 1946 that John learnt from several sources about Rose's fate. She had apparently been distraught by his rejection, her health had broken down and she developed tuberculosis. Then in the aftermath of an American air raid on Hong Kong on 1 December 1943 she was tragically killed by Japanese mortar fire.[25] The finality of her death expunged John's romantic vision of China, a country that had once fascinated and held him in awe. In the new postwar world he needed to put the past behind him. He never returned to China.

However, in the course of 1946 John made two crucial decisions: first, that he could not contemplate life in Malaya without a wife; and second, that he had found 'the right girl' within his parents' social set in Surrey.

At the end of July 1946 the War Office finally handed back financial responsibility for Col Davis to the Colonial Office, where John's request to join the Malayan Civil Service had been lodged since February. While mulling over the decisions he had made for the future, he let the summer and early autumn days drift by, until the likelihood of a recall to Malaya spurred him at last to confront Helen. If he had sensed it vaguely since childhood, he was now certain that they were 'made for each other'. They had always been candid with each other and both had survived the war years with remarkably little emotional scarring. They had much in common: no one could say it was a case of the attraction of opposites. Both were forceful, determined, self-reliant characters, attracting admiration from a circle of loyal friends of their own sex. They shared a taste for simplicity, for the natural world and an aversion to materialism and pomp. Only in one respect was John a passive, admiring bystander and that was when Helen discovered wells of creativity in herself from which a considerable artistic talent flowed.

In the end, everything happened in a rush. On 7 November it was announced in the *London Gazette* that Col John Lewis Haycraft Davis DSO had been promoted to 'Commander (Military Division) of the Most Excellent Order of the British Empire in recognition of gallant and distinguished services while engaged in special operations in South East Asia'.[26] A week later the personal notification arrived from the War Office, confirming his CBE (Commander of the British Empire). Among the Davis family and their friends John's award was received with immense pride and pleasure. Colin Mackenzie, head of SOE's India Mission, congratulated him with the firm assurance that 'it was more than earned'.

Buoyed by the honour, John was spurred into action. Helen was in Salisbury visiting her sister Elizabeth when she received his phone call, asking her to come home immediately. Helen demurred but her sister insisted she took the next train back home. Each instinctively anticipated the other's itinerary. As he descended from the bus in Sutton, Helen was greeted by the bizarre sight of John in a mackintosh with a Wellington boot sticking out of each side pocket. There had been heavy rain and the ground was soft, but, as he explained, he wanted to take her for a walk in the nearby woods so she needed heavy footwear. In this muddy setting John confidently proposed marriage and Helen, after an appropriate pause, accepted graciously. Their engagement appeared in the papers on

19 November. Delighted letters poured in from friends in England and Malaya, offering dual congratulations. The only impediment to celebration was Mr Ouin's failing health, which was causing the family some concern, so it was agreed that a quiet family wedding should be arranged as quickly as possible. The ceremony took place at Christ Church, Sutton, on Tuesday 10 December, followed by a small reception in the town. Helen wore a simple ice blue suit and hat. John decided against his colonel's uniform and medals in favour of a plain lounge suit. They agreed to forgo a honeymoon in the British Isles as they would soon be leaving for the Far East.

The New Year brought notice of three memorable events. First came an invitation to Col J.H.L. Davis CBE, DSO, to attend the royal investiture by King George VI at Buckingham Palace on 28 January 1947. A fortnight later John was informed that he was to return to duty by the first available passage after 15 February and his transfer to the Civil Service was in hand. Notification that they were to depart on 11 March on the *Otranto* filled Helen with 'sheer joy'. But she and John had another good reason to be excited. She was pregnant and the baby, due in October, would be the first of five Davis children born in Malaya.

Chapter 12

Regression to Conflict

In Malaya the press had wind of the fact that Col Davis was on the *Otranto*'s passenger list. On 3 April one paper sported the headline, 'Resistance Hero Back in Singapore'; a second carried a picture of John in uniform. Yet what should have been a happy return developed into a fortnight of melodrama. Immediately after landing Helen was rushed into hospital with a threatened miscarriage, just as John had orders from the Malayan Establishment Office to report immediately to Kuala Lumpur. Four days later, armed with an emergency bottle of brandy, they risked the journey north, to be met off the train at Kuala Lumpur by Richard Broome. Despite the acute accommodation problem in the capital, he and Tamsin had managed to find two spare beds, and 'surrounded by masses of friends who were marvellous' Helen recovered from her ordeal.

John was instructed to take over in May from Noel Alexander, a close friend from the pre-war Canton set. His position had a 'long-winded, pompous title, the Deputy Commissioner for Labour, Pahang, Trengganu and Kelantan'. To ease the transfer, Noel thoughtfully invited the Davises to join him on 24 April at the government bungalow in Bentong and stay until the official handover. The opportunity to talk proved invaluable to John, though for Helen the 50-mile car journey from Kuala Lumpur via the Genting Simpah pass, 'a wickedly winding road', was an excruciating introduction to the state of Pahang. Concerned that he was out of touch, John was glad to discuss the parameters of the Deputy Commissioner's job and to range confidentially over Chinese affairs and current political issues arising from the unpopularity of the government, the Malayan Union.

Malay hostility to the constitutional changes introduced by the Malayan Union had rapidly focused on three areas of concern. First, it was felt that the new constitution was antipathetic to Malay interests yet was foisted on the Sultans without proper consultation in a manner that flouted British traditions of diplomacy. Second, the introduction of a centralised system of government seemed an unwarranted attack on the sovereignty of the Malay rulers, fundamental as that was to Malay identity. Obviously centralisation also threatened the autonomy of the states, and with that the social and political status of the Malay elite. Lastly, the proposed extension of citizenship to non-Malay immigrant races, particularly to the Chinese, on specific grounds of birth, residence or naturalisation, was seen as another attempt to undermine Malay pre-eminence, which the British had hitherto upheld. The antagonism to the Malayan Union was, in fact, so intense that it inspired a new political consciousness among the Malays, leading to the formation of the United Malays National Organisation (UMNO) in May 1946. In consequence, even when the Malayan Union was abandoned in favour of a new federation conceding to Malay attitudes on citizenship and the sovereignty of the Sultans, the British and Malayan governments never fully regained the trust or respect of the Malay people.

In voicing his criticism of the Malayan Union John Davis picked out the lack of organised government support for the Chinese community, which had once been provided by the Chinese Protectorate. Looking back, 'it was a rattling good department', John recalled. However, the mandarins of the Malayan Planning Unit, who included Sir Edward Gent, the future Governor and High Commissioner, judged it to be inconsistent with the principle of a common Malayan citizenship, so it was abolished after the Second World War. At the same time the pre-war Labour Department, which had dealt exclusively with Indian labour, was transformed. 'All Labour affairs have been turned over to a greatly increased Labour department to which 90% of the Chinese speaking MCS have been sent. The other 10% are in a very small Chinese Affairs Department which deal in politics only,' but such men were 'up in the clouds', added John dismissively. In the postwar Labour Department the Chinese speaker 'is in effect the old Chinese protector but without the glamour and prestige of the name and with the disability of having to sully his hands with Indian affairs from time to time! In fact the degradation of the protectorate is in keeping with the general deterioration in government work and prestige throughout Malaya.' These astringent remarks were made safe in the knowledge that he was only seconded to the Malayan Civil Service and could still 'don a Sam Browne again' as a police officer, if the Malayan Civil Service terms proved unsatisfactory.

It was perhaps over-optimistic of John to believe that as Mountbatten's wartime representative in Malaya he would receive exceptional treatment from the Colonial Office, even though his 'very gallant record' had been personally acknowledged by Gent himself.[1] When the official letter arrived in June 1947 and the Secretary of State for the Colonies informed him that he was transferred as a Class IV officer, John was incensed, since that entailed a loss of five years' seniority. He knew that to turn down the offer would be ruinous for his career, and as he pondered his situation the explanation dawned. 'I have often been warned that I should certainly be gunned for helping the Communists in the war. I have always laughed at the idea but perhaps it is true after all!'

After his appeal to the Establishment Office was turned down in October 1947, John indicated his intention to take his case to higher authority – if necessary to the Secretary of State. But when a second response from the Establishment Office arrived just before Christmas in the form of a straight ultimatum, he was forced to accept their terms. 'I have beaten a strategic retreat,' he admitted, determined that though he had lost the battle he might still win the war. He set his sights on steady rather than spectacular advancement. He never nursed ambitions to reach the highest echelons of the Malayan Civil Service because, as he observed, 'the plums are always reserved for slobs who hang around Secretariats'. He was himself unwilling to pay that price, whereas 'they deserve them considering the awful paper life they lead!'

Bentong was very much to John's liking. It nestled in a little corner of Pahang State, a modest, largely Chinese township with a long main street lined with shophouses and the usual public buildings, a police station, District Officer's residence, Public Works Department, rest house and hospital.[2] Yet with only ten government officials (and four wives, including Helen) it was a small and self-contained little European community. And there were several other advantages. 'It is one of the most beautiful stations in the Peninsula, surrounded by jungle hills, cool to the point of being almost cold in the morning, and . . . pretty healthy.' They also had a small house and garden entirely to themselves, a priceless asset after Kuala Lumpur. High on a sloping site a little way out of town, the bungalow looked out over range after range of the Pahang hills, and 'we have two magnificent jungle pools 4 and 7 miles away for bathing'. At weekends there was a choice between a poolside picnic or a day spent in the garden, taming their 'complete wilderness'. John enjoyed the hard labour, leaving Helen to plant 'seeds, cuttings, orchids and other mysteries'.

All they lacked in Bentong was the company of old friends. However, John was still confident he and Helen would 'make a go of it'. They had the use of an old government car, since the Labour Commissioner's work involved a good deal of travelling. At the same time Helen began to learn Malay, determined not to fall into the languid lifestyle of the colonial *mem*, in addition to which she was soon persuaded by the District Officer to take on a little voluntary work, distributing welfare to the aged, orphaned, sick and needy from a corner of John's office.

As the weeks went by, John felt increasingly pleased with his position. 'I enjoy the independence of a small department with a headquarters which is not organised to bother you,' he told his father. 'The work consists of inspecting estates, mines etc., dealing with strikes, arguing the heads off all and sundry, and a fair amount of judicial work, settling disputes . . . As a sideline I am also an Adviser for Chinese Affairs, which gives me a certain amount of work to do with the political side of things.' He found himself continually dealing with unofficials and government departments other than the Labour Department.[3] However, with a predominantly Chinese workforce in his constituency, he needed to delegate work to a Chinese labour inspector. Luckily he had the assistance of an exceptionally able officer, Lau Yew Choon, as well as an Indian inspector to deal with Tamil workers. 'The main delight of the job is that it covers such a wide field,' he wrote, summing up his good fortune. Accepting that the three eastern states included large tracts of uninhabited, undeveloped rainforest, in terms of undertaking visitations they amounted to a massive territorial responsibility.

Although Malaya showed some signs of economic revival by May 1947, John saw it as a fragile recovery, set against a soaring cost of living and fluctuating international markets in rubber and tin. Production was aggravated by labour shortages and the infiltration of the trade unions by militant Communists out to promote industrial unrest. John was emotionally committed to Malaya – in his words, 'I am still a great believer in this country' – but he could see both sides of the political argument. He accepted that 'colonial empires were exploitative' and 'colonial territory only thrives economically because of the low standard of living of the majority of the inhabitants'; but 'directly you start raising the standard of living (or perhaps the bogus standard of increased wages) you throw away your trump card in world competition'. No sooner had John taken over in Bentong than a mid-year downturn in rubber prices prompted a widespread reduction in rates of pay and a rash of strikes. Two stoppages were on his patch, at the Telemang and Sabai estates, giving him his first experience of handling industrial disputes. His job was to ascertain whether regulations were being observed and, if necessary, to take appropriate measures against proprietors or managers who failed to fulfil contractual obligations; equally, he had to act against Communist agitators involved in alleged incitement or intimidation while operating as trade union representatives. Keen to be seen as acting even-handedly, John issued both sides a stern warning against intimidation. Within a fortnight there was a general return to work. Yet the bald, unacceptable fact was that after 300 stoppages in 1947 the countryside of Malaya was smarting from the effects of this 'Year of Strikes'. The country could not afford this trend to continue.

In John's view many trade disputes over contracts revealed the deficiencies of owners, managers and middlemen and the victimisation of labour. In a typical situation he faced 'a dozen labourers screaming for their wages, a sub-contractor admitting he owes them a great deal more than he does in order that he can squeeze more out of the contractor, and a contractor who is useless, probably criminal and anyway bankrupt'. Sometimes John had to intervene physically to ensure justice, as in the case of a Chinese-owned timber-felling company that had failed to pay its coolies their food entitlement and advance in wages. The complaint was only rectified after John drove to Kuala Lumpur and extracted Straits $2,000 from the timber purchasing offices of the Malayan Forestry Department to meet the labourers' arrears.

Since a good proportion of estates and businesses were Asian-owned or -managed, John relied heavily on his two Asian inspectors, while he spent many days and nights on visitations to the estates of European planters and managers. They lived in greater isolation than their counterparts in west Malaya and he admired their courage in pursuing an increasingly difficult, insecure and lonely job. But inspections had to be conducted rigorously, as John's succinct reports testify, with information on the state of buildings, size and ethnic mix of the labour force and contractors, rates of pay and benefits, crèche and medical amenities, health records, union involvement, labour relations, grievances and disputes. Frequently he was scornful of company policy, particularly of insurance companies. His eyes were opened by attending workers' compensation cases, which revealed a pack of 'downright swindlers' accepting compensation risk on workers whom they knew to be outside the scope of the compensation laws. 'That did not worry them,' he concluded: 'They pocketed the premium,' and he was just as critical of lawyers who 'knowingly worked through crooked agents'. In all, there was something of the Wild West about Pahang: it was still 'a pretty uncouth and inefficient state'.

Kelantan was little different, which explained the existence of trouble-spots like Gua Musang in the wild border area held by Chinese KMT guerrillas during the war, led by one Kok Choi. Afterwards, as headman of the district and with a fearsome reputation, he created considerable unrest among the Malays. Government policy on lawlessness was unequivocal. Satisfied that Kok Choi's record was 'not conducive to the safety, peace or welfare of the state', John ordered his deportation to China.[4]

These time-consuming cases and his frequent absences from Bentong made for a pressurised life spent rushing around 'in a cloud of dust, stink of petrol and [with a] splitting headache from the last argument one has dealt with'. There was also a 'vast mass of Force 136 stuff that still comes in – mostly begging letters for jobs or back pay'. Jim Hannah had warned him to expect a deluge of paper with requests for help, allegations of ill-treatment by the authorities, angry or obsequious letters, some even threatening. To bereaved fathers searching for explanations of their sons' deaths – cases such as Pat Noone and Cheng, Agent 108 – John could only offer sympathy. Yet, by implication, it was somehow generally assumed that his influence was supreme.

Some people came in person to speak to him. Occasionally, on their return at dusk from a jungle walk, John and Helen discovered the recumbent shapes of a couple of former bodyguards waiting on the verandah. These being hard economic times, they had come to ask a favour. All John could do was to drop a line to a friend or contact:

Dear Bob,

Bearer . . . Tsai Siew Chuen is an old pal of mine – 2½ years of jungling together – whom I can thoroughly recommend. Like so many of them he is untrained to any trade . . . If you can do anything to fix him up I shall be very grateful. I hate to see these fellows – grand chaps of their day – wandering around bewildered and becoming increasingly feckless as time goes on.[5]

But the most assiduous by far in his pursuit of John was Liew Yau, who claimed compensation in August 1947, as pensions and gratuities for the members of the Ex-Comrades' Association. John referred the claim to the Secretary for Chinese Affairs (SCA) in Singapore, who took it forward to the Colonial Secretary in Singapore, asking for it to be handed to Far East Land Forces (FARELF). The matter rumbled on, as the War Office and GHQ FARELF continued to saddle John with the problem. In December 1947 the Major General Administration FARELF asked for a full briefing from him. John wrote a seven-page document on the MPAJA and a commentary on Britain's outstanding obligations. He stated firmly his opinion that the general claim for back pay was settled at disbandment.[6] His final contribution to this saga was to serve as a conduit between the Ex-Comrades' Association and the new Federation government that replaced the Malayan Union on 1 February 1948, after Liew Yau asked him to transmit all the documentation on the ex-MPAJA claims to the Deputy Chief Secretary.[7] However, now, two and a half years after the end of the war, John was thoroughly tired of the whole business, including the game of musical chairs played by the civil and military authorities. Furthermore, he had also lost all patience with Liew Yau, who was still pushing the claims of 1,115 men – claims John considered to be bogus. As for the Ex-Comrades' Association itself, John was now convinced that it was quite simply and evidently 'a 100% political organisation and poisonously revolutionary at that'.

In September 1947 John had written home with a confusing picture of the political scene. Perceiving a marked deterioration in law and order, during the spring the British press had highlighted the incidence of intimidation producing a 'fear-laden atmosphere' in Malaya, and raised calls for action from Asians as well as British officials and planters. At the same time the attitudes of people like John and Jim Hannah were lambasted by traditional right-wing journalists: 'The idea which certain liberal-minded British had in the early days of the re-occupation, that the British would be able to continue cooperating with those left-wing groups which had given them useful help during the war, has long since been shattered.'[8] Six months later, John probed his parents as to how the press was then presenting the Malayan situation – 'I dare say the recent banditry scares have even filtered through to the home papers' – so he wanted to reassure them. 'Politically things are quietening down a bit, though in fact we are threatened with a public services' strike at the moment.' This kind of contradiction reflected not just John's uncertainty, but the colonial government's growing dilemma, how to plug the serious intelligence vacuum caused by the disappearance of Lai Tek the previous March. How did this affect the Communist leadership and what were the implications for the British and Malayan governments? Clearly even the political intelligence bureau, the Malayan Security Service, did not know that Chin Peng had been elevated to the leadership of the MCP as Secretary-General. In August John received a letter from the Malayan Security Service in Kuala Lumpur:

Dear Davis,

The following is an extract from an agent (a good one): 'Chen Ping [sic] @ Wong Boon Hua is now in charge of all the MPAJA arms dumps in Perak. He has in his possession maps showing the locations of the dumps that were originally kept by Low Mah.' There followed a brief physical description of the man. Then, 'He spends much of his time travelling round the country and is frequently in K.L. Said to be well known to Mr. J.L.H. Davis.' Do you recollect Chin Peng and did you know him well? Do you suppose he would be the type to cough up the goods if very discreetly approached and promised a handsome reward (which he would undoubtedly get if he played [ball]?)[9]

If this was the sum of the Malayan Security Service's fact-file on Chin Peng then it was a poor showing, simplistic, out-of-date and unfocused, the result of the division of intelligence between a political bureau and the CID. John had produced a precis on each of the Communist leaders at the time of disbandment and probably knew as much, if not more, about Chin Peng than any Englishman. Was he a man to sell arms secrets for money? The answer was No, and not simply because he was Secretary-General of the Communist Party: unlike some ex-guerrillas he would not do business with the Malayan government.[10]

Since John believed in the efficacy of softly-softly tactics, he decided on a low-key personal approach to his old ally. An opportunity arose when the War Office told him that Chin Peng (along with Ah Ng) had been awarded the OBE for his wartime services in assisting the British officers in Malaya. John was very pleased since he had been instrumental in producing supportive recommendations at Colin Mackenzie's request. Failing to reach Chin Peng in Kuala Lumpur – it was August and the Chinese leader was abroad on Party business – John wrote instead to his father, who had a bicycle and tyre business in Sitiawan, asking him to pass on his heartiest congratulations. He added that he would be pleased to receive a letter from Chin Peng 'telling me how he is getting on, or better still if he would pay me a visit should he ever have the opportunity of coming to Pahang'.[11] In his reply, Mr Ong stated he had passed on John's congratulations to his son and hoped that Chin Peng would write or visit in the near future.[12]

It seems that shortly after this Chin Peng did communicate with John at Bentong, for John noted down the gist of their conversation.[13] Chin Peng wanted to start a lorry haulage company, for which he needed a licence. The plan was quite ambitious, requiring several – ten or so – vehicles, and the purpose was to carry salt and fresh fish from Pangkor to Ipoh, Penang, possibly even Kuala Lumpur. There was a note saying that pigs and rubber might also be traded. He spoke of the 'possibility of drawing in others at Sitiawan', with the promise that a new company would be formed. John, of course, could only make appropriate enquiries, since Perak did not come under his jurisdiction. However, he indicated that a written reply should go to 'Wong Man Wa, 59 Klyne Street', the address of the Ex-Comrades' Association in Kuala Lumpur. John kept his word. In December he wrote to the Commissioner of Road Transport, Malayan Union, with a letter of introduction on behalf of 'Mr Wong Man Wa, OBE', and a covering letter with the concluding statement, 'I can thoroughly recommend him.'

On the face of it, John was taking a gamble. It could not have escaped his attention that a haulage firm operating between the towns of Kuala Lumpur, Ipoh and Penang would provide ideal cover for many purposes, not least a Communist nexus across north-west Malaya. On the other hand, he may have calculated that after years of rootlessness in the jungle Chin Peng was ready to settle down to build up a family business in the Chinese tradition. In any case, John had a very personal view of friendship, made more particular by being tried and tested in the heat of war. Whatever information or suspicion he nursed about Chin Peng's ultimate political intentions, he would always think of him as a remarkably brave individual to whom he owed his life, and that consideration overrode most others.

On 7 October 1947 Helen gave birth to a daughter, Patricia Ann, in Kuala Lumpur. The proud father assured his parents that at a month old, 'She is still a complete Davis . . . with an astonishingly expressive face'. His new status of fatherhood brought John deep satisfaction. 'Life is very full and very good,' he wrote in the spring of 1948. He and Helen had set themselves one principal objective, to emulate an English way of life. Gardening and walking remained their chief forms of relaxation. They avoided the club and the social round of dinner parties, relying instead on their friends to drop in casually whenever they liked.

One of John's friends who stayed with them at Bentong in late March was John Barnard, head of Perak CID. He came for advice, for since the end of the war Barnard had been gathering intelligence on the remaining KMT guerrillas known as the Malayan Overseas Chinese Self-Defence Army (MOCSDA). In the battle for law and order he was convinced that they posed as serious a threat as the MCP. In May the CID chief wrote to alert John to the fact that these nationalist guerrillas had already extended their control along the central mountainous spine around Bidor and the Cameron Highlands, which had been MPAJA territory and John's old stamping ground during the war. Now MOCSDA forces appeared to be expanding their activities and 'a couple of KMT big shots' had moved into the Bentong area. At the same time, Barnard hoped John might turn detective to unearth more information through his unorthodox connections. 'I know that this is not your line of country any longer but perhaps with your amazing contacts you might get extraordinary aid from [your] MPAJA pals who have no love for the [Overseas Chinese].' In return he invited John to join the police in 'some jungle bashing' in July.

Hannah's informers had also been monitoring the movements of the Perak Communists, and he felt John should be told of a recent development involving their ex-comrades of the 5th (Perak) Regiment. 'You will be sorry to hear, but probably not surprised', he told him in June, 'that a lot of our late little boys are melting back into the ulu in twos and threes and fours and have been responsible for one or two terrorist jobs within the last fortnight.' Indeed, rumours were rife that since May ex-MPAJA men had been leaving town and heading for the jungle to their training camps and arms dumps. The ringleader appeared to be 'that bastard Let Yong [sic]', whom Hannah reminded John had been on Col Itu's staff.

John was aware that the creation of an independent Communist republic was the basic goal of the MCP. However, he never believed it would be achieved because the conditions propelling Indonesia to popular nationalism were absent in Malaya. This fact had been accepted by the Communist leadership in 1945, when Secretary-General Lai Tek adopted a policy of peaceful agitation as the Party's *modus operandi*. Nor did John believe there was the slightest chance of the Communists seizing power by means of an 'armed struggle', which became party policy under Lai Tek's successor, Chin Peng. John found it strange that what was obvious to the MCP in 1945 was apparently forgotten in 1948, by which time there had been a significant improvement in economic conditions in Malaya. Though he saw the current epidemic of strikes in Singapore as 'particularly vicious', he put them down to a 'last fling' by the Communists rather than a call to urban revolution, for they had recently been 'losing ground steadily'.

However, in the course of May 1948 there was a worrying increase in shootings and armed robberies on the mainland, which the Malayan government treated as a serious rise in criminality, responding with arrests and anti-union legislation designed to proscribe the Pan-Malayan Federation of Trade Unions. On 9 June, a senior Communist Party member and head of the Political Committee, Liew Yit Fan, was arrested and subsequently deported to China. However, the words on the lips of most British civilians were still 'strikes' and 'bandits', not 'terrorism' and 'rebellion' or 'guerrilla warfare'.

By 9 June, however, the day of Liew Yit Fan's arrest, Jim Hannah observed to John that 'things are hotting up more and more every day and I think there will be a crop of hold-ups and murders before June is out'. It was a prescient remark. A week later, on the morning of 16 June 1948, in ruthless, efficient operations, three unarmed British rubber-planters were murdered in cold blood by Communist killer squads on their estates in the Sungei Siput area of Perak. Their deaths marked the tipping point. The European community was outraged, particularly by the death of the manager's assistant, 21-year-old Ian Christian, and public opinion now forced the Federation government to act decisively to stamp out lawlessness and violence.[14] A State of Emergency was proclaimed in parts of Perak and Johore. The following day it was applied to the remainder of those two states and then on 18 June extended to the whole country. The regulations accompanying the government's Declaration of Emergency brought in a swingeing regime of coercion and enforcement.

John was on a labour inspection in Kuantan at the time of the Sungei Siput killings. While there he received a telephone call summoning him back to Bentong with the unexpected request that in response to the national State of Emergency as soon as possible he was to take over as Acting Officer Superintending Police Circle (OSPC) West Pahang. Back in Bentong, John received a second call from Harry Harper, Pahang's Chief of Police. He was detained at Mentekab investigating an attack on the police station but had just received a message that the police station in Jerantut was also under attack. He asked John to deal with the incident.

Helen fought back her nervousness as John explained the situation. That night, with a small party of police volunteers and Lau Yew Choon as his second-in-command, John set out for the riverine settlement of Jerantut. At first light they paused at the approaches. The buildings, doors and windows barred, had an abandoned air and the silence confirmed the disappearance of the terrified inhabitants. They were soon joined, however, by some agitated police who emerged from hiding. John and his party guardedly entered the township, making for the police station. Inside they found one young Malay constable, trussed, immobile and in shock. After he was released John was able to piece together an account of what had occurred. The police station had been attacked by a gang of Chinese Communist bandits, perhaps twenty or thirty strong. They had seized three local *towkays* (businessmen) and taken them off with the police sergeant. The rest of the police had probably managed to escape into the surrounding jungle.

With a dozen men, Malays, Chinese and Sikhs, John instituted an immediate search of the area for signs of the perpetrators. It was not difficult to trace the bandits because no effort had been made at concealment and their tracks led up into jungle-covered hills. On one summit the police party found the remains of a camp and nearby the corpses of the three *towkays*. Since it was now full daylight they continued their pursuit, during which they surprised and captured one of the bandits. He was probably the lookout, because soon afterwards the police approached an old *atap* hut that had served as the attackers' overnight base. Intending to rush the camp, John and his men crept forward in silence until they were suddenly spotted at 20yds distance and the bandits scattered. In their flight two of the Communists were killed. The leader of the gang ran the wrong way and was caught helplessly in a swamp. John fired to wound the man, enabling him to be taken prisoner. So with their captives, the bodies of the *towkays* and some recovered loot belonging to local inhabitants, the party made their way back to Jerantut. John decided to stay until a patrol of soldiers from the Malay Regiment arrived to reinforce the local police, and the villagers dared to return to their homes. Only then did he hand over command and return to Bentong with his volunteers.

At first Helen had weighed the odds and counted the hours. She had a baby to protect, their bungalow had open access and their nearest neighbour lived a mile away, but she had two servants and two dogs on site and John had given her a gun to keep under her pillow. She made up her mind that if one dog barked in the night she wouldn't worry – a wild pig had probably broken into the garden – but if both dogs barked she would ring her neighbour. One night she heard both animals barking so she alerted her friend, who offered to come over immediately. But reassurance was all Helen needed. Nothing untoward had happened in Bentong during John's absence, and yet a sense of living with 'the Emergency' had come to West Pahang.

Chapter 13

Ferret Force and Aftermath

The Malayan Emergency was a war in all but name as the Communist campaign of terror escalated into a twelve-year conflict. The battlefields were isolated estate roads, dark rows of rubber, ugly mining camps, lonely police posts and the ubiquitous brooding rainforest. At its height an estimated 7,000 guerrillas, supported by a mass peasant organisation, the Min Yuen (Masses Organisation), were pitted against the Malayan government, backed by Malay and urban Chinese opinion and the might of 25,000 British and Commonwealth troops, over 60,000 police and a quarter of a million Home Guards.

For John personally the Emergency brought a dramatic reversal of roles. While leading covert operations in Japanese-occupied Malaya he had organised resistance and sabotage in cooperation with Chin Peng, the Communist chief in Perak. When the British re-occupied Malaya their friendship became harder to sustain, as the MCP, shielded by a united front of satellite organisations, set itself in political opposition to the colonial regime. In a dramatic switch of policy, however, peaceful agitation gave way in 1948 to a strategy of armed conflict aiming at popular insurrection. In July the MCP was again declared illegal and Chin Peng, the new Secretary-General, inevitably earned the sobriquet of Public Enemy No. 1. John found it a sad irony but he was bound to accept the logic that 'the rest of my career was concerned with the Emergency and defeating this man who had been my greatest ally and then became my greatest enemy'.[1]

The Sungei Siput episode in June was, in John's opinion, an act of overt terrorism, calculated to ravage public confidence throughout

Malaya. Although the Federation government imposed severe Emergency Regulations, these did not deter the Communist bandits from perpetrating more terror attacks, particularly where there was a concentration of Chinese, 'sickening, morale-breaking and effective' operations, such as the raid on Kulai village, the assault on the Batu Arang mining complex, in which five Chinese strike breakers were liquidated, and the 'liberation' of Gua Musang in Pahang. The victims were not simply British managers but anyone who might be thought to sympathise with the imperialists. 'Their method of murdering ordinary Chinese in villages on the pretext that they were police informers was terrorism,' John insisted angrily, as he pondered how to play the Communists at their own game. If he drew one conclusion from his experience at Jerantut it was the absolute necessity of a swift, determined response to counter acts of violence and intimidation.

The Emergency 'was when John came into his own', according to an officer of the Malayan Civil Service, Oliver Wolters, who observed him in action during those years. In his reluctance to court publicity John was inclined to let others take credit for his ideas and initiatives, but close friends were not deceived and believed his contribution to the government's anti-Communist initiatives was far more significant than present historical writing suggests. 'He was certainly the central figure in planning the long overdue counter-insurgency policy,' was Wolters' judgement of the strategy that ultimately defeated Communism in Malaya. And in the autumn of 1948 John Davis 'was entirely responsible for conceiving, promoting and leading Ferret Force', the first tactical initiative launched against the Communist guerrillas.[2]

John's first step was to contact two of his most knowledgeable friends, Richard Broome and Noel Alexander. They agreed to meet for an urgent brain-storming session and decided to ask someone else to join them. Bob Thompson was another Malayan Civil Service Chinese expert who had been with John and Richard in Ballygunge, Calcutta, in 1942; he had later been involved with Wingate's Chindits in Burma, where he had had experience of jungle warfare. Early in their discussions the friends agreed that existing Security Forces would be inadequate. Regular military units were undermanned and inexperienced in jungle operations. No matter how distinguished their record of military service, when 2 Guards Brigade arrived as reinforcements, few in their battalions could communicate with the local people or distinguish a bandit from an innocent villager. The rank and file of the rural police, predominantly Malays, were too open to intimidation. Bearing this in mind, John and his colleagues drew up a probable scenario.[3] They reckoned that the bandits or Communist terrorists – CTs, as they became known – were organised on similar lines to the wartime MPAJA guerrillas and would rely on the jungle for protection. From the security of camps and clearings along the foothills of Perak, Selangor and Johore, they could launch surprise attacks on estates, mines and communications in the western plain, withdrawing over the mountain spine, if necessary, to take cover in the jungles of Kelantan or Pahang. It was likely, too, that the Communist command system would be decentralised, leaving it to local commanders to take appropriate initiatives. This much John and his friends assumed from their knowledge of the wartime Communist model, but they found it difficult to believe that the Malayan People's Anti-British Army (MPABA) was as large, well-armed and motivated as the MPAJA.[4] Yet, as they worked out a counter-strategy, they were aware of the danger of complacency.

Bearing all this in mind, John explained his idea for a new strike force on Force 136 lines. It would set out 'to demonstrate appropriate jungle tactics', and thence 'to break down the bandits' feeling of ownership of the jungle' by *ferreting* them out from their cover. A draft proposal was worked out for a special kind of jungle force, which would have select military and police personnel, Europeans with special operations experience and hand-picked Asians.[5] They would work in teams, and as they penetrated the jungle they would aim to eliminate Communist killer bands on their own or in collaboration with regular forces. Their intention was to emulate the terrorists, operating in mobile cadres with local knowledge, and led by officers who had already proved themselves in resistance or irregular warfare. From these outlines John and his colleagues worked out a plan and filled in the essential details.

They proposed a multiracial force of 300 men, organised in twenty operational units of fifteen men to be placed in strategic areas. It could be run from a small headquarters in Perak by two officers, since it was assumed that each Ferret group would operate with maximum independence and freedom of action vested in the group commanders. It was estimated that two weeks' special training should ensure 'considerable efficiency' (because only exceptional types would be chosen as Ferrets) and they would be supported by Chinese Liaison Officers and interpreters.

To simplify the supply issue everyone would have to be prepared to live in jungle conditions on a basic rice diet. John never claimed that this was more than a temporary solution until the Security Forces could operate effectively, and given that it had yet to be costed, he accepted that modifications might be necessary. However, he and Richard saw it as the cheapest method of coping with the Emergency as well as the 'best and perhaps the only method of coping with Communist terrorists once they get into the jungle'. With the government floundering in indecision, and the High Commissioner about to be recalled (as a prelude to dismissal), they hoped someone in authority might see the virtue of their scheme.

The proposal sent to the Chief Secretary might easily have gone astray because sweeping changes were about to overtake the senior echelons of the administration and services. Ten days after the Emergency was declared, Sir Edward Gent flew from Singapore to London, only to be killed in a mid-air collision near Northolt just prior to landing. It would be three months before his successor, Sir Henry Gurney, took over the government from Sir Alec Newboult, the acting head of the administration. Meanwhile, at the outset of the Emergency, Col H.B. Langworthy, Commissioner of Police, had resigned on grounds of ill health, and Maj Gen Sir Charles Boucher, the recently appointed GOC Malaya, had yet to take stock of his command, which was very different from the familiar, conventional large-scale campaigns of the Second World War. Boucher's insouciant prediction that jungle operations in Malaya would be an easy challenge was an unfortunate introduction to the Emergency and scarcely filled old Malaya hands with confidence. Yet, after discussing the Ferret plan informally with the CO (Commanding Officer) of the Malay Regiment, Boucher appeared to be surprisingly enthusiastic. On 6 July it was brought to a meeting at Malaya District HQ, where it was presented as a proposal for the immediate organisation and formation of a Special Jungle Guerrilla Force for offensive anti-insurgent operations in the Federation.

Obviously there were many decisions and arrangements yet to be made, but in principle Ferret Force was given the go-ahead as a combined civil–military initiative with approval for five (later increased to six) operational groups.[6] Two patrols of Gurkhas and two from the Malay Regiment, each of some twenty men, were to be made available for each group. One of John's next moves was to make a list of possible 'bodies' after sounding out former Force 136 colleagues working in Malaya. In mid-July his loyal colleague, Lau Yew Choon, offered his services, the first Chinese to do so. Before the month was out ten ex-Force 136 volunteers had joined.[7] Most were in government posts, and by the beginning of September another dozen Europeans had come forward, including special Chinese and Dyak Liaison Officers.[8] The Army was willing to grant these officers temporary military status for three months initially, provided their civilian employer paid their salaries. In addition, group commanders were gazetted as acting lieutenants-colonel.[9] Some pitfalls remained. As a civilian volunteer John had no decision-making power over the appointment of civilians or their conditions of service: these were settled by the Deputy Chief Secretary and the central Recruiting Authority of the Federal Secretariat in Kuala Lumpur. And although he was the obvious man to lead planning and operations, basic practical decisions, such as siting Ferret Force at the Malay Regiment HQ near Port Dickson, were not in John's hands but were made on grounds of military convenience. The Army appointed an Administrative Commandant responsible for the force's training, assessment of their requirements and for issuing arms and equipment. John was soon to regret not being more fully involved in these matters and admitted it had been a mistake not to involve himself more actively at the planning stage. However, when he met the officer concerned, he was satisfied that the Army took Ferret Force seriously. Lt Col Walter Walker DSO was a man after his own heart, efficient, 'utterly straight', and a man of his word, who had commanded 4/8th Gurkha Rifles in Burma during the war.[10] John was happy to work alongside him.

In early August he and Richard Broome transferred themselves to Ipoh, leaving their families together in Seremban.[11] John was eager to be operational and take his Ferrets into rural Perak, a cauldron of bandit activity. As commander of the first group of Ferrets he had sixty-seven military and civilian personnel under his command, men of the Malay Regiment, Chinese Liaison Officers, signals, transport and medical orderlies. It was a fortnight before his second-in-command arrived, but Capt T.G. Hughes-Parry RE proved a keen and dependable addition to the team.[12] In September they were also joined by a party of Dyaks – skilled jungle trackers from Borneo – and Noel Ross, one of John's many close acquaintances, who was the Dyak Liaison Officer. In accordance with the agreed policy of decentralisation John made his own plans and left the other group commanders to make theirs.

Group No. 1 started by setting up camp in the caves south of Ipoh to straddle the insurgents' main north–south route. John listed his problems. Coming across a group of frightened, awkward aborigines indicated how hard the Ferrets would have to work to woo these people away from Communist influence. John also had technical difficulties with the W/T transmission, a lack of sufficient administrative support staff, an irritating shortage of size 12–13 boots for his Europeans and no cook to prepare the main meal for his men on their return from a twelve-hour march. But he was determined to be positive and in his interim report he assured Walter Walker that 'Morale is very high, surprisingly so in view of the obvious difficulties of cave life and I am very pleased indeed with everyone . . . Come up and see us some time.'[13] Walker noted John's complaints but regretted his inability to produce solutions. He too was bedevilled by staffing problems at headquarters and was frustrated by the inflexibility of his senior officers, who were trying to replace the Dyaks' no. 5 rifles with shotguns, although the Dyak trackers were proving excellent shots with the rifles. But Walker signed off cheerfully with the message, 'Good luck and good hunting.'

Success in hunting down the terrorists, as John knew, depended on a number of qualities and tactics, not least good intelligence, patience, alertness and rapid response. On the advice of friends in Perak CID he left one patrol where they were to keep watch on the caves, and transferred the rest of his group to the prime tin-mining region north of Ipoh, where there had been a number of Communist operations. The Ferrets set up camp a few miles west of Chemor, a notorious area. It was on the Chemor–Jelapang road that the general manager of the Muru tin mine, Ian Ogilvie, was murdered by eight CTs at the beginning of August. The first notable Ferret contact came when nine men of No. 1 Malay Patrol tracked a party of forty CTs through the night as they returned from another tin-mine attack. The Ferrets crept to within 10yds of a sentry post before the alarm was given. Screened by the dark the CTs fled, leaving behind a substantial quantity of ammunition and equipment. John was delighted and reported on the 'sterling qualities' of his Malays.

In the next five weeks his patrols carried out continuous forays along the jungle foothills in scrub and shoulder-high grass, searching for signs of enemy habitation and laying ambushes at strategic points. At Sungei Perlu they found a new bandit camp built on a wartime site. In the vicinity stood a lookout post camouflaged by high trees and huts for fifteen to twenty terrorists, which John concluded were used for night stopovers by special service units or killer squads. The camp and huts were burned to prevent their future use by the terrorists. Group No. 1's most serious engagement, however, took place in September, when three patrols of Ferrets searched behind Kampong Jalong for the bandit camp of No. 9 Patrol of the 5th (Perak) Regiment. En route to their destination they discovered four men hiding in huts whom they arrested for questioning. Later, after disturbing a lookout post, the Gurkha and Malay patrols gave chase through jungle until they reached a clearing where they came under persistent Bren and rifle fire. Well-screened by undergrowth, John estimated the terrorists as being of similar strength to his Ferrets. It was evident that the Communists were staging a planned rearguard action to enable their leaders and the occupants of the main camp to get away. While crossing a stream, A.G. Robertson, in charge of the Malays, was lucky to escape injury; the shots slightly wounded his scout. The opposition was persistent but John had no doubts the enemy would be dislodged. In fact the action lasted about forty-five minutes, and when the camp was abandoned the Ferrets were able to search the site for clues to add to the growing body of intelligence about the terrorists. John concluded that Kampong Jalong consisted of two camps, an established site used by No. 9 Patrol and a new one belonging to the recently displaced No. 3 (Tikus) Patrol. The Ferrets also picked up a quantity of equipment, clothing and a shotgun, and on another search a rocky hideout yielded Communist propaganda leaflets and trade union receipt books. There was evidence that here and in many areas, squatters and terrorists were living cheek by jowl with one another, indicating considerable collusion.

The last important find north of Ipoh occurred in early November, when Malay and Gurkha patrols of Group No. 6 under Richard Broome's command, searching in precipitous country a mile inside the jungle, discovered a major training camp and rifle range capable of accommodating 100 insurgents. In the next two days intermittent contact resulted in casualties on both sides but the Communists were finally routed when screaming Gurkhas charged after them into the jungle. This and other episodes were reported in *The Times*: 'We were given a terrific press,' John told his parents. Maj Gen Boucher publicly explained the purpose of Ferret Force and applauded its considerable achievement in striking at enemy morale. John was satisfied they had 'achieved a measure of quiet success both in organisation and operations', though he had doubts about whether this would be fully appreciated in all quarters.

His hunch was close to the mark. Even while praising the work of the Ferrets Boucher had already for some time decided to disband the force and warned John in a personal letter that reached him just as the press published its plaudits. The contents made John bristle. In a change of strategy each Ferret group would be phased out at the conclusion of its three months' enlistment, the last at the end of November.[14] On reflection, John admitted, 'We were fighting a losing battle from the first owing to the inexcusable failure of the government to release to us the officers we needed – in fact they gave us nine of a promised thirty – but the end was almost indecently hastened by our jack-in-the-box little general, who got over-excited about us in the beginning and then decided to write us off after only six weeks because we had not won his war for him.'

In his reply to Boucher John staunchly defended Ferret Force. 'Ferrets never failed as a military proposition,' and their continuing value was obvious, he insisted. The reason for winding them up was 'entirely the Government's failure to give support to recruitment'.[15] He did not mention a private concern, that as fresh troops arrived – and 2 Guards Brigade with 2nd Coldstream Guards, 3rd Grenadier Guards and 2nd Scots Guards, landed in Singapore in early October – the Army would want to keep civilians out of the frame. But the final blow to Ferret Force was dealt by Boucher when he decided to move Lt Col Walker to become Commandant of the new Jungle Warfare Wing of the FARELF Training Centre in Johore.

Nevertheless, Ferret Force had set certain precedents. In the coming months John pushed for the creation of police jungle squads and Chinese assault squads based on Ferret lines. The use of aboriginal trackers and of small infantry patrols became standard practice in jungle warfare. Ferret Force also inspired the Security Service's deep jungle operations in the 1950s. 'Ferreting', Boucher told John, 'will in future be done by a Ferret Company in every battalion or equivalent unit', which would be composed as far as possible of ex-Ferret Force personnel, and a Civil Liaison Corps would be recruited to assist the Army. At this stage John and Richard were invited by the general to assess the impact of the Ferrets. Boucher may not have expected John's terse observation that 'Army Ferrets' would not work. As to why, John forecast that 'Civil Liaison' would not attract appropriate recruits. 'Liaison and talk is not as interesting as operations and command. There will be the fear of being submerged by ignorant military personnel. The Civil Liaison Corps will not have the glamour of a "special force".' To sum up, 'The major difficulty will be twisting a war machine into a police job.' Instead, it was better to train special operations professionals: 'Professional ferrets must be used against professional bandits.'

John was pushing his luck. He must have known that generals would consider regular soldiers to be 'the professionals' and would not take kindly to advice from an ex-policeman-cum-irregular soldier. However, the Army had its own solution. To avoid closing the matter on a sour note, in the next round of public honours John received recognition for Ferret Force by being officially 'Mentioned in Despatches'.

From the disbandment of Ferret Force John's career seemed to be in the melting pot. With bluff paternalism Maj Gen Boucher had assured him in September that he had a key role to play in the Emergency. 'I do not know whether the Chief Secretary has written to you on these lines, but for your personal information, he is anxious to secure your services to run Chinese interrogation, which is at present very backward and needs someone of your calibre to take hold of it.' The key problem was the acute shortage of Chinese speakers, so in addition to police duties (except during active jungle service) John reverted to the role of intelligence officer, interrogating detainees or surrendered enemy personnel and interpreting captured documents. He knew the importance of this work: 'The SEP [surrendered enemy personnel] should be the most valuable anti-bandit weapon in existence. He is a mine of "direct action" information, history and local knowledge.'

However, committed as he was to intelligence work, John had no desire to be tied down to one field of activity. By some discreet string-pulling he managed to talk his way into a tailor-made post, combining military and police liaison duties. 'I float around as a sort of Adviser giving advice where it is not wanted,' he wrote, tongue-in-cheek. The advantage of this temporary job was its flexibility. In the early days of the Emergency poor communications between police and military hindered effective operations against the bandits. Called in as mediator, John could point to a specific area where the Security Forces should be working together. 'Police/Military penetration of the Telom, Bertam and Lemoi valleys is very overdue,' he advised officers in charge of the Gurkhas and Coldstream Guards, the OSPC Tapah and the Head of Special Branch collectively. Otherwise, he carried out on-the-spot assessments, assisted the police jungle squad in their strategies to win over the *orang asli* and met military commanders who were generally glad to have the benefit of his intimate knowledge of their operational patch. He made regular journeys to the local headquarters of the King's Own Yorkshire Light Infantry, the Coldstream Guards and 2/2nd Gurkha Rifles, particularly after a terrorist incident, when he was often able to advise on known bandit routes and on which trouble spots to concentrate searches.[16]

Warnings had come to John in mid-October of an impending escalation with well-conducted attacks on the military at Sungei Siput and Bidor. His cross-examination of two deserters enabled John to compile a dossier on the notorious killer squad, Lit Yong's Assault Company, who had been terrorising the Sungei Siput area.[17] The commander, Lit Yong, had commanded No. 4 Patrol of the 5th (Perak) Regiment of the MPAJA (the Kampar–Gopeng district) at the end of the Second World War and had taken over command of the MPABA in Perak at the start of the Emergency. His second-in-command of the Assault Company was Khek Fung, who had held the same role in No. 4 Patrol. The Assault Company was formed at Tanjong Rambutan from the elite of the Central Perak Anti-British Army, with the aim of carrying out major attacks on government forces, initially covering the Lintang–Jalong district. The group was 84 men strong and was armed with seven Bren guns, seven Stens, eleven Tommy guns, a trench mortar and a good supply of small arms and ammunition. John was able to compose a nominal roll of the Assault Company and to establish their movements between December 1948 and February 1949. They were in the rear of the main body of the Perak MPABA when they took action against 2/2nd Gurkha Rifles, who were tailing them. Two ambushes were set for patrols of 2/2nd Gurkha Rifles. The first on Christmas Eve was on the infamous Lintang road, the scene of the Sungei Siput murders back in June, and yielded valuable guns and ammunition to the killer squad. The second ambush, on the equally desolate Jalong road, left six of Lit Yong's men dead and two wounded, but the Assault Company carried on to Kuah in the remote Korbu valley. In January, however, the Assault

Company was having increasing difficulty securing and transporting food supplies. The decision had been made to withdraw the Perak MPABA eastwards across the central range into the wild jungle of Ulu Nenggiri, in southern Kelantan. After Lit Yong and his men decamped on 21 January, the Gurkhas struck back, making wide sweeps above the valley, exposing the two large Communist mountain camps at Kuah and Yong Yap, each capable of housing 150 men. But the terrorists had melted into the jungle. It is unclear whether Lit Yong and his men were making ultimately for the town of Gua Musang, which had assumed the elevated status of 'a liberated area', since it was seized and held for five days by the MPABA in July. An alternative refuge, John reckoned, was the area round the source of the Telom, east of the Cameron Highlands: he advocated more penetration of that region by military patrols. Another curious piece of intelligence he elicited was that Lit Yong's wife travelled with the main MPABA party. John had no knowledge of the subsequent fate of Lit Yong, and there was no further information on the Assault Company in his file, but according to Chin Peng himself, he was killed in action early in the Emergency in Kelantan.[18]

By December 1948 the number of terrorist attacks had dipped while the Communists began their re-grouping in Kelantan or West Pahang. There was some optimism among the British that the measures put in place since the declaration of the Emergency in June – the expansion of the Security Forces, especially of special constables, the Emergency Regulations and National Identity Card scheme, and tough military measures to punish those Chinese suspected of being insurgents (as in the shooting of villagers at Batang Kali) – were giving the initiative to the government. John felt that the Communist leadership headed by Chin Peng had underestimated Britain's counter-insurgency capacity. With official bulletins detailing a lull in bandit activity during December, he sensed the time was ripe for fresh government action. If Chin Peng was willing to enter into dialogue with John, then John would broker a face-saving arrangement with the British authorities.

He first broached the idea of a direct approach in strictest confidence with Jim Hannah, who was a regular house-guest at the Davises' house in Ipoh. Hannah was also one of the small band of Britons who knew the Chinese leader personally. While accepting the chances of his old ally taking the bait were probably slim, it seemed a case of nothing venture, nothing win. But he needed official clearance to take the idea further. On 21 December John dropped a note to his Special Branch contact, Ian Wylie, at CID HQ. Two days after Christmas Wylie sent a cautious but quietly encouraging reply. 'If it worked it could definitely be made into something,' he told John, 'possibly on the old Chang Hung lines – which would suit us down to the socks.' Wylie assumed that John was planning to repeat Special Branch's brilliant coup of the 1930s when they had planted Lai Tek – alias Chang Hung – as a British agent, contrived his election as Secretary-General of the MCP and secured a unique source of regular, often invaluable, intelligence. John took Wylie's response to be official approval for putting feelers out to Chin Peng. He had already decided on a simple, friendly letter, unconditional and without recrimination. The outcome was difficult to predict. John wrote to Chin on New Year's Eve 1948:

Dear Chin

I have heard nothing from you for some time now and am wondering what has happened to you. I can only guess that you may feel it better to keep out of the way during the Emergency in view of your wartime connection with the MPAJA. It does seem a great pity however that our old friendship should be broken due in circumstances which are outside both our control and I should be very pleased indeed if you will write me a letter telling me how you are so that our connections may not be broken. I am sending this through your relatives as I have no address of yours.

Yours sincerely,
John Davis[19]

John waited patiently for some weeks but there was no reply. He was not to know that Chin Peng and a small band of bodyguards had just embarked on a five-month jungle trek from the Cameron Highlands to new party headquarters 10 miles east of Mentekab.[20] Out of touch with the world, it is questionable whether he ever saw John's letter. In fact the first communication John received regarding Chin Peng was a letter from E.C.S. Adkins, the SCA in Singapore, in March 1949.

This contained information that must have aroused John's suspicions. On 22 December 1948 Maj Wu Chye Sin OBE, alias Ah Ng, leader of the

Dragons on John's first 'Gustavus' operation, had approached a Malayan Civil Service officer named G.W. Webb in Singapore with a bold suggestion that was uncannily like John's in general substance and timing. John never discovered if he had picked up hints from Hannah, but Wu Chye Sin offered the use of his good offices to the government to contact Chin Peng. Claiming to know the wartime Communist leaders intimately, Wu Chye Sin suggested that through his agents 'we should do a deal with the bandit leaders . . . if they could be brought into the fold and given some sort of jobs the whole trouble might be cleared up very quickly and a lot of money saved'. He assumed the Communist leaders could be bought if they were offered big enough bribes in the form of lucrative posts. A deal was patently preferable to death in action or by judicial sentence, and if no deal were done, it was Wu Chye Sin's opinion that the Emergency 'would drag on for years'.

Meanwhile, Webb had gone on home leave. In his absence there was no response to Wu Chye Sin's proposal until February 1949, when a version of the interview somehow reached the ears of the Governor of Singapore and the Colonial Secretary. Their reaction was almost manic. This was a matter 'of the greatest importance', no less than 'a scheme to end the Emergency'. From their offices frantic telephone messages were sent to Adkins, the SCA, asking for elucidation. He took the matter just as seriously. He had always believed that if the government had been more generous to the MPAJA veterans, many would never have joined the MPABA. If those veterans, together with the labour leaders who were persuaded by propaganda to support the Party, could be prised from the terrorist ranks by offers of fair terms, only a hard core of ideologues and gangsters would have opposed the British. Yet Adkins was clearly puzzled why Wu Chye Sin had never broached John directly, but had sought a sympathetic hearing in Singapore. Was it, he wondered, because John Davis knew too much about this man?[21] Be that as it may, Adkins was told towards the end of March 1949 to contact John and arrange to fly to Ipoh to brief him. The authorities were intent on passing the buck, he warned John, and had ordered him 'to put the whole matter in your hands'. Their meeting was brief but useful, and shortly afterwards Adkins sent John a copy of Wu Chye Sin's original statement, which had just arrived by air from Webb. It was now up to John to interview Wu Chye Sin and make it clear that he was officially pre-empting his interference in the matter.

On 6 April John questioned his former 'Gustavus' colleague at length, going over his statement with a fine-tooth comb. Wu Chye Sin repeated that the only way to halt the Emergency was through a treaty with the Communist leaders. He claimed to be able to contact them and felt hopeful because Chin Peng was 'a good man'. The sole obstacle was the British commitment to the death sentence for all terrorists. Would the authorities compromise on this? John parried by indicating that the government was not simply set on stopping the rebellion but on crushing Communism by destroying morale at the grass roots: 'snowballing surrenders from bottom up'. The government itself would not negotiate. However, if any of the leaders wished to make contact, John insisted it should be done in his name – with Wu Chye Sin perhaps acting as his agent to make arrangements. After several days Wu Chye Sin came back to report his lack of success to his superior. It came as no surprise, for John was sceptical from the start that Wu Chye Sin could persuade Chin Peng to default, but he informed Adkins, 'I will keep the line open through Wu Chye Sin – just in case.'

There was a short postscript to this wild-card attempt to end the Emergency. Some months later, in December 1949, John reported an alleged sighting to Claude Fenner of the Federal Special Branch. 'A contact of Jim Hannah says that he saw CTP [Chin Peng] in King Street, Penang, one day about a month ago. CTP was on the pavement and the contact did not speak to him as he was passing in a car. This information was given quite casually as the contact had no idea of the significance of CTP. It may therefore be true.'[22] It was known that Chin Peng had family connections in Penang and had visited the island in the past, but ensconced in the fastnesses of Pahang, with communications inhibited by the Security Forces, it seemed inherently unlikely that he would have risked crossing the western plain and the Penang Straits. That was the last purported link with Chin Peng until 1955. For the rest of the insurgency he remained as elusive as the Scarlet Pimpernel.

Chapter 14

Chinese Affairs

The arrival in Malaya in October 1948 of Gent's successor, Sir Henry Gurney, brought hopes of progress in the conduct of the Emergency. Although he lacked previous experience of Malaya, Gurney was shrewd, intelligent and humane, all qualities that John Davis respected. In turn, he found John an exceptional officer, a fluent Cantonese speaker with a rare understanding of the Chinese and brimming with ideas and the energy and determination to implement them.

John regarded the Emergency as a Chinese phenomenon brought on by a total loss of confidence on the part of the Chinese community in the British colonial system. After the old custodial machinery of the Chinese Protectorate was abolished and the Federation Agreement abandoned the Chinese to the status of second-class citizens, Malayan Chinese were convinced 'we [the British] intend to hand over the government to the Malays within ten years – and who will dare say they are wrong?'[1] Yet even assuming, as John did, that the Communists would be defeated, half a million Chinese remained to pose another challenge to the administration. Here was a rootless fringe society, 'a vast unabsorbed and not understood rural population who have never seen the government, have no interest or confidence in it and couldn't care less about it', but needed to be controlled: a situation encapsulated in the expression, 'the squatter problem'.

Chinese squatters were a by-product of the 1930s slump, but during the Japanese Occupation their number had greatly increased as thousands fled from the towns to find refuge in and around the jungle. They survived by growing food under the hidden eye of the MPAJA. After the Liberation many stayed with their families on the jungle margins or the periphery of mines, estates and forest reserves. They grew vegetables and cash crops or picked up work as tin or rubber labourers. The majority were young and uneducated. Many were disaffected and would obey whoever could enforce obedience, a situation that the MCP could usefully exploit because, as John put it, 'the Communist knows them, has studied them, speaks their language and in many cases is related to them'. And 'showing their true satanic colours', the Communists used propaganda and coercion to extract money and food supplies and 'twist the . . . sentiments of the squatters into a feeling of hatred and antagonism' towards the authorities.[2] In effect, the Emergency forced the Malayan government to bring the squatters under its control, and the solution devised was a system of transfer and resettlement. As one of the earliest advocates of the policy John played a significant part in planning, advising and assessing a historic process that would transform Malaya's socio-economic profile.

Before the end of 1948 John was tipped off by David Gray of the Federal Labour Department that he would be front-runner for a new Chinese Affairs post in Perak. The High Commissioner was sufficiently concerned about the squatter issue to set up a special Federal advisory body in December, which John was invited to join.[3] Chaired by the Chief Secretary, it was to examine the facts, recommend the main outlines of a resettlement policy (taking account of the thorny legal issues of land tenure and illegal occupation) and advise the government on necessary legislation.[4] Gurney also asked each State government to investigate its particular squatter problem and put forward recommendations that he hoped would result in a uniform countrywide policy. John undertook to prepare a specification for a Squatter Settlement Officer under the Federal SCA, to be responsible for the success of federal policy and to secure the confidence and cooperation of State governments.[5] Those close to him at home would recognise the high expectations behind his jocular modesty.

For some time now I have been talking 'big' about the squatter problem, and I have recently been told . . . I am to settle the squatter problem in Perak! It serves me damn well right, of course, for talking too much. I went down to K.L. to ask them what I was to do and was told that it was for me to tell them that! So now I am to learn how to fail gracefully. The only spark of light is that at the same time I have been put on a 'squatter' committee for the

Federation, where I can continue to talk 'big' and help formulate the policy
which I know I cannot carry out.

Perak was a special case among the Malay states in that half its population
was Chinese – 50 per cent, compared with 40 per cent of Malays. The state
had pioneered a pre-war scheme for squatter *padi*-planters and in November
1948 resettled pro-Communist squatters from the Sungei Siput area at
Pantai Remis in the Dindings. But in observing the Perak situation John
knew the squatter problem would not be easily resolved. Political tension
between the State and Federal authorities, galvanised by antagonism over
the Malayan Union, was on the increase over matters of procedure and
State rights. Most of all, the governing Malay elite distanced themselves
and their State governments from responsibility for the terrorists, believing
that the onus for all aspects of the Emergency, including the Chinese
squatters, lay with the Federal government. Gurney, on the other hand,
thought the State governments were failing to cooperate with the Federal
government and were over-indulgent to Malay interests, to the detriment
of the Chinese or Indians. All the while, to sustain the war against the
Communist insurgency the High Commissioner and the Federal authorities
were carrying an impossible financial burden of Straits $250,000 per day
by 1948–9.

Meanwhile, a separate Perak Squatter Committee was set up to decide
on state policy.[6] Although John was a member of both this and the
Federal committee, the chairman was the forceful Malay Mentri Besar
(Chief Minister), Dato Panglima Bukit Gantang, who later left the UMNO to
lead the Perak National Party, and instinctively favoured the Malays over
the Chinese. John had no doubt that the Federal Squatter Report, which
appeared in January 1949, would not suit the Malays, 'who want to use
fire and sword against all Chinese'. In fact, it was John's misfortune to take
charge of Chinese affairs when an ambitious politician from the Malay elite
dominated Perak, and solutions to the integration of the Chinese squatters
into Malayan society were being hindered by Malay procrastination and by
the complacency or intransigence of British officials.

While he waited for news of the post in Chinese Affairs, John was keen
to try out an idea he had devised of enlisting 'ordinary Chinese' to share
the responsibility of defending their own community. He worked out
a prototype for anti-terrorist operations: the Chinese Assault Squad, a

15-man unit of Chinese special constables, tough types from the Sungei Siput mines, including some with KMT or Triad connections. Command of the first squad went to John Litton, a Chinese-speaking Malayan Civil Service cadet and one of John's former Ferret Force colleagues. After some obstruction in the Federal Secretariat the squad was ready by the end of January for undercover operations. Their orders were to regain control of the tin-mining area of Kinta, which had been virtually lost to the Communists since the start of the Emergency. For its intelligence-gathering operations they disguised themselves as terrorists, infiltrated the scattered squatter camps to elicit information and acted as *agents provocateurs* to identify members of the Min Yuen, the support organisation of the MRLA. Unfortunately, Litton's squad were just proving themselves when he was transferred to China. For some weeks his men languished, until an experienced European sergeant took charge and revived morale and discipline. After their intelligence work was praised by the Federal SCA, four more squads of ex-KMT guerrillas were raised in 1949 and drafted to Grik to protect northern Perak from Communist forces.

In the meantime, on 1 February John was transferred officially from the Labour Department to Chinese Affairs. Shortly afterwards he received the all-clear to undertake the organisation of a Squatter Office within the Perak State Secretariat in Ipoh, with a brief for 'policy, propaganda, advice and general supervision from the Chinese point of view'.[7] In addition to a clerk and an interpreter, he was promised the assistance of two high-calibre, Chinese-speaking officers. Given the shortage of Chinese speakers throughout the administration, John contacted his excellent former assistant, Lau Yew Choon, inviting him confidentially to be Chinese Affairs Officer in Ipoh. Lau agreed, only to find his secondment from the Civil Liaison Corps was blocked by other Malayan Civil Service officers. John had to fight his corner with terrier-like persistence, and it was only after a fortuitous meeting with Gurney that his staffing crisis was resolved. As a Chinese Affairs Officer for Perak Lau Yew Choon proved a considerable asset in the drive to integrate the Chinese into rural society, helping to win over the influential Chinese to establish citizens' committees in country areas, a public relations task he performed with tact and efficiency.

The High Commissioner had responded to John's appeal partly because he was concerned at the apparent failure of the states to implement the Federal Squatter Report. In May 1949 Gurney asked the State governments and British Advisers to make squatter resettlement their first priority, but John found the Mentri Besar increasingly uncooperative. He was alarmed, too, by the latter's apparent desire to orchestrate Chinese affairs himself.[8] The minister ignored opportunities for a proper investigation and discussion of the squatter solution for which John had been appointed. As to the land question, John felt the Perak State government was reluctant to issue Temporary Occupation Licences to squatters and was far more interested in the problem (of squatters occupying Malay reservations) for political rather than for security reasons. Underlining his unease in graphic terms, John wrote with a degree of bitterness, 'At present I feel very much a squatter on a Malay reserve.'[9]

There was another reason for unease in the British community after the middle of 1949, signs that the conduct of the Emergency had run into a stalemate. Even some of John's earlier certainty had waned. The Communists had successfully exploited incidents involving unarmed squatters and the Security Forces to play on the fears of the Chinese community. In addition, the prospect of a Communist victory over the Nationalists in China's civil war had undoubtedly raised MCP morale and reinforced the spectre of Communism as a dynamic force in the Far East.

In John's view a reassessment of the government's approach to the Chinese in Malaya was certainly needed. He had discussed the situation endlessly with colleagues, and after attending a conference of Chinese-speaking officers on 14 August he worked on a personal analysis of the Emergency with a strategy to win over the Chinese people. 'The new approach must cover a much wider field' than security operations, he argued. Government must be brought to the rural population. 'The objective is now not so much the crushing of the rebellion but the settling of the whole question of the government, welfare and future of the Malayan Chinese Community. In order to obtain the new perspective H[is] E[xcellency] must widen his sources of information and redistribute the balance between "security" and "administration".' Passing this idea on to Oliver Wolters as 'roughed up' stuff, John could not have foreseen that in less than a year it would become a basic tenet of the so-called Briggs Plan.

At this point a call came from the Chinese Secretariat in Kuala Lumpur that the High Commissioner wanted to see John at 11 a.m. on 23 September 1949. Twelve days earlier the Communists had shown their contempt for the Federal government by attacking the railway town of

Kuala Krau with a force of 300 men. Gurney had to admit 'things are not going too well' and new initiatives were needed. John was being offered a rare chance to expound his ideas on the Emergency direct to His Excellency rather than through the Secretariat. Wolters had incorporated John's thinking into a collective memorandum, 'A review of the civilian and operational aspects of the Emergency'. The Chief Secretary accepted it and urged the High Commissioner to discuss it further with John and others in Kuala Lumpur. As a result, a request came from the High Commissioner for an outline structure for the Chinese community's involvement in anti-bandit operations. John responded with a three-phase rolling plan of 'Self-Protection' for the rural Chinese.[10]

However, after a month of government silence John's patience wore thin. He learned from the CPO (Chief Police Officer) Perak that his proposals on Chinese assault squads had not yet been approved by Nicol Gray, the controversial Commissioner of Police. He challenged the police chief to tell him what advice he should give officers administering 'difficult' areas. This was passed off as a rhetorical question: no answer came.

The Federal authorities knew their Chinese policy was adrift. 'The whole problem of the future of Chinese Affairs wants thinking out afresh,' Gurney told the Chief Secretary on 22 October for the umpteenth time, as he sought ideas from the SCA, Edward D. Fleming. At Fleming's request John, with other Chinese speakers, addressed the problem of structure with another memorandum, which went to the Federal chiefs on 4 November. They recommended the creation in the framework of each State administration an SCA post, a China-trained State officer with recognised authority as a member of the EXCO (State Executive Council) and as Chairman of the State Chinese Advisory Board. He should advise the State government and State officers on Chinese Affairs, as well as assisting State and District Officers to train Chinese officers attached to District Officers. The Chinese Affairs Department in Kuala Lumpur should remain, the secretary serving as Adviser on Chinese Affairs to the Federal government. Fleming moved fast to incorporate this paper into his department's official response to the High Commissioner's request.

A few days later John found himself at a top-level meeting at King's House in Kuala Lumpur to discuss the future of Chinese policy.[11] Approval was given to the setting up of Chinese Affairs branches under a senior Chinese-speaking officer in Johore, Perak, Selangor and Pahang. To John's probable relief 'it was agreed that Mr J.H.L. Davis should be Secretary for Chinese Affairs in Perak'. His only awkward moment came when Graham Black, the compliant British Adviser, warned that the title might not be acceptable in Perak, obliquely referring to the political sensitivities of the Mentri Besar. However, John was less interested in political niceties than in progress on the ground. In the run-up to Christmas he immersed himself in plans for Chinese Affairs branches in each state. Again he pressed the case for high-calibre Federal recruits for the posts of Chinese Affairs Officers and Junior Chinese Affairs Officers. In parts of rural Perak there was a desperate need for officers to deal with squatters, he told Perak's Malay State Secretary, and there was no time to lose to get new structures in place.

In January 1950 the Emergency slipped into a new phase of Communist activity, marked by the overall doubling of government, Security Forces and civilian casualties. In addition, the Communists were buoyant when early in the same month the Labour government in Britain gave official recognition to the People's Republic of China. It was not just the expatriate British who were incensed, but the whole anti-Communist Malayan community, as fears were voiced of a weakened war effort and an influx of Communist consuls into Malaya. John offered a partial solution. 'I do think that a particularly violent anti-Communist effort both on the political and military front should be planned . . . in order to jerk the Chinese back into line again.'[12] Edward Fleming, the SCA, took his suggestion seriously, confirming to John that 'a violent anti-bandit effort is being planned'. The 'effort' was an Anti-Bandit Month campaign launched in February–March 1950 to rally the Chinese and the country's opposition to the Communist cause.

Fleming was not the only senior officer to call on John for help with Emergency initiatives. From the Defence Department came a request for ideas for improving the training of the Security Forces for 'rooting out and destroying bandit gangs – and anything else you think important, such as psychological warfare, would be of immense value'.[13] The Defence Secretary wrote for advice on the treatment of surrendered enemy personnel held at Batu Gajah Gaol. After inspecting the detainees John sent in a full report with his recommendations. The Federal Economic Secretary wrote personally about the government's draft Development Plan.[14] The CID continued to call on John to interrogate Chinese suspected of having sensitive information. Even when he was home on leave he was asked by the Colonial Office to brief Hugh Carleton Greene of the BBC on Chinese matters, before Greene's secondment to the Malayan government to advise on anti-Communist propaganda.

Squatter issues, however, remained John's central concern. To his chagrin, unnecessary dilly-dallying delayed the EXCO's acceptance of the Perak Squatter Committee's report and scotched hopes of starting to implement their Resettlement Plan until after the Anti-Bandit Month, by which time he expected to be out of the country.

Problems tended to interact. The fifty-three citizens' committees set up in Perak were in serious need of protection, particularly those in areas of Communist activity. John advised the CPO Perak, John Barnard, to station a Chinese jungle squad in the area, but little had been done when a fresh Communist assault began in February 1950. Besides the burning down of Simpang Tiga, there were three murders and three armed hold-ups in broad daylight within a few miles of Ipoh. One of the dead was a Chinese citizens' committee member; and seven committees in the area remained completely unprotected. With a shortfall in troops and police, the logic for John lay 'in arming the good Chinese (Auxiliary Police) against the bad (CTs)'. He pressed Edward Fleming hard on the matter of Chinese self-protection, reminding him of his earlier scheme, which was stillborn because John dared to push for higher pay for the Chinese.

When Fleming raised the idea of Special Chinese Squads again, Gurney offered to meet John the next day at Ipoh aerodrome to discuss the issue. John suggested to Gurney an interim target of 50–100 men and an optimum number of 300. All in all, he was greatly encouraged by their discussion. The High Commissioner gave his approval to the Special Chinese Squads, subject to Barnard's agreement, and to top up funding of salaries by the Chinese community.[15] When Barnard agreed to the establishment of three or four Chinese squads for the Ipoh area, and the prominent Chinese politician, Leong Yew Koh, representing the Chinese, approved the raising of extra revenue by a special cess, the vital provision for self-protection was finally in sight. There were now grounds to hope that the first operations of Perak's resettlement plans would begin in March, provided, that is, that the State government would guarantee the appointment of several Junior Chinese Affairs Officers to assist the District Officers. The District Officers themselves were at the ready, and John assured them that 'we hope shortly to be faced with a heavy programme of squatter settlement'.[16] Preoccupied with launching the squatter operations, John was totally unprepared for the blow conveyed the next day by Barnard.

John's proposal for up to 300 Chinese recruits was turned down flat, as were jungle squads made up 100 per cent of Chinese; instead, a limit of 25 per cent Chinese was to be applied to any squad. Barnard confirmed this was not his decision but a political judgement based on fear of Chinese defections to Communism. John was livid, suspecting immediately the hand of the Commissioner of Police, Nicol Gray. He was scathing about the limit of Chinese personnel of squads to 25 per cent, and writing to the SCA, he asserted: 'Such squads will be quite useless because . . . unless the Chinese influence in the squad is dominant they will not be able to gain the confidence of the Chinese population which is the main reason for their formation. In any event I do not wish to have any hand in recruiting policemen who will be suspect as potential traitors.'[17] Amid the flurry of communications reaching and leaving the Squatter Office was a note from the High Commissioner agreeing 'this is wrong'. Gurney supported John by minuting the Commissioner of Police that he should have been consulted.[18] Reading the rebuke in the High Commissioner's hand, John felt vindicated, but only partly mollified. Gurney, of course, wanted to resolve the fiasco without undermining his own or his officers' authority.

John had mixed feelings as he looked back over the previous fifteen months. In personal terms he and Helen had many good memories of this first postwar tour.[19] Yet no matter how stimulating it was to deal in turn with different sectors – the Army, the police, the Civil Service, Chinese of varying socio-economic backgrounds and Malay officials – it tended to be frustrating and irritating in the end, and the prospect of imminent home leave became extremely attractive. Before that, however, John had been asked to speak on Radio Malaya for the Anti-Bandit Month initiative and since it was a chance to publicise the plans for squatter resettlement, the hottest topic of the Emergency, he agreed to do so. On 4 March he recorded his talk. When it was broadcast a fortnight later he and his family were on the high seas and Perak's Chinese Affairs were in the experienced hands of Noel Alexander. Meanwhile, the direction of the Emergency, and the implementation of the squatter policy in particular, would become the responsibility of a new Director of Operations, Lt Gen Sir Harold Briggs.

❖ ❖ ❖

John's absence from the Malayan scene coincided with the most significant time since the Japanese surrender in 1945. All hopes were resting on the success of the Briggs Plan to end the insurgency and settle the Chinese problem once and for all. Briggs came with a high reputation as a commander in the Burma campaign, but he was charged with a civilian role under Gurney, that of coordinating the efforts of the Security Forces and the civil administration. Shortly after the introduction of the Briggs Plan, war broke out in June 1950 between the two Republics of North and South Korea, which escalated when the United States intervened to back the South and China supported the North. Initially Malayans were fearful that this was the beginning of another phase of Communist expansion, but as events turned out 'there was a brilliant silver lining to this particular dark cloud'.[20] The war produced an insatiable demand for raw materials, including Malaya's two prime commodities, rubber and tin. This prompted an immediate rise in prices and created, in the medium term, a phenomenal economic boom. It was the massive funding made possible by the prodigious profits of the Korean War that financed Briggs's ambitious plan and ultimately enabled it to succeed.

John was alerted to this sudden swing of fortune when their luxury liner called at Colombo on the way back to Malaya. The Federal Establishment Office had left messages that after disembarking at Singapore he was to call at squatter settlements in Johore and Negri Sembilan on his way back to Ipoh to take up his old position. The latter would imply a substantial commitment to squatter resettlement, but there was no indication of advanced plans for a State Chinese Affairs Department, John noted, nor mention of an SCA. Instead, he was told, 'Much water has flowed under bridges since your departure on leave, and the conception of the squatter resettlement has radically altered. More important, the Federal Government is now prepared to make available for the purpose funds to an amount previously undreamt of.'[21]

Lt Gen Briggs's first innovation was to separate the running of the Emergency from the civil administration. A hierarchy of war cabinets was established at District, State and Federal levels, machinery that would bypass normal channels of administration. Another early directive reinforced all the staffing recommendations that John had pushed urgently before his leave. At State level there would be Chinese Affairs Officers responsible to the State and to the Federal SCA, and at District level, Junior

Chinese Affairs Officers under the State SCA and District Officers. The main
innovation, however, was the resettlement of the squatters. The programme
was essentially a team effort, John maintained, a view endorsed by an ADO
in South Perak who was himself actively involved.[22] 'The Briggs Plan was
in essence a tidying-up and refinement of what had already been in many
minds' and could only have been devised with a wealth of assistance from
experienced police and administrative officers, including Chinese experts.[23]

The squatter resettlement process began in earnest in June 1950 while
John was home on leave but it was still at a basic stage when he returned
to Malaya. The transfer of villagers over long distances had fallen out of
favour: the aim was to re-group squatters reasonably close to their original
homes and workplaces. The new settlements of *atap*-roofed huts were
protected by high wire fencing and police posts, and later by Home Guards,
and regularised by government officers. Under Briggs the process became
a series of well-organised, joint civil–military operations. Many additions
and refinements would be made over time, one of the most crucial, in
January 1951, being the introduction of food controls to deprive terrorists
of supplies from the Min Yuen.

John in the meantime was back on the road – so his diary for 1950
confirms – sorting out problems, meeting squatters, attending the Perak
State War Executive Committee (SWEC) and the Chinese Advisory Board
meeting. The young ADO, Mike McConville, newly 'immersed in shifting
squatters', remembered the cheerful figure of John Davis driving down
from Ipoh frequently, but unlike some officious visitors, he was always very
welcome and extremely helpful. Before the end of 1950 the Davis family
was allocated a pleasant family-size house in Garland Road, Ipoh. It suited
their needs admirably, especially after the birth of William John Ouin Davis,
on 21 January 1951. As his fortieth birthday drew near, John summed up
his good fortune: 'a nice house, good friends and now a son'.

Among their new friends was Rex Madoc, CO of the Royal Marines in
Ipoh, whose brother Guy Madoc had been a close friend since he and John
sailed out together in 1930–1. The Royal Marines' CO in Kampar was
another keen walker and supplied bodyguards for Sunday excursions. To
John walking was not a simple matter of taking exercise: British credibility,
he believed, required British officers to be seen outside the confines of
the towns. Rowland Oakeley recalled an occasion when John persuaded
him 'to go on a "show the flag" walk and lent him a rifle'. After driving

to Gopeng, the pair 'walked [several miles] back through smallholdings with a few squatters to the main road, accompanied by large numbers of headmen with shotguns and special police with rifles'. It was not a very interesting walk – they saw no bandits – but, concluded Oakeley, 'One has confidence in John that he knows what he is doing', and repeatedly luck was on his side.[24] On another occasion the Davises were on their way to Parit for Sunday lunch with ADO John Loch and his wife Daphne when a bus behind their car was targeted by terrorists. The two Johns, with a posse of police, gave chase, but after a further exchange of fire the CTs fled from a Davis frontal assault.[25]

The security situation was deteriorating by the end of 1950. 'Bandits are far more active,' John noted, and in the south of Perak a killer gang under Yong Hoi was proving 'cleverer and more vicious'. At the turn of 1950/1 the Marines were targeted twice in the Kampar–Gopeng and Cameron Highlands areas, sustaining five fatalities among nine casualties. In 1951 there were over 6,000 terrorist incidents and though the CT casualties more than doubled, the loss of 1,195 killed or wounded in the Security Forces was the worst of the Insurgency. Since the government had become more proactive, John attributed the soaring violence to a tacit popular acceptance of the Emergency and a decline in personal initiative.

The year 1951 was not the best for John. Although he had reorganised the Chinese Affairs Department in Perak, he felt frustrated by lack of recognition and weary of the intransigence of the Mentri Besar and the pusillanimous responses of the new Federal SCA.[26] He warned the latter of the Mentri Besar's tactics to subsume Chinese Affairs as 'an appendage of the State Secretariat'. On 10 August John boldly minuted the Malay State Secretary, 'I will call myself Secretary for Chinese Affairs from now on', and then informed the Federal SCA that he intended as his next step to take over the Federation's Chinese Affairs staff in Perak and absorb their title and the duties of Perak's Adviser, Chinese Affairs.[27] He was still involved in finalising the schemes for Chinese Affairs Officers and Resettlement Officers when he heard a rumour that he was to be transferred to Penang. Against this uncertain background he was considerably affected by two traumatic occurrences, one private and personal, the other public and political.

In April 1951 Helen broke the news to John that their three-year-old daughter had a malignant tumour in her left eye that required immediate surgery. She was admitted to the Bungsar Hospital in Kuala Lumpur.

Shocked and stressed, both parents testified to the other's exemplary courage and to the fighting spirit of their little girl. When the crisis passed there remained ongoing problems of after-care, and it was some while before life returned to something like normality.

The second blow came on 6 October. Sir Henry Gurney was on his way up the mountain resort of Fraser's Hill with his wife and secretary when his Rolls-Royce was ambushed on the Gap Road by an independent platoon of guerrillas. With instinctive chivalry Gurney stepped from the car to draw their fire and was immediately gunned down. The High Commissioner fell dead at the roadside. As the news percolated to the outside world Malayans were stunned. The operation had been carried out with patient precision and awful irony, for the terrorist leader, Siew Ma, had been trained at the Oriental Mission's No. 101 STS in Singapore.[28] The only event John could recall that was comparable to this in its demoralising impact was the sinking of the *Prince of Wales* and *Repulse* by the Japanese in the Second World War. For the first time in two decades he wondered whether being in Malaya 'was worth it all', as the public tragedy of Gurney's death compounded personal anxieties for his daughter and his career. In the closing weeks of 1951 John felt that life had become unusually bleak.

Chapter 15

One of Templer's Men

The prospect of a move to Penang sustained John's morale, since it promised 'a completely fresh outlook' and 'the work would be very different and more congenial'. However, the Federal SCA, R.P. Bingham, had a particular interest in the appointment, since he was Penang's Resident Commissioner-designate, and he pointed out to John that Penang would not constitute promotion and Selangor was a possible alternative. John made it clear, however, that he would definitely prefer Penang to Selangor.

Then, a week before their September date for moving, John was casually told that the transfer was off, as was the Selangor option. Instead, he was to establish a new training school for Resettlement Officers. 'A task for an MCS cadet,' he growled in disappointment as it dawned on him that he was being taken off Emergency work and redirected to routine administration, something he had always dreaded. Impelled by fury, he drove down to Kuala Lumpur to protest, returning confident that he would be switched to something else.[1] However, he had been taken aback to be assured by certain officers that the decision had Gurney's support. That was something John never had the chance to test. An appeal to the High Commissioner to reconsider his case was soon irrelevant, for within ten days Gurney was dead, assassinated on that fateful drive to Fraser's Hill. When the dust had settled John came to the conclusion that he had been let down by the Federal SCA in Kuala Lumpur. He suspected that his uncompromising minute of 10 August to the Perak State Secretary on the smouldering issue of his status as SCA had alarmed Bingham, and their relationship never recovered from that rough passage.[2] In any case John's image as a man of action, robust, outspoken and unorthodox, was hardly likely to commend him to an office-based career administrator of the old school.[3]

John's close friends could scarcely believe that he was to be sidelined from Emergency matters, but only family members knew his disappointment brought on a dose of 'lethargic depression'. Fortunately, the next Federal SCA, David Gray, was much more on the Davis wavelength, and after John was assured that his new job was only for six months, he braced himself to become an educational planner. The original hope of siting the training school at Port Dickson (which held out the prospect of sailing weekends with friends) fell through for lack of accommodation, but John was reasonably happy with the second choice of Taiping, which he had known since the 1930s as quite a healthy place, with excellent walking in the vicinity. In October he moved the family from Ipoh to the Taiping Rest House, but the pleasant views over the Lake Gardens to Maxwell's Hill could not make up for the appalling food and the upsetting regime of living out of suitcases.

As soon as possible they escaped up the Hill, and John took to daily commuting to his office which, as he observed, was 'in the Museum, rather appropriately'. Here, as director-designate, he worked on preparations for the school, which would be located on Rifle Range Road. The accommodation was of basic military standard, with three long huts with plank walls, asbestos roofs and concrete floors, including sleeping quarters, living rooms, office, stores, and lecture hall. Furnishings were simple but adequate. The opening day was scheduled for 7 January 1952, when the first crash course was due to start. It was difficult to be enthusiastic working on one's own, but just before Christmas an assistant arrived – an ex-mission teacher from China and a youth movement instructor in England. A.R. Allen was an immense support to John and won his regard and gratitude. He was also a keen companion on jungle walks. With his sense of purpose recharged, John devised an intensive eleven-day course for the trainee resettlement officers, designed 'to occupy every moment of the students' time with talks, lectures and discussions, liberally interspersed with physical exercise and practical demonstrations' and the Outward Bound ethos.[4]

Meanwhile, in the middle of November 1951 the Davises moved into their official home in Museum Road. The house was vast, 'a ridiculous tumbledown old mansion' that was highly labour-intensive, at a time of acute shortage of domestic servants. And there was another complication: early in 1952 it was confirmed that Helen was expecting another baby.

Personal matters aside, John detected the heightened tension in the country following Sir Henry Gurney's sudden removal from the scene and the mounting anti-Chinese feeling among Malays. In Britain people were driven by election fever as the pendulum swung away from Attlee's postwar brand of socialism. In Malaya an inevitable period of caretaker government under Vincent del Tufo and a swift succession of retirements among senior figures in the Security Forces – including Briggs and Gray – fuelled expatriate fears that the handling of the Emergency was again drifting without direction. When the new Conservative Colonial Secretary, Oliver Lyttelton, arrived in Singapore at the beginning of December to take stock of the situation, he admitted it was appalling, far worse than he had ever imagined, thanks to the structural shambles of the Federation of Malaya. It seemed an irony that the Federal Agreement had been intended to placate the Malay people and stabilise the country after the debacle of the Malayan Union. From its inception on 1 February 1948 John had been an arch-critic of 'this fantastic constitution and complete administrative mess up'. Now, it seemed, the Colonial Office voice was echoing the Davis mantra. Lyttelton lambasted the confused structure, bedevilled by the introduction of the member system, with no lines of definition 'to show where politics, civil administration, police action, administration of justice and the like end and where para-military or military operations begin'. And, unforgivably, it was an administration 'that operated at a leisurely peacetime pace'.[5] Little wonder that despair had settled on the communities of British, Malays and loyalist Chinese.

Yet John's deepest private fear was *not* that the Communist insurgency would succeed, but that the British would concede overall control of political policy prematurely and that a Malay-dominated government would take over the country and set up a form of oriental despotism. His was a singular view. 'Against this background the actual war with the Communists assumes an almost minor importance,' he suggested.

The portents were irredeemably black. 'Everything is deteriorating and particularly the morality and integrity of the government service.' For this reason he held out little hope that Gurney's successor would be able to control the Malays. Instead, he feared that 'he won't be able to lift a finger to push our three-quarters Malay State administrations around'.[6] In fact, John was to be proved wrong on this point.

The choice of Gurney's successor was obviously a subject of burning interest and importance. John reported a lot of talk about Montgomery, though he felt 'such a big noise' would be inappropriate. The decision would be finalised in the New Year. Meanwhile, the debate over strategy rumbled on as the Colonial Secretary and his team travelled the length of Malaya for consultations with representatives of various interest groups and communities. Anticipating that the SCA would be one of those consulted, John prepared a paper headed 'Notes for a memorandum on the need for reform in the Administration of Malaya', which he passed on to David Gray. The document was a strongly argued commentary on the administrative structure and the resulting 'jealousies' and 'destructive competition' between State and Federation. On this assumption it offered practical recommendations to increase efficiency in the main areas of administration.

Gray evidently used these 'Notes' when he produced a memorandum on the Emergency, which he handed to Lyttelton's Parliamentary Secretary, Hugh Fraser. At the same time, in his capacity as Chairman of South Perak DWEC (District War Executive Committee), Oliver Wolters ventured to present the Colonial Secretary with another memorandum outlining a view of what he judged was 'necessary to put emergency policy on the right tracks'. He had discussed the contents with John during a quick visit the latter made to Tapah. Wolters's paper, 'The Chinese and the Emergency', focused on the subject of the Home Guard, which Lyttelton had already prioritised. He made it clear that his memo was effectively the same strategy document on Chinese Home Guards and jungle squads that John Davis had submitted to Gurney back in September 1949. He concluded by recommending to the Colonial Secretary that 'a Chinese-speaking officer with military experience be attached to the staff of the Director of Operations for the specific purpose of doing this . . . I know of only one officer of the Malayan Civil Service supremely qualified for this assignment. He is Mr J.L.H. Davis, CBE, DSO, MCS.'

It was probably crucial that John's name was put before Lyttelton at this moment, on the eve of the appointment of Gen Sir Gerald Templer, GOC Eastern Command, as the new combined Director of Operations and High Commissioner of the Federation of Malaya. Templer was an unknown soldier to many Malayans. However, an officer of immense experience and a formidable personality, he came with a directive granting him combined civil and military powers that had been denied to his predecessors, Gent, Gurney and Briggs. He was given two major tasks, to restore law and order by taking full operational command during the Emergency; and to assist the Malayan people to achieve a united, self-governing, democratic nation. The statistics indicate his success in directing the containment of the Emergency, and by winning 'the hearts and minds of the people' Templer not only articulated a powerful concept that has become an enduring political ideal, but considerably advanced the goal of a modern Malayan state. His achievement was all the greater in view of some unyielding scepticism that a soldier with absolute power could successfully handle a blend of political, social and economic problems. So having promised Prime Minister Winston Churchill that he would do his best, Templer was a man with a mission when he flew into Kuala Lumpur on 7 February 1952. It was a poignant moment, for the British world was rocked by the sudden, early death of the King, George VI.

One of Templer's first actions was to meet the civil servants who would be instrumental in carrying through his policies, beginning with the senior officers of the Malayan Civil Service. As a member of the Chinese-speaking group, John was summoned to Kuala Lumpur. Their initial face-to-face encounter was unsettling for John, who admitted to Helen that he did not know what to make of Templer. Had he known that the new supremo's wartime spell with SOE had been 'like a breath of fresh air' and that he had 'enjoyed shocking the Establishment', John would probably have warmed to him instantly.[7] It came out later that both men were strong advocates of Intelligence as an arm of the security services. In his time as Director of Military Intelligence (1946–7) Templer had vigorously supported an officer reserve in the Intelligence Corps, and by coincidence not long before the general's arrival in Malaya John had been notified of his own appointment to the Regular Army Reserve Officers of the Intelligence Corps, with the substantive rank of major.[8] Be that as it may, as the major studied the face of the general at their first meeting in Kuala Lumpur, he saw 'a very strange fellow', 'a curious, nervy individual' with 'pointed, sharp' features, a thin moustache and the brightest of eyes. But behind the penetrating gaze there was a tough, even harsh quality, an intimidating character whose mordant tongue and vivid language would unquestionably make him some enemies in Malaya.[9]

By a gradual process John's reservations were dispelled. In May, three months after the general's arrival, John wrote home, 'I see Templer from time to time and like him . . . he has made a very great difference to morale already.' Yet at that point he still had his doubts. 'He has not yet shown signs of doing much on the political side and I wonder if he ever will even try to get a grasp of it . . . By and large I should say that he is not a great man, but he is the kind of man we need – he has jolly well got to be anyway. We cannot go on waiting for ever.' Four months later John could still crack a joke to his parents at the general's expense – 'he talks an incredible amount of nonsense in private' – but his respect for Templer had grown enormously. 'Never, never has Malaya had a better chance than under this man. He is utterly tireless . . . and . . . is undoubtedly the most impressive – and frightening – man I have ever met. As a gentleman give me Gurney every time. To end the Emergency give me Templer.' In the end, like many Malayans, John succumbed entirely to the general's charisma. Even though he observed facetiously that this leader 'binds you with flattery and then sucks you dry', he recognised in him an extraordinary gift for motivation, for vitalising the energies of all kinds of people. Four decades later, reflecting on the transformation of Malaya between 1952 and 1954, John Davis was not ashamed to admit that he hero-worshipped Gerald Templer.

On a personal level John also knew that the progressive upturn in his career, which began soon after Templer's arrival, was due substantially to the general's backing. Early in 1952 he was relieved to be told that a transfer to a Chinese Affairs post in Johore was on the cards. Their lifestyle in Taiping had become an increasing strain – in her pregnant condition Helen had found their huge, rickety folly quite intolerable – so she and the children moved temporarily to Maxwell's Hill, where John joined them whenever he could. Then Johore was suddenly forgotten as John learned that 'a certain job' had been earmarked for him in Kuala Lumpur. His only professional concern in leaving Taiping was the interruption it might bring to the Assistant Resettlement Officer courses, which were still evolving. With typical generosity he offered his help to the next director of the training school, Richard West, and continued to contribute to the lecture programme and make himself available for consultation. However, he was excited by news that he was being moved to an unusual position. So when Noel Alexander offered John accommodation for the family in his house in Kuala Lumpur, John seized the moment, and they moved there on 15 April.

It was apparent that one of Templer's primary concerns was the welfare of the rural communities still evolving from squatter camps. Under Briggs and Gurney these were 'the Chinese resettlement areas', but pointedly Templer insisted that this rather soulless nomenclature be replaced by a simple and more optimistic title, 'New Villages'. It was the 'hearts and minds' of the 'New Villagers' that Templer first set out to win. By March 1952 there were some 410 of these villages in existence, varying in size and distribution. In Perak over 170,000 people had been resettled, whereas in Trengganu the number was a mere 624, reflecting the fact that most New Villagers were Chinese, although there were some purely Malay settlements and some with a proportion of Indians.[10] The economic profiles of the villages also differed, some being purely agricultural communities, others industrial, generally mining villages, but the majority being dependent on a mixed economy. In order to take stock of these developments with all their many implications Templer appointed John to be Malaya's New Villages Liaison Officer (NVLO). His brief was to advise the general on 'all matters affecting the well-being and security of the New Villages' and the future development of rural Malaya. John took his promotion to the post as an acknowledgement by Templer of his expertise in both Chinese and Emergency matters.

After pioneering the need for after-care and development policies since 1949 he was at last being offered the opportunity to influence their implementation.[11] He would have the ear of Templer and his senior officers, since he was to make 'periodical reports to His Excellency the High Commissioner on the progress of resettlement at such intervals as His Excellency may direct', and he would automatically be a member of the Chief Secretary's committees on resettlement matters. On issues of security he was to be responsible to Gen Sir Robert Lockhart, Templer's Deputy Director of Operations, and on all other matters directly to the Chief Secretary, to whom he was to make policy recommendations.

On 24 April a public statement of John's new position was put out by the Acting Chief Secretary to all senior State and Settlement officers. 'Mr Davis will be expected to travel widely throughout the Federation and to examine closely all aspects of resettlement work in order that he may become a useful agent for the dissemination of ideas and experiences on the progress between the various States and Settlements.' John had wanted him to add that 'it is believed that many good ideas have not been properly exploited and many failures have been unnecessarily repeated because of the lack of any coordinating agency'; but he had to content himself with a concluding request that State and Settlement authorities should 'make the fullest use of Mr Davis's advice and assistance in all aspects of his work'.

In pursuit of a good story the local press made the most of John's promotion; but since they did so without interviewing or even contacting him he reacted very badly, cursing 'an appalling piece of newspaper publicity' in the *Straits Times*, which described him as 'a Superman and father and mother of 400 villages'. He was just as annoyed, however, when a rival paper referred to him unflatteringly as 'a humble official'. It was not the humility John deplored but the word 'official', 'because at the training school I made a particular point of decrying the word "official" as indicating an officious little bounder wrapped up in his own self-importance'. However, ignoring John's reaction, those who knew him were delighted by his promotion and highly entertained by the novel thought of John Davis being cast in the role of Superman and thrust into the public spotlight. With his close friends Richard, Noel and Jim Hannah, John enjoyed a special private joke, but frankly he was relieved when public interest waned.[12] Templer had set him a challenge and he was keen to get on with it.

The High Commissioner had made it clear that he wanted to see the New Villages become flourishing, permanent communities that would be the building blocks of a cohesive, governable, democratic society. From this time 'Community Development' replaced 'Resettlement Areas' as the new buzzwords. In presiding over continuous social improvement John would have to take on board a range of matters, setting up representative institutions, education for citizenship and social welfare, ensuring the provision of services such as Home Guards and peripatetic medical care, and amenities from clean running water to lighting, roads and schools. He was asked to be 'particularly concerned with the co-ordination of the work of voluntary associations in the New Villages which is expected to expand considerably'. By these the Chief Secretary meant not simply bodies such as the Malayan Chinese Association (MCA), but missionary organisations, the Red Cross, the St John Ambulance Brigade, the Boy Scouts and Girl Guides and the Women's Voluntary Service, of which Lady Templer was patron.

John took these voluntary services very seriously, aware that he needed every scrap of help he could get. He kept an admiring eye on the achievements of the 'Red Cross girls' who worked in the New Villages and the Malay *kampongs* and put up with infinite discomfort, 'living close to the ground' so that they had a real understanding of the country. He had great respect, too, for the dedication of a group of Christian missionaries who had been forced out of Communist China and were working among the Malayan Chinese of Johore. At Rengam he met Mr and Mrs Wicks and at Kluang three women missionaries, qualified nurses who offered to help with medical cases. But one elderly English missionary in the township of Yong Peng particularly impressed John. Seventy-year-old Miss Griggs had spent her life in the part of southern China from which many of Yong Peng's Chinese had originated. This gave her special kudos with the people, who had a reputation for being notorious troublemakers. John was convinced that with money, effort and good Malayan Civil Service personnel, there was immense scope for replanning Yong Peng. He recommended the clearing of the west-side slum and concentrating development to the east, with a new water supply, plans for 400 new houses and a Chinese school with twenty-eight classrooms, enough for 1,000 pupils. He described Yong Peng as 'the most important outstanding resettlement project in Johore', and after revisiting it in December 1952 he was satisfied by the smooth progress in both slum clearance and resettlement.[13]

Such improvements could only take place with the cooperation of a great many individuals, from the Executive Secretaries and other members of SWECs to senior police officers, District Officers and Resettlement Officers. In addition, John consulted a range of professionals, surveyors, planners, public works officers, education experts and administrators. After his first round of inspections, John noted significantly, 'the importance of proper planning strikes me forcibly everywhere'. From this point he regularly consulted with Concannon and Buck, government town planners, but he was also much impressed by the work of a survey officer named Bruce serving in Johore. He pressed for the adoption of his village schemes, and consequently 'Bruce planned' became a label synonymous with model planning. In another field of legislation – notably the Village Councils Bill, an important plank in the 1952 legislative programme – John had certain reservations about transforming village committees into local councils with financial and elementary judicial competence, and he found an unexpected ally in Harold Bedale, a visiting local government expert.[14] They were mutually supportive during the wrangling generated by the bill, sharing views on voting rights and citizenship, and there was no doubt about Bedale's respect for John's 'great experience' of Malaya.

As NVLO John received a flood of papers and memoranda for information or for comment on subjects as diverse as land tenure and land reserves policy, local government legislation, racial integration, Home Guards, village halls and food cultivation. But his main priority was to undertake a comprehensive schedule of inspections of the New Villages, for only by seeing them for himself could he test the criteria for successful New Village development that he had devised at the training school.[15] In late April 1952 John made preliminary visits to Selangor, Perak and Penang, followed in early May by tours of Johore and Malacca. During the rest of 1952 he covered every state of the Federation, compiling confidential reports on each village visited. These inspections enabled him to judge whether and where the government's massive financial investment was bringing social and economic improvement to the original resettlements. It gave him considerable satisfaction to walk over the ground in the company of District Officers, local resettlement staff and police officers, while scrupulously observing what had been achieved and what still needed to be done, both the success stories and the failing villages that might require resettlement a second time.

His investigations took John away from Kuala Lumpur for the first part of the week, usually until Thursday; he then returned to the capital for the rest. Processing the information from his travels in the office and incorporating it into directives or recommendations was less to his taste. He complained of being short of clerical staff, of being unable to understand secretariats or write minutes, and 'K.L. was completely stewed up in paper and pomposity'. His strength lay in interpersonal communication and strategic thinking. 'I can talk quite well and authoritatively – thus giving people a feeling of confidence in my ability to get things done . . .' but, typically, to avoid sounding boastful, adding, 'At times I came perilously near being a fraud.'

That was patently not the opinion of Gen Templer, however, who was delighted with John's performance and told Lyttleton, 'Davis is absolutely first class in a new appointment called "Liaison Officer, New Villages". He is responsible to me for all coordination and everything in respect of all New Villages . . . He spends nearly all his time travelling round them and coming back and telling us here what is going wrong.'[16] Templer could empathise with John's efforts, for between 1952 and 1954 he himself notched up 30,000 miles by air and 21,000 by road in his determination to meet the people and win them over from Min Yuen influence to the government side.

There were still outstanding problems associated with the New Villages and in 1952 unquestionably many still fell short of the achievements of the best as the economic boom came to a halt. John was particularly concerned about the shortage of good agricultural land in mining areas such as the Kinta valley, over which the Malay-dominated State governments still retained jurisdiction. However, by the advent of 1953 there was growing confidence that the Security Forces had at last secured a grip on the Emergency and Templer decided the time was ripe for two fresh reviews, one of armed services policy, the other a parallel analysis of civil affairs. He wanted a group of three or four Malayan Civil Service officers to undertake the second review and produce a punchy report.

Some months earlier Templer had asked John for his ideas on the essential reorganisation of New Village administration at State level. John's response was unequivocal: the Executive Secretary was the key figure in efficient New Village development. He should have a dual role as Secretary of the SWEC and Secretary of a State New Villages Development Committee responsible to the EXCO, as a move towards the integration of Emergency and development administration.[17] Templer doubtless remembered John's constructive reply, for he suggested him as a member of the new civil review team, with Rowland Oakeley; J.A. Cradock, a former District Officer in Perak; and Ian Blelloch, British Adviser, Perak, a senior Malay specialist. At their first meeting on 12 January 1953 John observed Templer's managerial style with keen interest, as he summarised what he believed had been achieved so far in Malaya. Then he posed the question: was legislation being properly implemented? ('We must look for the gaps,' said Templer. 'See where we are not going fast enough.') In addition, what had been achieved for the people? And in view of the government's 'spectacular' assistance to the Chinese, what had been done for the Malays and what could be done to eliminate the danger of their alienation? Templer then revealed his intention of forming a standing committee under his own chairmanship to deal with the development of Malay welfare. This led on to his thoughts on a tentative projected timetable for representative institutions: local councils were to commence in 1953, State elections were to start in 1954 and be completed in 1955, and Malayan national elections were to start in 1956. Winding up their session, Templer reiterated he wanted brief ideas for innovation.[18] The committee collectively highlighted three desirable initiatives for the future: a major road-building policy, a large-scale programme for providing water supplies – both these would directly benefit the Malay *kampong* communities – and a massive investment in the educational provision of English schools with hostel accommodation for both sexes.[19]

By the time the report was submitted, John was eagerly anticipating a spell of home leave. The whole family had been ill at various times in 1952. The new baby expected in August was born prematurely in June and she lived only twelve hours. John and Helen were both hospitalised in September, suffering from sub-tertiary malaria. On recovering John returned to a hectic schedule of work. He had picked up other commitments, notably examining officials in Malay and officers in Cantonese, the latter at the government's Chinese Language School at the Cameron Highlands, where the director was his friend of China days, Robert Bruce. On 12 February John returned from a New Village visitation to Kelantan to find Helen and the children ill, but he hesitated to warn his parents they might have to delay their departure.

Then suddenly other events forced his hand. 'Yesterday [the 13th] a bombshell was thrown at me,' he confessed. 'I was asked it I would consent to postpone my leave and act as British Adviser in Pahang for three or four months.' It was quite unexpected, 'One of those freak things that turn up from time to time.' Someone had to cover the interval between W.C.S. (Charles) Corry's retirement and J.A. Harvey's taking over as British Adviser. John remembered 'both old warriors who were there at different times when I was in Bentong'.

As a Malayan Civil Service officer John knew he had been paid a signal honour. The offer still awaited the Sultan's consent, but John was unperturbed, since by implication he already had Templer's approval. The decision had to be made promptly. John accepted, since to have refused would have seemed ungracious and politically inept. 'We have decided to treat it entirely as an adventure,' he said in a private aside. So John would ride his luck.

Chapter 16

The Honourable Mr John Davis

On 5 March 1953 John flew to Kuala Lipis, the capital of Pahang, to meet Charles Corry for the official handover. He was taking on what was traditionally one of the most senior Malayan Civil Service positions in the field, where his diplomatic skills and understanding of Malay politics would be publicly tested. He also knew his performance would be appraised by Templer. Someone had warned him not to expect too much, 'that I am not getting my foot on the ladder and have not a hope of repeating the performance for many years to come'. For all that, John was buoyant about the future: 'They have . . . consented to consider making me a District Officer next tour, which is what I want, as it puts me ultimately in the B.A. [British Adviser] line.'

Pahang was an appropriate posting for John. He was familiar with the terrain and the Malays of the east coast from his pre-war police service in Kuantan and Pekan. As Assistant Labour Commissioner based in Bentong he dealt with the state's postwar economic and social problems, and more recently as NVLO he had toured Pahang comprehensively. As part of his survey of the New Villages, in October 1952 he had visited a number of remote Malay riverine settlements, including some regrouped villages upriver from Jerantut ferry, and had been struck by their inadequate defences. Keen to rectify the impression that Malay interests were being neglected by the government, he wrote in his report: 'If there is little we can do for these Malay villages by comparison with the great deal we do for the Chinese ones, I feel at least the Government should ensure frequent visits by the Government officers in charge of them.'

Five months later he found himself pondering some very different matters, the responsibilities of a British Adviser. As he admitted, the fact that he had never even been a District Officer meant there were many gaps in his knowledge of basic protocol and procedure. Leaving nothing to chance he had scribbled down a list of questions to fire at Corry. How should he handle the Malay administration, the Sultan, the Mentri Besar and the Malay elite, the Tunkus? How should he set about informing the Sultan of his intentions? What precisely were the British Adviser's functions and position on the EXCOs and LEGCOs (Legislative Councils)? When and where was it essential to speak Malay? And conversely, how should he deal with visits by Templer, His Excellency the High Commissioner, and Sir Donald MacGillivray, the Deputy High Commissioner? He had questions, too, about the SWEC; given his temporary British Adviser status, would he be Chairman? John also wanted particular tactical advice. 'What, if any, moves were to be resisted?' To avoid making *faux pas* he had to know the scale of hospitality and entertainment that he and Helen would be expected to provide, the conventions to observe while travelling in or outside Pahang. And he needed clarification as to the customary toasts at formal dinners, the rules governing the British Adviser's membership of clubs, the conventions about going to private houses, and for John what was a seriously practical matter: what was the attitude to wearing shorts and hats?[1]

Charles Corry, charming and smooth-mannered, presumably answered these concerns, for John was soon at ease and the handover proceeded as planned. There were four days of farewell functions during which the new Acting British Adviser met Pahang's Chief Minister, and John formed an instantly favourable impression of the latter, confirming that he and the Mentri Besar would get on well together. During the social junketing he was also introduced to the rest of the European community, including John Clifford, the SWEC Executive Secretary, finding to his satisfaction that he liked him too. It was also encouraging to find he still had friends in Pahang dating from his spell in the Labour Department. However, John was far less convinced by the attendant ceremonial pomp, which he had always found a bore. 'We have got to reduce it', he confided in a letter home, 'both because we cannot stand it and also cannot afford it.' In any case, Helen had her own spontaneous style as a hostess, applying all her natural friendliness to the task of making visitors feel welcome. One person who greatly appreciated this was Bishop Henry Baines, whose episcopal duties brought him periodically on visitations to Pahang. She admitted, however, to a certain strain in managing 'servant trouble' among the Residency staff.

Nevertheless, taking everything into account, they could not help but be pleased with their new surroundings. The Residency exuded space and gracious living. It was a capacious mansion with a lovely garden. They were supported by numerous servants and provided with an official chauffeur-driven Humber, enabling their own middle-aged Chevrolet to be well rested. There was, in addition, a desirable 'perk', a state bungalow at Fraser's Hill, where they could take a break from work and entertain their friends.[2] Finally – although John would have considered it in the worst possible taste to mention it – he was now officially addressed as 'The Honourable Mr J.H.L. Davis CBE, DSO'.

On the night following the Corrys' departure there was an understandable touch of smugness on John's face as he sat in his office surrounded by three telephones, though 'Heaven knows where they go to'; there were also 'masses of maps . . . and photographs of kings and queens and sultans'. In spite of his known dislike of formality, John soon took 'quite kindly to long white linen trousers, tie and coat when necessary', and demonstrated that he could host a cocktail or dinner party with aplomb. In addition, he was 'perfectly at home when the Sultan came to stay'. But the greatest test for the Davises came in June with the celebration of the coronation of Queen Elizabeth II, when they threw a party for 700 local children, followed by an evening reception at the Residency for 250 people of Pahang.

Thanks to Corry's long experience in the Malayan Civil Service, John inherited solid relations with the Malay leaders in this Malay-oriented State. Like all British Advisers Corry had a diminished role after the Federal agreement, but he had built a good working relationship with the Mentri Besar, Mahmud bin Mat, and his successor, Tengku Panglima Perang. For many years he also enjoyed a close friendship with the Sultan, who had taken a stand against the Communists in the Emergency and notably against the all-Malay 10th Regiment of the MRLA, which operated in Pahang. This must have reassured John as he settled into office, though at first he affected some apprehension. He had expected the Sultan to be 'difficult', to refuse to speak English, and to squander the money in his hands.[3] Happily there was no evidence at all of awkwardness between the Acting British Adviser and the ruler. John could converse with the Sultan in Malay, and at the end of his term as British Adviser, he and Helen were invited to Pekan for the Sultan's birthday celebrations on 24 June, and a fortnight later to a dinner in the *Astana* on the eve of their departure.

Despite his unaccustomed exposure to Pahang society, John's overriding responsibility remained the Emergency. During 1953 anti-guerrilla operations were concentrated on Pahang, as intelligence sources indicated that the Communist leader, Chin Peng, with the Politburo and MRLA HQ staff, were almost certainly hiding in one of their jungle camps deep inside the state. In October 1951 the MCP had issued new directives in response to charges from their own side that their policy of sabotage, destruction and intimidation was alienating, not winning over the people. The new directives redefined Communist strategy, placing equal weight on political and military activities.

However, thanks to the Briggs Plan, by 1953 the flow of food and medical supplies from the Min Yuen to Chin Peng's guerrillas had slowed down. Hunger drove the MRLA ever deeper into the interior to clear patches of rainforest for growing crops, but deprivation siphoned off Communist morale. Starvation and deficiency diseases were clearly factors contributing to the increasing number of surrendered enemy personnel and 'total eliminations' in that year. Greater cooperation between the armed forces and Special Branch brought success to many local operations, coupled with the significant build-up of the Security Forces. Air reconnaissance sorties located possible Communist campsites in conjunction with ground operations by special detachments of Commonwealth troops and the Police Field Force (PFF). The tide was turning in favour of the government in Kuala Lumpur.[4]

John's friendship with Chin Peng and his understanding of the Communist mentality meant that he had a special contribution to make to the Pahang SWEC's counter-insurgency plans. Templer understood this. One of the general's innovations had been to instigate an Army Operational Research team to analyse Communist jungle tactics. During a visit to Pahang in April 1953 he agreed that John should vet their research papers and comment on their findings in the light of his Force 136 experience. Two days in May were set aside for round-table talks with Maj Gen W.P. 'Bill' Oliver, Templer's Chief of Staff, and other officers, but on returning the papers John was honest enough to admit there was nothing he could add. He gave all credit to the officers: 'All aspects [of jungle warfare] seem to have been thoroughly considered.'

Successful military operations depended on SWEC planning using information provided by Special Branch. Intelligence sources had placed the Communist Secretary-General and his headquarters staff first near Raub and then hiding in the Bentong area, but in fact this information was already out of date, despite the improvements in intelligence since 1948. Chin Peng has since confirmed that he had moved his headquarters from Bentong to Raub in 1952 and a decision to leave Raub was taken later that year. While plans were laid by the Security Forces to search out and eliminate the MCP leaders and hardcore members of the MRLA of West Pahang, the latter had already moved on north. Their plan was to make for the safety of the Cameron Highlands, to a remote site north of the Sungei Telom, which they reached by February 1953.[5]

British intelligence had latterly picked up indications of the northerly movements of Chin Peng and his staff, who were settling into another temporary camp on the Perak border just as John took over the British Adviser's responsibilities in Pahang. Shortly afterwards, the RAAF targeted the Communists' hillside camp in a ferocious attack that killed two of Chin Peng's personal bodyguards. This close shave convinced the Secretary-General that Pahang had become too dangerous and he had no choice but to seek a safer haven in northern Perak. So as John was settling down in Kuala Lipis, Chin Peng and his fifty-strong party decamped and embarked on a two-month slog through the wilds to the little town of Grik. Even here they discovered that food shortages were acute and security had been penetrated by Special Branch, so they had to push on further. Finally, in July 1953, as John handed over the reins to John Harvey, Pahang's next British Adviser, Chin Peng and his comrades were moving towards yet safer refuge across the jungle-wrapped border with southern Thailand.[6]

During the four months from March to July, while John was Acting British Adviser, anti-terrorist searches in Operations 'Cato', 'Matador' and 'Sword' were carried out in Pahang. Although they were unable to locate or destroy Chin Peng's headquarters, John was able to confirm at the

SWEC meeting on 19 May that a dozen Communist guerrillas had been captured. However, the downside of the crumbling terrorist presence was a macabre incident in Kuala Lipis. John and Helen had no idea that their well-meaning *Amah* had taken their little daughter to the town police station, where the body of a terrorist killed by the Security Forces had been put on public display. The innocent five-year-old was petrified by the sight and long term the trauma left her emotionally scarred.[7]

In July 1953 John's service in Pahang was followed by a much-needed spell of home leave. Looking back on this tour, beginning in 1950 with Sir Henry Gurney as High Commissioner, John noted, 'It has been a funny time, mostly very hectic and interesting, partly very depressing.' The demoralising loss of Gurney had been overtaken by the succession of a conspicuously different leader. Gerald Templer had renewed John's sense of purpose and assuredly enlisted his aid in the crucial battle to win the hearts and minds of the Malayan people.

Almost five months away in England gave John the rest and stimulus he needed. Just before Christmas 1953 he took the family to Paris for a few days, and it was only after the New Year celebrations that he began to think seriously about the situation in Malaya. On 21 January, when they landed back in Singapore, he found he had a few days' grace before taking up his next post. He and the family set off by train on the Davis version of a royal progress, to be greeted first by a mass of friends at Kuala Lumpur and then some more at Ipoh. Finally they reached Prai and took the ferry across to Penang, spending the night at the celebrated E. & O. Hotel. 'Home' would be the official residence across the Penang Straits at Butterworth. They moved in on the next day, 25 January 1954, when John began a spell of two years and four months as SDO Province Wellesley.

While being shown around, John realised that his new post carried a multitude of responsibilities. He took the news philosophically, assuming 'that a great deal of trouble has been taken to give me the job which it is felt I should experience – in the nicest way and place possible'. Since most of his police contemporaries appeared to be prospering – Guy Madoc, for instance, was now Templer's Director of Intelligence – it was important for John's self-esteem to taste more success in the Malayan Civil Service. He soon discovered, however, that he was expected to perform three full-time jobs simultaneously. As SDO he had seniority over the other Province Wellesley District Officers; but he was also District Officer in his own parish of Butterworth, and he had to cover the routine work of another District Office that was lying vacant. His work included responsibility for land and rural affairs and Emergency administration. Finally, in addition to official membership of the Settlement Council, he became chairman of the newly elected Butterworth town council, taking on 'the introduction of responsible local government, town planning and development, and local government administration'.

They had been in Butterworth for less than a month when Helen began to worry about the effect of this workload on John's health, which took the form of some unpleasant and persistent symptoms. To save his sanity John decided he would have to demand some assistance. But he had barely thrown off the virus when he inadvertently offended R.P. Bingham, the Resident Commissioner and his senior officer in Penang, from whom he received a stern written rebuke. To start with there was no 'Dear Davis', for John had committed a serious sin of omission by failing to arrange for someone to meet the Resident Commissioner when he crossed the Straits from Penang to land at Butterworth.[8] There was no point in arguing the toss: John took it on the chin. But in bold red letters he added an instruction to his secretary. 'Better have a personal file – in which such oddments can be put.'

To John's palpable relief he was allocated another District Officer in May. De Vries was 'an extremely nice fellow, a Eurasian aged 47 and very experienced'. His presence may not have reduced John's personal workload, but it restored some efficiency into the running of the province and 'makes me feel more comfortable', John admitted. He also recovered his physical fitness. It was as well, for besides his full complement of administrative duties, he had become involved in one of Templer's personal counter-insurgency initiatives, the Special Operations Volunteer Force (SOVF).

Indeed, Bingham's rebuke was delivered when John was in Kuala Lumpur, having been summoned to King's House for a meeting with the High Commissioner on 8 March to discuss SOVF.

These volunteers were ex-terrorists of the MRLA who had surrendered to government forces and offered their services for special jungle operations against their former comrades. Most were Chinese, but a few were Indians, mainly rubber-tappers or labourers. Some had fought as guerrillas against the Japanese. However, after years of harsh existence in the jungle, many guerrillas had grown weary of the fanaticism, excessive discipline and political brainwashing and were prepared to be 'turned' by a government that offered them good terms of service. They were given three months' intensive training before being organised into platoons of fifteen under a British police officer, their objective to seek out and kill MRLA terrorists. Their success rate against former comrades was remarkable.

After the story of the SOVF was publicised in the press in February 1954, Templer took up the idea of holding a conference to pick the brains of these ex-CTs on a range of issues, such as propaganda and tactics. A two-day conference was consequently arranged for early March involving ten platoon sergeants and four British officers, two from the police and two administrators.[9] Instead of following a formal agenda there would be guided general discussion. From the Chief Secretary's office a request went out to the Settlement Secretary, Penang, and through him to the Resident Commissioner, that 'H[is] E[xcellency] is . . . very keen that John Davis should take the chair at this meeting, as he has knowledge of several branches of Government and would be a first rate man to lead the discussion . . . We apologise for always trying to steal your Senior District Officer; but if you have the best, you must expect to pay the price!' John duly chaired the conference, which picked up a number of specific concerns. From these he highlighted the main issues that needed addressing to make general improvements in the SOVF.[10] John found the SOVF sergeants 'a refreshing group' for, having renounced Communism, they had gained a sense of purpose from their new role.

One outcome of this conference was an interesting paper analysing current government policy and tactics for accelerating the surrender rate of terrorists. Templer was pleased with the results. He instructed that there should be a second conference at the end of April involving surrendered MCP members. John was again to be Chairman and the High Commissioner attended the opening at Bluff Road, Kuala Lumpur. The participants were Special Branch officers and two groups of nine former Branch Committee Members and nine former District Committee Members of the MCP who had surrendered in the previous eighteen months. The wide-ranging discussion was to include operational tactics of the Security Forces, food control and the CTs' sources of supply, psychological warfare, the treatment of surrendered enemy personnel and the relationship between the CTs and secret societies. The report was sent to Templer on 3 May. In his covering letter John was his usual honest, direct self.

> Your Excellency . . . The conference was not a success and we quite failed to get 'under the skin' of these men. We did not sense any antagonism but rather a lack of interest in anything but their individual well being . . . We also noticed that they were hyper-sensitive about being called 'traitors' . . . To sum up, it struck us that this group of men were steadily, though probably unconsciously slipping back into a Communist frame of mind, because they had been given nothing to replace it.[11]

Although he detected a difficult psychological challenge he would not presume to have the solution. Nonetheless, John's opinion was still valued, since two days later he was asked by Alec Peterson, the Director-General of Information, for his view of a proposed propaganda leaflet to be used in a tactical drop on CTs in the Kluang area of Johore: this was proof that he could still make a contribution to the 'psywar'.

Province Wellesley, John said with pleasure, was 'a much smaller and more civilised area than I have been accustomed to, no jungle but much prettiness'. The Butterworth residence, with its 'dilapidated charm', sea breezes and 'incredible views across the Strait to Penang island', was a perfect place for parties and became the family's favourite home.

In the past John's work in the secret services had relieved him of the round of entertaining expected of a senior officer of the Malayan Civil Service, and he and Helen were still adjusting to these social responsibilities while they were at Butterworth. Among their first guests were the Templers, whose aircraft had to make a forced landing at Butterworth aerodrome with engine trouble. The first John knew of it was a phone call at 5 p.m. to say the two were on their way to the residence with Gerald Templer's Military Assistant. This prompted some feverish improvisation in their evening menu and in the preparation of beds, complicated by the fact that seven-year-old Patta Davis was in the throes of dengue fever. However, their guests were 'really delightful', said John. 'We wouldn't allow him to put a tie on and gave them bacon and eggs for dinner. They said they enjoyed it – and we certainly did – it was obviously a great relaxation from formality for both of them.'

Three months later Lady Templer paid her second and last visit to Province Wellesley. The general's period of service was coming to an end and they were preparing to leave Malaya shortly after, on 31 May. 'A detailed programme had to be arranged so that every minute [was] filled, part in our district and part in Kulim [South Kedah]. It meant a luncheon party and full afternoon, cocktail party here and the ADC to dinner . . .' It so happened they did see the Templers once again, at a wedding in Kuala Lumpur. John, resplendent in Malayan Civil Service full dress, gave away the bride, who had worked as secretary of the Women's Institute, which was Lady Templer's special interest.[12] After the wedding John attended a Force 136 reunion dinner where he had to introduce the guest of honour, Lt Gen Sir Geoffrey Bourne, Gerald Templer's successor as Director of Operations. It was an emotional occasion. John believed that in a true consideration of Malaya's best interests, Templer's departure was premature; and with 'the slightest relaxation' of Emergency initiatives, a new flare-up of Communist activity might result. Without wishing to cast doubt on either Lt Gen Bourne or Sir Donald MacGillivray, who was to succeed Templer as High Commissioner, John anticipated a reaction in the public mood: 'New men have got to prove themselves against a reputation that they obviously cannot emulate.'

Although the level of terrorist activity had diminished significantly under Templer, he knew, and John knew, that the Emergency still had some way to run. Until recently the border area of South Kedah–Province Wellesley was highly vulnerable to terrorist attacks, particularly the road from Kulim to Serdang, but in April 1954 Templer noted that for the first time in almost six years there was no record of an incident in Penang or Province Wellesley in the daily situation report.[13] Just before the Templers' departure, however, Neville Godwin, CPO Kedah, was killed in an ambush on the road leading to Kedah Peak, an area where John enjoyed walking. He had known Godwin, a tall, powerfully built figure and a highly experienced officer, for over twenty years. 'It was a great tragedy,' he wrote, 'one of these isolated incidents which we are warned are bound to happen from time to time.'

At the end of 1954 another attack occurred just half an hour after the Davises returned to Butterworth from local leave at Fraser's Hill. According to John:

A couple of Communist gunmen walked into a Chinese inspector's house at Nibong Tebal – about 25 miles from here – and tried to kill him and three young schoolboys who were in the house – fortunately none fatally. That meant organising another 'drive' which I do hope will produce some results. In Province Wellesley we are right down to the hard core but just don't seem to be able to finish them off. They do little in return – this was only the third incident this year and in fact we have contacted (and killed) them infinitely more times than they have done anything against us – but while they remain, the whole population is upset and frightened and any sign of relaxation and the whole situation slips again.

If the Insurgency seemed to be a permanent backcloth to life, there were special events that temporarily pushed it out of people's minds. On 21 August 1954 the Davises' second son, Humphrey Haycraft Davis, was born in the general hospital in Penang. Both parents were 'awfully pleased with him'. He was christened in Kuala Lumpur in the presence of lots of old friends, and the Lochs threw a party to celebrate the occasion.

As to public affairs, as SDO John was much involved in the election process that marked the transition to self-government, starting with the town council elections held on 4 December 1954. Butterworth, he observed, was 'a fairly conservative place and nothing very exciting happened', but 'we are rather proud that this is one of the two towns in the country which holds out against the Alliance . . . which at present is sweeping the country'.[14] While John was not personally hostile to the Tunku Abdul Rahman's Alliance Party, he took the very English political view that the effect would be 'pretty unhealthy because there will be virtually no opposition when we start political government in Kuala

Lumpur next year'. As they prepared for the Federal elections in April 1955, he took his electoral duties in his stride. 'I am becoming quite an expert in elections . . . as we have had town council elections, the Penang settlement elections and in two months we shall have the Federal elections. I am the Returning Officer for this area which means that I have to see they go alright. Fortunately they have done so far.'

The year 1955 brought promises of other changes. Butterworth was 'building up rather rapidly, as it is to be the HQ of the Commonwealth Brigade'. The RAF station was also expanding, with greater RAAF involvement. On the other hand, the country was entering a critical stage in its progress towards Independence, and for the first time Europeans began to talk openly of retirement or redundancy. In his private thoughts John accepted that a question mark probably hung over his prospects. He felt the urge to hang on, even though 'everybody seems to think the BAs' [British Advisers'] jobs will be the first to pack in'. He was under no illusion about the new trend. 'The line now is *specialisation* – economic secretary, financial secretary etc. which is no good to me. So I suppose I shall be on the top line for abolition terms – and I do not particularly want to be abolished!'

It seemed a pity now that the early strain of his job had gone. Relations with Penang were relaxed while David Gray was Acting Resident Commissioner in 1955. The young SCA in Penang, Brian Stewart, was a congenial colleague. They had also formed a new circle of friends among the residents of Butterworth. John had grown deeply attached to the place, not least the timeless quality of the view from the residence:

> The sea is lapping the sea wall fifty yards away and there are about five big ships in harbour, two Blue Funnel and odd cargo vessels . . . The most noticeable feature of Penang from here is a clock tower which is our time keeper . . . It is sunny, odd fishing boats are passing by, no one is in a great hurry and it is very beautiful . . .[15]

This tranquil scene was in evident contrast with the pace of John's working life. 'We have hit a spell of hard work and social functions – odd navies, Colombo planners, Australians (Army, Navy and Air Force!)', he wrote in cryptic mode. The load of official invitations and requests to dine with visiting VIPs, to give talks, take part in ceremonies and conferences, was heavier than ever. However, while it was time-consuming to attend the school sports at Bukit Mertajam or a pageant at the Light Street Convent in Penang, it was scarcely onerous. It was not just schools that made claims on his time: so, too, did the armed services, with requests that the SDO should attend the Battle of Britain Dance in the RAF officers' mess or lend support to the Ex-Services Association of Malaya.

The highlight of the District Officer's calendar, however, was Province Wellesley's Annual Poppy Day Dance in November, traditionally held at the District Officer's Butterworth Residence. The Emergency temporarily forgotten, this was a fancy-dress occasion for letting down hair in well-tried colonial style. In 1955 John and Helen reversed their roles. John wore his wife's black skirt and stockings, his own white shirt and brown shoes, a black net scarf and some red, artificial roses at his throat, and to top it, a white hat with a huge bow in the front, from under which appeared a mass of brown parcel string representing hair. Pushing a doll around in the family pushchair, his face painted with makeup, he looked revolting, Helen confirmed. Meanwhile she was dressed in John's everyday work clothes, including a topee, and sported a walking stick and burnt-cork moustache.

Helen admitted that she much enjoyed the experience of being District Officer for a few hours, especially as one of her self-imposed duties was to greet the Resident Commissioner and his small accompanying party on their arrival at the Butterworth residence.

Chapter 17

Baling

It had become a Davis tradition to spend Christmas with a house party of friends and 1955 was no exception. As soon as Boxing Day was over and their guests were departing, John prepared to leave Butterworth for the little frontier town of Kroh near the Thai border. This would be the starting point of an operation, code-named 'Pink Gin', that had been in the throes of preparation for months. John was to be the operational go-between for an unprecedented dialogue involving the Communist leader, Chin Peng; the Chief Ministers of Malaya (Tunku Abdul Rahman) and Singapore (David Marshall); and Dato Tan Cheng Lok, the leader of the MCA. A secret game plan had been skilfully devised behind the scenes by Col Hubert Penrose, staff officer in the headquarters of the Director of Operations, Lt Gen Sir Geoffrey Bourne, and it would be carried out under the command of Assistant Police Commissioner T.B. 'Tommy' Voice. John Davis's responsibility was to ensure that operational contacts between the Communist and governmental representatives were effected smoothly and safely.

By 1955 the British-led Security Forces were confident that they were in control of the 'shooting war'. As a measure of their success they pointed to the growing number of White Areas freed from Communist influence, which suggested that it was time for a different approach, a political offensive to bring about the conclusion of the Emergency.[1] Hitherto it was

assumed that political independence could only come about after the end
of the Emergency. Templer had timetabled the first Federal elections for
1956 or 1957, but under pressure from the UMNO–MCA Alliance, the
new High Commissioner, Sir Donald MacGillivray, agreed to bring forward
election day to 31 July 1955. Once this date was settled, as a prelude to
Independence the Alliance leader, Tunku Abdul Rahman, called on the
Malayan government to hasten the end of the Emergency by offering an
amnesty to surrendering guerrillas. The British authorities were hostile,
however, seeing this as opening the way for Communist penetration of
Malayan political life, and talk of the amnesty was dropped.

At this point, May–June 1955, Chin Peng launched his surprise counter-
move, a Communist peace offensive in advance of the Federal election. The
MCP Secretary-General arranged for a letter to be forwarded to the main
Malayan political leaders, offering to negotiate a peace settlement on the
basis of the amnesty proposals. The offer, however, was abruptly rejected
by Tunku Abdul Rahman as a tactic to disrupt the imminent election.
The Tunku had seized the initiative back again. In the heady atmosphere
of Election Day, 31 July, his Alliance Party swept to power in a landmark
victory, with fifty-one seats in the LEGCO out of fifty-two. Then on
9 September, pledging support for a swift end to the war in the aftermath
of victory, the Tunku, now Malaya's Chief Minister, threw his support
behind a magnanimous Federal declaration of amnesty.[2] It was obvious
now that the Communist Party's anti-colonial stand had been usurped by
the Alliance Party. To save face Chin Peng responded with letters to the
Tunku, to David Marshall, Chief Minister of Singapore, and other political
leaders, proposing talks to end hostilities. Tunku Abdul Rahman agreed to
talk, but ostensibly for the purpose of clarifying the amnesty arrangements.

In view of the complications of setting up a meeting, preliminary 'talks
about talks' were held between 18 October and 16 December in Klian
Intan and Kroh. Envoys from both sides – Chen Tien acting for the MCP
and Ian Wylie, Deputy Commissioner of Police, for the Federal government
– thrashed out the pre-conditions. The government representatives made
clear that, before and during the talks, media access to the Communist
representatives would be strictly limited. The English school at the little
town of Baling was chosen as the venue for the conference, which was to
take place over two days on 28–9 December. The time limit was due to the
fact that Tunku Abdul Rahman had been invited to London at New Year

for crucial constitutional talks with the Colonial Secretary, Alan Lennox-Boyd, on a timetable for Independence.

Significantly, no British officer was to be present at the conference table at Baling, despite the overriding role of British military and police in planning the talks and implementing all the arrangements. Although the British authorities in Kuala Lumpur still had a controlling hand in security and defence matters, some members of the administration, notably in Special Branch, were worried that Chin Peng would manipulate the Tunku at Baling and would try to inveigle the MCP into a political role. Within the Alliance Party suspicion grew that the British government was also dragging its feet over Independence. In fact, this was not the case. The Colonial Secretary was ready to cooperate with the Tunku in moving towards decolonisation, having been persuaded that it was in Britain's long-term strategic interest to do so, hence the importance of the forthcoming New Year talks in London. Consequently, in a gesture of good faith the High Commissioner was empowered by the British government to announce that the continuation of the Emergency would *not* be an obstacle to Malayan Independence.

Such, in brief, was the interactive chain of events that were the backcloth to the Baling talks. The Davis papers show that John's involvement was written into the plans from an early date, probably in August.[3] He said later, 'I had known for some months that if these talks came off I should be wanted to do the meeting part,' a somewhat inelegant reference to his selection as Conducting Officer to Chin Peng's party.

However, since the decision had been taken at the highest level that 'all orders and instructions . . . should be given verbally and by visits of officers' and nothing should go out in writing, there is no way of knowing who put forward his name.[4] Possible police candidates – Guy Madoc, Claude Fenner, Bill Carbonell, Ian Wylie, Harvey Ryves – were all his long-standing friends and knew about the special relationship that John had enjoyed with Chin Peng during the Japanese Occupation. All would agree that more than anyone John would have the trust and respect of the Baling participants. At any rate, almost two weeks before the preliminary talks started, at a top-level meeting on 6 October of senior police, Army and air force officers in Police HQ in Kuala Lumpur, an outline plan for security arrangements referred specifically to 'Davis' as 'Conducting Officer'.[5] Furthermore, at the Klian Intan discussions John's name came up again as a potential 'hostage' to guarantee the safe conduct of Chin Peng and his personal staff, but the idea of hostages was subsequently scotched by Chin Peng himself.

Meanwhile, it was clear to everyone involved in the planning and execution of the Baling meeting that security would be a critical issue throughout the Communist leader's presence on Malayan soil. Even with a ceasefire in operation over 400 square miles along the North Malayan–Thai border and the guarantees and provision for protection for himself and his party, as Britain's Public Enemy No. 1 Chin Peng was a potential target for assassination. There were countless Malayans who perceived the Communist leader as a ruthless fighter responsible for some 10,000 deaths. On the other hand, it was difficult to predict the direction of an attack. The Communist record of treachery and revenge suggested death might come from friend or foe.[6] It was not until 1998 that a former Military Intelligence Officer mentioned an MI5 plot to eliminate Chin Peng in the jungle. Chin Peng also heard that the officer commanding the Kroh District was associated with a plan to ambush and kill him, a proposal quashed by the British authorities in Kuala Lumpur.[7] Had John known about such a decision, he would have refused to approve or cooperate in an act of alleged counter-insurgency during a ceasefire. Sometimes he doubted if the conference would get off the ground at all, with so many issues on which compromise was unlikely or impossible: 'There was so much preliminary parleying beforehand that I thought it would all wash out and it came as quite a surprise in the end.'[8]

Finally, however, the arrangements for the Baling talks were confirmed. Chief Ministers Tunku Abdul Rahman and David Marshall would represent the Federation of Malaya and the settlement of Singapore, with a doyen of the Chinese community, Dato Tan Cheng Lok. Chin Peng would be accompanied by his second in command, Chen Tien; Rashid Maidin, a Malay representative; and his personal staff. John's orders were unequivocal. He had a dual obligation to facilitate the safe conduct of Chin Peng and his party, combined with a public relations role, 'a clear duty to keep relations reasonably sweet in order to make the conference possible'. He was *not* to carry 'any responsibility or concern in the conference or negotiations'.[9]

On 27 December John made sure he reached Kroh in good time to contact the 3rd Malayan PFF, who were to provide his contact and road escorts. Command HQ had issued instructions to police commanders to 'give him every assistance and pay particular attention to his advice'.[10] However, to ensure there would be no hitches on his part, he ran again through his detailed instructions on the security and conference arrangements. This kept him away from all the journalists who were 'buzzing around' Kroh – in particular a posse of eleven Chinese reporters from whom he managed to conceal himself, though they were packed into a small room next to his in the local hostelry. The next morning he was up before dawn and soon ready to join John Penly, the PFF commander, the contact party and road escort personnel. It was pleasantly cool and John sat in an open jeep as they headed out of Kroh in convoy. Passing through Klian Intan, the column of vehicles was met by expressionless or hostile stares from the local Chinese, but John dismissed fears that he might be in danger. 'I have never been so well escorted in my life,' he said, 'not for security reasons so much as to proclaim that he [Chin Peng] was coming to us and not on equal terms.'[11]

A short distance from Klian Intan was the prospective contact point. Rising out of a dark green sea of dense jungle, Gunong Paku was an inhospitable outcrop with an eerie atmosphere, a hot, dry, flattened hilltop that reminded John of the harsh landscape bordering the Red Sea. Although this location had been proposed by Chin Peng's emissaries to be the meeting place, the police braced themselves for a capricious switch of plan at the very last moment. Tin was still mined in the area, but to play safe the local tin workers were cleared from the scene and roads were closed off. The workforce at the Rahman hydraulic tin mine, arriving just after dawn, was taken out again in a lorry, and access to the Kwong Leong mine was barred. From 7 a.m. the Klian Intan road to Kroh and Baling was closed to all civilian traffic for half an hour before and after the police escort drove through.

Promptly, the company of 2nd Malayan PFF set up a camp of improvised tents in a large defensive circle around the exposed summit. John walked under escort to the contact point, armed with a loudhailer to announce his presence. He was to sum up the significance of the scene:

The high, bare hill, covered with a truly formidable array of troops, up near the Siamese border, waiting for my old friend, Chin Peng – for the last seven years our deadliest enemy – who was coming out of the jungle under a flag of truce to meet the Prime Minister of Malaya and discuss surrender.

At about 10 a.m., the meeting time, we saw a couple of figures climbing up
over the mine. It was not Chin Peng but Chen Tien, his sort of go-between,
and a messenger [Lee Chin Hee] . . . He told me Chin Peng was coming down
but was late, as he could not walk fast. So four or five of us strolled down the
hill to the mine edge to wait for him, and he turned up an hour or so later.
He was little altered except very much heavier . . . [he] could only move very
slowly from the effects of beri-beri. But it was a thrill to see him again.[12]

The pleasure was evidently mutual and in Chin Peng's case mingled
with surprise. 'I met Davis just outside the jungle fringe among old mine
tailings,' Chin Peng recalled. 'To me he looked unchanged. Still as fit as
ever. Tough. Seemingly not a day older. Davis, dressed in light cream shirt
and shorts, held out his hand and as I moved forward to shake it, he said
to me in Cantonese, "Long time, no see."'[13]

A report in the *Straits Echo* that the meeting was 'icily formal' was a piece
of inaccurate propaganda. Both men understood that a public welcome was
out of the question, and the sizeable police and military presence around
Gunong Paku indicated yet again how seriously the authorities took the
security issue. But John's discreet appearance as Conducting Officer was
planned to reassure Chin Peng, to be a guarantee, in John's own words,
that the Communist leader 'was not being led into a trap' since 'we hadn't
let each other down before'. All the same, this meeting was not an occasion
for reminiscing. There were formalities to go through before they left the
contact point, and a witness noticed Chin Peng's 'rather wintry smile' as
John introduced him to John Penly and a couple of senior police colleagues.[14]
The Communist leader was accompanied by a small, unarmed party, which
included his cook, orderly, aides and secretaries. Once identities had been
established, it was the Conducting Officer's duty to brief Chin Peng on the
arrangements affecting his main bodyguard and his personal escort party.
These covered plans for security, accommodation, the timetable and transport
to and from the conference site, 20 miles away in the Baling English school.

The bodyguards were to remain camped out of sight in the obscurity
of the jungle, though they would be covered by the police escort, who
were to remain at their posts in the vicinity. To boost their self-esteem,
the Communists had originally exaggerated the number of uniformed
guerrillas in Chin Peng's bodyguard, but in the end only a platoon of
twenty accompanied him to Gunong Paku. At an early stage John needed

to identify the guards' commander, who would be acting as Liaison Officer to the police escort. According to a senior British NCO present, he was 'an evil-looking character with a Mauser pistol stuck in his belt and a stolen British carbine slung over his shoulder'. As for the guards, they 'were hard men, in patched khaki drill uniforms' but their weapons were in good condition and he had no doubt they 'would not hesitate to use them'.[15] Perhaps to defuse the situation, John assured Chin Peng that his bodyguard would not be interfered with unless they provoked an incident. However, they should *not* try to make contact with the local people, nor follow Chin Peng's party nor move towards the roadhead: any movement or deviation, day or night, by the bodyguard would constitute a breach of the ceasefire terms. Meanwhile, since John's police escort was to provide them with rations for the duration of the talks and the following ten days, boxes of tinned food and rice were handed over. Finally John asked Chin Peng to allow John Penly and a number of unarmed signallers entry to set up a telephone contact between the police escort and the Communist bodyguards, in case it was decided to send a courier back into the jungle.

With the protocol settled, at around 11.20 a.m. the two parties emerged from the jungle edge. Acting on orders, John had checked the Communists were unarmed before they set off by jeep for the mine workshop. There they transferred into police pick-up trucks, which took them down the dusty Gunong Paku road to the Tanah Hitam junction. At this point John, Chin Peng and his party transferred to Bedford police vans with bench seats and, protected by an armoured column, they drove along the winding route to Baling. On the way occasional groups of inquisitive villagers watched the cavalcade, but the passengers were obscured from view by window blinds. At the approaches to Baling a crowd of 200–300 lined the road, waiting good-humouredly to see the Communist leader. But as they reached the entry to the school grounds, John suddenly faced an alarming situation. 'I experienced for the first time what being in the international publicity limelight can mean. This meeting had caught on as world news and representatives from almost every country were present and the popping of flash light bulbs was quite terrifying.'

Everything possible had been done to ensure effective security control. In the school grounds 'a special wired camp had been made, full of every conceivable kind of police and military staff officers, technicians, W/T sets and goodness knows what. Fortunately, of course, the public and press

were not allowed in – except the press at special times and under control.'
However, 'I thought we were never going to get there ourselves as a huge
crowd of curious onlookers, who had collected at the gate, surged forward
to get a closer glimpse and nearly smothered us . . . We were almost
immediately enveloped in literally hundreds of flashlight photographers.'
Then came the worst moment when, amid the confusion, the vans stalled
while manoeuvring the sharp turn through the entrance. Luckily the
situation was saved by the massive police presence.

John had spotted that Chin Peng was thoroughly enjoying the publicity.
Even a simple newspaper headline, 'Red Boss in Blue Shirt', gave him
welcome attention. On the other hand, having worked for so long in the
secret areas of government, John mistrusted the integrity of newshounds.
The Baling talks had created an unparalleled stir, and even the newsreel
produced by the Malayan Film Unit – part of the government propaganda
machine – 'drew large crowds of Chinese, and Chin Peng was applauded
when he appeared on the screen'.[16] Yet when images of the youthful leader
appeared on cinema and television screens, the sturdy, protective frame of
his Conducting Officer was close by, wearing a calm, confident expression,
implying that everything was going to plan.

In the spirit of the ceasefire a strangely civilised atmosphere prevailed
in the conference area, now designated 'a protected place'. It was after
12.30 p.m. when the Communist delegates arrived at the Baling school
campus: obviously the original plans for a morning session had been quietly
shelved. John escorted Chin Peng's party to their billet, a modern brick-
built bungalow, shielded on the far side by trees. 'All I had to do was to
see that they were alright as they were isolated from the rest of the camp,'
John remarked. Their needs had been anticipated. On each 'guest' bed a
toothbrush, toothpaste, soap, a towel and a mosquito net were laid out. Chin
Peng asked if they might also have clean underwear, and a messenger was
sent to the local shops to buy singlets and underpants, which were presented
free of charge. Food and utensils had also been provided, and soon the
sounds of chopping wood and smoke from the chimney indicated the cook
was preparing a meal. John slipped off, reappearing at 1.30 p.m. with two
large loaves. Instinctively, Chin Peng checked the windows before opening
them, taking note of the extent of the barbed-wire fencing around the key
areas. Two armed policemen were stationed behind the billet and picked
marksmen were in position throughout the conference zone.

The venue for the talks, which were to begin at 2.30 p.m., was in a teaching block a short walk from the Communists' quarters. The Malayan government team led by the Tunku had just arrived, and members of it were standing beside one of the two long, parallel tables that were freshly covered in white cloths. When Chin Peng entered the conference room, followed by Chen Tien and Rashid Maidin, John formally introduced the participants. After this the waiting pressmen were given five minutes' access to the room to take photographs of the scene, while John retreated to an adjacent room. He shared this anteroom with two armed police guards, a staff officer, personal secretaries to the Chief Ministers, and certain 'recording personnel'. Since the British were excluded, John took it that Special Branch had bugged the conference room with microphones.[17] All he had to do was listen for his summons, one ring of a bell, indicating an adjournment had been requested. In the event, there were two short breaks, but it had long grown dark when talks were ended on the 28th. Chin Peng and his colleagues returned to their billets for an early night.

Publicly and privately John never admitted to inside knowledge of the dialogue taking place that day. 'My protégés were quite well behaved,' he wrote later, but 'Chin Peng got very morose', suggesting that things had not gone well for the Communists. The media had picked up the same signal at the end of the first day. To reach out to his adversaries Chin Peng made his ultimate offer, that if the governments of the Federation and Singapore secured self-determination in respect to internal security and national defence, the MRLA would be able to cease hostilities. However, it became clear the next day that neither side would concede their initial positions. The Communists' offer to lay down arms was still hedged by conditions on which there was no compromise, and the recognition of the MCP as a legitimate political party was rejected by the Tunku, who became convinced that Communism and Malaya could never coexist. The *Singapore Standard* blamed Chin Peng and his parting shot, 'We would never accept surrender at any time and will continue the struggle to the last man.' From there the prospect of peace collapsed and 'it all ended somewhat abruptly': the conference broke up without an agreement just before 1 p.m. on 29 December.

The relief felt by many Malayans was in profound contrast to the sense of anticlimax and despondency on the Communist side. John's charges were reluctant to return to Gunong Paku, since their bodyguards would not be expecting them yet. He, on the other hand, being sceptical of the media's good faith, wanted 'to get Chin Peng's party out of the publicity atmosphere of the camp' and finally persuaded them to return that afternoon with their Conducting Officer and police escort to their contact point. It was then agreed that some of the party could rejoin the main bodyguard in the jungle. Chin Peng, however, asked if he and his small escort could stay at Gunong Paku for the night under the ceasefire terms and join the main party the next morning. To meet his request, an extra tent and blankets were brought from Kroh police station and a dinner of fish curry and rice prepared for the unexpected guests. For the cooks, a platoon of Malayan police constables, it was a bizarre situation, for they had spent years hunting these same Communist terrorists in the jungle. But for the two wartime allies there was a chance to drop their reserve in the privacy of the tent and, in Chin Peng's words, to 'talk over the good old days when we at least played at being on the same side'.[18]

Such harmless reminiscing, however, was not all that was on the agenda. There was a hidden sequel to the Baling talks, a contingency strategy, involving John. He said later, 'The odd thing was that I don't think he [Chin Peng] wanted to go back,' while managing to conceal his own intent to have a serious dialogue with Chin Peng. At the prospect of the guerrilla war reopening, neither the Communist side nor the Tunku and his Alliance Party had won the peace. The one individual who might conceivably salvage it at the eleventh hour was John Davis. It would certainly be a long shot and would depend partly on his ability to rekindle his old rapport with Chin Peng. And what better time or place to begin talking than during the hours of darkness, in the privacy of a shared tent close to the jungle edge at Gunong Paku, where John stressed, 'We could breathe free air again, as no press was allowed within miles'?

The identity of the instigator of the stratagem remains a well-kept secret. The Colonial Secretary, Lennox-Boyd, was a pragmatic politician, prepared to defer to the man on the spot, which suggests a British Malayan source, arguably the Head of Intelligence or the Head of Special Branch, in liaison with the Director of Operations and the High Commissioner.[19] Certainly, John would not have acted unilaterally. Someone contacted him, and leaving nothing to chance he scribbled down the gist of his verbal instructions on a scrap of paper. The first order was imperative: the 'Chin Peng meeting must be secret'.[20] It must also be clear that it was an initiative of the British in government, not that of the Alliance Party or its leader. The basis would be the terms of the 9 September amnesty which offered those who surrendered and gave up Communism the chance to redeem themselves and resettle in Malayan society or depart to China. Two developments had changed the climate surrounding the amnesty offer: first, government food control measures were driving more guerrillas to give up, and second, the Malayan public was less interested now in the terms offered to the Communists, so as an inducement to Chin Peng it would be possible to 'concede something to freedom' by way of human rights and liberties. But the immediate priority for John was to secure agreement on 'surrender terms'. 'Get [these] fixed early' was his unequivocal order.

It was a delicate task. The starting point was the dialogue in Baling: in the seclusion of their tent John took careful note of what Chin Peng told him.[21] From the start, 'things had not gone too well for the Communists'. There had been a 'lot of talk' leaving 'definite impressions', but Chin Peng could not understand why there was 'no negotiation zeal', why the Tunku and his colleagues made no effort to bargain or compromise, which was what he had expected of negotiations. He had told the Tunku that if peace were agreed he still hoped to 'form some [sort of] organisation' resulting in political involvement. Meanwhile it was the threat of internment and police investigation of his members that troubled him most and was a 'very real difficulty' in reaching an agreement.

Acting on the directive that surrender terms were the top priority, John tried to persuade Chin Peng to recognise that his forces would undoubtedly be defeated. If he could accept this, the next step would be to find a reasonable climb-down position. Chin Peng prevaricated, then reiterated the issues constituting a stumbling block to a settlement.[22] The amnesty terms were intolerable to committed Communists, he said. The government had stated it would conduct investigations leading to unlimited internment, but Chin Peng saw capitulation, investigation and indefinite internment as the 'whole difficulty'. These would impose unacceptable humiliation and loss of face on his people; and the Malayan government should know that they were entitled to their pride and self-respect. He had no problem with the setting aside of weapons but *not* to the implication of 'surrender'. And with his intense dislike of exploitative colonialism, Chin Peng firmly identified the British as the Communists' real enemy, blaming them for pushing for surrender.

However, as he admitted to John, on certain matters there was room for clarification and possible compromise. Chin Peng agreed there might be 'limited "dispersal" [and] detention' of the Communists, but he argued that their investigation should be conducted in private and not in public where they would face cross-examination in a court trial. For this reason he also wanted to know more 'about [the] Police reporting system'. He was concerned, too, about losing a cross-section of supporters. The repatriation of surrendered Communist personnel had come up with the Tunku and there was 'talk of most going to China but a few must stay – [a] few hundreds – not just privates but sample types'. Chin Peng himself did not want to go to China, but he expected China to accept numbers of the guerrillas. Later Chin Peng began talking about a 'working committee' with all types represented, including one or two guerrillas, 'to arrange who goes to China and who stays'.

Moonlight filled the night sky as the pre-conditions for some sort of agreement seemed to emerge. John was certain that Chin Peng 'emphatically wants to stop fighting'. He was ready for peace, admitting that the 'constant moving [was] making life difficult'. The Communist leader also repeated his disappointment at the outcome of Baling. When the Tunku had said the talks were an opportunity to clarify the amnesty terms but not to negotiate, Chin Peng thought he was indulging in diplomatic sophistry. He had expected the conference to produce a settlement. As for his enemy, the British, Chin Peng came as near as he could to an apology for the Sungei Siput murders, admitting they were a bad mistake for which he had to accept ultimate responsibility.

The next question was how to turn the pre-conditions into an agreement to end the Emergency. At this point the memories of the two ex-comrades diverge. Chin Peng says he turned down John's proposal to continue their negotiations in the jungle under special escort, and the serious talk stopped there.[23] John has no recollection of such a proposal. Instead, his secret notes suggest they worked out a method for disengagement based on the freedom of movement. Chin Peng would come out of the jungle and sign a provisional agreement, after which he or his representatives would go to the various committees whose task was to decide on the relocation of all Communist personnel. Government transport might be used in the task, which would take about a month to implement. Chin Peng was confident, however, that his people would cooperate and come out of the jungle – except the few who preferred a life of banditry.

Turning to the matter of contact, John had already been working on a system that allowed written contact twice monthly, on the first and fifteenth of the month, starting on 15 January 1956. A 'post-box' for dropping letters would be situated in an agreed position about 20yds from the entrance to the Gunong Paku site, the area being cleared of Security Forces on the specified dates. Two of Chin Peng's trusted staff who had been at Baling were named as potential couriers. On the promise that there would be 'no deliberate ambushing of messengers', these two, Onn Chin Hee and Kwee Ching, were to leave a message from their leader between the hours of 10 a.m. and 4 p.m. The receipt of a letter would then activate a response from the British authorities. A special announcement was to be broadcast on three successive nights on Radio Malaya after the 9.30 p.m. news in English: 'Will Mr Harold Slocum, last heard of in Singapore in 1954, please get in touch with Police Headquarters?' was to signal government approval.

It was late into the night when the discussion ended. They were in relaxed mood and continued to talk around the clock, going over old times well into the small hours. A short time later John gave the press a wickedly sanitised version. 'We had a casual talk during the night. But there was nothing to it,' he told the reporter from the *Straits Times*.[24]

At dawn both men were up in preparation for their departure and John took Chin Peng down to his escort, waiting at the perimeter point. The Communists had accepted a couple of 24-hour food packs for the journey but declined further rations. An NCO dog handler with 2nd Malayan PFF noted that Chin Peng looked uneasy: he put it down to the threatening appearance of his heavily armed PFF colleagues lining the ground from the mine edge to the jungle edge. 'And then,' said John, 'there broke one of those stupid little incidents that the Communists so love manufacturing':

Chen Tien – the No. 2 – thought he must save some face so asked that the escort should retire over the brow of the hill in order that they should not see where the party went – a ridiculous suggestion, as you cannot see a yard into the jungle anyway, and both they and we knew exactly the path they were taking for the next 2 miles. Anyway, we had promised not to follow them for ten days! However, it would be nice from their point of view if they could say that the escort had retired at their bidding. This had to be strongly resisted, of course, and fortunately was solved quite easily by my offering to follow them personally as far as they liked for their security, knowing of course that I was absolutely safe. They accepted this way out of the deadlock and I went about

¼ mile into the jungle when Chin Peng, who really is a bit above nonsense of this sort, thanked me very much and most anxiously pressed his escort on me to see me safely back to our people! It took a lot to persuade him that I was perfectly capable of finding my own way through the jungle for ¼ mile! So we parted amicably. I was very sorry to see him go.

John retraced his steps to the waiting police escort. It was around 11.15 a.m. when he returned to Kroh in the company of two police colleagues, H. Middleton, OCPD Kuala Kangsar, and Geoffrey Turner, OCPD Kroh. Not surprisingly he felt distinctly dishevelled and asked to have a wash and shave. The next stop, by helicopter, was Baling and from there Davis travelled to Kuala Lumpur for an extensive de-briefing. Claude Fenner telephoned Helen to put her in the picture, and John was back in time for New Year's Day.

A fortnight later John received official thanks for the part he had played at Baling. A letter from the Director of Operations, Lt Gen Sir Geoffrey Bourne, enclosed a copy of the High Commissioner's appreciation and thanks. Both acknowledged John's 'considerable part in making a success of the arrangements'. Bourne had added a few words: 'Dear John . . . Thank you particularly for the very special, and by no means unrisky part which you played in meeting Chin Peng in the jungle. I'm glad it went off so smoothly. Yours sincerely, Geoffrey Bourne.'

Was there an allusion in the double negative to an assassination plot in which John might have been caught in crossfire? And what of the chimerical order John had been given to induce the Communist leader to surrender? Whether John, or the British officers who had put him up to the plan, had any serious expectations of persuading Chin Peng to comply, is impossible to tell, since the combination of ingrained discretion and a failing memory put a seal of silence on the subject after 1955. In reality, there was no response from Chin Peng's side at the Gunong Paku letterbox, nor any from the government on Radio Malaya. By February John knew that the time for a sudden surrender by Chin Peng to the offer he had brokered had been overtaken by other dramatic political developments. On 8 February it was agreed at the London conference that Malaya should have immediate de facto self-government and August 1957 became the target date for an independent federation of Malaya. That same day the amnesty granted to the Communists in September ceased. Once it was known that British and

Commonwealth troops would remain on Malayan soil, the MCP withdrew their conditional offer of peace made at Baling. Violence was renewed and the Malayan Emergency entered another phase. John reconciled himself to the growing certainty that Chin Peng 'would never have given in without obtaining a substantial amount of recognition which he would have skilfully turned to his advantage in a future political war'.

Chapter 18

Triumph in Johore

The British government's acquiescence in forwarding the date of Malayan Independence to 31 August 1957 triggered a period of significant change implicit in the process of decolonisation. Malayanisation of the structure and personnel of government, of institutions and of Malaya's industries and businesses, was the order of the day, and members of the expatriate community began to face a bleak future in which they would be redundant, retired, retained on temporary contracts or redirected to other parts of the Empire, where change moved more slowly.

John had four months to serve as SDO after the conclusion of 'Pink Gin' before he was due another four months' home leave. A month before he left in May 1956, Tunku Abdul Rahman paid a formal visit to Province Wellesley. Although John had seen him at Baling, they had never had a conversation, but as he drove the Tunku around in his car that day, he instantly warmed to the Chief Minister's urbane candour and charm. He was a man to admire, but as Chin Peng found, a difficult protagonist.

On his return to Malaya in November John was appointed to the temporary position of Acting SCA for the Federation of Malaya, a job he would have coveted a few years earlier when the SCA was one of the senior positions in the Malayan Civil Service. Now, however, in the light of Malayanisation it was becoming increasingly irrelevant. Listening to the talk in Kuala Lumpur, he was aware of 'an awful feeling of no future and unrealism in the air' and had low expectations of his career. Like many British Malayans he agonised about the choice ahead: whether to cut and run with a good settlement, or to stay as long as the Malayan government would employ him. He chose the latter, because he still loved Malaya.

During December John had the opportunity to revisit Pahang's east coast with all its pre-war sentimental memories. He drove across in the old Chevrolet by the new Temerloh–Maran link road to Kuantan, now the state capital. 'I had tea with the old Mentri Besar and his wife whom we were so fond of in Lipis,' he said reflectively.

Although John's job in the Federal Chinese Secretariat was only a holding operation, it was not without incident. He felt obliged to keep a watchful eye on two potentially destabilising developments. One was the simmering pro-Communist subversion in Chinese middle schools, which had produced an alarming wave of sit-ins and riots in Singapore since 1954, and the other the resurgence of the Chinese secret societies that gave cover to Mafia-type gangsterism and racial strife. In 1956 it had seemed possible that Penang might go down the Singapore route, when there was a serious riot after two days of civic celebrations and processions by Georgetown's predominantly Chinese population. The trouble was caused by young secret society hooligans who targeted Malay bystanders and provoked street violence. Law and order was only restored with military aid and the imposition of a curfew.[1] The Federal government was rightly concerned about a possible liaison between the secret society fraternity and the Communist Party. To help his friend, Guy Madoc, the Director of Intelligence, who was making an urgent appraisal of the events, John asked Brian Stewart, SCA Penang, for all possible information on the background to the riots and the support of secret societies. He also wanted to know more about a recent hostile sit-in at Penang's Chung Ling High School, which only ended when the police moved in with tear gas. The SCA and the Penang authorities were determined to prevent a breakdown of civil discipline of the kind triggered by Communists among students in Singapore.

Against this background of Communist-inspired urban unrest John was asked by the EXCO to undertake a special investigation. He agreed to re-examine the case of a Chinese teacher, Liow Yong, who had appealed against the Director of Education's refusal to register him as the headmaster of a Kuala Lumpur middle school on the grounds of 'public interest'. A secret report showed that Liow Yong had a history of left-wing activity in Sitiawan, where he had taught the young Chin Peng and supported the Communist regime in China. While there was no evidence of Liow

Yong's direct connection with the MCP during the Emergency, the police considered him a security risk. In weighing the evidence of the conduct of Special Branch and Liow Yong's tendencies, John displayed his innate fairness, but he suspected that, in the climate of school disruption, the EXCO would reject the appeal.

After Christmas John heard that in January he was to take up a newly created post in Johore. He knew little of the job except that it was 'to replace the British Adviser in so far as he did most of the handling of the emergency in the state', excluding the customary authority and prestige of the British Adviser. Then, a few days later, it was confirmed as a 'new temporary post of State Secretary (Emergency), Johore, on MCS Superscale F', which would last until July 1959. After making arrangements with the Permanent State Secretary, John was to take over just before the departure of the present British Adviser, David Somerville, on 21 January.[2]

There was still much to clarify. He had no detailed job description, no word on accommodation, no reassurance about his status: instead disquieting hints of 'some political bother'. He took this to mean that to soothe Malay feeling, the State government might whittle down the status of his post 'for fear that it may be like continuing the BA [British Adviser] under another name!' But it was a risk John decided to take, and once he had made up his mind to accept, he immediately arranged to go down to Johore. Helen accompanied him on the trip, for as well as John's hectic round of meetings it gave them 'an excuse for a general snoop around' and 'the chance to make a joint decision if we find any snags there'. In fact they were greatly reassured by their kind reception from both Europeans and Malays.

Although the Mentri Besar was customarily the nominal SWEC Chairman, John, as his titular deputy, was to be *de facto* Chairman and Executive Officer of the Combined Departmental and Services Committee. Consequently he would be responsible for the administration of the Emergency and conduct of operations throughout the state. It was the biggest challenge of his postwar career, and he carried it off with imperturbable efficiency.

The Emergency was still a very live issue in Johore, which was home to around 500 guerrillas. From northern Johore, the Regional Commander of the South Malayan Bureau, Hor Lung, directed terrorist operations in the southern half of the country. He was sustained by a hierarchy of support bodies made up of armed and active terrorists. They in turn depended for their food and other supplies on the Min Yuen. Communist activity, however, was widely scattered, so that although the government focus was on Johore by 1956, the Security Forces had to extend operations to the Malacca and Negri Sembilan borders, and east to the China Sea to include parts of Mersing and Pekan districts. By the time John took over the direction of the Emergency in Johore, Communist action had also become spasmodic. This was partly because communications between Chin Peng's headquarters in Thailand and Hor Lung's cadres in southern Malaya had been effectively severed, and the leadership in central and southern Malaya had been weakened in 1956 by the deaths of two key members, one of whom, Yeung Kuo, was the MCP Vice-Secretary-General.[3] It was little wonder that the total strength of the Communist forces had fallen by the turn of 1956/7 to 2,000 guerrillas. It was left to Hor Lung to rally his depleted and dispersed units with the assistance of some friendly aborigines and elements in a Min Yuen that was increasingly penetrated by Special Branch.

Since a number of key decisions had been taken by the Johore SWEC several months before John's appointment, it was his task to implement them successfully. The targeting of North Johore was to be a prelude to a principal aim of creating a 'White' corridor linking Johore with Perak by the time of Independence. The first target in the drive to clear North and Central Johore of terrorists was the district of Segamat, the scene of countless ambushes and atrocities in the early 1950s. The terrorists in this area had relied on workers in the local rubber estates and New Villagers for their food supplies, but all this was set to change irreversibly as Federal Priority Operations swung into play. After Segamat attention would next turn to the once notorious hotbed of Communist support in the Yong Peng–Bekok area, and ultimately to South Johore, south of Kluang, to Kulai, Pontian and Kota Tinggi.

In pursuing a policy of Federal Priority Operations John had certain advantages. It helped greatly that he already knew some of the senior officers whose support he needed, such as Jack Slater, CPO Johore; Alan Blades, the Police Commissioner in Singapore; and Brig Walter Walker, the dynamic OC 99 Gurkha Infantry Brigade Group, with whom he had worked on Ferret Force. By coincidence they both arrived in Johore in 1957 and found themselves working on SWEC. John had a lot of time, too, for the OC 26 Gurkha Brigade based in Segamat, Brig David Powell-Jones, 'a highly intelligent, subtle, humorous Welshman'.[4] Sandwiched between his work at Johore Bahru and in the districts, John attended meetings of the Chief Minister's Emergency Operations Council in Kuala Lumpur and had consultations with the Director of Operations and his civilian staff, notably Walter Lucas, who was soon to become another good friend.

Looking back, John realised that the visitations he had made as NVLO gave him invaluable knowledge of Johore's townships and rural settlements, as well as a shrewd sense of the main guerrilla strongholds. He also had the vital support of a well-honed committee structure, both at the headquarters in Johore Bahru and in the operational districts. To the latter he gave advice, explaining tactical decisions and settling disagreements with a firm but tactful hand. Occasionally, when personality clashes or strong differences of opinion occurred, John turned to troubleshooting. As it happened, just after he arrived, a serious disagreement between the State Home Guard Officer (SHGO) and the Yong Peng police was lowering morale and efficiency.[5] His solution was a long, constructive talk with the SHGO, which set reconciliation in motion. Observing him in action, the Administrative Officer of the Segamat District Committee concluded that no one was better than John at taking on the challenge of the job. 'His qualifications were unbeatable. As a pre-war Malayan Police officer, wartime Army colonel in command of the Malayan component of Force 136 and postwar Malayan Civil Service administrator, he combined personal experience of the three services whose work he was now co-ordinating, with intimate knowledge of the enemy.' And not least, 'he was a very nice, hardy, cheerful, common-sensical, considerate man to work for'.[6]

At his arrival in January 1957 John Davis inherited immediate responsibility for an ongoing operation, code-named 'Cobble'. This was a major food denial operation aimed at weeding out the 132 CTs still remaining in the twenty, largely Chinese, villages of Segamat District.[7] Phase I had begun in the previous July when he was on leave, and he arrived as Phase II was scheduled to start, with the simultaneous arrest of sixty known Min Yuen food suppliers on whom the guerrillas depended. At the same time, tighter curfews were imposed on the district and the number of security personnel – Home Guards and police – was increased to man the gate checks and body searches. These were routine measures used countless times before. 'Cobble', however, marked a precedent in Johore with the introduction of Central Cooking, the ultimate form of food control. Rice was cooked in guarded central kitchens and issued twice a day to the inhabitants of the New Villages and estate labour lines, consumption being confined to the village perimeter. There was a simple reason for this unpopular and draconian measure. Cooked rice soon turned sour in a tropical climate so it would be inedible well before reaching the hands of hungry CTs, who were driven to desperate solutions, including surrender. Two months into Phase II John wrote that 'the emergency is going quite well here at the moment. We are having a lot of success which I hope will continue.' Three killings and one surrender from the Selumpur branch amounted to a good start.

'Segamat was only one of five or six inter-connected little wars he [John Davis] had to deal with,' Segamat's Administrative Officer explained, because to eliminate the personnel in each Communist Party district or branch required a tailor-made strategy.[8] As Phase II of 'Cobble' got under way, Johore SWEC operations were extended. In the neighbouring district of Batu Pahat, Phase I of Operation 'Shoe' – the preliminary gathering of vital intelligence – was started as a basis for operational planning. Central Cooking was introduced into the townships of Paloh in July, Yong Peng in September and Labis in November, as full-scale food denial was phased into Operation 'Shoe' in the second half of 1957.

If Central Cooking was a highly effective weapon of state control in the war against terrorism, the rewards system ran a close second. Bribery proved an effective method of persuading CTs to surrender and provide information leading to the death, capture or surrender of their comrades. The notion of betrayal for financial reward was as old as it was abhorrent, but to entice a starving colleague to abandon the jungle and the Communist cause for a tidy sum seemed a less messy way of ending the conflict than by ambush or aerial bombing. This was particularly the case when loudhailers, voice aircraft messages and millions of leaflets offered an escape route and the handling of the surrendered personnel was carried out ever more efficiently by Special Branch.

In the ensuing months [after intensive food denial and Central Cooking] there was a small, erratic trickle of surrenders. The Rhodesian African Rifles [sic] killed a couple of CTs in an encounter in Labis. A detached company of the Rifle Brigade based on Jementah steadily eroded the strength of the

'Johore–Malacca Border Committee' based on and around Mount Ophir. Meanwhile, 2/10th Gurkha Rifles laid an ambush in Bukit Siput New Village, acting on Special Branch information that four CTs intended to penetrate the perimeter wire of the village by night to collect food. The Gurkhas got them on the second night, killed five instead of the expected four, and made friendly criticism of the numeracy of Special Branch.[9]

After this the dispirited remnants of the Min Yuen were rounded up easily. In the meantime the elimination of nine CTs of the Selumpur branch was a serious blow to the Segamat district committee. The leader, Ming Lee, who had escaped death twice in ambushes, finally quit and surrendered to the authorities. His defection and that of Party officers marked a new stage in the story of the Emergency in Johore.

As Operations 'Cobble' and 'Shoe' progressed, John was philosophical about his growing workload, the inevitable result of the drain of experienced European officers at the approach to Malayan Independence. 'One cannot help wondering whether wiser statesmanship, particularly on the British side, would have avoided this,' he reflected. In April 1957 he lost his assistant – but right-hand man – on the Johore SWEC. As he put it, 'Now the BA [British Adviser] has gone I have taken his part on the Committee, but now also the Executive Secretary – the top and the bottom!' Quite a number of close friends of the Davises were also on the point of departure, hoping to establish themselves in new careers before the trickle of unwanted colonial administrators became a flood. In August, as Merdeka (Independence Day), fast approached and the last farewells were said by friends, John admitted that he felt 'very much on the edge of a volcano'.

Fortunately they were diverted by being drawn into Johore's official preliminaries to Independence Day. On the High Commissioner's final visit to Johore on 22 August, Helen was deputed to look after Lady MacGillivray, and John had invitations to various State functions. These included lunch at the palace of the Tengku Mahkota, the Sultan's eldest son, followed by a 'dreary visit' to the BBC relay station, which His Excellency had decided would be more interesting than the launch trip downriver to a Malay *kampong*, which John had suggested. Finally, in the evening, 'Johore surpassed itself with a terrific reception at the Astana Besar, the Great Palace that was reserved for State functions,' which included 'the grand reception room furnished entirely in glass'. John was unusually fulsome in praising 'the glitter of uniforms and evening dresses and sashes and medals'. Even he conformed, wearing his CBE on his collar until told by a great friend, the local brigadier, 'that on such occasions it should only be worn in insignificant miniature on the breast'.[10] For all that, John long remembered the occasion as a great Malay triumph, 'a most brilliant and successful show'.

Their last engagement before Independence was to welcome the returning Sultan Ibrahim, a venerable octogenarian, at Singapore docks. He displeased his fellow Malays by declining to attend either the 'jollifications' in Kuala Lumpur or the State ceremony in Johore Bahru. But one man who *did* accept his official invitation to the Independence Day celebrations was Gerald Templer, who combined it with a sentimental visit to Yong Peng. The first John knew about this was a telephone call, asking him to make the necessary arrangements.

> I motored up to Kluang where he was staying the night with the Gurkhas. I waited for him beside a helicopter while he walked down the road lined with soldiers. All he said to me was, 'Hullo, John,' just as if we had met yesterday. We climbed in and were off on the 15-minute journey to the village . . . [where] he was met by a crowd of old friends of all nationalities and marched to the village hall to the strains of the village band. Here he gave one of his old talks, praising them here and ticking them [off] there and completely forgetting he was no longer the High Commissioner . . . After his talk he was piled into an open lorry with his old pals and they took him to show him the improvements to the village . . .

It was the tightest of schedules. In no time Templer had to be whisked back with John to Kluang aerodrome where, after a quick farewell, the general climbed into his aircraft and was gone. John had contributed to a highly successful public relations occasion. 'Certainly Yong Peng liked it,' he said with satisfaction, 'not least Miss Griggs, the elderly English missionary, who had instigated the visit by writing to Templer in England to say the villagers insisted he should come.'

And so to Merdeka, Independence Day, 31 August 1957, an historic moment when the Federation of Malaya became an independent democratic state presided over by a sovereign paramount ruler. For the British an era of political influence in the Far East that dated back to 1786 was finally over. For the people of Malaya a new era was beginning. The principal celebrations took place by right in the new Merdeka Stadium in Kuala Lumpur, before an ecstatic crowd, amid 'much pomp and circumstance and goodwill'. Although it was not the volatile situation predicted by some administrators, in some areas formalities were limited to a proclamation and flag-raising ceremony. Elsewhere celebrations depended on local initiatives.[11] In Johore Bahru John remembered being awakened around midnight on the 30th by a loudspeaker blaring the speeches being made in Kuala Lumpur. There was a little cracker-firing, then it fell quiet. The next morning he donned his Malayan Civil Service full dress for the last time and went down to the *padang* (an open, grassy space) to witness the Proclamation of Independence. He and Helen took the children, despite some rumours of racial trouble, which John dismissed out of hand. 'It was quite an impressive little ceremony with a guard of honour and a band and plenty of glitter among the onlookers. The proclamation was read by the Deputy Mentri Besar as the rest were in Kuala Lumpur. The children were delighted with the salute of guns . . . In the evening we went into the town to see the illuminations which were really very fine.' All around the country similar scenes were enacted to celebrate Malaya's Day of Freedom.

Happily, none of the adverse consequences of Merdeka predicted by European Jonahs occurred. John found that 'work here in Johore is the same as ever and the "government" set-up unchanged and very pleasant'. In point of fact he struck up excellent relations with the Johore administration, and it was a measure of his warmth towards his new colleagues that in 1958 he alerted his parents that 'three very good friends of ours, Syed Zainal, Abdullah, and Charles Lowe with their wives are on leave in England now and . . . I have asked them to call on you'.[12]

In the second half of 1957 there was more diplomatic jockeying between the Communist leader and Malaya's Chief Minister to bring the Emergency to a close. In the run-up to Merdeka the prospect of coupling independence with peace gained public appeal and Tunku Abdul Rahman was under some political pressure to meet Chin Peng for talks. This coincided with a letter sent from the MCP to Chinese organisations putting forward conditions for peace negotiations. In the afterglow of Merdeka, however, the Tunku renewed surrender terms to assist the flow of desertions from the Communist ranks. Chin Peng's next move came in mid-October, when in a letter to the Chief Minister he indicated his readiness to take part in talks after a preliminary meeting of their representatives.[13] The Tunku in turn was willing to discuss means for ending hostilities, and in anticipation of preliminary talks John was asked to act as government envoy or contact officer to meet Chen Tien, the Communist representative. A verbal approach must have preceded the secret confirmation John received from Johore's Chief of Police on 12 November. In an operation code-named 'Changol', John was to be ready to fly from Singapore via Kuala Lumpur to the contact area, accompanied by another government officer.[14] The little border town of Kroh was the likely venue. A follow-up letter marked 'Top Secret and Personal' from the Secretary for Defence and Internal Security confirmed John's appointment as official emissary to contact Chin Peng if preliminary talks were held. The other Malayan Civil Service officer, Che Yeop Mahidin, a Malay, was to accompany him. However, when a month had elapsed without further word from Chin Peng, Tunku Abdul Rahman sent him an ultimatum on 6 December, giving him until the end of the year to send his emissary to arrange the meeting. In a note dated the 11th and posted from Province Wellesley, Chin Peng offered to send Chen Tien and Musa Ahmed to meet the government's representatives, but he repeated his absolute refusal to consider surrender terms. Consequently, on 22 December the Tunku finally turned down Chin Peng's request for a meeting. Operation 'Changol' came to nothing. John focused his attention once more on military tactics to end the war.

To some extent this episode impacted on Operations 'Cobble' and 'Shoe' taking place in Johore. For a potential surrendered enemy person to receive a reward and lead the Security Forces back to his former camp was a high-risk move, one he would be disinclined to take if talks between Chin Peng and the government were likely to take place. But the question still remained, how long could 'ragged, hungry, fugitive, apprehensive' CTs, who were 'increasingly suspicious of the reliability of their own comrades', hold out for peace or surrender?[15] Starvation stared them in the face. The last man to give up in West Segamat MCP district was so desperate that he paid Straits $100 to a small boy for one banana.[16]

By the last quarter of 1957 the Communist war effort in North Johore was crumbling. On 4 December Ah Chien, the senior figure in the Johore–Malacca Border Committee, indicated his desire to defect, and with a handful of companions he was brought out by an officer of the Cheshire Regiment. The western part of 'Cobble's operational area was cleared. Some supplies were still reaching the South Malayan Bureau from Segamat district and there were Communist survivors in the Yong Peng–Bekok target area of Operation 'Shoe'. Nevertheless John was satisfied: 'We are certainly getting a grip of the Emergency and have reduced the problem in Johore by a half over the last year.' Before the end of 1957 the Johore SWEC, with John at the helm, decided the time was ripe to extend priority operations to South Johore, where almost a hundred terrorists were still thought to be lurking in the jungle. In the preliminary planning of Operation 'Tiger', launched on 1 January 1958, John had the full cooperation of Brig Walker and his battalion commanders of 99 Gurkha Brigade, in addition to the support of police, Special Branch and 'psywar' services. By mid-April, Phase I operations aimed at the Kulai and Pontian areas had resulted in the elimination of a Communist cell.

Meanwhile, in February, among the guerrillas who opted to surrender in North Johore were four members of the group supplying Hor Lung's headquarters. This gave the Segamat DWEC, and Special Branch in particular, a rare opportunity to exploit the situation to 'turn' the CTs against their comrades, to the detriment of the head of the South Malayan Bureau. The professionalism of the Security Forces was about to pay off. Nevertheless, not even a born optimist like John Davis would have forecast the 'miraculous disintegration' of Communist organisations in Johore that happened in the spring and summer of 1958.[17]

The first step caught everyone by surprise, even Brig Powell-Jones, the Gurkha commander in Segamat. On 5 April a call from Special Branch alerted 'P-J' to the greatest catch of the Emergency. An unprepossessing figure in singlet and underpants had presented himself at the police post at Kampong Tengah New Village, but refused to reveal his identity until he talked to Special Branch. The disenchanted character was Hor Lung, the senior Malayan terrorist in the field, by all accounts a dedicated, fanatical, intelligent and incorruptible Communist. More to the point, his defection raised the possibility of mass surrenders: 'If the secret of his surrender could be kept he was the one man who could bring out every surviving terrorist in Johore.'[18]

Only a small number of officers from Special Branch, the military, the SWEC and the District Sub-Committee in Segamat were involved in planning and implementing the steps by which Hor Lung enticed his comrades from their deepest hideouts. Through his influence some local leaders came in from the jungle: Lee Tuan of the North Johore Regional Committee; Ah Chiau, District Committee Secretary of Pontian district; and Kim Cheng, who ran Yong Peng for ten years and in turn brought out twenty members of No. 7 Independent Platoon. Hor Lung himself worked under discreet protection. 'The essence of his success lay in his knowledge of terrorist dispositions and habits, his own personal authority, and the fact that his defection was unsuspected,' wrote a participant of 'Dogpatch', the name the Segamat team gave to the Hor Lung operation. To this one should add the contribution of the 'puppet-master' of the operation, Ken Larby, the Head of Special Branch, Johore, and Hor Lung's support team, which included 'Special Branch officers dressed as CTs and a young National Service officer whose job . . . was to help with any rough stuff that might develop'. In return for his services, Hor Lung received Straits $247,000, making him seriously rich. Those he induced to surrender also received generous rewards.

In the weeks after Hor Lung's defection John's responsibilities intensified. Phase II of Operation 'Tiger' began on 15 April, ten days after Hor Lung's surrender, its objective to destroy the South Johore Regional HQ, commanded by a formidable adversary, Ah Ann. The plans had already been laid with Brig Walker and the Johore SWEC, with John in the chair. The hope was that by a combination of aerial bombardment, intensive patrolling and protracted ambushes, the terrorists would be killed, betrayed or induced to surrender. Simultaneously, at the other end of Johore, the exploitation of Hor Lung's surrender was well under way. To make sure his blandishments had a chance to take effect, John indicated to the Segamat team the need for a softly-softly approach. He also indicated when and where adjustments to routine operations should be made, so that Hor Lung's jungle journeys to bring out CT defectors would not be impeded by accidental encounters with the Security Forces, and outside the jungle no suspicious abnormalities in anti-terrorist activities would be discernible. His instructions were always couched in clear, unvarnished language. 'A larger military presence here. Relax searching and food control there . . . Keep the level of psychological warfare constant, no more, no less, in Labis and Bekok. Put the squeeze on the Gemas Bharu Branch. Take it off again . . .'[19]

This secret, patient process continued for four months until the enemy's strength on the order of battle in the Segamat DWEC operations room had been reduced to nil. 'The Emergency is clearing up fairly rapidly now', wrote John of the Johore situation. A parallel operation in southern Perak, launched after the defection of a regional political commissar in October 1957, took until April 1959 to achieve a target of 170, of which 112 were surrendered personnel.[20] In North Johore by August 1958, to the 132 guerrillas who were killed, captured or had surrendered in the last phase of 'Cobble' could be added 28 more, making a total of 160. In the opinion of an officer who had worked under him for eighteen months, this had been 'a complex production orchestrated with great skill and wisdom by John Davis, the Deputy Chairman of the Johore SWEC'.[21]

In August 1958 the government felt able to declare the whole of North Johore a White Area. The Defence Minister, Dato Abdul Razak, visited Yong Peng to make the announcement. Operation 'Cobble' was formally wound up and with it the Segamat DWEC. By the end of August, 58 of the 96 guerrillas in South Johore had also been eliminated, leaving only the hard-core CTs of the South Johore Regional HQ. Operation 'Tiger' was concluded at the end of the year with the final clearing of South Johore. With the whole state declared a White Area, this was a time of genuine celebration. A generation of Malayans who had reached adulthood knowing only a society that was subjected to violence, deprivation and fear, would enjoy peace as well as freedom in the first time in their lives.

As the surrenders climaxed in Johore John was pondering his future. While he was wondering whether it would be symbiotically linked with the results of 'Cobble', 'Shoe' and 'Tiger', he received a timely official approach: would he consider repeating what he had done in Johore in the northern state of Kedah? In reality the Malayan government was offering him a high-level post until mid-1960. John agreed, on condition of first taking some home leave. Above all, he wanted the chance to introduce the latest addition to the family to his English relatives. The birth of Ralph Thomas Humphrys Davis on 14 June had been completely overshadowed by the spectacular collapse of the Communist insurgency in Johore, although John did remember to put an announcement of his third son's arrival in the *Straits Times*.

The last three weeks before leaving were crammed with engagements. A press conference on 26 August in Kuala Lumpur was followed later that day by a party in Segamat thrown by the Administrative Officer, Michael McConville, to mark the end of Operation 'Cobble'. On the 31st, the first anniversary of Independence, a special tea party was held in Johore Bahru. Within the week John gave his last talk to a group of Chinese Affairs Officers on the Emergency and counter-subversion, and there were still meetings of the State and District Committees to attend right up to the eve of their departure.

The night before he retired as Deputy Chairman Johore SWEC John received a telegram from 99 Gurkha Infantry Brigade. It said:

PERSONAL FROM BRIG. WALKER TO MR DAVIS. IT HAS BEEN A GREAT PLEASURE SERVING IN SOUTH JOHORE UNDER YOUR DIRECTION. THE GUIDANCE AND WISE COUNSEL WHICH YOU HAVE ALWAYS GIVEN US HAS I AM SURE BEEN THE MAJOR REASON FOR THE GREAT SUCCESSES ACHIEVED IN JOHORE OVER THE LAST FEW MONTHS. FROM MYSELF AND MY STAFF AND 99 BRIGADE I SEND YOU BEST WISHES FOR YOUR LEAVE AND FOR SUCCESS IN KEDAH.

With this ringing endorsement from a fighting Gurkha commander, John, with Helen and the children, flew off from Singapore the following day.

Epilogue

John knew that Kedah would be his last tour. The Malayanisation of the civil service had rightly advanced to the point where only 60 European administrators were left, whereas formerly there had been 400. The survivors, John wrote, were 'a few of the more carefree youngsters who have learnt to love the country and foolishly cannot drag themselves away' or 'second-raters on the make or old fogies long in the tooth which the government is too kind to kill off (and I am afraid I am one of the last category – aged 48!)'.

A staunchly Malay state, Kedah was full of surprises. The western belt was a land of flat, open *padi* fields, offering striking views eastwards to the distant hills. 'The countryside is wonderfully beautiful – absolute contrast to Johore,' wrote John enthusiastically. 'Sunrise is often unbelievable.' On 23 January John reached Alor Star, the seat of the Sultan of Kedah and the State government, where he would be based in his capacity as Acting Chairman of Kedah SWEC. As with Bentong, he found the 'very small town' atmosphere hugely appealing. Even the weather was welcoming in the first few days. 'Lovely . . . very dry and bright with a good breeze blowing', no matter that it would turn very hot, heavy and humid a month later.

John's first priority was to meet the senior members of the State government and of the SWEC, the chief of police and Brigadier Upjohn, the officer commanding the infantry brigade, consisting of four battalions of the Royal Malay Regiment. In a busy first week there were social engagements with VIPs, operations briefings, tours to meet Kedah's District Officers and the Mentri Besar, from whom John was taking over a range

of responsibilities. The Emergency in Kedah was small-scale in comparison
with Johore and he began with his characteristic complaint, 'I cannot
see much of a job!' In fact, he soon learned that for some while there
had been no firm *civilian* direction of counter-insurgency policy in Kedah:
instead, the state had been run by the police and the Army. The Mentri
Besar, Dato Syed Omar, was 'a most courteous, kindly and understanding
man' but he was no longer young and was partially sighted. After John's
arrival he seldom attended the operational meetings of the SWEC. To assist
the work of the SWEC John relied on Maj Alex Mineeff, the experienced
Military Intelligence Officer attached to Special Branch, who had moved
up with him from South Johore; the young, vigorous and utterly honest
Scottish police chief, H.W. Strathairn; the Federal Infantry Brigade; and
'one brigadier who looks askance at an interfering stranger'.[1] This was
Brig G.R. (Bob) Turner Cain. John appreciated his soldierly directness and
Turner Cain understood John's dislike of brass and chrome; and since they
held similar views of Thai cooperation, they were soon on good terms. In
the SWEC office John relied on the assistance of Shamsudin, 'a very good
fellow' who handled the Land Development work, and Miss Lee Ai Tin, his
confidential clerk, who managed all the secretarial work with efficiency
and charm.

Once John had taken stock, the situation in Kedah caused him no great
concern. Terrorist activity had patently dwindled to almost a standstill.[2] In
the strategic border area of Kroh–Baling (where the south-east corners of
Kedah and North Perak abutted the border with Thailand) the Operations
War Executive Committee was 'shaping well' under its chairman, the ADO,
Osman Khairrudin; and the activities of the South Kedah Security Forces
were already reduced to patrolling. There had been 'no incidents in the
whole of Kedah since June 1958 . . . and no incidents outside the border
areas for a very long time indeed'. John estimated that forty guerrillas were
operating in Kedah, of whom twenty-two in Central Kedah were already
being targeted. In theory these numbers were too low to make them viable
targets for elimination; in practice he hoped to succeed.

In the meantime, in May 1958 a major food denial operation,
Operation 'Jumlah', was set up in Central Kedah to cut off supplies to
the remaining terrorists and induce them to surrender. John took over
this initiative although he was sceptical as to whether it could succeed
in a rich rice-growing area like Kedah. In fact, the operation achieved

seven 'eliminations' by December 1958. After that there were no contacts with the CTs, nor had Special Branch any information of any terrorists in Central Kedah. All the same, John concluded that the emergency measures – curfews, police checks, controls on movement and food storage – should remain in force. The last operational success in Kedah State came in March 1959, a few weeks after he assumed his SWEC co-ordinating role, when the Security Forces killed three CTs at Changloon, near the Kedah–Perlis border. In future the guerrillas remaining in Kedah were likely to be couriers or members of small contact groups, but not fighting units.

It was the border region with Thailand, with its 100 miles of undeveloped mountain jungle, which constituted the outstanding problem for the Malayan government. Despite a decade in which various initiatives had been tried, John could tell that aspirations had not produced results.[3] In 1957 a start had been made on winning *kampong* and aboriginal people from their past association with the Communists by a key road-building programme to bring government services and amenities to rural communities. But guerrillas on the Malayan side still had no difficulty evading capture, slipping by uncharted jungle paths across into southern Thailand.[4] When John arrived in Kedah he found liaison with the Thais was conducted by two CPOs sitting together monthly on a small committee. 'Relations were good but the liaison was limited to minor operations by the odd PFF platoon over the Border.'[5] Here there were neither food restrictions nor controls, but 30,000 Chinese inhabitants ready to give material support to fellow Chinese. It was obvious to John why the borderlands had not been sealed to the Communist guerrillas, but he was reluctant to publicise it for political reasons.[6]

The hope of a breakthrough came at the end of July 1959, when John went to Kuala Lumpur for further talks about the Thai–Malay border issue. He admitted confidentially:

> The talks sounded good but I am afraid they mean very little. The main object of the Thais was to have a good time . . . I understand the scale of entertainment one gets under similar conditions in Siam is absolutely magnificent! They don't seem to have the same sort of Treasury that we have . . . The talks were meant to ginger up operations in South Thailand where all our terrorists have gone. We have a long-standing arrangement with the Siamese that our police – but not our soldiers – can operate over the border

against them . . . The principal object of these talks was to get them to take action and if possible to persuade them to use soldiers – the police are useless. They have only given us half a promise . . . As far as I am concerned the only difference is that our liaison over the border . . . will now be part of my responsibility.

On 2 August, in a gesture of cooperation, John was invited to fly with the Thais over the virgin jungles of the Bentong salient, where Communist camps had existed since 1953. The main outcome of the July talks, however, was the formation of the Border Operations Committee, with John chairing the Malay side. The Malay authorities hoped that this body would deliver Thai cooperation for specific police and military anti-terrorist operations on Thai soil. There were further conferences in September and December 1959, but John was still frustrated by the inability of the Thai military and police to cooperate with each other.

By the beginning of 1960 the DWECs of both South and Central Kedah no longer met regularly. John reported:

There are some 500 well-armed, well-fed and well-led CTs in South Thailand. They are not in any way aggressive although they live in the most elaborate and best-fortified camps I have yet seen. They are busy divesting themselves of 'weaker brethren' and preparing to 'sit it out' till the political tide changes. I do not personally think they are in much of a position to influence the political tide in this country one way or another and for that reason I do not think they are really of any great significance. Nevertheless it is very uncomfortable to have them 'leering' at us from over the border and we have to try to eliminate them or at least take preventive action to keep them outside our territory.

The kind of action he had in mind would place greater emphasis on intelligence and continuing use of PFF patrols; but he knew the only lasting solution lay in sustained diplomatic cooperation between the Malayan and Thai governments, leading to more joint activity by their Security Forces.

Meanwhile, the need to rationalise the administration of the operational area of Kedah SWEC was another matter on John's mind. In 1959 a White Area had been created in the coastal plain and the area between Kedah Peak and Province Wellesley. Further inland a very similar, so-called 'Relaxed Area' was delineated.[7] In the east the operational area remained 'Black', in the sense that a theoretical skeleton food control and curfew were still in place. The area was equally divided into two zones. The northern half, John admitted openly, was 'a mess administratively and I do not know what to do about it'.[8] Fortunately, the southern zone was functioning well. But it was still necessary to maintain military framework operations in the border area of North Kedah, to check terrorist forays across the border and to support operations in the Sadao area of southern Thailand, where Chin Peng's guerrilla headquarters were sited.

The prospect of progress improved near the end of John's tour when the Thais appointed an experienced police officer, Maj Gen Chan, as task force commander. Michael McConville, who succeeded John, confirmed that Chan was 'the only Thai with, approximately, his heart in his work';[9] and John noted in his diary that 'Chan does seem genuinely determined to do something effective and of course we shall back him to the hilt'.[10] Ultimately the resolution of the border problem depended on effective liaison between Chan and Kedah's chief of police and their successors.

In June 1959, amid this long-running saga of Malay–Thai border relations, John received a highly gratifying piece of news. In celebration of the *Agong*'s (King's) birthday he was to be honoured for his contribution to the ending of the Communist Emergency in Johore with the award of a new Federation medal, the JMN (Commander of the Order of the Defender of the Realm). On 12 November he travelled down to Kuala Lumpur with Helen for the investiture and received his medal from the *Yang di-Pertuan Agong* (Malaysia's sovereign ruler) himself. This honour was followed three months later by notification that in celebration of the coronation of the new Sultan of Johore, he was to receive a second medal, for his work in Johore, the SMJ (Faithful to the Crown of Johore). These would be carefully kept with his British wartime awards of CBE and DSO, a Mention in Despatches and his two pre-war police commendations for service in the Federated Malay States Police Service.

News of his JMN had unfortunately coincided with a severe attack of fever, thought to be dengue. 'I am getting rather close to the exhaustion point for the tropics which is about thirty years,' he wrote a little wearily. Other medical problems affected him later in the year, but he had already faced up to 'the fact that I am redundant and it is really quite unfair to expect the government to find me another job'. On 30 September he gave notice that he wished to leave the service in March 1960, after which he would be entitled to three months' final leave, ending on 20 June.

In the meantime, decisions on the revised regulation of the border area were being finalised in Kuala Lumpur by the Emergency Operations Council. John was duly informed of the proposed new arrangements in a draft paper he received on the eve of leaving Malaya. Kedah SWEC would ultimately become the nucleus of a new Border War Executive Committee (BWEC) with responsibilities for a newly defined 'Border Security Area', covering 'a fairly deep, irregular belt along the whole of the Thai border from Perlis to Kelantan'. This body would also be charged with implementing cross-border operations with the Thais. In other words, as BWEC Chairman, John's successor would inherit a geographically extended version of his old remit based in Alor Star and would take over the formal meetings of the Thai–Malayan Border Committee. He would work in conjunction with other committee members, the chief police officers of Perak and Kelantan and the brigadiers of the Malay and Commonwealth Brigades.

John was greatly relieved that the proposals were eminently sensible, and he was satisfied that Kedah would be in good hands. With only about 100 guerrillas left in the country in March 1960, and a token force across the border, it had seemed the right moment for him to bow out. Besides, by now the Malayan people as a whole were confidently anticipating the formal end of the state of Emergency. It came at last on 31 July 1960, in a government declaration that marked the cessation of twelve years of internal conflict.

The voyage home in the spring, followed by his official retirement from Malayan government service in the summer of 1960, drew a line under the three decades of John Davis's adult life in the Far East. For the following forty-five years the Davises lived first in Kent and then in Sussex. In May 1961 John took up the position of General Secretary of the Kent Council of Social Service, which he held until his retirement in 1974. It was a happy choice, based on Folkestone and so close enough to the wide arc of Malayan friends in the Home Counties, with the benefits of sea and country. His passion for the jungle and the vibrancy of the tropical light was superseded by his youthful love of the South Downs and the pale, cool palette of temperate England.

In 1931 John Davis had been one of a stream of young middle-class Englishmen who looked to the colonies for a rewarding career. The British in Malaya were still serenely confident in those days of the benevolent paternalism of the Empire, oblivious to a changing world in which Malaya was moving unknowingly but inexorably towards a catastrophic war. When the conflict broke out in 1941 existing hostilities were suspended – the enmity between Great Britain and the Chinese MCP, and between the Communists and the Chinese Nationalist supporters of the KMT – as they all faced a common enemy in Imperial Japan. From 1941 to 1945 John was immersed in the special operations to foster resistance to the Japanese Occupation of Malaya. With the support of his friend Chin Peng and the cooperation of the leaders of the MPAJA, Force 136, under John's command, eventually prepared for the restoration of British rule.

Trust, especially in people of another culture or race, tended to be a matter of expediency. John's wartime experiences, however, linked him directly with three prominent Chinese leaders. His friendship with Lim Bo Seng was genuine, though all too short-lived, to his regret. Little is known of John's personal or professional relations with Lai Tek, the highest-ranking Communist in Malaya. As a professional spy and triple agent, Lai Tek's masterly opportunism hoodwinked comrades, allies, even enemies, and against the odds he outwitted others to save his own skin. However, the ultimate exposure and downfall of the Secretary-General in 1947 at the hands of Chin Peng reinforced John's resolute determination to maintain total silence over his connections with Lai Tek.[11] Paradoxically, he felt much more comfortable with Chin Peng, the man who was to become Britain's chief enemy – and consequently his own – in the long Communist struggle for the soul of Malaya. John could never forget that during the war he owed his life and the continuing existence of Force 136 to Chin Peng's vigilance and protection. Although he had no illusions about the Chinese leader's innate hostility to British colonialism, their comradeship in the jungle enabled each to continue to respect the other even as enemies during the Communist Insurgency. Sixty years after the end of the war Chin Peng was still unequivocal in his regard for John. He wrote in his memoirs, 'Since we first met I had formed perhaps the closest association I would ever strike with a European . . . I had always liked Davis, indeed admired him . . . he [Davis] was brave and energetic, perfect for the extraordinarily dangerous job he did in Malaya during the war.'[12]

In 1963 echoes of another Englishman's connections with Communism broke upon the British nation, when it was disclosed in Parliament that a senior government officer and double agent had defected to Soviet Russia. His exposure was much overdue. Kim Philby had infiltrated the SIS, rising to became head MI6 officer in Washington at the height of the Cold War. John felt mixed emotions at the news. Though their relationship belonged to the distant past, Kim Philby, the son of an Indian civil servant, a nice, sporty, extremely clever boy, had been John Davis's best friend at the prep school, Aldro, before Kim won a scholarship to Westminster and John went to Tonbridge. Philby's story now reopened all the issues that Lai Tek's duplicity had once raised in John's mind. Philby had been educated in the same tradition of duty, loyalty and patriotism as John but was allegedly responsible for the deaths of numerous unnamed Allied agents. Lai Tek had betrayed Communist comrades and John's KMT Intelligence network to the Japanese Kempeitai. Later, during the Malayan Emergency Communist guerrillas perpetrated the vicious killing of Chinese, Indians, Malays and British. Planters, estate workers and managers, villagers, young police constables and National Service conscripts – men, women and children – fell victim to the Communists. Although most incidents were organised at local level by subordinates, it was Chin Peng as their Party leader who ultimately carried the blame. John detested the violence and duplicity he observed over twenty years, but he remained resolutely non-judgemental. Experience had taught him that the truth was rarely a matter of simple explanation.

In 1989 as people power tore down the state armour of Communism in Eastern Europe, crucial preliminary discussions were under way to end the 41-year-long struggle between the MCP and Malaysia and Thailand. Accordingly, on 2 December 1989 Chin Peng, the MCP leader, who in different circumstances might have become Malaya's Ho Chi Minh, agreed to end all armed activity. He pledged loyalty to the *Yang di-Pertuan Agong* and to the laws and constitution of Malaysia. He praised the Malaysian government's spirit of understanding and compromise that allowed the

MCP to claim they had won peace with honour. Others in Malaysia, however, believed the accords resulted from the close cooperation between Malaysia and Thailand, particularly on security matters, which John Davis had identified as essential to peace and tried to put in place in 1959–60.

In 1994, when Chin Peng's initial hopes of living in Malaysia foundered, he settled in southern Thailand. Subsequently he travelled to Australia and Britain, giving media interviews, academic seminars and undertaking archival research.[13] During the summer of 1998, the fiftieth anniversary of the outbreak of the Malayan Emergency, Chin Peng gave an interview to BBC television on the rebellion against British rule. He let it be known that he would welcome the opportunity to meet John Davis, his old friend and adversary, again. On hearing this there was great excitement in the Davis family. For as long as Patta and her brothers could remember, 'Chin Peng' had been a household name that figured prominently in their father's stories about Malaya. They were also aware of the high respect in which he was held by John. In Humphrey Davis's words, to meet Chin Peng 'was like the Second Coming'. So when the message arrived they all saw it as a chance to rekindle the trust and friendship that had been extinguished by the rough justice of politics.

There was some delay and uncertainty over the arrangements, which were allegedly handled by the middleman who first traced John's whereabouts. Chin Peng, however, stated later that he personally telephoned Davis.[14] Although he had agreed to a reunion, before the day arrived John became increasingly anxious, even fearful, of the face-to-face encounter being planned. It was the reticence of an 87-year-old man, suspicious of ideologies and politicians and nervous of the passage of time upon his own faculties: after all, forty-three years had slipped away since they last talked at Baling. He had always respected other men's beliefs, but he could see no virtue now in raking over old ideological ground or becoming involved in a post-hoc discussion of Communism. He wanted to remember Chin Peng as a wartime friend and ally, not as the leader of the Malayan Communists. 'I have to be very careful to keep the two aspects of him strictly apart in my mind,' he explained, otherwise their meeting might end on a distinctly sour note. He was also worried about the Official Secrets Act and the possibility that he might be drawn into revealing highly sensitive matters, such as his Special Branch role in running Lai Tek.

As he pondered, John decided that for his peace of mind he should protect himself by laying down certain conditions. First, the meeting would take place in his own home. Second, to guarantee everyone's privacy there should be no journalists present, nor should anyone be told of the arrangements. And third it was to be a purely personal occasion, that is to say, without any official standing.

On these terms Chin Peng was invited for an informal lunch.[15] He accepted and was accompanied by his niece, 'a very pretty lady'. With John and Helen were their son Humphrey and his wife Dilla, who were there to represent the younger generation of the Davis family. John himself was to do the honours by greeting his guests off the London train at Shoreham and driving them back to his Sussex home. He has never revealed the language they used in their first exchange of words at the station, but sitting in the lounge of their bungalow they talked throughout in English, while Helen served a sandwich lunch.

As Humphrey Davis gazed across at the two friends reunited, he was conscious of a historic moment he would never forget. He was deeply impressed by Chin Peng's impeccable manners, by his charm and politeness and the natural confidence of a man of evident intellect. In stature he was quite heavily built, and taller than Humphrey expected after seeing youthful snapshots taken in 1945 that were in his father's wartime album. For a part of the time the discussion in the lounge flowed very politely around family matters as the two veterans swapped family photos. But looking out through the picture windows to the walnut tree gracing the front lawn, their conversation turned naturally to the English weather: and that was where John ensured it remained.

Humphrey sensed strongly that Chin Peng was all the while itching to turn the talk to a more serious note, but John manfully resisted. At one point Chin Peng implied that he would like to meet John again at a later date but John was evasive and nothing more was said. For the rest of the time they reverted to 'idle chit-chat' until it was time for Chin Peng and his niece to take their leave.

The whole occasion had been conducted with diplomacy, civility and decorum. Politics had been outmanoeuvred and sleeping dogs left to lie. John must have felt relief and satisfaction as he drove his Chinese visitors back in time to catch the London train. In the end their departure was restrained and unremarkable. It was on the platform of Shoreham railway station that the two incomparable old warriors said their final farewells.

Afterword

A Tribute from Chin Peng

John Davis died peacefully on 27 October 2006 in his ninety-sixth year. On hearing of his death, Chin Peng responded from the other side of the world with a message to the Davis family, which included a personal tribute to John. He asked that the latter might be read out publicly at John's Funeral Service, which was held at All Saints' Church, Grayswood, Haslemere, on Monday 6 November 2006. In accordance with his request, the tribute was duly read by John's nephew and godson, John Davis.

REMEMBERING JOHN DAVIS

Many people tend to believe that friendships cannot bridge the divisions of international conflict – particularly in situations where those with close bonds of trust and understanding find themselves in bitterly opposing camps. I would quietly differ from this viewpoint. I would even go as far as to suggest that perhaps there might be a lesson for our troubled world today in the decades-long relationship that has existed between my friend, John Davis, and myself.

It is not that we were in constant touch with each other throughout this time. Historical circumstances determined that this was not to be. But these very historical circumstances also determined that at no point in our lives, once we had met and worked together, would we ever forget each other.

I well remember the day John Davis and I first came into contact. It was 30 September 1943. The place was Segari beach on the Malacca Straits section of Perak State in Japanese-occupied Malaya. John was there to establish links to the outlawed MCP – the only active anti-Japanese Resistance group then in existence in the country. After initial introductions, John presented me with his credentials – a letter signed by Adm Louis Mountbatten, head of Britain's Ceylon-based SEAC. I was there representing the Perak State Committee of the MCP.

That initial meeting forged an association that was at first expedient. We both wanted to rid Malaya of a common enemy. But both of us ultimately realised that the period of being allies in a common cause would eventually come to an end. And it did.

But I can never forget my time together with John in the Malayan jungle. I remember him as an implacable leader in the most harrowing of circumstances. On one occasion, in the Bidor region of southern Perak, John and I, together with a band of MCP guerrillas, had gathered to recover a joint personnel and arms drop by RAF aircraft. Things went terribly wrong. Parachutes landed in wrong areas. Arms landed where personnel should have been and vice versa. And to top it all, we came under heavy Japanese machine-gun fire. I was 20 years old at the time. John was in his early thirties. I had never encountered such a sustained attack before and perhaps for the first time in my life I knew the feeling of real fear. I looked across at John and he appeared calm and in control. This is the picture of John Davis that has stayed on my mind all these years.

John was also a man of principle and I recognised that very early on. I came to appreciate it when our guerrillas became his group's Security Force at the hill-top Blantan camp. I knew it when the MCP signed the Blantan Agreement with SEAC on 26 February 1945. This tied his cause and mine to an honourable agreement, albeit of limited duration.

I knew it when I saw him again during the Malayan Emergency. We renewed old ties at the so-called Baling peace talks in northern Malaya from 28–9 December 1955. Sadly, these failed. Because of our wartime association, John had been deputised to look after me at Baling during the MCP's negotiations with Malaya's Tunku Abdul Rahman and Singapore's David Marshall. John escorted me to and from each bargaining session. My onetime ally was now my enemy. We both acknowledged this fact. But at no point during that Baling episode did I feel any personal hostility on his part. Neither did I feel any antagonism towards him. We strongly differed on matters of politics and principle, but there was still great mutual respect that precluded personal enmity.

The world moves on. Visions and goals likewise modify and change from all perspectives. So when I visited the United Kingdom in 1998, I sought out my old friend John Davis. It was my way of showing my deep gratitude for a man who, despite being vehemently opposed to my anti-British colonial struggle, always treated me fairly and decently. You cannot ask more of a man or a friend. John Davis is a great loss to this troubled world.

One final thought. When John and I got together in Britain that day in 1998 he gently laid down the ground rules for our reunion. 'Chin Peng,' he said, 'let's just talk about the good old days.'

And that is how I will always remember him – John Davis in the good old days.

Chin Peng

2 November 2006

Appendix 1

Glossary of Acronyms

ADO	Assistant District Officer	DWEC	District War Executive Committee
AJA	Anti-Japanese Army		
AJU	Anti-Japanese Union		
AJUF	Anti-Japanese Union Forces	EXCO	State Executive Council
ALFSEA	Allied Land Forces, South East Asia	FANY	First Aid Nursing Yeomanry
AMS	Ashkar Melayu Setia (Loyal Malay Army)	FARELF	Far East Land Forces
		GLO	Group Liaison Officer
		GLT	Group Liaison Team
BMA	British Military Administration	GOC	General Officer Commanding
BWEC	Border War Executive Committee	HQ	Headquarters
		ISLD	Inter-Services Liaison Department
CBE	Commander of the British Empire		
CCAO	Chief Civil Affairs Officer	KMT	Kuomintang (Nationalist Party of China)
CID	Criminal Intelligence Department		
CO	Commanding Officer	LEGCO	Legislative Council
CPO	Chief Police Officer		
CT	communist terrorist	MCA	Malayan Chinese Association
		MCP	Malayan Communist Party
DSO	Distinguished Service Order	MCS	Malayan Civil Service

MOCSDA	Malayan Overseas Chinese Self-Defence Army	RN	Royal Navy
MPABA	Malayan People's Anti-British Army	RNVR	Royal Naval Volunteer Reserve
MPAJA	Malayan People's Anti-Japanese Army	SACSEA	Supreme Allied Command South East Asia
MRLA	Malayan Races Liberation Army	SAS	Special Air Service
		SCA	Secretary for Chinese Affairs
		SDO	Senior District Officer
NCO	non-commissioned officer	SEAC	South East Asia Command
NVLO	New Villages Liaison Officer	SHGO	State Home Guard Officer
		SIS	Secret Intelligence Service (MI6)
OBE	Order of the British Empire		
OC	Officer Commanding	SOE	Special Operations Executive
OCPD	Officer Commanding Police District	SOVF	Special Operations Volunteer Force
OSPC	Officer Superintending Police Circle	STS	Special Training School
		SWEC	State War Executive Committee
PFF	Police Field Force		
'the Plen'	Plenipotentiary of the MCP	UMNO	United Malays National Organisation
RA	Royal Artillery		
RAAF	Royal Australian Air Force	VE	Victory in Europe
RAF	Royal Air Force	VIP	Very Important Person
RAMC	Royal Army Medical Corps	VJ	Victory over Japan
RASC	Royal Army Service Corps		
RE	Royal Engineers	W/T	Wireless Telegraphy

Appendix 2

Glossary of Foreign Words

Agong	King
amah	children's nursemaid, Malay/Chinese
atap	nipa palm thatch
Dato	general male non-royal title of distinction, lit. grandfather
Dyak	aborigines from Borneo, known as skilled jungle trackers
Hailam	Chinese immigrants originating from the island of Hainan, off the coast of China
Inche	a polite form of address for untitled Malays
jelutong	rubbery tree resin, ingredient of chewing gum, found in tropical jungle
kampong	village/rural settlement
kaput	head
mem	wife of a European male/lady of the house
Merdeka	Independence Day
orang asli	descendants of the aboriginal people of the Malay Peninsula
padang	an open, grassy space (usually in an urban setting)
padi	rice/ricefields
prahu	multi-hull sailing ship of Malay origin
sampan	small rowing boat
stengah	drink of one half whisky, one half soda, popular with Europeans
sumatra	sudden gale blowing across the Malacca Straits to Malaya
Teochew	Chinese immigrant community and dialect originating in South Min, an ancient Chinese community facing Taiwan
Temiar	a Malay aboriginal tribe

tongah	light pony trap
tongkang	a light boat used for transporting goods by river
towkay	wealthy Chinese businessman/manager
Tunku	Malay prince/title of a member of a Malay ruling house
Yang di-Pertuan Agong	Malaysia's head of state and sovereign ruler (lit. 'he who is lord and king')

Appendix 3

Place-names of Geographical Derivation

Ayer	water (e.g. Ayer Busok)
Bagan	jetty/landing stage for merchandise (e.g. Bagan Datoh)
Batu	stone/rock/mile post (e.g. Batu Anam)
Bukit	hill (e.g. Bukit Mertajam)
Gunong	mountain (e.g. Gunong Batu Puteh)
Kampong	Malay township/settlement (e.g. Kampong Chaah)
Kota	fort/fortified town (e.g. Kota Bharu)
Kuala	river mouth/estuary/confluence (e.g. Kuala Bernam)
Pulau	island (e.g. Pulau Pangkor)
Simpang	junction of more than two roads (e.g. Simpang Tiga)
Sungei	river (e.g. Sungei Besi)
Telok	bay/wide stretch of water (e.g. Telok Anson)
Ulu	headwaters of river/hinterland/up-country/remote jungle area (e.g. Ulu Nenggiri)

Notes

PROLOGUE

1. National Archives of Singapore, Oral History Centre: John Davis, interview with Miss Tan Beng Luan, 7 April 1984.
2. *Ibid.*
3. Where possible, for simplicity's sake, the Chinese agents are called by their wartime aliases.
4. In addition, their packs included utensils, spare clothing, maps and private items. The official record (TNA: PRO H55/165) states that a Mark III W/T set was also taken in by Davis in Operation 'Gustavus I' and buried on the beach before the party set off, because it was too heavy to carry inland. But John Davis's own accounts, including his report on Operation 'Gustavus'/'Pirate', make clear this was not the case. He had only a small portable receiver. A cumbersome Mark III set was not brought in until August 1943 in Operation 'Gustavus III'.
5. Ah Ng picked up information about search parties. See R.N. Broome, report on 'Gustavus', Appendix D, John Davis personal papers.

CHAPTER 1

1. Capt Robert Charles Loveday, Senior Surveyor of Public Works in the Chief Engineer's Office, Singapore, was at the centre of a conspiracy involving European and Chinese building contractors. Of the installations erected in Singapore, Johore and Penang, it was found that, for example, some machine-gun posts were substandard and potentially dangerous. Loveday was said to

have benefited personally by *c*. Straits $169,000. At his trial he was cashiered and sentenced to two years' imprisonment in Changi Gaol, Singapore.

2. Letter to John Davis from Edmond Bunnens, 15 July 1996, John Davis personal papers. It is known that John Davis approached a fellow police officer, Inspector Edmond Bunnens, for assistance in finding a non-European contact inside the naval base. With the help of a friend who worked there, Bunnens gave John details of a Chinese employed in the gun shop.

3. A decision of the Chiefs of Staff in 1928 was responsible for the misjudgement. See Elphick, Peter and Smith, Michael, *Odd Man Out: The Story of the Singapore Traitor*, Hodder & Stoughton, London, 1993, pp. 5–6.

4. His aliases included Chang Hung, Wong Kim Geok, Wong Show Tong and a British name, Mr Wright.

5. I am grateful to Mr John Loch, formerly of the Malayan Civil Service, for alerting me to this aspect of John Davis's top-secret work. A very close friend from 1949, he was explicitly given this information by John in about 1992, some fifty years after the events, when it was exempt from security protection. At the age of 81 John Davis still had an excellent memory, and he was reluctant to allow this piece of information to die with him. Members of the Davis family consulted by the author have confirmed that, while they were not told explicitly, the information has the ring of truth.

6. Out of twelve secret intelligence organisations (excluding the police and liaison groups already mentioned), SIS and SOE are the most significant for John Davis's career: see Cruickshank, Charles, *SOE in the Far East*, Oxford University Press, Oxford, pp. 169–70.

7. Denham had a distinguished career in the Far East as Inspector-General of Police in Malaya and as managing director of the Anglo-Dutch Plantation Company in Java.

8. Foot, M.R.D., *SOE 1940–46*, BBC, London, 1984, p. 9.

9. John had learnt about the terrain and the indigenous tribes who lived in the mountainous spine from a fellow passenger on the outward voyage. Pat Noone was a Cambridge anthropologist based at the Perak museum in Taiping. He and John also shared a love of outdoor pursuits.

10. In 1938 John and a Malayan Civil Service friend, Robert 'Skip' Harris, climbed both these peaks. John could find no record of the height of Yong Yap, nor of its having been previously explored. However, he found it 'a very beautiful and awe inspiring cone'.

CHAPTER 2

1. Barber, Noel, *Sinister Twilight*, Collins, London, 1968, p. 28.
2. The Kuantan incident, i.e. the false report of an enemy landing and Adm Sir Tom Phillips's ill-fated diversion, had disastrous consequences. See Elphick and Smith, *Odd Man Out*, pp. 48–52.
3. Churchill, Winston S., *The Second World War*, vol. 3 of 6 vols, Cassell, London, 1948–54, p. 551.
4. The Special Branch officer Innes Tremlett, a Chinese specialist like John Davis, confirmed that Lai Tek was 'the Communist Party's most secret and revered personality. He is known to Davis, myself and one or two others.' See TNA: PRO HS 1/109.
5. Reported in Spencer Chapman, F. *The Jungle is Neutral*, Chatto & Windus, London, 6th impr. 1963, p. 27.
6. I am very grateful to two experts, Anthony Short and his correspondent, Leon Comber of Monash University, for their assistance with this matter. In an e-mail from Comber to Short, 22 September 2005, Comber states: 'It's correct that John Davis and Spencer Chapman did have a meeting with Lai Tek . . . when the Brits were planning to insert communists as stay-behind parties in Malaya.'
7. Cole had served in Kemaman before the war and volunteered for the dangerous mission on his own. With a knapsack of grenades on his back, he headed into Trengganu and handed them over to a tin-mine manager he knew, promising to return with arms and ammunition. He never reappeared. Later it was discovered that he had been captured by the Japanese and, as a prisoner of war, sent to Thailand, where he died on 31 May 1943.
8. Micky McNamara had been a friend since 1932 and their early days in Pahang. At this time he was OCPD Kuala Lumpur, based at Campbell Road police station.
9. In his memoirs Sheppard stated that Vincent Baker was so demoralised by orders to flood the mine that had been his life's work that he refused to be involved in the covert operation. But in *Pai Naa*, the story of Vincent's sister, Nona Baker, it is clear that Baker agreed to Sheppard's request and put forward Tyson, Cotterill and Fonseca, the mine's Singhalese electrician, as willing operatives. See Thatcher, Dorothy and Cross, Robert, *Pai Naa: The Story of Nona Baker, MBE*, Constable, London, 1959.
10. Letter from Maj M.C. ff Sheppard to Col J.H.L. Davis, 27 October 1945, asking the latter to question a Chew Kwok Yin before an inquiry to be held

at Kemaman. The account of the SIS/ISLD mission is based on John Davis's recollections recorded on a cassette, 13 March 1979, and as presented in conversations with the author.

11. Sheppard managed to retrace his steps and drive back to Singapore. He was admitted immediately to the General Hospital and diagnosed with tropical typhus or Japanese river fever, probably acquired on the Bundi walk. He was still ill when Singapore fell, so spent the rest of the war as a prisoner of war.

CHAPTER 3

1. Maj Rosher had been ordered to leave Malaya for India on 10 January. His successor was Capt L.P.T. Cauvin, alias Maj Barry.
2. Allen, Charles, *Tales from the South China Seas*, Deutsch, London, 1983, repr. Abacus, London, 1996, p. 258.
3. The hills around Tampin offered a base for sabotage operations, and the MCP was traditionally strong in the area and could be relied on to support the fighters with food and intelligence.
4. Cross, John, *Red Jungle*, Robert Hale, London, 2nd edn, 1975, p. 20.
5. The SIS/ISLD had set up a training school in Kluang, but it was short-lived, thanks to the swift Japanese advance. In addition to SOE's Chinese guerrilla group, a small European party under Capt T.M. Smyllie and a Dutch contingent of guerrillas also infiltrated the vast Labis palm oil estate just two or three hours before Japanese troops reached Labis.
6. Broome, Richard, 'A Memoir (Wartime Experiences)', Richard Broome personal papers, p. 27.
7. Barry's instructions were to remain in Malaya until further orders and set up a W/T station behind enemy lines. His experiences and those of some of his unit were recounted in part by Robert Hamond: see *A Fearful Freedom*, Leo Cooper, London, 1984.
8. The official historian Charles Cruickshank, in *SOE in the Far East*, gives the figure of 163 guerrillas infiltrated by 31 January 1942, siting them at Tenang, Ayer Hitam, Pontian Kechil, Kluang and Kota Tinggi. Richard Broome states that seven dumps and five Chinese parties were left behind. John Davis's personal papers indicate there were only four parties of guerrillas, at Serendah, Tampin, Kampong Chaah and Kota Tinggi. See Broome, *A Memoir (Wartime Experiences)*.
9. The *Empress* had brought much-needed reinforcements, troops, guns and equipment for the 18th Division. After superhuman efforts, most of the troops

were rescued, but all the armour and equipment were lost in the blazing ship.

10. Jamal had accompanied John on his recent infiltration operations and wanted to follow him on the Sumatran operation. Ah Chuan, who was friendly with Jamal, refused to be left behind in Singapore on Richard's departure.

11. Richard attributed the incident to a classic case of a clash between civilian and military tradition. The outcome might have been very different if the news had reached the *Hin Lee* that John and Richard were no longer civilians. They had received emergency commissions as second lieutenants in the Indian Army with effect from 5 February 1942 as they left Singapore the first time!

12. In fact, spearheaded by Japanese paratroops, the attack came four days later.

13. The decision to go to Sepang was influenced by talking to two British soldiers and a Chinese schoolmaster at Bagan Siapiapi. The latter had bought a *sampan* (rowing boat) and hired a young Chinese boatman to bring the soldiers across the Malacca Straits from Sepang. All four men now offered to return with John and Richard.

14. Two Chinese reached Sumatra with reports of five senior British officers and some 300 soldiers waiting for boats on Malaya's west coast, and Malays were being organised into search parties and paid Straits $5 per head.

15. Although the terms of the Dutch capitulation were unknown to Warren, he feared they might include handing over British personnel to the Japanese. To ensure the departure of the sailing ship *Sederhana Djohanis* remained unknown to the Dutch, he imposed absolute secrecy on the venture.

CHAPTER 4

1. Holwell, Lt H.E., RNVR, 'Escape from Singapore and Voyage to India on the *Djohanis*', John Davis personal papers. Colleagues gave slightly different measurements in their accounts. See also Brooke, Geoffrey, *Alarm Starboard! A Remarkable True Story of the War at Sea*, Patrick Stephens, Cambridge, 1982, and Skidmore, Ian, *Escape from the Rising Sun: The Incredible Voyage of the 'Sederhana Djohanis'*, Leo Cooper, London, 1973.

2. Skidmore, *Escape from the Rising Sun*, p. 114.

3. He had been general manager of the Socfin company estates at Labis, in Johore, and took a territorial commission in the King's Own Scottish Borderers.

4. Ah Chuan's full name was Loo Ngiap Soon. Jamal bin Daim was Constable No. 3632, Federated Malay States Police Service.

5. Holwell, 'Escape from Singapore', p. 19.

6. Skidmore, *Escape from the Rising Sun*, p. 114.

7. In 1981, in correspondence with Charles Cruickshank, John reiterated: 'It would be unfortunate if he [Campbell] was described as being in command in an official history.'

8. In Easter week a substantial Japanese naval force containing five aircraft carriers and other ships of war entered the Indian Ocean in preparation for an invasion of Ceylon. A major air attack on Colombo resulted in considerable damage to the dockyards and shipping in the harbour. Over a few days two British destroyers, a merchant cruiser, two heavy cruisers, HMS *Dorsetshire* and HMS *Cornwall*, and the aircraft carrier HMS *Hermes*, were sunk.

9. In the obituary of Frank Brewer CMG, OBE, a former Dalforce officer and prisoner of war, written by John Davis in 1987, he spoke of the Bangka debacle as 'a disaster of horrifying magnitude, the details of which only became known at the end of the war when survivors emerged from the prison camps'.

10. They also wanted to settle the futures of Jamal and Ah Chuan, to whom everyone on the *Sederhana Djohanis* owed a debt of gratitude. For the time being Ah Chuan decided to stay with Richard, but through the good offices of Denis Ambler, formerly of the Malayan Education Service, now a commissioned officer in the Royal Berkshire Regiment, Jamal enlisted as a private in the regiment.

11. Broome, *A Memoir (Wartime Experiences)*, p. 59.

12. John repeatedly defended what he believed were its achievements and reminded Cruickshank, author of *SOE in the Far East*, of the obstacles presented by the civil and military authorities to its proposed initiatives. He pointed to the establishment of the STS at Tanjong Balai, the infiltration of European and Chinese Communist parties and the setting-up of an escape route via Sumatra to India. He told Cruickshank bluntly: 'I think you are too critical of the OM. Everything that happened in Malaya [subsequently] was in fact started by the Oriental Mission' (draft copy of letter to Charles Cruickshank, *c.* 1983, John Davis personal papers).

13. Mackenzie was a product of Eton and King's College, Cambridge. An officer in the Scots Guards, he lost a leg at Passchendaele and became a member of the board of J. & P. Coats, the textile firm, while still in his twenties. Significantly, he enjoyed a close friendship with Lord Linlithgow, the Viceroy of India.

14. For the record, when John was ten, he had spent some months with his family in Simla, the summer capital of the Raj, when his father was appointed general manager and director of the Alliance Bank in Simla.

CHAPTER 5

1. Among those whom John recalled were Maj R.E. Forrester, from Burma; Bob Thompson, from Hong Kong; Jack Knott of No. 101 STS, Singapore, who had ended up in Calcutta after escaping via Rangoon, Lashio, Kunming and Chungking; and Brian Passmore, of the *Hin Lee* and the *Sederhana Djohanis*.

2. Broome, *A Memoir (Wartime Experiences)*, p. 63.

3. On his father's death, Lim Bo Seng had taken over the family business as brick and biscuit merchants. Before the outbreak of the Second World War, he made his name by organising a strike of 4,000 workers at the Japanese iron mine at Dungan and by rallying Chinese labour behind the Singapore government as a member of the Mobilisation Council and head of the Labour Service. It was during his escape from Singapore that he met Basil Goodfellow, but from Ceylon Lim Bo Seng and his colleague flew to China, only to be sent by the KMT back to India to take charge of the Calcutta seamen.

4. For instance, on locating a 26-year-old Chinese Naval Armaments Supply Officer with seven years' experience working at Singapore Naval Base, John and Richard were telegraphed by their chief to recruit him immediately and start him on W/T training. John kept a record of his searches and tactics in an old blue exercise book, which is among his personal papers.

5. Z Force was a special unit formed in Hong Kong in 1939 to prepare for covert operations in the event of the colony's occupation by a hostile power.

6. Goodfellow was aware of the anti-British, pro-American feeling among senior KMT figures since Gen Chiang Kai-Shek's expulsion of the China Commando Group early in 1942: see Cruickshank, *SOE in the Far East*, pp. 77–9.

7. Richard Broome's opinions are expressed in *A Memoir (Wartime Experiences)*, p. 62.

8. Hudson, a 36-year-old Oxford man, had risen high in J. & P. Coats before the war, and was Mackenzie's choice to represent SOE's Far Eastern Section in London. After he arrived in Ceylon in January 1943, Hudson found he had a political battle on his hands to establish the viability of Group B, which included an Anglo-Dutch Section and an Islands Country Section, in addition to the Malaya Country Section.

9. See Cruickshank, *SOE in the Far East*, Appendix I, p. 266, for a diagram of the organisational structure of Force 136.

10. In Colombo John was introduced to a former rubber-broker, Walter Fletcher, 'a very remarkable and most amusing character'. Fletcher was peddling an

intelligence-gathering and rubber-smuggling scheme and was looking for agents, hence his interest in John. But he was to make his name later over a massive and highly lucrative black-market scam in China, involving precious stones, gold watches and drugs, netting some £77 million for the Allied war effort in the Far East. Fletcher was later knighted and after the war became MP for Bury, Lancashire.

11. Out of a total of 233 Chinese recruited by the SOE directly by this route, 107 were Malay-speaking Dragons, and, of these, 46 were satisfactorily deployed on operations in Malaya; these included the first party recruited by Lim Bo Seng in Chungking. See Cruickshank, *SOE in the Far East*, p. 13.

12. Tan Chong Tee, *Force 136: Story of a WWII Resistance Fighter*, Asiapac Books, Singapore, English edn, 1995, p. 41.

13. John argued, 'As to the question of submarines, all we ask for is

    1. A guarantee of the use of patrol submarines for Phase I and II

    2. A guarantee of ditto for Phase III in the event of success of Phase I

    3. In the event of complete success of our operations a periodical but not necessarily monthly submarine

    4. In the event of failure that a submarine will have a look for me at my alternative rendezvous on the next patrol after Phase II.'

John gives no date to his draft, but it is clearly a direct response to Basil Goodfellow's letter of 21 March 1943, marked 'Most Secret'. See correspondence relating to India Mission, 1942–3, John Davis personal papers.

CHAPTER 6

1. The Dindings comprised Pulau Pangkor, the Sembilan Islands and a mainland strip around the Dindings River. They were part of the British colony of the Straits Settlements until returned to Perak in 1935. Lumut was the chief town and port for the coastal trade in fish, rubber and coconuts.

2. John Davis, lecture notes on his Malayan experiences, 1962, John Davis personal papers.

3. Ah Lim and Tan Tieng Song were aliases for Tan Chong Tee. Shek Fu (sometimes spelled Shi Fu) was the alias for Yi/Yee Tiang Song, and Lee Choon or Chuan the alias for Liang Yuan Ming.

4. A little later they would be known as the MPAJA.

5. Kratoska, Paul H., *The Japanese Occupation of Malaya: A Social and Economic History*, Hurst & Co., London, 1998, pp. 293–4.

6. Cheng Kiang Koon, alias Sing Fa and Dang Sing Huat, was simply 'Cheng' to the British party.

7. Operating from jungle camps, the AJA groups were active in Selangor, Negri Sembilan, North and South Johore, Perak and West Pahang, although the first two had since been dissipated under Japanese military pressure.

8. Cheng was entrusted by John to convey his report on AJUF and other valuable information to Tremlett and to pass on his own knowledge of Malaya in his debriefing.

9. R.N. Broome, report on 'Gustavus', Appendix A, John Davis personal papers.

10. In the course of the attack *c.* 50,000 tons of shipping were sabotaged. The Japanese were outraged and thirty innocent European men and women in the Changi internees' camps came under suspicion of possessing and using a W/T set and aiding and abetting the operation. Imprisoned in savage conditions, they were interrogated by the Kempeitai, and a number died from their torture. This notorious episode, known as the Double Tenth, showed the futility of large-scale sabotage attacks.

11. John Davis, report on 'Gustavus'/'Pirate', p. 1, John Davis personal papers.

12. Cheng Ji Non, a businessman and owner of the Teng Tin Fishery, secured identity papers for Ah Ng, who subsequently invited him to be manager of the commission agency. The other man was Lee Shu Yeh, Secretary of the Overseas Chinese Association, the principal agency set up by the Japanese to control the Chinese community.

13. Mo Ching or Muk Ching – alias Moh Wing Pan – was given the cover name Ah Seng.

14. See R.N. Broome, report on 'Gustavus', Appendix B, John Davis personal papers.

15. *Ibid.*

16. Spencer Chapman, *The Jungle is Neutral*, p. 223.

17. Shinozaki, Mamoru, *Syonan – My Story: The Japanese Occupation of Malaya*, Asia Pacific Press, 1975, Times Books International, Singapore, 1982, p. 111.

18. The reason for the failure of 'Gustavus VI' is puzzling. The shore parties may have been blocked by a heavy Japanese presence, or a misunderstanding may have occurred between Ah Tsing and Ah Ying about who was to take over the rendezvous arrangements. Curiously, neither John nor Richard includes the operation in their official reports, but John does include it in a checklist of operations that he wrote many years later.

19. A plan for an 'Emergency Gustavus' operation had been requested by John

before he left Ceylon, to reinforce the existing team or, *in extremis*, to evacuate the Davis–Broome party.

CHAPTER 7

1. The document was signed by Lt Gen Henry Pownall, Chief of Staff SEAC, and was post-dated 26 November 1943.
2. Imperial War Museum, Oral History, Department of Sound Records: Richard Broome in 'Two Men in the Jungle', broadcast on Radio 4, 24 January 1984.
3. Sabotage operations would include attacks on shipping, dockyards and the fomenting of labour trouble.
4. John agreed to promote the transfer of Chinese instructors as soon as the transport problem could be resolved. In the interim Chinese students would be sent from Malaya to India to train as instructors. The introduction of European instructors at a later stage would be investigated: see details of proposals and decisions of the Blantan Agreement, reproduced on pp. 78–9.
5. See R.N. Broome, report on 'Gustavus', p. 46, John Davis personal papers; Chin Peng, *My Side of History*, as told to Ian Ward and Norma Miraflor, Media Masters, Singapore, 2003, p. 26.
6. Chang Hung agreed in principle but argued that since the question of extending cooperation beyond the invasion period had not been raised at his briefing, it was outside his terms of reference. The clause was, in fact, added as a codicil to the Agreement, to be subject to ratification by the full General Committee of the MCP, AJUF and AJU.
7. R.N. Broome, report on 'Gustavus', Appendix D, p. 46, John Davis personal papers.
8. Terms of cooperation, Blantan Agreement.
9. Subhas Chandra Bose first went to Germany to win support for Indian nationalism, but when the Nazis turned lukewarm he shifted his allegiance to Japan. Leaving Europe by U-boat in February 1943, he transferred to a Japanese submarine off Madagascar and proceeded to Japan, where he wooed that country's leaders before flying to Singapore on 2 July.
10. TNA: PRO HSI/2020.
11. The details of their fate only emerged after the Second World War, when Pat Garden, another of Spencer Chapman's party and a fellow prisoner of war in Pudu Gaol, gave John the full story. Vanrenan and Graham were brought in as captives and over several months (with another of their team, Bill Harvey, and

others) they conceived the brave but wild idea of a group break-out. Garden feared that Vanrenan had an unrealistic idea of large-scale Chinese support for the Resistance. But with three others he risked his life covering for his friends. Unfortunately, though the escapees got away from Pudu in September 1942 they were re-captured within days. Vanrenan and Graham were ambushed at Kampong Jauda Baik, just over the pass to Bentong, and were summarily beheaded at Kuala Lumpur.

12. For nearly a year, Quayle, a New Zealander, and the two 'old men', Chrystal and Robinson, both rubber-planters, stayed with the Perak guerrillas at Ulu Slim and then Kampong Chemor. In 1943 Robinson died of malaria and dysentery. Chrystal, increasingly sickened by the rigidity of Communist methods and their anti-British ideology, went off to join a KMT Chinese group at Pulai in Kelantan. Noone, meanwhile, had proved useful to the Communists by acting as a liaison between them and the aborigines – *orang asli* – persuading the latter to act as guides and lookouts to warn the guerrillas of Japanese movements. But Noone also tired of the Communist mentality and returned to his old stamping ground at Jalong, where his Temiar wife, Anjang, had a clearing for growing food. Finally Quayle, weakened by ill health, decided to try and link up with John Davis and the Force 136 team, which he did in March 1944.

13. In 1981 Charles Cruickshank, the historian of Force 136 and author of *SOE in the Far East*, sent John Davis lists of Oriental Mission Europeans who took part in left-behind parties, indicating their fate where known. Of the forty-two Europeans named in eight parties, fourteen had been killed or died in Japanese hands; the remainder were prisoners of war in Malaya, Siam or Sumatra.

14. Cross, *Red Jungle*, pp. 141–2.

15. National Archives of Singapore, Oral History Centre: John Davis, interview with Miss Tan Beng Luan, 7 April 1984; Imperial War Museum, Oral History, Department of Sound Records, 'Two Men in the Jungle', broadcast on Radio 4, 24 January 1984.

16. R.N. Broome, report on 'Gustavus', John Davis personal papers; Imperial War Museum, Oral History, Department of Sound Records, 'Two Men in the Jungle', broadcast on Radio 4, 24 January 1984.

17. Chin Peng, *My Side of History*, p. 16.

18. Operation 'Remarkable' was an extension of the 'Emergency Gustavus' sorties, although John said later the name was quite unknown to him. He took a dim view of the fact that it brought in ISLD agents with Force 136 personnel.

19. Soh Hun Swee was a very long-standing friend and Lim Bo Seng had high hopes of his assistance. The other two, a banker and a schoolmaster, were Ong Pia Teng and Koh Chee Peng. See TNA: PRO HS1/108, report of Tan Chong Tee.

20. The women were greatly embarrassed by the ablutionary habits of Japanese officers. When a stark-naked officer, fresh from a shower, entered the room where Ah Tsing was held, they departed in haste.

21. There is some discrepancy surrounding Ah Ng's arrest and subsequent conduct. After the Second World War John was told, on the word of Ah Han, Ah Lim and Shek Fu, that he was picked up six days before the other KMT agents, at Simpang Ampat. See letter from J. Hannah to John Davis, 20 September 1947, John Davis personal papers, and TNA: PRO HS1/108, report of Tan Chong Tee. This differs in some detail from Richard Broome's account, but together they provide a narrative of the events of the last fateful days of March 1944. See R.N. Broome, report on 'Gustavus', Appendix D, John Davis personal papers.

22. R.N. Broome, report on 'Gustavus', Appendix D, paragraph 19, John Davis personal papers.

23. The details of Noone's death were revealed after the Second World War. Black Lim had been broadly correct. In November 1943 Noone was walking northwards with his wife, Anjang, and two Temiar men, Busu and Uda, when the latter, driven by passionate jealousy and desire for Anjang, attacked the Englishman. After knocking the revolver from Noone's hand, Uda killed him with a blowpipe. The two *orang asli* then buried his body according to Temiar custom at Kuala Wi. Since the Temiar were a peace-loving, non-violent people, shame and fear imposed a curtain of silence over the episode, and for a long time talk of Noone's death remained taboo. See Holman, Dennis, *Noone of the Ulu*, Heinemann, London, 1958, and Noone, Richard, *The Rape of the Dream People*, Hutchinson, London, 1972, for Pat Noone's story.

24. R.N. Broome, report on 'Gustavus', p. 28, John Davis personal papers.

CHAPTER 8

1. John Davis personal papers, lecture notes, 15 June 1962.

2. The figure varied. For example, Black Lim and Spencer Chapman returned to camp in June–July, and in early September John gave Cheng – Agent 108 – permission to leave Gurun to rejoin the Sitiawan guerrillas and monitor enemy movements along the coast.

3. Spencer Chapman, *The Jungle is Neutral*, p. 308.
4. There is little doubt that Spencer Chapman resented John's position as designated SEAC representative and Head of the Force 136 mission to Malaya, since he was younger than Freddy and had been junior to him in the Oriental Mission.
5. Letter to John Davis from Mrs Lim Bo Seng in Singapore, 29 December 1946, John Davis personal papers.
6. R.N. Broome, report on 'Gustavus', p. 11, John Davis personal papers.
7. National Archives of Singapore, Oral History Centre: John Davis, interview with Miss Tan Beng Luan, 7 April 1984.
8. Cross, *Red Jungle*, pp. 141–2, 148, 166, 196–7. Cross was under the impression that the Force 136 party had known about the ISLD unit for very much longer. After the war Cross wrote to John to remonstrate about his apparent lack of interest in the ISLD offer of cooperation. However, John was following orders on security and had acted quite properly.
9. Spencer Chapman, *The Jungle is Neutral*, pp. 319–20.
10. Only Spencer Chapman was exempt: by an unfortunate piece of timing Freddy had been struck down by another serious attack of fever, diagnosed by John as tick typhus.
11. Secret and confidential letter from 'Jackie K.' to John Davis, n.d., John Davis personal papers, but from the context it would seem to have been delivered by Lim Bo Seng, who for some reason did not bring the Mark II plan with him to Blantan.
12. Three months earlier Col Peter Fleming, the explorer and brother of the thriller writer Ian Fleming, had been called in to assist with transmissions to Capt (later Gen Tan Sri) Ibrahim bin Ismail. After being captured with his SOE party in Kelantan, Ibrahim bin Ismail was engaged in a protracted and highly dangerous game of deception of his Japanese captors.
13. 'Tit-us' referred to the tight stretch of his shorts over his buttocks whenever he bent down.
14. The legend was repeated in the BBC Radio 4 programme, 'Tales of the South China Seas', broadcast on 24 January 1984; see Imperial War Museum, Oral History, Department of Sound Records 8431/6.
15. Letter from Geoffrey Bence to John Davis, 26 January 1984, John Davis personal papers, prompted by his hearing the Radio 4 programme. A FANY was a member of the volunteer First Aid Nursing Yeomanry, who had been approved for service as W/T operators, cipher clerks and confidential

secretaries in the Far East at the end of 1943. The FANY section at the large Colombo station was formed in July 1944.

16. Featuring the name Maj John Lewis Haycraft Davis, Indian Army, attached 6th Rajputana Rifles, his full citation reads: 'Major Davis has been employed in operations of great hazard since December 1941. After the initial stages of the Pacific War he was cut off in Sumatra and helped to sail a small craft across 1,000 miles of ocean to Ceylon. In May 1943 he led a team of native agents into enemy-occupied territory, making a blind landing on an unknown coast. He returned to India with valuable information and subsequently went back again in July 1943 and re-established contact with his agents. Since then he has remained in enemy-occupied territory undertaking work of a perilous nature with great skill and perseverance. For the last two years this officer has rendered outstanding services under difficult and dangerous conditions entailing a life of discomfort in dense and fever-ridden jungle with the ever-present threat of discovery and death at the hands of the enemy. The success of the operation led and directed by Major Davis has been due almost entirely to his ability, courage, resourcefulness and determination in exceptionally difficult circumstances, which are deserving of the highest order.'

17. Force 136 found that ISLD had been given priority for the next mission to Malaya.

18. Imperial War Museum, Oral History, Department of Sound Records 8431/6: 'Tales of the South China Seas', first broadcast on BBC Radio 4, 24 January 1984.

19. Ah Chuan wanted to serve with Richard in Malaya. Lacking a formal education, he was initially turned down as a volunteer for the Malaya Country Section, but he persisted and was finally admitted to Singarh. However, he aspired to a specialised role and trained as a W/T operator. His selection for Operation 'Funnel' fulfilled his ambition.

20. The mail brought John good and bad news. The latter concerned his brother Geoffrey, a submarine surgeon-lieutenant in the Royal Naval Volunteer Reserve, posted missing at sea and presumed killed on active service just after D-Day in June 1944, when John's fate had reached its nadir. On the side of good news was the birth in 1944 of two nephews for John, and his further promotion.

21. For example, see Signals 393, 394 and 3598, secret exchanges between the Chiefs of Staff and Mountbatten regarding the Resistance movements in Malaya, and the British government's postwar constitutional plans for the country, copies of which are to be found among John Davis's personal papers.

22. TNA: PRO HS 7/165, history of Force 136 operations in Malaya.

23. TNA: PRO HS 1/115, progress report, 7 July 1945.

24. To ensure their salvation Ibrahim committed the 'Oatmeal' party to a daring exercise in double deception with the Japanese for the rest of the war.

25. John was told this by Richardson and Headly in 1978. He had been wrongly informed that Jamal had died of illness in India.

26. R.N. Broome, report on 'Gustavus', John Davis personal papers; author's italics.

27. Cruickshank, *SOE in the Far East*, p. 200; also, a draft letter from John Davis to Malcolm Brinkworth, BBC producer, 23 October 1982, John Davis personal papers.

28. Handwritten transcripts of these and other ISLD signals are contained in a wartime exercise book (without cover or title) among John Davis's personal papers.

29. Cruickshank, *SOE in the Far East*, p. 254.

CHAPTER 9

1. R.N. Broome, report on 'Gustavus', John Davis personal papers.

2. TNA: PRO HS 1/107, Appendix C, record of decisions taken at conference, 17 April 1945.

3. R.N. Broome, report on 'Gustavus', p. 48, John Davis personal papers.

4. John Davis, report on 'Gustavus'/'Pirate', John Davis personal papers.

5. TNA: PRO HS/1/109, paper by Innes Tremlett on the organisation and central direction of the AJA.

6. TNA: PRO HS/1/107, Operations 'Gustavus', 'Pirate', 'Funnel', 'Carpenter'.

7. The strength of each patrol was estimated as 100 men, or 150 in strategic places. Each was to be armed with fifty-four carbines, forty-two Sten guns, twenty-seven Browning automatics and a small number of grenade-throwing rifles, Bren guns, anti-tank rifles and demolition stores.

8. The officer was Maj D.R.W. Alexander; see TNA: PRO HS/1/107.

9. See, for example, a draft letter from John Davis to the author Ian Trenowden, 6 May 1977, John Davis personal papers.

10. Imperial War Museum, Department of Documents, 67/165/1: Lt Col D.K. Broadhurst, report on Operation 'Galvanic'/'Guitar'.

11. These were the figures quoted in John Davis's interview with Miss Tang Beng Luan, 7 April 1984, held at the National Archives of Singapore's Oral History Centre.

12. Imperial War Museum, Department of Documents, 67/165/1: Lt Col D.K. Broadhurst, report on Operation 'Galvanic'/'Guitar'.

13. *Ibid.*

14. A draft marked 'Secret', 'The Disbandment of Guerrilla Forces in Malaya', is among John Davis's personal papers.

15. A SEAC document of 22 August forecast that the MPAJA 'was the likely source of trouble because its 'hard-core elements' were 'communists who hold extremist and anti-imperialistic views and are known to support the idea of an Independent Republic of Malaya'. See Cheah Boon Kheng, *Red Star over Malaya: Resistance and Social Conflict during and after the Japanese Occupation of Malaya, 1941–1946*, Singapore University Press, Singapore, 1987, p. 163.

16. See, for example, TNA: PRO HS 1/114, letter from Col Leslie Sheridan, an SOE staff officer, to Edward Gent, Colonial Office and later High Commissioner of Malaya 1946–8. John was, of course, unaware of this correspondence, which contained unwarranted allegations about his judgement.

17. There were two conditions. Force 136 officers were *not* to accept enemy surrenders, nor were they to take over responsibility for law and order from the Japanese.

18. This account of the Serendah incident is dated 2 September 1982, but there are several versions in his papers, and variant accounts were told by others there, such as Broadhurst; see Imperial War Museum Department of Documents 67/165/1, Lt Col D.K. Broadhurst, report on Operation 'Galvanic'/ 'Guitar'. Jimmy Robertson's account appears in Shennan, Margaret, *Out in the Midday Sun: The British in Malaya 1880–1960*, John Murray, London, 2000, pp. 296–7, where there are additional remarks made by John Davis to the author in 1999.

CHAPTER 10

1. The commander of the Japanese military police in Tapah wrote to Hannah (5 September 1945) giving bogus accounts of Lim Bo Seng's treatment and of the release of the KMT 'spies' on 25 August 1945. See John Davis personal papers.

2. TNA: PRO HS/1/108, report of Tan Chong Tee.

3. The Communists suspected Cheng of being a traitor, and after the Japanese surrender he was tricked into leaving Ipoh to return to camp near Sitiawan, but was killed by a senior member of the MCP. See Tan Chong Tee, *Force 136*, p. 102.

4. Shinozaki had been imprisoned by the British in 1940, but while serving in the Japanese civil administration in Singapore in 1942–5 had been appalled by the barbaric treatment of the Singapore Chinese.

5. Two Japanese swoops on the Singapore Town Committee of the MCP in August 1942 and April 1943 resulted in the elimination of most members of civic and commercial circles. The notorious Batu Caves incident destroyed many of the rising Communist leaders on the mainland. Lai Tek unaccountably missed the slaughter, and his miraculous escape fuelled the myth of the 'Great Survivor'. Overt hints of Lai Tek's treachery in a denunciation by Wong Yeh Lo, a fellow MCP informant, first appeared in the Penang press in September 1945, but in May 1947 his record was unmasked by Chin Peng. In 1953 the saga of Lai Tek was publicly aired by Maj Isaacs in an article, 'Wright helps Japs to trap Reds at Batu Caves', in the *Malaya Mail*, 31 August. See also Cheah Boon Kheng, *Red Star over Malaya*, pp. 82–97.

6. Imperial War Museum Oral History, Department of Sound Records, 8726/4: interview with Col John Davis.

7. Ziegler, Philip, *Mountbatten*, Collins, London, 1985, p. 314.

8. Imperial War Museum Oral History, Department of Sound Records, 8726/4: interview with Col John Davis.

9. The Morib fiasco was partly the responsibility of the secret intelligence team from Combined Operations Pilotage Parties, who had carried out secret exploration of the coast in June; in addition, second-grade maps from India were used.

10. The Communist guerrillas in the Kuantan area were a tough challenge, as Freddy Spencer Chapman discovered. Acting as Civil Affairs Officer in East Pahang he twice turned to John for assistance. On 6 September John allocated a Gurkha Support Group to Spencer Chapman as back-up; on another occasion the guerrilla leaders were brought from Kuantan to Kuala Lumpur to be verbally disciplined by Chin Peng.

11. The conclusion of the report on Force 136 operations in Malaya: see TNA: PRO HS/7/165.

12. J. Davis, report to Malaya Command on Negri Sembilan situation after visit, 9 November 1945, John Davis personal papers.

13. Richard Broome referred to them as 'the brutal and licentious BMA' to John.

14. A top-secret copy of the personal message from the Commander Force 136 to all Force 136 Liaison Officers with AJA, 23 October 1945, is among the John Davis personal papers.

15. Secret memorandum, 'The Disbandment of Guerrilla Forces in Malaya', n.d., John Davis personal papers.

16. At the disbandment conference, chaired by Lt Gen Sir Miles C. Dempsey, were Lt Gen O.L. Roberts, GOC XXXIV Corps; Brig H.C. Willan, Deputy CCAO; and Col V. Purcell, Principal Adviser on Chinese Affairs. The provisional date for disbandment, fixed on 11 September, was 1 December. The 23 September meeting laid down the conditions under which the MPAJA, KMT and AMS guerrilla units remained under BMA command. All MPAJA personnel would be paid Straits $30 a month with effect from 14 August 1945, and to induce the uncontrolled but armed guerrillas to join a recognised formation and reap the benefits, a sum of Straits $150 per head was offered on immediate surrender of arms. The terms of the final pay-off and gratuity were to be decided later. See secret memorandum, 'The Disbandment of Guerrilla Forces in Malaya', n.d., John Davis personal papers.

17. V. Purcell, Remarks on W.819/29/49 (Draft history of MPAJA), 8 October 1949, John Davis personal papers.

18. *Ibid.* 'First of all they insisted on being made into a permanent military force to succeed – or augment – the Malay Regiment. Then they brought up political questions but received no encouragement on this score. They wanted political undertakings from the British government. After that they concentrated on "re-settlement" – they did not want "jobs" so much as capital grants to set them up in business.'

19. There were some tragic-comic moments, such as that at Johore Bahru, when the band of 2nd Cameronians clashed with two highly persistent buglers in the AJA band; and at Bentong the Thunderbolts and Spitfires flew so low over the ceremony that they drowned out the Sultan of Pahang's speech and blew all the flowers off the grandstand. See secret memorandum, 'The Disbandment of Guerrilla Forces in Malaya', n.d., p. 8, John Davis personal papers.

20. Weapons issued and recovered are listed in the secret memorandum, 'The Disbandment of Guerrilla Forces in Malaya', n.d., Appendix C, John Davis personal papers, but Chin Peng claimed an additional 5,000 were secreted away in the jungle for later use. See Chin Peng, *My Side of History*, p. 138.

21. Letter from D. Headly to John Davis, 30/19/97, John Davis personal papers.

22. 'We must succeed in Malaya', Mackenzie argued, 'and see to it that . . . there is no development here, even in a small scale, resembling those in French Indo-China or the Netherlands East Indies.' Top-secret message, 23 October 1945, John Davis personal papers.

23. John Davis, report on Operation 'Gustavus', John Davis personal papers.

CHAPTER 11

1. Secret memorandum, 'The Disbandment of Guerrilla Forces in Malaya', p. 10, n.d., John Davis personal papers.

2. *Ibid.*

3. Listed in the 'Malt' accounts for December 1945 is a mention of financial 'rewards' to Chin Peng, Chang Hung and Liew Yau, and the sum of Straits $450, the cost of a farewell dinner in Kuala Lumpur, on 12 December for the MPAJA leadership: see John Davis personal papers.

4. Soon Kwong, MCP head in Kuala Lumpur, had been arrested on 12 October on charges of extortion in early September, i.e. before civil justice was officially reinstated. In the last of three trials he was sentenced by three BMA officers to four years' hard labour on 2 January, four days before the medals ceremony in Singapore. In a conversation with the author in May 2000 John Davis spoke of his 'bitterness' over this incident. See also Chin Peng, *My Side of History*, pp. 149–55.

5. Secret memorandum, 'The Disbandment of Guerrilla Forces in Malaya', pp. 9–11, n.d., John Davis personal papers.

6. John was asked, for example, what should be done about the 52 Dragons who were no longer operational but were still living in Kuala Lumpur, costing a defunct Force 136 some £600 per week.

7. Letter from Jim Hannah to John Davis, 4 November 1946, John Davis personal papers.

8. Letter from John Davis to the SCA, 11 August 1947, John Davis personal papers.

9. Short, Anthony, *The Communist Insurrection in Malaya, 1948–1960*, Frederick Muller, London, 1975, p. 37.

10. Stubbs, Richard, *Hearts and Minds in Guerrilla Warfare: The Malayan Emergency 1948–1960*, Oxford University Press, Oxford, 1989, p. 207.

11. For Dickinson this was a very sensitive subject. The hardship of internment in the Second World War had forced the end of his career, when he was advised to retire on health grounds.

12. 'I consider I shall not be able to maintain and develop contacts with the Chinese to the fullest advantage if I remain in the Police Force,' he wrote in his application to the Secretary of State for the Colonies, 4 February 1946.

13. Letter from John Davis to A.H. Dickinson, 22 January 1946. I am grateful to Mrs Fenella Davis for alerting me to the letter, supplied to her by Peter Elphick.

Dickinson's reply of 29 January 1946 – see below – is among the John Davis personal papers.

14. At the termination of the BMA Gent became Governor of the Malayan Union on 1 April 1946. Later, from 1 February 1948, he was High Commissioner of the new Federation of Malaya.

15. The fact that the name of Lau Mah was on the list of visitors was not a good augury, for even during the war he had been known in Perak as being militant and anti-British.

16. Since there is no record of a meeting it is impossible to prove what Purcell told John. It could be that he wanted to impart revelations about Lai Tek; or possibly the MCP decision to create a secret jungle army for future anti-colonial action, as opposed to the open, official but disbanded MPAJA.

17. Letter to John Davis from Nona Baker, 7 July 1946, John Davis personal papers.

18. Hannah had a lucrative post with the Perak River Hydro-Electric Power Company, based in Ipoh.

19. First letter from Jim Hannah to John Davis, 4 November 1946, John Davis personal papers.

20. The cache was discovered on 28 February, according to *The Times*, 8 March 1947.

21. Letter from Chin Peng to John Davis, 11 February 1947, John Davis personal papers.

22. Chin Peng, *My Side of History*, pp. 187–91.

23. Comment by a former colleague, J.D.H. Neill, 6 December 2006; the opinion of Prof Jeffrey Richards, the distinguished social historian, in conversation with the author, June 2004.

24. John was affected by the news: 'I am still very, very fond of her and common sense and decency cannot quite master my feelings . . . I do hope she has got a really decent chap – she deserves one,' he told his parents.

25. Letter (damaged) to John Davis from Rose's sister, Mae Lam, 12 or 22 April 1946; letters from sister Yee Lok (Alice Lam), 23 May 1946, and brother Paul Lam, 26 May 1946; letter from T.E. Jackson, Hong Kong, 13 April 1946; John Davis personal papers.

26. The full citation covers John Davis's war service from the time he made a blind submarine landing on the west coast of Japanese-occupied Malaya in August 1943. For much of the next eighteen months he was out of contact with SEAC. After W/T contact with Ceylon was established on 1 February 1945

'it was possible to piece together the story of his achievements since the time he entered the country. He had established excellent relations with local Chinese guerrillas and had spent much time and energy in training them and organising them along disciplined lines. He was immediately appointed senior Force 136 Liaison Officer to the Resistance movement in Malaya and in that capacity has achieved outstanding results. He established close and cordial relations with the HQ of the Chinese guerrilla movement and it was almost entirely due to his personality and diplomacy that the Supreme Commander's directive to the Resistance movement was accepted in toto. During the build-up period when . . . all operations connected with the introduction of British personnel stores, W/T stations, etc., were accelerated to the capacity of the air lift available, Colonel Davis was a tower of strength in ensuring that guerrillas who had not hitherto been contacted were briefed to receive British Liaison teams and ordered to carry out their instructions. All matters of policy in Malaya have been referred to Colonel Davis for interpretation and he has never failed to pass on the directions of the Supreme Commander of Force 136 in such a way that they have been acceptable to the Resistance Forces. He has from time to time rendered most useful suggestions on policy which in nearly all cases have been adopted. Largely due to his example and initiative the patrols which had received Liaison teams under his guidance were shortly before D-Day disciplined fighting forces capable of rendering assistance to the invading forces, who, owing to their Communistic leanings, might tend to take the law into their own hands in the interval between the Japanese capitulation and the arrival of British forces . . . but it is no exaggeration to state that where Colonel Davis has been in personal contact with the patrols . . . there has been nothing but complete cooperation, excellent discipline and a willingness to carry out the Supreme Commander's directive to the letter, very often in spite of most aggravating circumstances. Colonel Davis has made an outstanding contribution to the maintenance of law and order in the areas of Perak, Selangor, Negri Sembilan, Johore, in which he had direct personal contact, and the discipline of the AJUF and complete cooperation of AJUF Central HQ has been very largely the result of his personal influence.'

CHAPTER 12

1. In his letter, Gent not only offered his congratulations to 'Colonel Davis' but assured him of his support: 'I will do what I can about your wish to transfer to the MCS.' Letter, 7 March 1946, John Davis personal papers.

2. During his time at Bentong John learned from the Tamil doctor and Chinese nurses at the hospital about the fate of the Vanrenan–Graham party in 1942, particularly the fate of Nugent, who was brought in wounded by the Japanese. Nursed back to good health at Bentong Hospital, and discharged as fit, he was taken away to be executed as an enemy agent. See letters from John Davis to Tom Evans, 20 October 1994, and to Pat Garden, 14 June 1995, John Davis personal papers.

3. 'Unofficials' were the non-governmental sector, such as people in commerce, business and the professions.

4. According to the Banishment Enactment of 1913 this was done in the name of the Resident Commissioner.

5. Letter from John Davis to Bob (later Sir Robert) Thompson, 15 July 1947, John Davis personal papers.

6. Any remaining claims could only come from the original 160–165 guerrillas trained at No. 101 STS, who deserved gratuities on a par with members of Dalforce. To these John added the dependents of those men killed and wounded while under British orders, a very small number listed in the Liaison Officers' reports. As to claims made by Liew Yau on behalf of another 950 guerrillas recruited as No. 101 STS trainees, John was adamant that these were not authorised and were without foundation. See John Davis, Memorandum, 4 February 1948, John Davis personal papers.

7. Letter of John Davis to the Deputy Chief Secretary, 23 April 1948, John Davis personal papers.

8. *The Times*, 8 March 1947.

9. Secret and personal letter to John Davis from the Malayan Security Service, Suleiman Building, Kuala Lumpur, 21 August 1947, signature illegible, John Davis personal papers.

10. Chu Sun Leung offered his services to John Davis as a professional arms hunter in the Tapah–Bidor area. John passed his name on to Harvey Ryves, the Malayan Security Service officer in Perak. A pencilled draft letter from John Davis to Harvey Ryves survives, n.d., but from context autumn 1947, John Davis personal papers. Further letters followed but the Malayan Security Service missed the boat: Chu Sun Leung wrote in December to say the Communists had enlisted him for special work in Sungei Siput.

11. A pencilled draft letter from John Davis to Mr Wong Sing Piaw a.k.a. Ong Sing Pio, n.d., John Davis personal papers.

12. Letter to 'Mr John Davis, Bentong', from Ong Sing Pio, Ban Hong Leong &

Co., 36 Lekir Road, Sitiawan, Importers and Exporters of Motor and Cycle Accessories and stockists of Bicycles, Tyres and Oils, 18 September 1947, John Davis personal papers.

13. In a small black notepad kept for jotting down messages and important bits of information.

14. Even Chin Peng could not justify the murder of Ian Christian, who was due to leave for another position the next day. He attributed it to an over-zealous local group of Communists who operated independently of the state commander. See Chin Peng, *My Side of History*, pp. 215, 222. Richard Clutterbuck ascribes the murders to a unit of the 5th (Perak) Regiment of the MPABA, which was commanded at that time by Lit Yong. See Clutterbuck, Richard, *Riot and Revolution in Singapore and Malaya 1945–1963*, Faber & Faber, London, 1973, p. 168.

CHAPTER 13

1. Imperial War Museum, Oral History, Department of Sound Records, 8400/4: interview with Col John Davis, Reel 8.

2. The opinions of the late Prof Oliver Wolters of Cornell University, who was an expert in Chinese Affairs in the Malayan Civil Service during the Emergency and knew John Davis well. See letter of O. Wolters to the author, 16 August 2000.

3. In a memorandum on the idea of Ferret Force, written by Richard Broome on 28 June 1948, John Davis personal papers.

4. To widen the organisation's appeal the title MPABA was soon dropped in favour of MRLA.

5. Richard Broome acted as Minuting Secretary and produced the memorandum on this Special Jungle Guerrilla Force for suppression of terrorism, dated 28 June 1948, but made it clear that it represented an amalgam of the participants' ideas, though primarily those of John Davis, if Wolters was correct. The new organisation became known as Ferret Force.

6. Issues to be decided included size and composition of the force, equipment, communications, accommodation, medical issues, pay and leave. John wanted to involve as many former Force 136 officers as possible, but there was also the issue of police and Army recruits to be settled. Should retired or seconded officers, or those due for release, be considered? Should there be direct enlistment from the UK? What proportion of Malays, Chinese, Gurkhas

or Punjabis could join the other ranks? Could Dyak trackers from Borneo be employed? See secret agenda for meeting, 6 July 1948, John Davis personal papers.

7. The ten included John himself, Richard Broome, Bob Thompson, Jim Hannah, James 'Jimmy' Hislop, F.A. Olsen, I.C. Hinton and A.T. Dutton.

8. O.W. Wolters joined as a Chinese Liaison Officer, but unfortunately twenty-one possible volunteers, including GLOs from Force 136, Douglas Broadhurst and Derek Headly, could not secure secondment from their civilian work to join: see various nominal rolls, Force Ferret [sic]; nominal roll, European civilians, 6 September 1948; nominal roll, Army officers ex-Force 136; and nominal roll of Europeans not available for Ferret; John Davis personal papers.

9. Government servants seconded to Ferret Force were to be paid by their existing departments. An advance of Straits $200,000 was made available in mid-July for immediate expenditure, but was later revised upward to Straits $398,000.

10. Pocock, Tom, *Fighting General: The Public and Private Campaigns of General Sir Walter Walker*, Collins, London, p. 71.

11. In John's absence from his post in Bentong, the Labour Office bungalow was occupied by his temporary successor, Tom Mackie. While their husbands were away on Ferret Force service, Helen joined Tamsin in the Broomes' home.

12. In addition to Capt Hughes-Parry, Group No. 1 team command included A.G. Robertson of the Malayan Customs Service and Donald Grant of the Malayan Forestry Department, formerly of Force 136, in charge of the Malay companies, and Lt R.S. May and Lt Baxter, in charge of the Gurkhas.

13. Interim report, Group No. 1, 12 August 1948, John Davis personal papers.

14. Boucher explained: 'My policy for the future is to break up Ferret Groups as their agreement runs out, to send the Army personnel back to their units, to move the Federation government servants to other jobs in which their services will be of the greatest use in the present emergency, and to allow civilians to return to their civil jobs.' See letter to Col J.L.H. Davis, CBE, DSO, OC Group No. 1, Ferret Force, 16 August 1948, John Davis personal papers.

15. A note by John Davis on the continuing need for Ferrets, n.d., John Davis personal papers.

16. For example, John kept in regular touch with Max Wood, ADO Batu Gajah, who commanded a police squad working to bring the aboriginals over to the government side.

17. All the information about Lit Yong and his company is contained in a secret paper by John Davis, dated 7 March 1949 and headed 'Perak MPABA Lit

Yong's Assault Company', John Davis personal papers. Tanjong Rambutan is situated by the Kinta River and on the main rail route just south of Chemor.

18. Chin Peng, *My Side of History*, p. 139.

19. A draft in pencil of the letter is among John Davis's personal papers. In order not to arouse suspicion John's address was given as the Labour Office in Bentong. It was addressed to Wong Man Wa, the Chinese leader's most frequent alias. In line 1 'worrying' has been deleted in favour of a less emotive word, 'wondering'.

20. Chin Peng, *My Side of History*, p. 243.

21. Wu Chye Sin – alias Ah Ng – was a complex and volatile character, as John discovered over time. He and Richard Broome were highly complimentary about Ah Ng's contribution to the organisation of the SOE intelligence network in Ipoh and greatly regretted that Wu Chye Sin was captured and incarcerated by the Japanese when the network was broken up. After the war John was instrumental in Wu Chye Sin's award of the OBE. It was not until 1946 that John learned how during his captivity three of his fellow prisoners claimed to have seen him collaborating with his Japanese interrogators. John never publicly commented on this allegation and others concerning his probity, nor on Wu Chye Sin's unpopularity with the Chinese community in Ipoh after the war. He did make two criticisms of him, however: one in an undated letter on a War Damages claim, in which John roundly repudiated the substance of Wu Chye Sin's claim for compensation, and secondly that he proved 'financially unreliable since the War' after his partnership with his wartime colleague, Ah Han, was dissolved in 1946. It is interesting that in his memoirs Chin Peng attributes the betrayal of Force 136's intelligence network to Wu Chye Sin. See Chin Peng, *My Side of History*, p. 108.

22. John Davis was among a select number who knew in 1949 that Chin Peng was the Secretary-General and leader of the MCP; it did not break in public until September 1951.

CHAPTER 14

1. John's prediction, made in a letter to his parents on 17 December 1948 (John Davis personal papers), reflected Chinese unease.

2. Script of a broadcast by John Davis on the squatter problem, 17 March 1950, John Davis personal papers.

3. The members of this Squatter Committee were the Chief Secretary; Deputy Mentri Besar, Johore; the State Secretaries of Perak and Selangor;

A.B. Ramsay, Acting British Adviser, Kedah; J.D. Murray, Commissioner of Lands; Chong Yow Shin; and J.L.H. Davis. The first meeting was held on 14 December 1948 in Kuala Lumpur.

4. The committee published its report on 10 January 1949; John predicted that it would not please the Malays.

5. John Davis's paper, 'The Functions of a "Squatter" Settlement Officer', 21 December 1948 (John Davis personal papers), emphasised the important status of the officer for the future. The Squatter Settlement Officer would be responsible for links with the Chinese community and its leaders, propaganda and general supervision in an advisory capacity of all large-scale executive action in connection with squatters. He should have a staff of five, including two Chinese Affairs Officers, whose primary task would be to bring the government to the squatters.

6. The Perak Squatter Committee consisted of the Mentri Besar (Chairman); J.G. Black, British Adviser, Perak; Inche Mustapha Albakri, the First Assistant State Secretary; R.H. Oakeley, Adviser on Chinese Affairs; J.S. Ferguson; Toh Eng Hoe; Raja Omar bin Raja Ali; Inche Mahmud bin Sheik Abdul Majid; J.A.E. Morley, Secretary to the British Adviser (Committee Secretary); and J.L.H. Davis, Assistant State Secretary.

7. Knowing that in dealing with Malays and Chinese imposing titles were symbols of authority, John was disappointed by his nondescript title of Assistant State Secretary (B) in charge of Chinese Affairs.

8. For example, Bukit Gantang wanted to change the Advisory Board to a small elite group and to control the Chinese Committee's deliberations and decisions.

9. Letter from John Davis, State Secretariat, Ipoh, to E.D. Fleming, SCA, Kuala Lumpur, 2 June 1949, John Davis personal papers.

10. The plan was as follows. Phase I would empower local Chinese Assault Squads to occupy and take control of a squatter area. As government representatives the Squads would inspire the local people to see officialdom as supporting and protecting them against the Communists and from improved public morale and confidence a flow of information about terrorist groups was envisaged. At the same time the administration would begin to take root with visits from District Officers, Chinese Affairs Officers and officials of the MCA. Phase II would centre on the appointment of a Chinese headman for each area and the election of a committee. The headman would be in charge of 100–1,000 houses and have personal knowledge of all householders. As chairmen of their local committees they should be made to feel a permanent part of the administration and aids to

the police on security matters. In the final phase the headman would be expected to assist in the organisation of armed auxiliary police to replace the Assault Squads as community protectors. The new auxiliaries would be co-ordinated with the regular police force under the local OCPD. Once this organisation was set up, with a headman and committee responsible to the District Officer, backed by their own auxiliary police, a system of responsible Chinese self-protection would be in place. 27 September 1949. See proposal for the development of a plan for Chinese self-protection, John Davis personal papers.

11. Present were the High Commissioner; the Chief Secretary; the SCA; the British Advisers for Perak, Selangor and Negri Sembilan; the Commissioner for Labour; the Deputy Commissioner of Police; the Resettlement Officer, Selangor; Bernard Davis, an Assistant Secretary, Colonial Office; and the Assistant Secretary (B), Perak, Mr J.L.H. Davis CBE, DSO.

12. Author's italics.

13. Letter from Robert Thompson to John Davis, 30 July 1949, John Davis personal papers.

14. Letter from J.A.E. Morley to J. Davis, 17 December 1949 (John Davis personal papers), asking 'if you could look through and think about the draft [of the government's Development Plan] and send me any comments you may have, I'd be extremely grateful'.

15. John kept pencilled notes of this interview, which also covered a number of political issues, such as the question of Communist consuls. He also kept a record of various follow-up conversations and letters between 11 February and 3 March 1950.

16. Author's italics.

17. Letter from John Davis to E.D. Fleming, SCA, 24 February 1950, with attached note from Fleming to Davis, 3 March 1950, John Davis personal papers.

18. His Excellency the High Commissioner's minute to the Commissioner of Police, 3 March 1950, John Davis personal papers.

19. Lasting friendships were struck with two couples, in particular: John Loch, ADO Parit, and his wife, Daphne, and Rowland Oakeley, Deputy Commissioner for Labour in Perak and a Chinese specialist, whose wife, Diana, shared a love of art with Helen.

20. Stubbs, *Hearts and Minds in Guerrilla Warfare*, p. 107.

21. Author's italics.

22. Michael McConville was ADO Tapah, responsible with his colleague Michael Codner for organising resettlement areas in South Perak, such as Bidor Station New Village and Chenderiang.

23. Letter from Michael McConville to the author, 15 October 2001.

24. Extracts from Rowland Oakeley's letters to his wife, Diana, sent to the author 27 March 2004.

25. Loch, John, *My First Alphabet*, John Loch, Marlborough, 1994, pp. 29–30.

26. Approval of the plan to reorganise Chinese Affairs was given by the Sultan of Perak on 27 November 1950 on the advice of the EXCO, but John Davis was not notified until 13 February 1951.

27. The full extent of John's dissatisfaction was made clear in his letter to R.P. Bingham, Federal SCA, 10 August 1951 (John Davis personal papers): 'You know my views on the subject. I consider you should insist that the SCA has the status of a State head of department responsible direct to MB [Mentri Besar] before the ACA [Adviser on Chinese Affairs] is abolished and your staff and their functions are handed over to the SCA. If the SCA's office is to remain a branch of the Secretariat then the SCA is a subordinate of the State Secretary and a minor state official incapable in my opinion of carrying out the functions envisaged for his office. Furthermore, in this subordinate position he is unlikely to be considered for a seat on the Council of State or on the EXCO. In my opinion he should automatically be on the Council of State.'

28. Chin Peng, *My Side of History*, p. 287.

CHAPTER 15

1. John was given to understand that the Penang posting was scotched because of 'a silly intrigue – not aimed at me . . . and at the same time someone invented but he did not think out the idea of this school. It was all too easy – the embarrassment of what to do with Davis was settled – just the man for the job.'

2. See Chapter 14, note 27.

3. Rowland Oakeley, who knew both men well, explained why there was tension between them: they were chalk and cheese. 'It was inconceivable to me that Bingham would go touring round the Chinese squatters with a rifle and a squad of armed headmen . . . it was the old trouble of the new man, with . . . new ideas, against the establishment, operating under a new situation, the Emergency.' Letter to the author, 10 April 2004.

4. A 'Preliminary Report on the Training School for AROs at Taiping' was written by John, as Director, and sent to the Director of Operations, Gen Sir Robert Lockhart, in Kuala Lumpur, 31 January 1952, John Davis personal papers. This details the situation, buildings, staffing, aims, curriculum assessment and

proposals for future courses, modifying the length to sixteen working days and catering for various grades of officers working in local administration.

5. Chandos, Viscount (Oliver Lyttelton), *Memoirs of Lord Chandos*, Bodley Head, London, 1962, pp. 366–7.

6. John's letters to his parents, 22 December 1951 (John Davis personal papers), just after Lyttelton's visit.

7. Cloake, John, *Templer: Tiger of Malaya*, Harrap, London, 1985, p. 143.

8. Notification from the War Office, Stanmore, Middlesex, 7 November 1951, the date from which John's appointment took effect.

9. Among his bitter critics were the Commissioner-General for South East Asia, Malcolm MacDonald, and the retired Malayan Civil Service officer-turned-academic, Victor Purcell, an authority on China.

10. The size of the villages ranged from 30–40 families to 1,500–2,000 families. Statistics for 30 April 1952 in appendix to a directive on Federal finances by the Secretary for Defence, 26 June 1952, and proposals for the administration of resettlement areas, March 1952, John Davis personal papers.

11. See, for example, the rolling plan John put forward at Gurney's request in September 1949 for involving Chinese villagers in self-protection and rural administration. See also Chapter 14, note 10.

12. John received a letter addressed to 'Most Exalted Superman', a very clever, amusing parody of a begging letter, almost certainly written by Richard Broome, who had great literary versatility.

13. NVLO confidential notes on visit to Johore, 8–12 December 1952, John Davis personal papers.

14. Harold Bedale OBE, town clerk and solicitor of the Borough of Hornsey, Middlesex, was commissioned to write a report on the establishment, organisation and supervision of local authorities in the Federation of Malaya.

15. John devised a ten-point list, a condensed version of Templer's fifteen points. Cloake, *Templer: Tiger of Malaya*, p. 275.

16. *Ibid.*

17. Confidential memorandum from NVLO to Chief Secretary, 1 July 1952, John Davis personal papers.

18. R.H. Oakeley, notes on the meeting with His Excellency the High Commissioner at the King's House, Kuala Lumpur, on 12 January 1953, dated 13 January 1953, John Davis personal papers.

19. R.H. Oakeley, on behalf of Cradock, Davis and Blelloch, secret report to His Excellency, dated 12 February 1953, John Davis personal papers.

CHAPTER 16

1. These and other questions were listed by John Davis in his diary for 1953.

2. While taking a June break, they managed to entertain Noel Alexander, the Lochs and Richard Broome there. John and Richard had attended 'a rather good' Malayan Force 136 reunion at the Hotel Majestic, Kuala Lumpur, before proceeding to Fraser's Hill.

3. John was harking back to an episode that happened twenty years earlier, when as a young and untried OCPD, but acting on orders, he tried to stop the Sultan from squandering state monies.

4. Under Briggs and Templer, particularly the latter, the armed forces had been much increased. British and Malay troops had been reinforced, a multiracial Federation Regiment formed by units from a number of Commonwealth countries, in addition to eight battalions of Gurkhas, a Fiji Infantry Regiment (raised specifically to serve in Malaya), two battalions of the King's African Rifles, an SAS contingent from Rhodesia, the Sarawak Rangers, skilled trackers and head hunters, and troops and air crew from Australia and New Zealand, including a squadron of RAAF.

5. Chin Peng, *My Side of History*, pp. 319–20.

6. *Ibid.*, pp. 321, 323–6.

7. The child was utterly traumatised by the sight of a corpse in *rigor mortis*. Quite unable to tell her parents what she had seen, she clung frantically to her mother, who was hosting a dinner party that night. It was only when her own children were grown up that Patta felt able to tell her mother what she had seen.

8. Letter from R.P. Bingham, Resident Commissioner, Penang, to J.L.H. Davis, SDO Province Wellesley, 9 March 1954, John Davis personal papers.

9. One man present was Maj Isaacs, formerly of Military Intelligence, now Head of the Psychological Warfare Section of the Information Services. John and he had last met in Singapore in 1945.

10. The conference report, 9–10 March 1954 (John Davis personal papers), summarised the recommendations, for example on surrender policy, operational role and greater tactical use of the SOVF in an underground (Q Squad) capacity.

11. Typed letter, marked secret, from John Davis, SDO Butterworth, to the High Commissioner, King's House, Kuala Lumpur, 3 May 1954, John Davis personal papers.

12. The bride, Margaret Graham, was the daughter of a great friend of Basil Goodfellow. 'I was supposed to look after her when she came out as Secretary of the W.I.', wrote John, but 'in fact I was on leave and so she decided to get married', her husband being Dermot Barton of the Malayan Civil Service. The Templers hosted the reception, one of their last, in King's House.

13. Cloake, *Templer: Tiger of Malaya*, p. 260.

14. A provisional alliance between the two communal parties, the UMNO and the MCA, formed in 1952 to fight Dato Onn bin Jafaar's Independence for Malaya Party, became formalised and enlarged in 1953 with the addition of the Malayan Indian Congress Party.

15. There was a clock in their residence, but the Davises preferred to rely on the clock across the water to tell them the time, although this necessitated using binoculars. John's enthusiastic descriptions were devised partly to try to persuade his parents to visit Malaya, which his father did from late 1955 to March 1956.

CHAPTER 17

1. White Areas were those districts where Communist activity had virtually ceased and the government exercised sufficient control as to warrant the suspension of Emergency Regulations relating to food controls, curfews and movement on roads, as the first steps to a return to normality.

2. He offered that those who surrendered would not be prosecuted for any offence connected with the Emergency that was committed under Communist direction, including murder.

3. The Colonial Secretary, Alan Lennox-Boyd, visited the Federation that month and John's diary shows that he had consecutive appointments with Lt Gen Bourne, the Director of Operations, and Bill Carbonell, the Police Commissioner, during the last week in August. See John Davis personal papers.

4. Marked top secret, minutes (in John Davis personal papers) of a meeting held at Police HQ, Bluff Road, at 1400 hrs, 6 October 1955, to consider a plan for a meeting between the Chief Minister, Federation of Malaya, and Chin Peng, Secretary-General of the MCP, p. 9.

5. *Ibid*. The minutes indicate a high degree of readiness on the part of the police authorities, since Chin Peng's letters asking for a conference were not sent out until 2 and 4 October.

6. For instance, leaders like Lai Tek and Ah Kuk were eliminated by Communists and Lau Yew and Lieuw Kon Kim by the Security Forces.

7. The assassination plots are discussed in Chin, C.C. and Hack, Karl (eds), *Dialogues with Chin Peng: New Light on the Malayan Communist Party*, Singapore University Press, Singapore, 2004, repr. 2005, pp. 180–2. Also see article on the internet by Dennis Wombell, 'The Baling Peace Talks, 28th to 29th December 1955', which explores the implications of an assassination plot.

8. John Davis, letter to his mother, Gertrude Davis, 2 March 1956, John Davis personal papers.

9. *Ibid.*

10. DEF.Y. 48/12/55, Operation 'Pink Gin': arrangements for contacting and escorting Chin Peng's party, John Davis personal papers.

11. Letter from John Davis to his mother, Gertrude Davis, 2 March 1956, John Davis personal papers.

12. John told many versions of this episode. This extract is taken from a lecture given at Tonbridge School, his *alma mater*, in 1962. See John Davis personal papers.

13. Chin Peng, *My Side of History*, p. 371.

14. Jackson, Staff Sgt, RAVC, 'We had Chin Peng to Supper', *Journal of Royal Army Veterinary Corps*, Vol. 27, No. 1, spring 1956.

15. *Ibid.*

16. Cited in Stubbs, *Hearts and Minds in Guerrilla Warfare*, p. 227.

17. There had been no mention of recording equipment at the preliminary talks. Harvey Ryves, director of Special Branch, admitted the British were involved in 'dirty tricks' at Baling, although he did not specify their nature: telephone conversation with the author, August 2002.

18. Chin Peng, *My Side of History*, p. 387.

19. Murphy, Philip, *Alan Lennox-Boyd: A Biography*, I.B. Tauris, London, 1999, p. 104.

20. Author's italics.

21. John made scribbled notes of this conversation on a second scrap of paper.

22. John wrote two pages of pencilled notes, elaborating the rough points on the scraps of paper, recounting this critical conversation with Chin Peng prior to his de-briefing in Kuala Lumpur. The notes summarise the main thrust of Chin Peng's thoughts, 29–30 December 1955. See 'On Government Service: PINK GIN', John Davis personal papers.

23. Chin Peng, *My Side of History*, pp. 387–9. Chin Peng allegedly rejected John's proposal on security grounds but he may have begun to worry that an agreement with a British officer would make him party to a diplomatic coup by the white colonials on the eve of the London conference.

24. *Straits Times*, 31 December 1955.

CHAPTER 18

1. I am indebted to Brian Stewart CMG, MCS, who was then SCA Penang, for giving me a detailed account of the 1956 riot.

2. Letter to John Davis from W. Fox, Federal Establishment Officer, Kuala Lumpur, 2 January 1957, John Davis personal papers.

3. The Political Commander of No. 7 Independent Platoon, Goh Peng Tuan, died in a fierce air raid on his camp near Kluang early in 1956, and this was followed in August by the loss of Yeung Kuo.

4. The description given by Michael McConville, the then Administrative Officer, Segamat, in a letter to the author, 19 September 2001.

5. Correspondence between John Davis and Rex Wait, Executive Secretary DWEC, Batu Pahat, January 1957, John Davis personal papers.

6. The opinion of Michael McConville, Administrative Officer Segamat, who was in a position to judge John's management of people, after seeing him in action at Segamat DWEC.

7. Segamat District had a mixed Chinese and Malay population of 37,000. For a detailed account of Operation 'Cobble', see Clutterbuck, *Riot and Revolution in Singapore and Malaya*, Chapter 13.

8. Letter from Michael McConville to the author, 2 March 2001.

9. McConville, Michael, 'Experiences of a Malayan Civil Service officer during the Malayan Emergency', unpublished manuscript, p. 202.

10. John bowed to his superior knowledge. The local brigadier was Philip Townsend, brother of Gp Capt Peter Townsend.

11. For a summary of the situation at Independence, see Shennan, *Out in the Midday Sun*, pp. 342–4.

12. Syed Zainal was State Information Officer for Johore, while Abdullah was State Secretary and Charles Lowe, a Eurasian, was State Finance Officer.

13. The latter was dated 12 October but it was brought from South Thailand through jungle to Kedah and was posted on 4 November in Alor Star. The Tunku's response was made on 8 November.

14. Addressed to the Deputy Chairman, Johore SWEC, the message read: 'IN THE EVENT SUDDEN EMERGENCE FROM JUNGLE OF CHEN TIAN [*sic*] MR DAVIS NOMINATED BY GOVERNMENT TO ACT AS CONTACT OFFICER DAVIS TO BE PREPARED TO FLY AT SHORT NOTICE FROM TENGAH TO POINT OF CONTACT POSSIBLY CALLING K/L ON WAY FOR BRIEFING IF TIME PERMITS DAVIS MAY BE ACCOMPANIED TO POINT OF CONTACT BY

ONE OTHER GOVERNMENT NOMINEE THIS OPERATION WILL BE CALLED CHANGOL PLEASE ACKNOWLEDGE': John Davis personal papers.

15. McConville, 'Experiences', p. 213.
16. Draft press release, n.d. 'North Johore Bandits Face Disaster – Success of Operation "Cobble"', p. 2, John Davis personal papers.
17. Short, *The Communist Insurrection in Malaya*, p. 490.
18. This and the following unattributed comments on the Hor Lung episode are from Michael McConville, who was personally involved in the operation. See McConville, 'Experiences'.
19. See, for example, the letter from John Davis to Michael McConville, marked secret and personal, 1 April 1958, John Davis personal papers.
20. Clutterbuck, *Riot and Revolution in Singapore and Malaya*, pp. 255–7.
21. McConville, 'Experiences', p. 217.

EPILOGUE

1. Maj Mineeff became Military Intelligence Officer with the Kedah contingent of Special Branch at Police HQ, Alor Star. He was invaluable to John for his experience in implementing SWEC policies at district and circle levels, and for his contribution to formulating policy at Kedah SWEC when John was in the chair.
2. Draft paper on the future of the Emergency operation in Kedah, n.d., John Davis personal papers.
3. A border agreement concluded between Malaya and Thailand in 1949 was intended to facilitate police investigations and prevent guerrillas from taking refuge from the police of one country in the security of the other. Further steps were taken under Templer, with the formation of the Frontier Intelligence Bureau in Penang and later the formation of a Malay–Thai Special Branch team at Songkhla. Finally, CTs were to be targeted in a series of joint PFF operations by Malay and Thai police.
4. Two independent guerrilla platoons, No. 4, from North Kedah, and No. 5, based at Kulim, withdrew across the Thai border in 1959.
5. Kedah SWEC, recommendations and instructions from John Davis on handing over to his successor, Michael McConville, 1960, John Davis personal papers.
6. John told his successor, McConville, 'I am not going to write at length about *our delightfully ineffective relations with the Thais.*' McConville soon understood: 'The Thais were charming specialists in constructive lethargy and

[participating in discussions] was pretty frustrating stuff, laced with touches of low comedy.' Letter from Michael McConville to the author, 20 March 2001.

7. It could not be designated a White Area because of its proximity to the border and the fact that the CTs had not been eliminated, but merely cleared out to Thailand.

8. The difficulty arose because police and military control had to be centred on Alor Star, but the area was outside Alor Star District and the Chairman (of North Kedah Operation Circle WEC) had no Emergency responsibilities whatsoever.

9. Letter from Michael McConville to the author, 28 March 2001.

10. Scraps of a diary of last days in Kedah, January/February 1960, John Davis personal papers.

11. Chin Peng, *My Side of History*, pp. 187–91.

12. *Ibid.*, pp. 15, 388, 390.

13. See *Dialogues with Chin Peng: New Light on the Malayan Communist Party*, ed. C.C. Chin and Karl Hack, Singapore, 2004; on the internet, Dennis Wombell, 'The Baling Peace Talks, 28th–29th December 1955'.

14. Chin and Hack, *Dialogues with Chin Peng*, p. 178.

15. In August 1999 John Davis told the author briefly about this meeting with Chin Peng. He hitherto regarded it as top-secret information.

Sources

This study derives substantially from the Davis archive for which there is no catalogue. Initially I found in two very large containers *c*. 170 manila and coloured files, folders, large envelopes and sundry packages containing a great variety of papers and notebooks. Since this material was in no particular order and the titles on the cover did not always relate to the contents, every item had to be checked. It would be too time-consuming to detail the full range of subjects covered in each file, folder or envelope, except to say that such diverse material, some typed, much handwritten, covered the period from the approach of the war with the Japanese in December 1941 to John Davis's retirement in 1960. The contents were in the form of correspondence, lecture notes, valuable personal recollections of the Second World War and its aftermath, and a unique batch of wartime records, memoranda, rough notes and accounts.

John Davis's practice of keeping briefing notes and personal jottings and holding draft copies of letters he sent (even those he occasionally withheld) has proved a considerable bonus. In addition he retained his personal copies of official papers relating to SOE/Oriental Mission and Force 136 marked 'secret' or 'top secret', and a substantial number of confidential documents to and from various government departments relating to the administration of Malaya and the Emergency, such as surveys, policy papers, directives, minutes of meetings, reports, maps, and captured Communist documents and Special Branch material. Among his papers, too, are learned articles and manuscripts sent to him for his professional opinion; with them are drafts of John's comments to the authors.

In addition to the containers mentioned, there is a separate collection of postwar volumes of John Davis's official diaries and Helen Davis's domestic/social diaries, which continue well beyond John's retirement from Malayan service. A third container yielded a variety of small notebooks, exercise books, address books, accounts, passports and a mass of family letters and records. A number of separate boxes contained personal letters and cards, several photograph albums, packets of loose photographs, photocopied newspaper cuttings and printed booklets and other published material. Overall, the *c.* 525 letters written by John Davis to his parents back home in England proved the most exciting find. The most useful were the 155 from Malaya between 1941 and 1960 (with *c.* 25 letters by his wife Helen to his parents). Quotations in the text that have not been endnoted all come from these family sources.

Over the years John Davis exchanged copious letters with his European friends and colleagues in the administration and Security Forces (*c.* 325 letters) and government officials in Kuala Lumpur and the Colonial Office (*c.* 280), which shed interesting light on the strains and stresses of work as an officer in the police, the wartime SOE and in the postwar Malayan Civil Service. Additionally there are letters to and from Asian colleagues and friends, the media world and journalists and academics. The archive also includes a number of recorded interviews and video tapes from the Imperial War Museum and the National Archive in Singapore. Finally, like many long-term colonial servants, John Davis had a considerable photographic collection, upon which I have been able to draw for the illustrations.

UNPUBLISHED MATERIAL

Broome, Richard, 'A Memoir (Wartime Experiences)', unpublished manuscript, Richard Broome personal papers

Holwell, Lt H.E., RNVR, 'Escape from Singapore and Voyage to India on the *Djohanis*', John Davis personal papers

McConville, Michael, 'Experiences of a Malayan Civil Service officer during the Malayan Emergency', unpublished manuscript

Ryves, Harvey, 'Seventy Days', Ryves papers. Copy lent by Fenella Davis

Wynne, Mrs Nancy (Mrs Bateson), 'Letters from Malaya to her family in Hull, 1940–41', University of Hull Centre for South East Asian Studies

Email correspondence between Anthony Short and Leon Comber of Monash University, September 2005

OTHER ARCHIVAL RECORDS

Imperial War Museum

Department of Documents

67/165/1. Lt Col D.K. Broadhurst, report on Operation 'Galvanic'/'Guitar'

85/40/1. Maj R.N. Broome, Ms log of voyage in the native prow *Sederhana Djohanis* from Sumatra to India, 8 March–14 April 1942

Con Shelf. Capt G.A. Garnon-Williams RN, top-secret papers and reports of British personnel left behind or landed in Malaya 1941–5

01/10/1. Maj I.A. McDonald, report on Operation 'Galvanic'/'Guitar'/'Brown'

Oral History, Department of Sound Records

11288. George Brownie of ISLD, recollections, 12 May 1990

8400/4. Interview with Col John Davis

8401/1. Interview with Mrs Helen Davis

8726/4. Interview with Col John Davis

10724/3. Interview with Col John Davis, *Post-War Malaya*

8431/6. 'Tales from the South China Seas', originally BBC Radio 4 programme, compiled by Charles Allen; 'Two Men in the Jungle', interview with Richard Broome and John Davis, 19 May 1983

The National Archives

TNA: PRO HS/1/107. Operations 'Gustavus', 'Pirate', 'Funnel', 'Carpenter'

TNA: PRO HS/1/108. Personnel reports (including record of activities of Tan Chong Tee)

TNA: PRO HS/1/109. Chapman and Broome reports; personnel; memorandum by head of Malayan Country Section, Force 136 on Resistance forces in Malaya on the eve of the Japanese capitulation, 15 August 1945

TNA: PRO HS/1/114. General intelligence: policy, progress reports

TNA: PRO HS/1/115. General intelligence: policy, progress reports

TNA: PRO HS/1/200. Reports on Subhas Chandra Bose and the Indian National Army

TNA: PRO HS/7/165. History of Force 136 operations in Malaya

TNA: PRO H55/165

TNA: PRO HSI/2020

National Archives of Singapore: Oral History Centre

John Davis, interview with Miss Tan Beng Luan, 7 April 1984, on his wartime
    experiences
John Davis, interview with Miss Tan Beng Luan, 10 July 1995, on political
    developments in Malaya, 1945–65

BBC Television

SOE: Arms and the Dragon
The work of the Special Operations Executive in World War II against the Japanese
    in Malaya and Singapore, 1987 (23 October 1984)

East Special; Malaya, the Undeclared War, 1998
The Communist Emergency in Malaya 1948–1960

PUBLISHED SOURCES

Alexander, Stephen, *Sweet Kwai Run Softly*, Merriotts Press, Bristol, 1995, repr.
Allen, Charles, *Tales from the South China Seas*, Deutsch, London, 1983, repr.
    Abacus, London, 1996
Barber, Noel, *Sinister Twilight*, Collins, London, 1968
Barber, Noel, *The War of the Running Dogs*, Collins, London, 1971
Barker, Ralph, *One Man's Jungle. A Biography of F. Spencer Chapman, DSO*, Chatto &
    Windus, London, 1975
Bayly, Christopher and Harper, Tim, *Forgotten Armies: Britain's Asian Empire and the
    War with Japan*, Allen Lane, London, 2004
Bayly, Christopher and Harper, Tim, *Forgotten Wars: the End of Britain's Asian
    Empire*, Allen Lane, London, 2007
Brooke, Geoffrey, *Alarm Starboard! A Remarkable True Story of the War at Sea*,
    Patrick Stephens, Cambridge, 1982
Chandos, Viscount (Oliver Lyttelton), *Memoirs of Lord Chandos*, Bodley Head,
    London, 1962
Cheah Boon Kheng. *Red Star Over Malaya: Resistance and Social Conflict during and
    after the Japanese Occupation of Malaya, 1941–1946*, Singapore University
    Press, Singapore, 1987
Chin, C.C. and Hack, Karl (eds), *Dialogues with Chin Peng: New Light on the Malayan
    Communist Party*, Singapore University Press, Singapore, 2004, repr. 2005

Chin Kee Ong, *Malaya Upside Down*, Federal Publications, Singapore, 1946

Chin Peng, *My Side of History*, as told to Ian Ward and Norma Miraflor, Media Masters, Singapore, 2003

Churchill, Winston S., *The Second World War*, vol. 3 of 6 vols, Cassell, London, 1948–54

Cloake, John, *Templer: Tiger of Malaya*, Harrap, London, 1985

Clutterbuck, Richard, *Riot and Revolution in Singapore and Malaya 1945–1963*, Faber & Faber, London, 1973

Clutterbuck, Richard, *The Long Long War: The Emergency in Malaya 1948–1960*, Cassell, London, 1966

Cross, John, *Red Jungle*, Robert Hale, London, 2nd edn, 1975

Cruickshank, Charles, *SOE in the Far East*, Oxford University Press, Oxford, 1983

Elphick, Peter and Smith, Michael, *Odd Man Out: The Story of the Singapore Traitor*, Hodder & Stoughton, London, 1993

Elphick, Peter, *The Far Eastern File: The Intelligence War in the Far East 1930–1945*, Hodder & Stoughton, London, 1997

Foot, M.R.D., *SOE 1940–46*, BBC, London, 1984

Getz, Marshall J., *Subhas Chandra Bose: A Biography*, McFarland, North Carolina, 2002

Gough, Richard, *SOE Singapore 1941–42*, William Kimber, London, 1985

Hamond, Robert, *A Fearful Freedom*, Leo Cooper, London, 1984

Heussler, Robert, *Completing a Stewardship: The Malayan Civil Service 1942–1957*, Greenwood Press, Westport, Conn./London, 1983

Holman, Dennis, *Noone of the Ulu*, Heinemann, London, 1958

Holman, Dennis, *The Green Torture: The Ordeal of Robert Chrystal*, Robert Hale, London, 1962

Jackson, Staff Sgt, RAVC, 'We had Chin Peng to Supper', *Journal of the Royal Army Veterinary Corps*, vol. 27, No. 1, Spring 1956

Keay, John, *Last Post: The End of Empire in the Far East*, John Murray, London, 1997

Kratoska, Paul H., *The Japanese Occupation of Malaya: A Social and Economic History*, Hurst & Co., London, 1998

Loch, John, *My First Alphabet*, John Loch, Marlborough, 1994

Lowe, Peter, *Great Britain and the Origins of the Pacific War: A Study of British Policy in East Asia, 1937–41*, Clarendon Press, Oxford, 1977

Miller, Harry, *Jungle War in Malaya: The Campaign Against Communism 1948–60*, Arthur Barker, London, 1972

Miller, Harry, *Menace in Malaya*, Harrap, London, 1954

Murphy, Philip, *Alan Lennox-Boyd: A Biography*, I.B. Tauris, London, 1999

Noone, Richard, *The Rape of the Dream People*, Hutchinson, London, 1972

Onraet, Rene, *Singapore: A Police Background*, Dorothy Crisp, London, 1947

Philby, Kim, *My Silent War: The Autobiography of Kim Philby*, Collins, London, 1989

Pocock, Tom, *Fighting General: The Public and Private Campaigns of General Sir Walter Walker*, Collins, London, 1973

Purcell, Victor, *Malaya: Communist or Free*, Victor Gollancz, London, 1954

Purcell, Victor, *Memoirs of a Malayan Official*, Cassell, London, 1965

The Register of Tonbridge School from 1861 to 1945, ed. H.D. Furley, 1951

Robertson, Eric, *The Japanese File: Pre-War Japanese Penetration in South East Asia*, Heinemann Asia, Singapore, 1979

Shennan, Margaret, *Out in the Midday Sun: The British in Malaya 1880–1960*, John Murray, London, 2000

Sheppard, Tan Sri Dato Mubin, *Taman Budiman: Memoirs of an Unorthodox Civil Servant*, Heinemann, Kuala Lumpur, 1979

Shinozaki, Mamoru, *Syonan – My Story: the Japanese Occupation of Malaya*, Asia Pacific Press, 1975, Times Books International, Singapore, 1982

Short, Anthony, *The Communist Insurrection in Malaya, 1948–1960*, Frederick Muller, London, 1975

Skidmore, Ian, *Escape from the Rising Sun: The Incredible Voyage of the 'Sederhana Djohanis'*, Leo Cooper, London, 1973

Spencer Chapman, F., *The Jungle is Neutral*, Chatto & Windus, London, 6th impr. 1963

Stenson, M.R., *Industrial Conflict in Malaya: Prelude to the Communist Revolt of 1948*, Oxford University Press, Oxford, 1970

Stewart, Brian, *Smashing Terrorism in the Malayan Emergency (1948–1960)*, Pelanduk Publications, Selangor, 2004

Stubbs, Richard, *Hearts and Minds in Guerrilla Warfare: The Malayan Emergency 1948–1960*, Oxford University Press, Oxford, 1989

Tan Chong Tee, *Force 136: Story of a WWII Resistance Fighter*, Asiapac Books, Singapore, English edn, 1995

Thatcher, Dorothy and Cross, Robert, *Pai Naa: The Story of Nona Baker, MBE*, Constable, London, 1959

Thompson, Robert, *Defeating Communist Insurgency: Experiences from Malaya and Vietnam*, Chatto & Windus, London, 1966

Trenowden, Ian, *Operations Most Secret: SOE: The Malayan Theatre*, William Kimber, London, 1978

Woodburn-Kirby, Maj Gen S., *The War against Japan*, 5 vols, HMSO, London, 1957–69

Ziegler, Philip, *Mountbatten*, Collins, London, 1985

Newspapers and Internet

Article about MPAJA arms dumps, *The Times*, 8 March 1947

'Wright helps Japs to trap Reds at Batu Caves', *Malaya Mail*, 31 August 1953

Dennis Wombell, 'The Baling Peace Talks, 28th to 29th December 1955', internet

Interview with John Davis, *Straits Times*, 31 December 1955

Index

Please note: the spelling of names of people and places reflects usage in the colonial period.